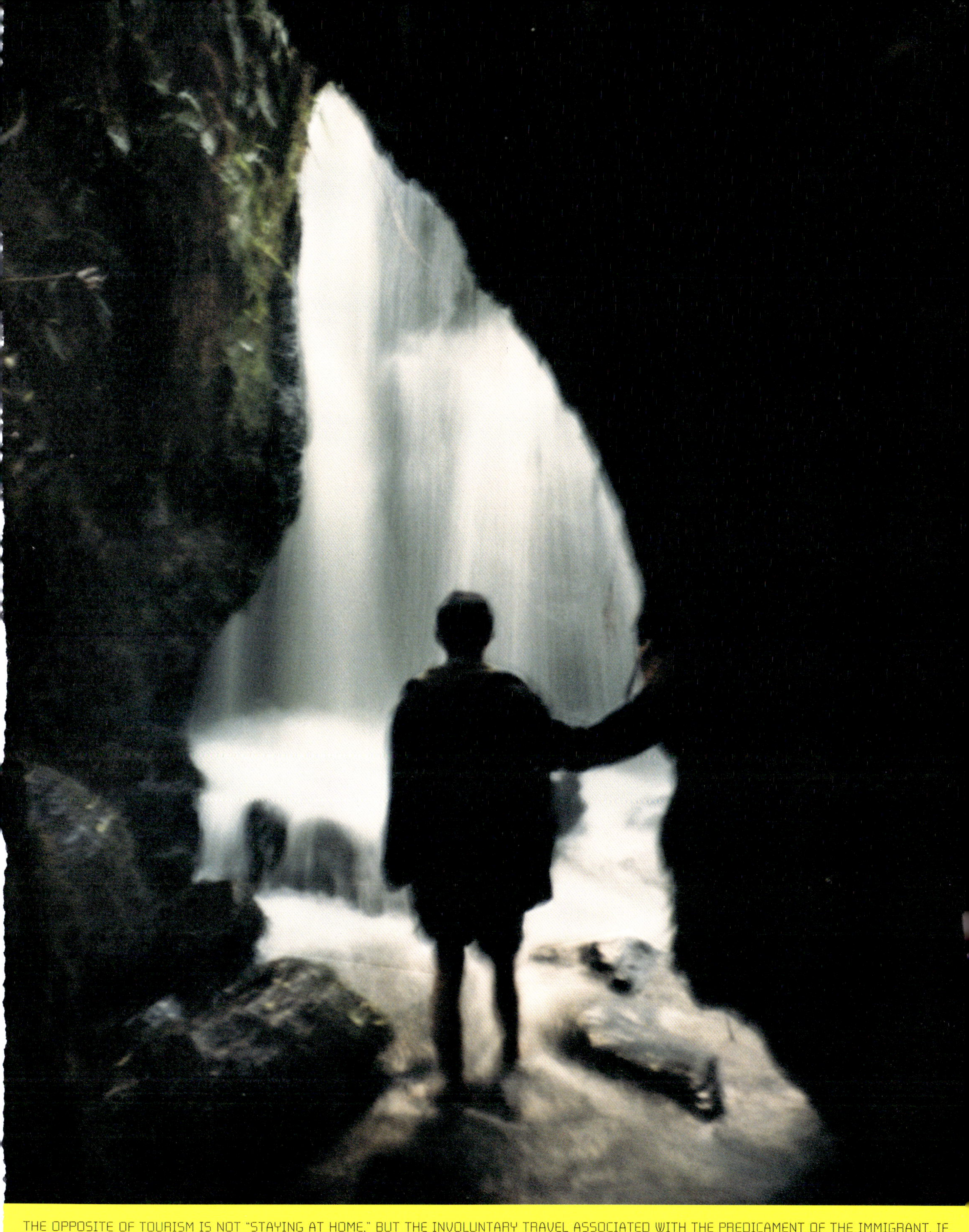

THE OPPOSITE OF TOURISM IS NOT "STAYING AT HOME," BUT THE INVOLUNTARY TRAVEL ASSOCIATED WITH THE PREDICAMENT OF THE IMMIGRANT. IF

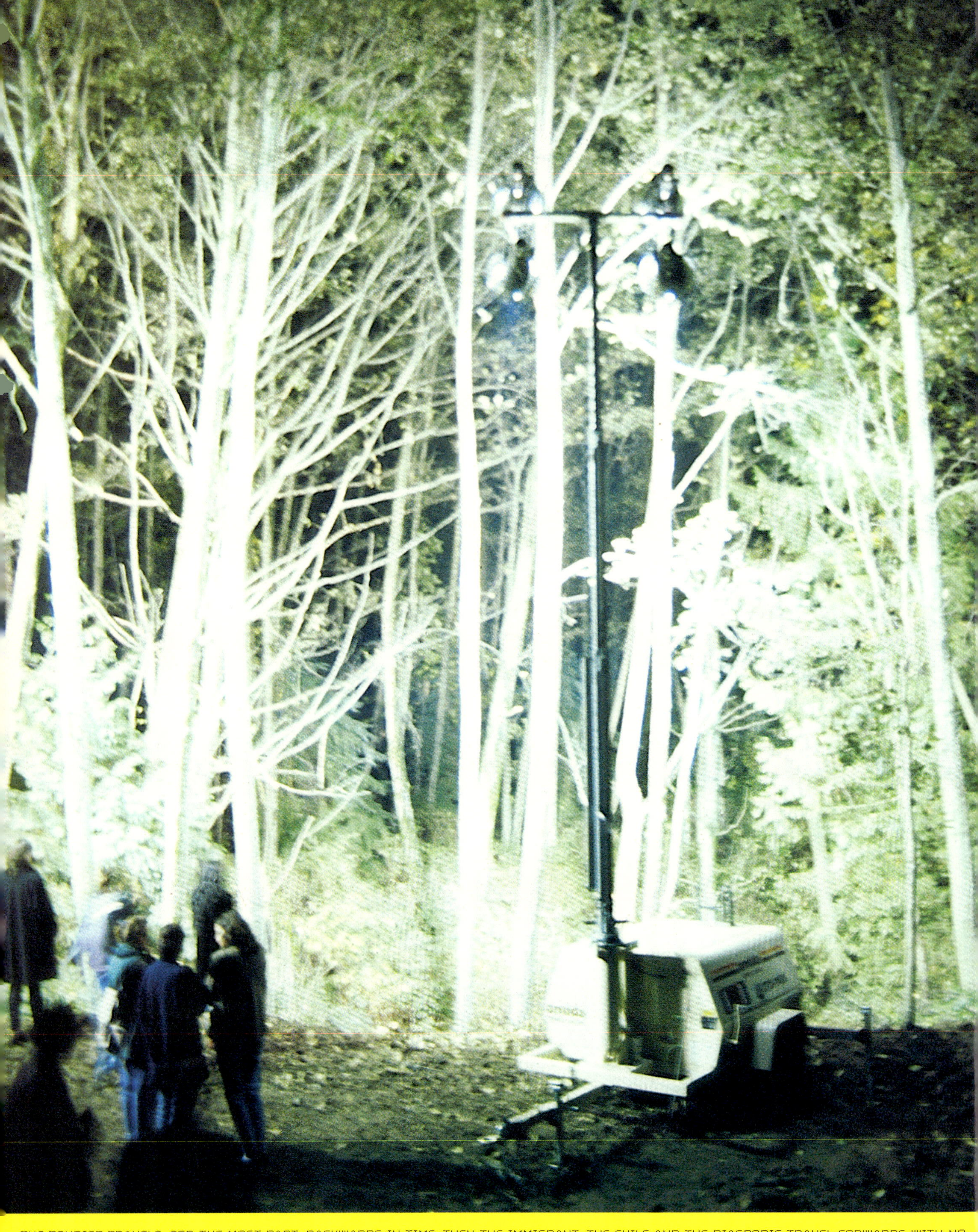

THE TOURIST TRAVELS, FOR THE MOST PART, BACKWARDS IN TIME, THEN THE IMMIGRANT, THE EXILE AND THE DIASPORIC TRAVEL FORWARDS WITH NO

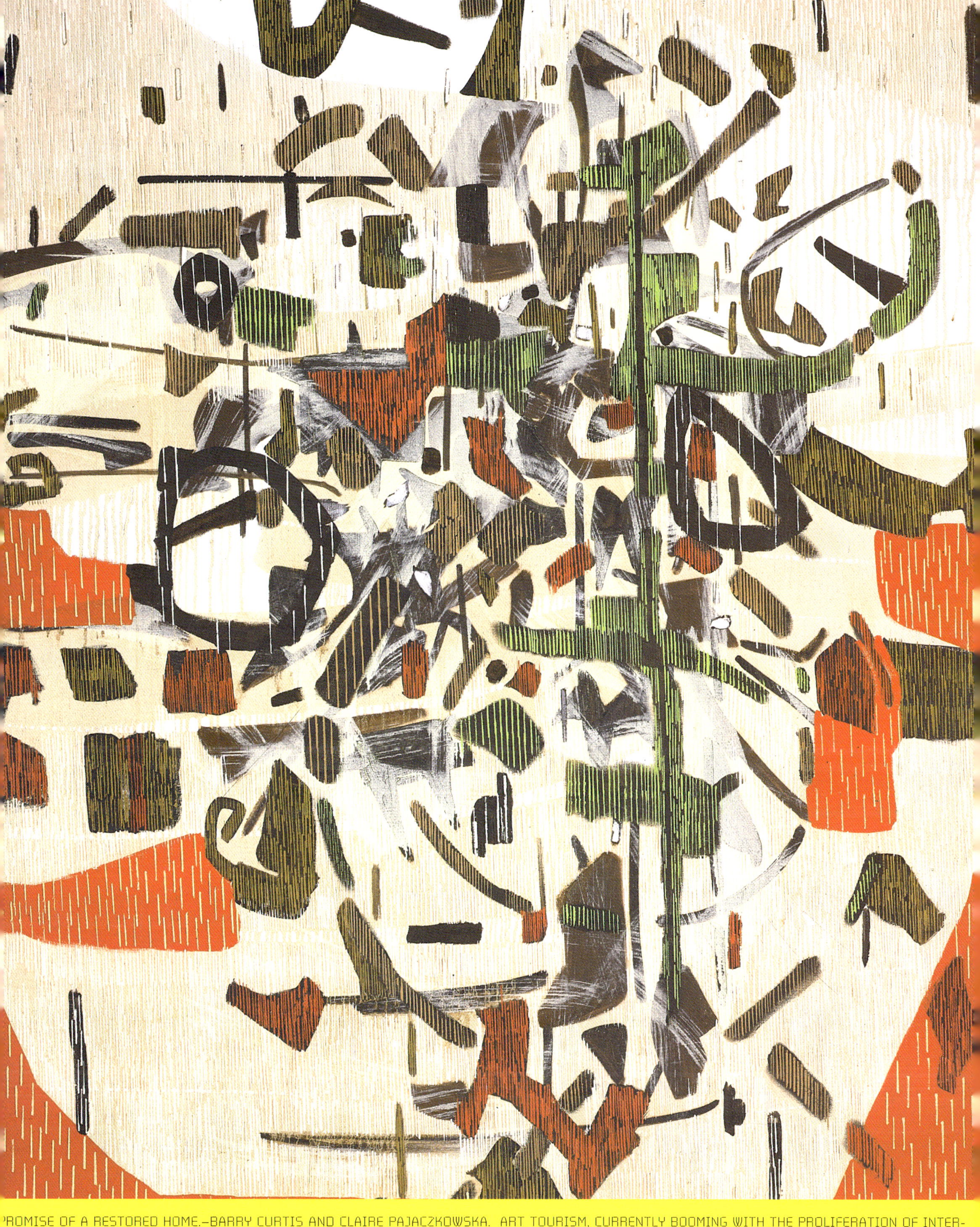

PROMISE OF A RESTORED HOME.–BARRY CURTIS AND CLAIRE PAJACZKOWSKA. ART TOURISM, CURRENTLY BOOMING WITH THE PROLIFERATION OF INTER-

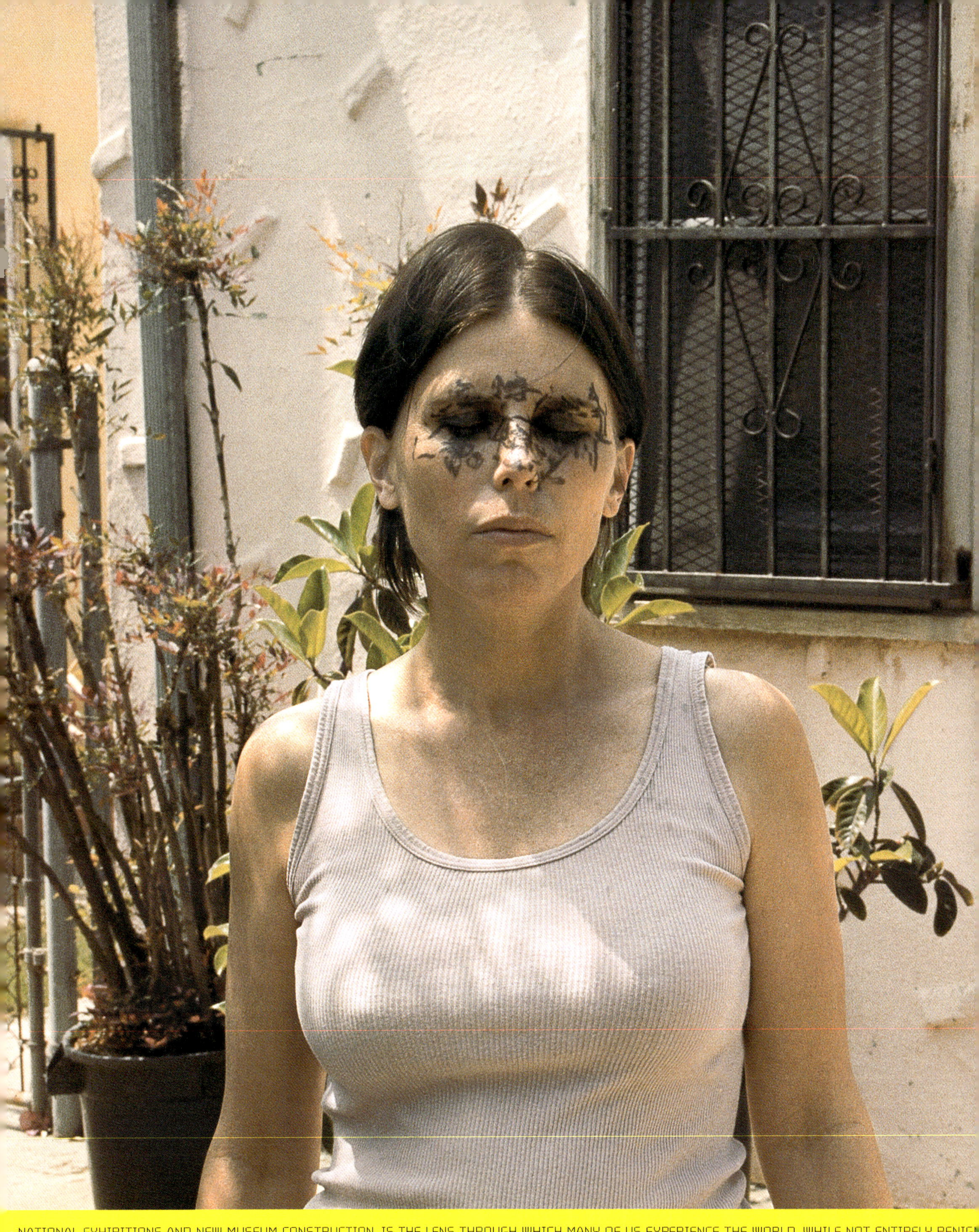

NATIONAL EXHIBITIONS AND NEW MUSEUM CONSTRUCTION, IS THE LENS THROUGH WHICH MANY OF US EXPERIENCE THE WORLD. WHILE NOT ENTIRELY BENIG

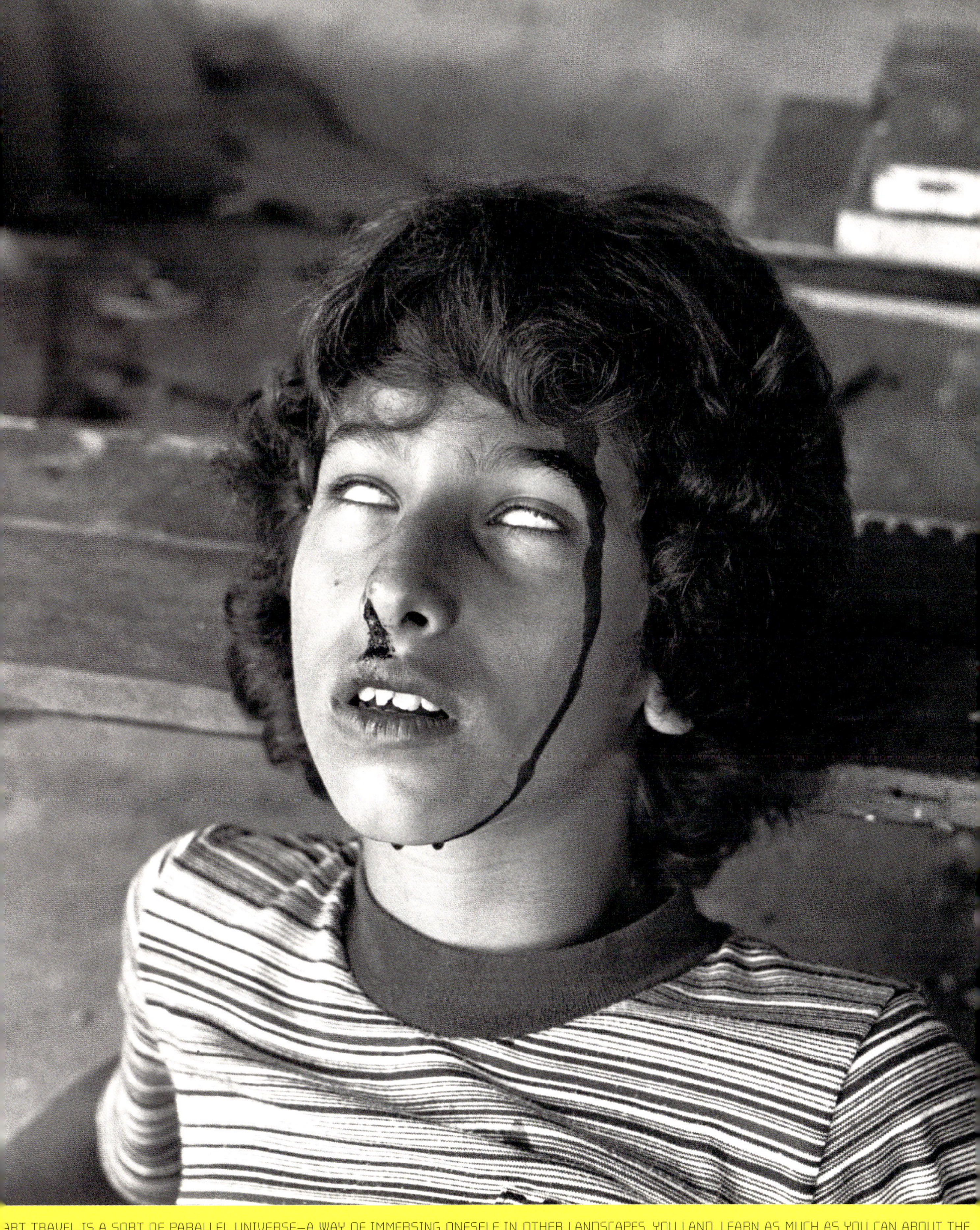

ART TRAVEL IS A SORT OF PARALLEL UNIVERSE—A WAY OF IMMERSING ONESELF IN OTHER LANDSCAPES. YOU LAND, LEARN AS MUCH AS YOU CAN ABOUT THE

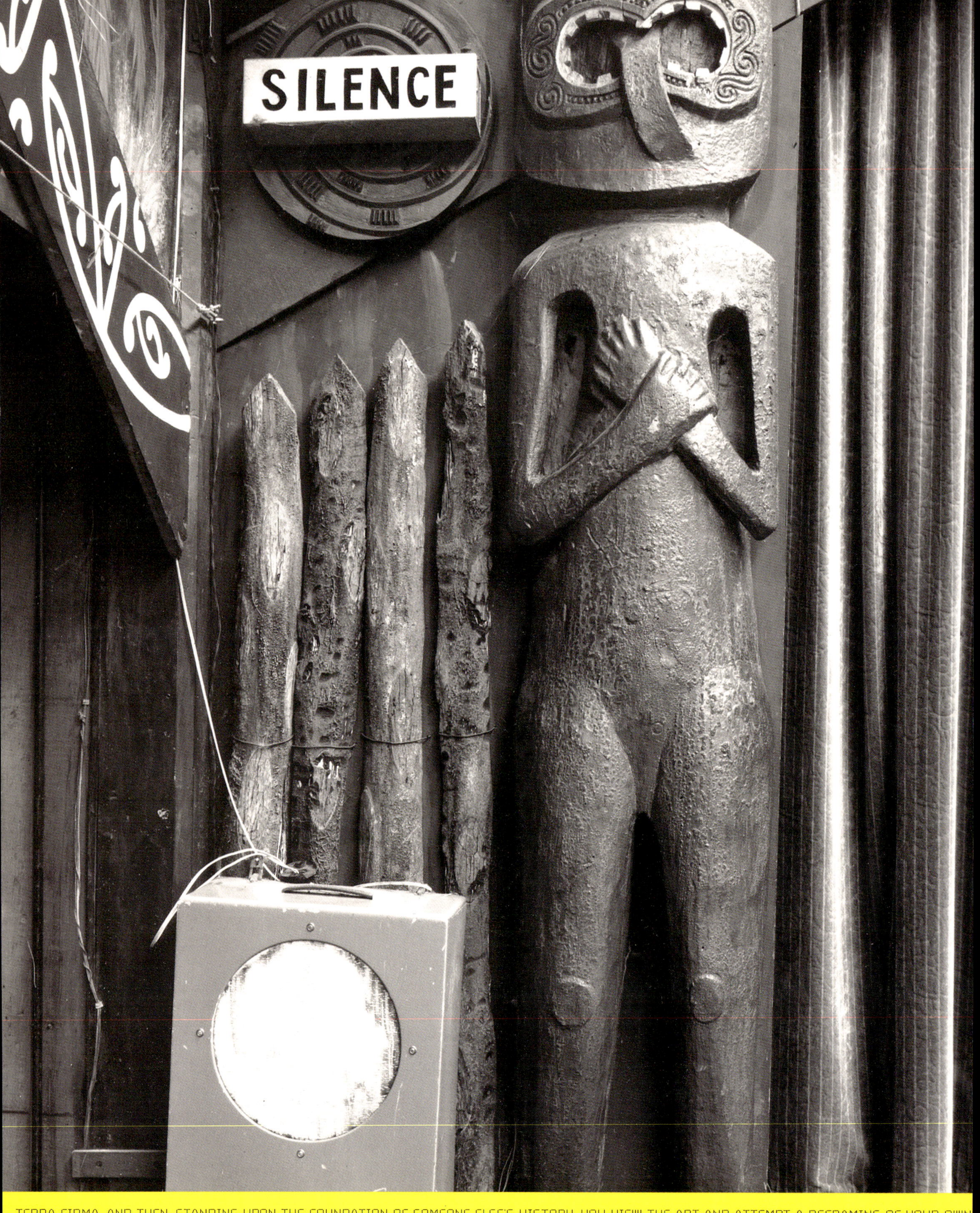

TERRA FIRMA. AND THEN, STANDING UPON THE FOUNDATION OF SOMEONE ELSE'S HISTORY, YOU VIEW THE ART AND ATTEMPT A REFRAMING OF YOUR OWN

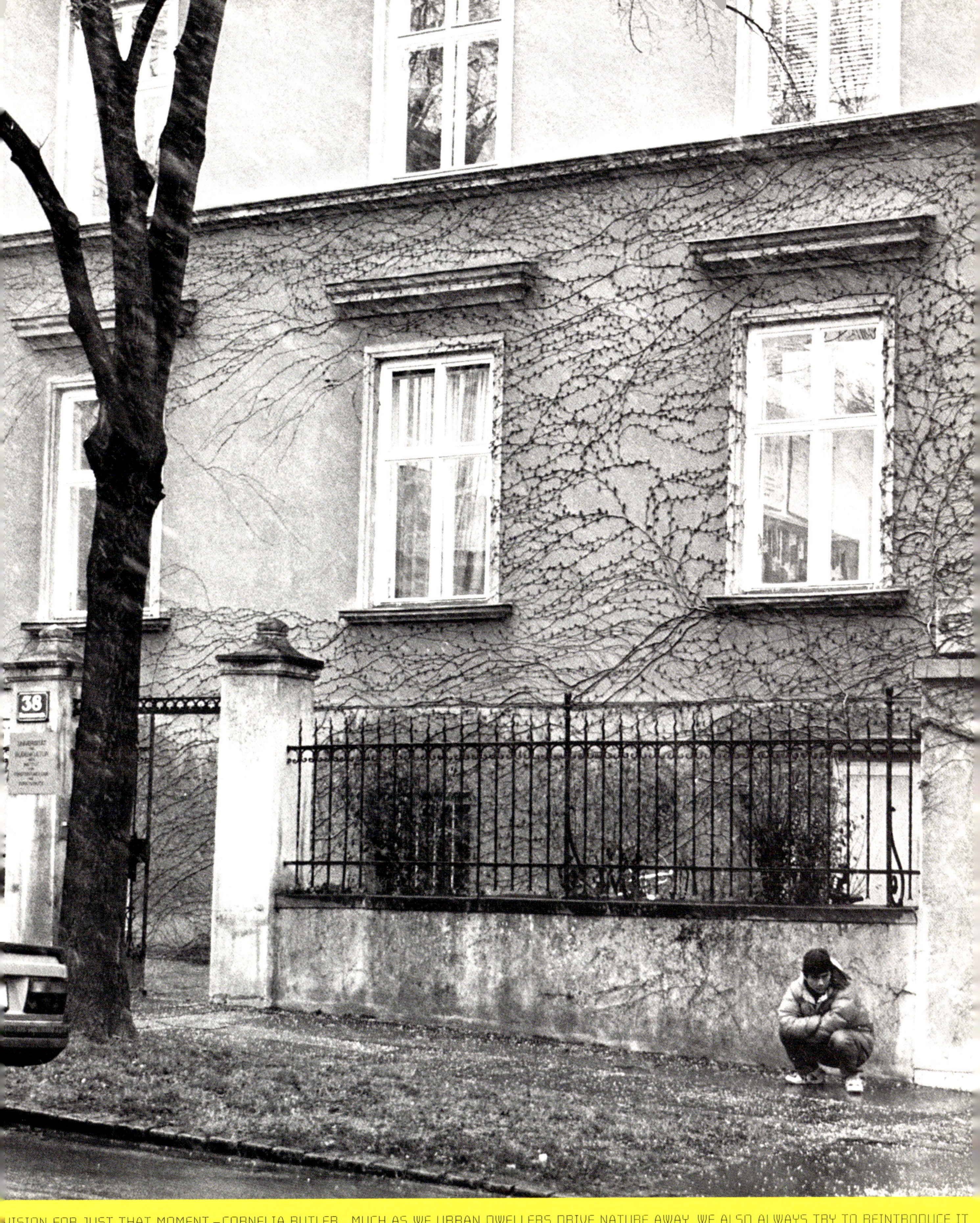

VISION FOR JUST THAT MOMENT.–CORNELIA BUTLER. MUCH AS WE URBAN DWELLERS DRIVE NATURE AWAY, WE ALSO ALWAYS TRY TO REINTRODUCE IT

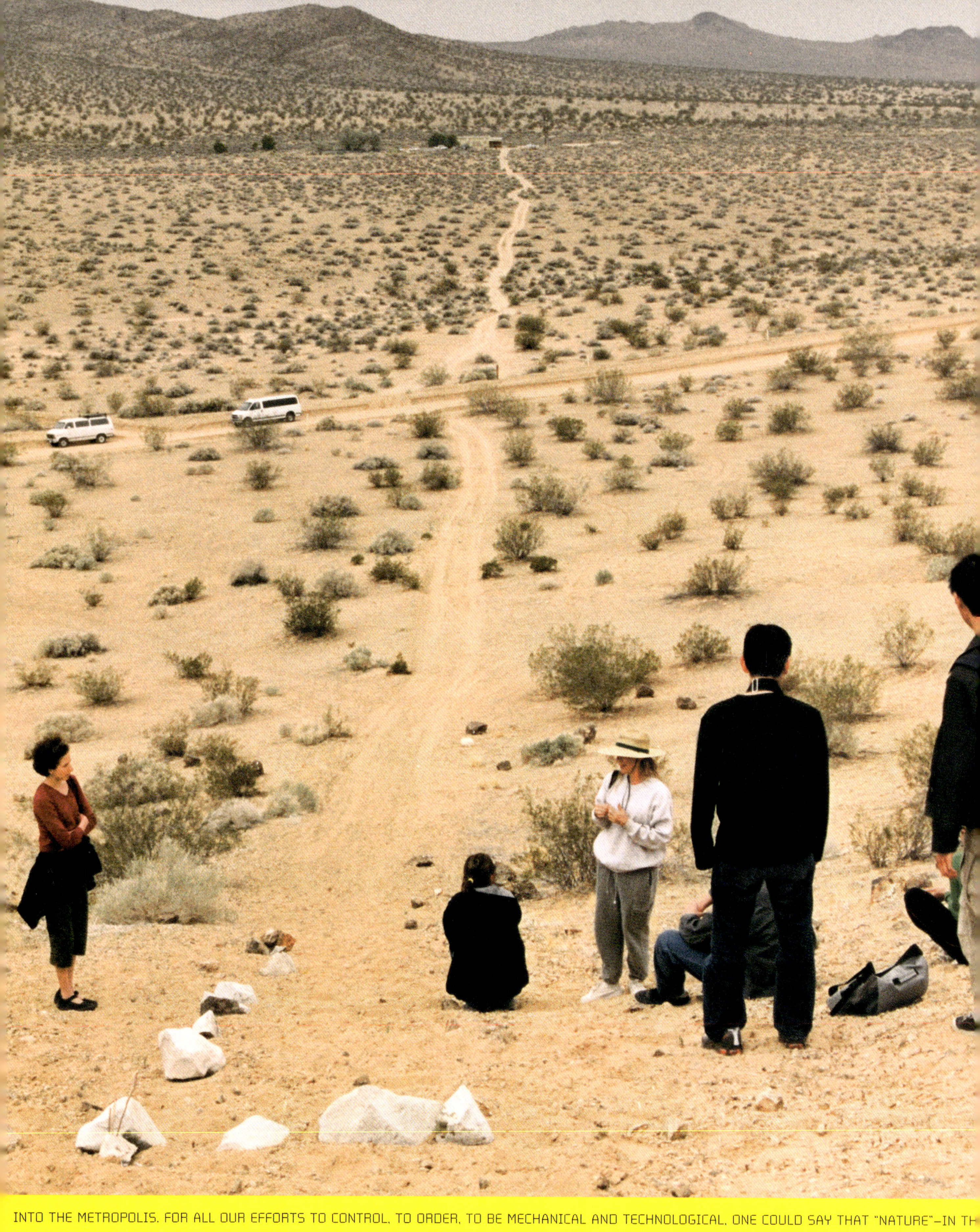

INTO THE METROPOLIS. FOR ALL OUR EFFORTS TO CONTROL, TO ORDER, TO BE MECHANICAL AND TECHNOLOGICAL, ONE COULD SAY THAT "NATURE"—IN TH

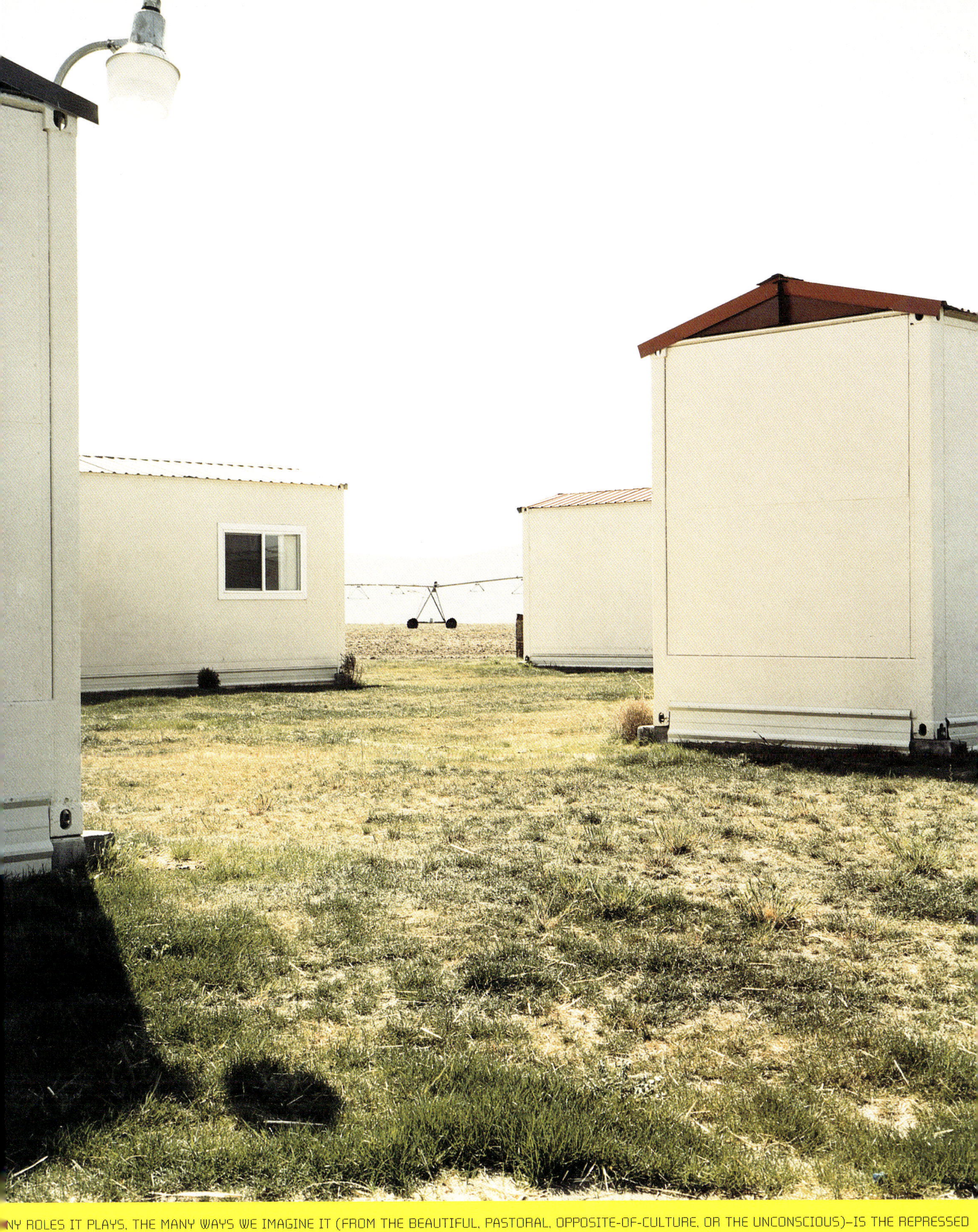

NY ROLES IT PLAYS, THE MANY WAYS WE IMAGINE IT (FROM THE BEAUTIFUL, PASTORAL, OPPOSITE-OF-CULTURE, OR THE UNCONSCIOUS)—IS THE REPRESSED

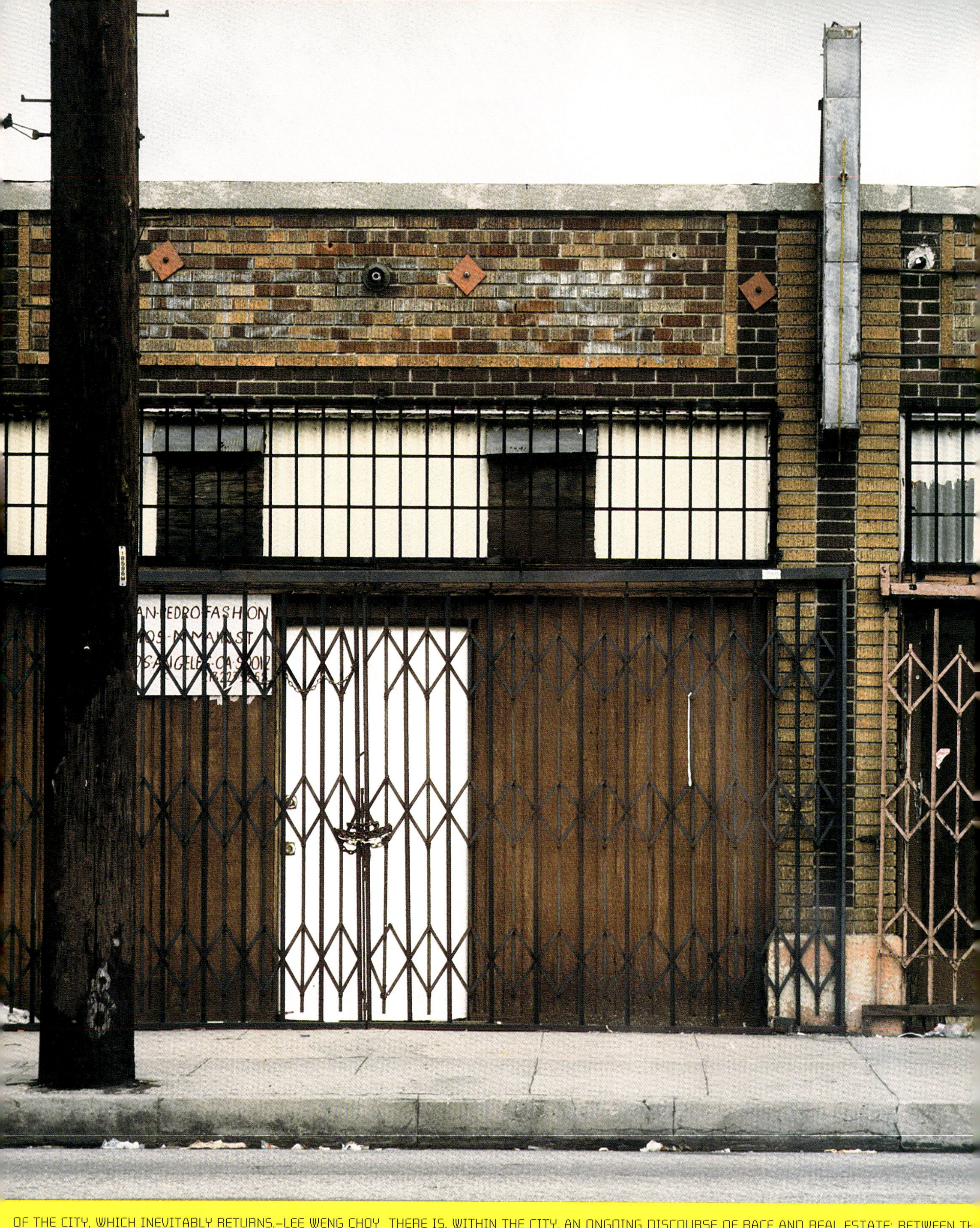

OF THE CITY, WHICH INEVITABLY RETURNS.–LEE WENG CHOY THERE IS, WITHIN THE CITY, AN ONGOING DISCOURSE OF RACE AND REAL ESTATE; BETWEEN TH

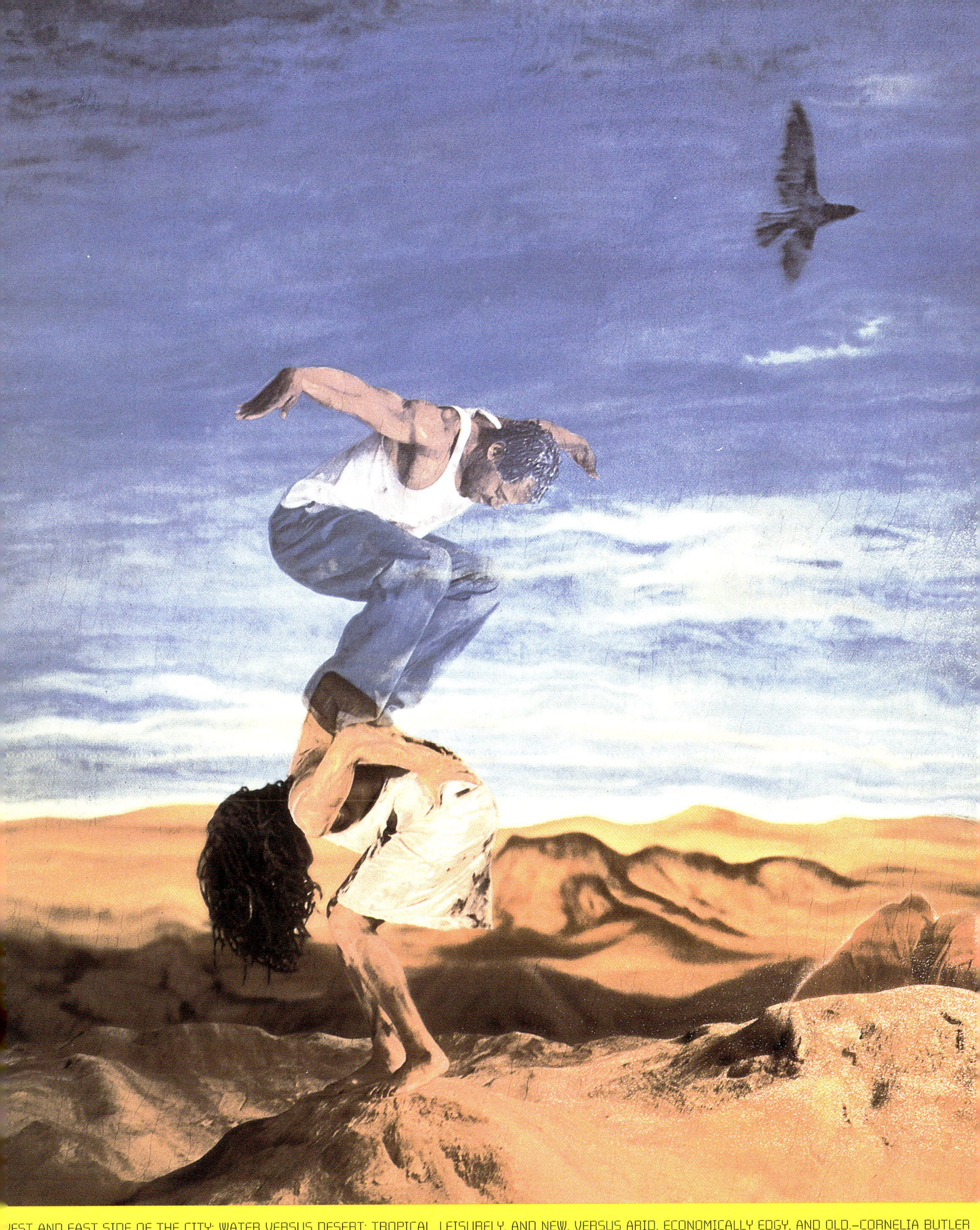

VEST AND EAST SIDE OF THE CITY; WATER VERSUS DESERT; TROPICAL, LEISURELY, AND NEW, VERSUS ARID, ECONOMICALLY EDGY, AND OLD.—CORNELIA BUTLER

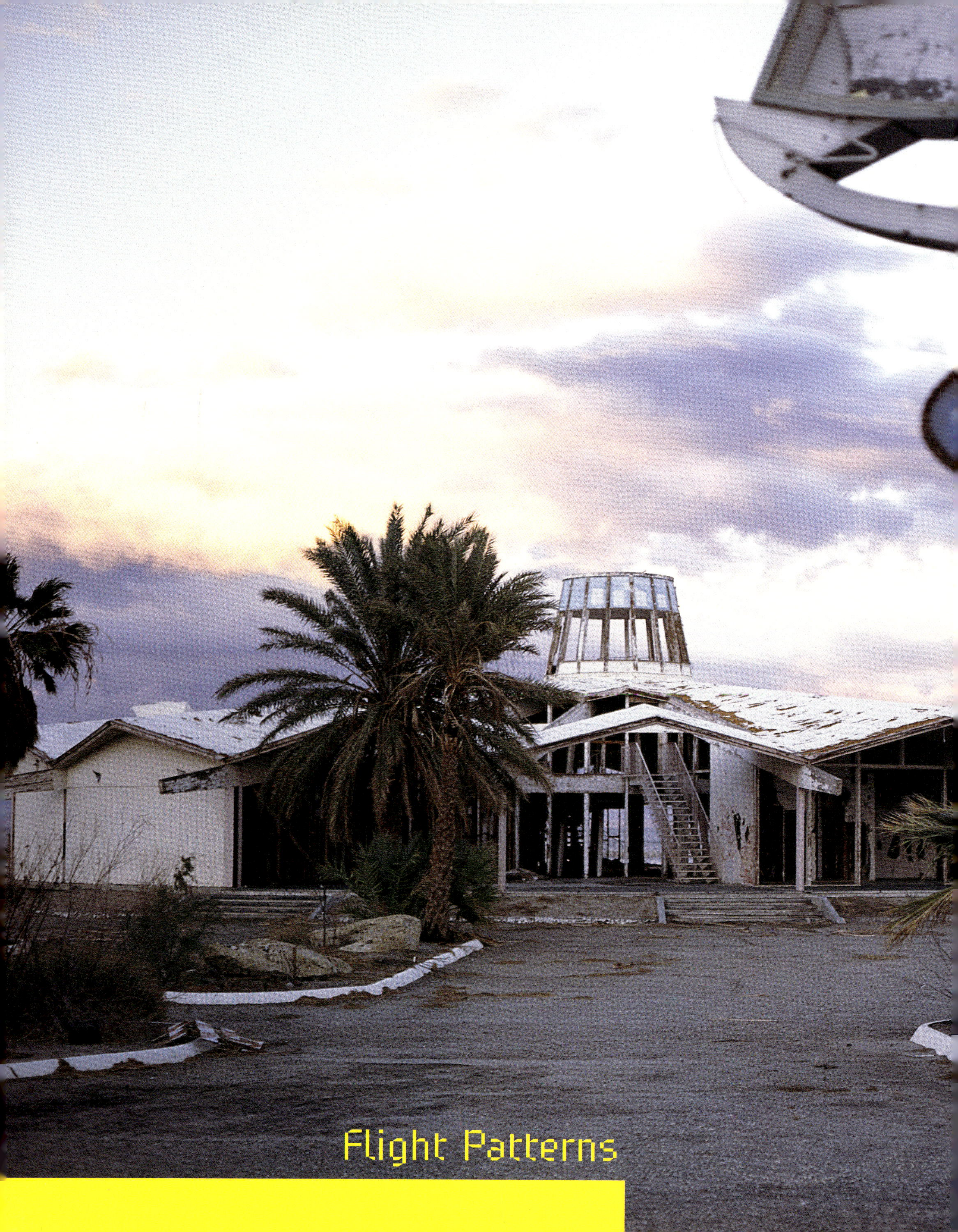

Flight Patterns

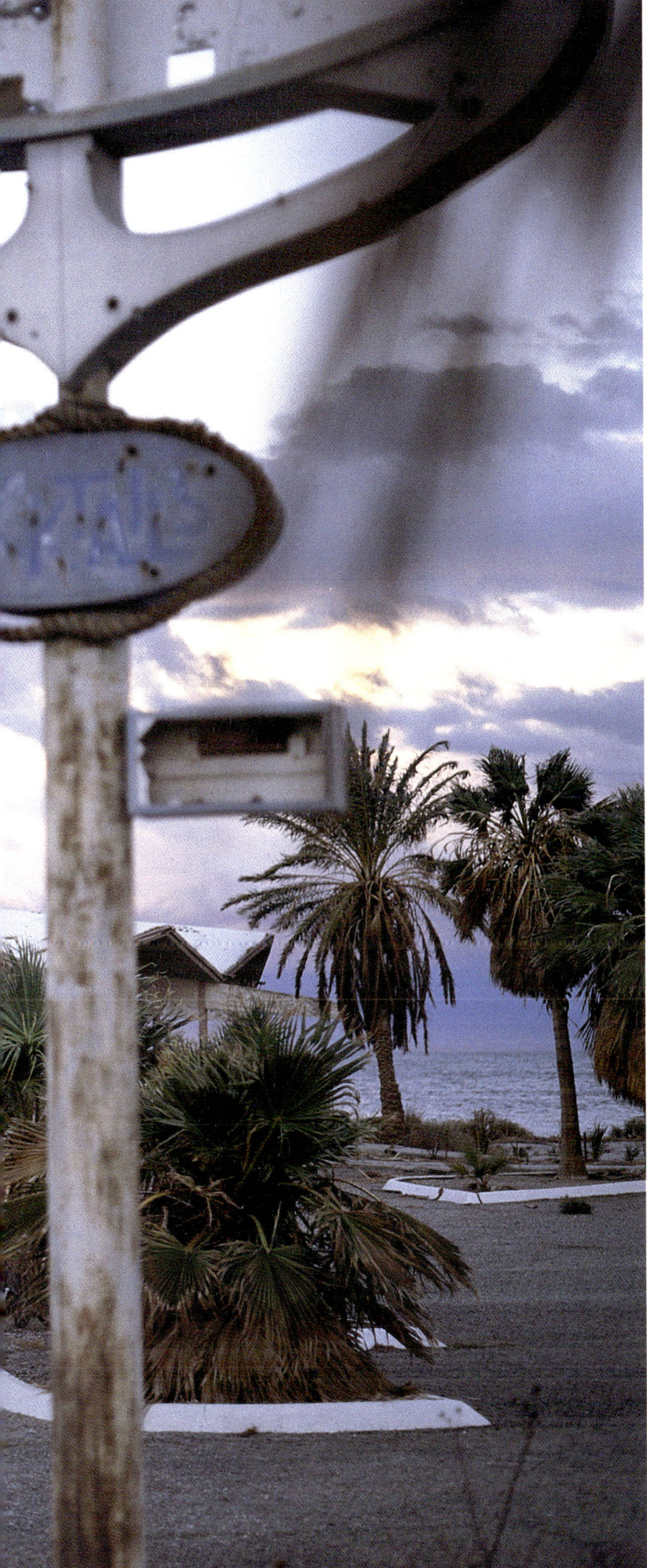

Laurence Aberhart
Doug Aitken
Center for Land Use Interpretation
Miles Coolidge
Caryl Davis
Christina Fernandez
Simryn Gill
Rodney Graham
Anthony Hernandez
Gavin Hipkins
Igloolik Isuma Productions
Tim Johnson
Rachel Khedoori
Roy Kiyooka
David Lamelas
Simon Leung
Tracey Moffatt
Lee Mullican
Paul Outerbridge
Michael Parekowhai
Allan Sekula
Yuk King Tan
Glen Wilson

Essays by
Cornelia H. Butler
Lee Weng Choy
Francis Pound

Organized by The Museum of Contemporary Art, Los Angeles
Sponsored by the Fellows of Contemporary Art

This publication accompanies the exhibition "Flight Patterns," organized by Cornelia H. Butler and presented at The Museum of Contemporary Art, Los Angeles, 12 November 2000–11 February 2001. This exhibition and its accompanying publication are sponsored by the Fellows of Contemporary Art. Additional support has been provided by Audrey M. Irmas, Creative New Zealand, The MOCA Projects Council, the New Media Project, and Erik and Heidi Murkoff.

Promotional support has been provided by KLON-FM 88.1.

Contributors

Cornelia H. Butler is Associate Curator at The Museum of Contemporary Art, Los Angeles.

Lee Weng Choy is an art critic based in Singapore. He has written for various art journals, magazines, books, and art catalogues, including *ART AsiaPacific, Nine Lives: 10 Years of Singapore Theatre, Singapore: Views on the Urban Landscape,* and *The Third Asia-Pacific Triennial of Contemporary Art.* Lee is presently an Artistic Co-Director at The Substation arts center in Singapore.

Francis Pound is a writer, curator, critic, and art historian who currently teaches art history at the University of Auckland. He has published numerous articles, catalogue essays, and books, including *Frames on the Land: Early Landscape Painting in New Zealand* (1983); *The Space Between: Pakeha Use of Maori Motifs in Modernist New Zealand Art* (1994); and *The Stories We Tell Ourselves: The Paintings of Richard Killeen* (1999).

Editor: Stephanie Emerson
Assistant Editor: Jane Hyun
Editorial Assistant: Elizabeth Hamilton
Designer: Michael Worthington
Design Assistants: Sara Cummings, Adam Michaels
Type Design: Batterie by Lee Schultz
Printer: Cantz, Ostfildern, Germany

The Museum of Contemporary Art, Los Angeles
250 South Grand Avenue
Los Angeles, California 90012

Fellows of Contemporary Art
777 South Figueroa Street, 44th Floor
Los Angeles, California 90017-2513

Available through D.A.P./Distributed Art Publishers
155 Sixth Avenue, 2nd Floor
New York, New York 10013
Tel: (212) 627 1999 Fax: (212) 627 9484

ISBN: 0-914357-76-X
Library of Congress Cataloging-in-Publication Data
Flight patterns / essays by Cornelia H. Butler, Lee Weng Choy, Francis Pound.
p. cm.
Catalog of an exhibition held at the Museum of Contemporary Art, Los Angeles, Nov 12, 2000–Feb. 11, 2001.
ISBN 0-914357-76-X (hardcover)
1. Multimedia (Art)--Pacific Area--Exhibitions. 2. Pacific Area--In art--Exhibitions. 3. Landscape in art--Exhibitions. I. Butler, Cornelia H. II. Lee, Weng Choy. III. Pound, Francis, 1948- IV. Museum of Contemporary Art (Los Angeles, Calif.)
N7399.7 .F58 2000
709'.04'007479494--dc21
00-056073
Printed in Germany

DIRECTOR'S FOREWORD

The Museum of Contemporary Art has a well-established history of organizing provocative thematic exhibitions that address complex issues of our visual culture. "Helter Skelter: L.A. Art in the 1990's;" "Pure Beauty: Some Recent Work From Los Angeles;" "A Dialogue About Recent American and European Photography;" "Uncommon Sense;" and "The Power of Suggestion: Narrative and Notation in Contemporary Drawing" all evolved out of the very personal investigations and passions of individual curators and from dialogues with the artistic community. These exhibitions attempted to name elusive but important concerns emerging from particular moments of cultural production.

"Flight Patterns" began as a proposal solicited by the Fellows of Contemporary Art, a deeply valued group of patrons in Los Angeles who have long supported the work of California artists through their generous sponsorship of exhibitions and publications. With their initial support, Associate Curator Connie Butler has developed an exhibition that both contextualizes the work of artists working in this region and engages in an international dialogue with work by artists from elsewhere in the Pacific region. The exhibition's theme—rethinking the topographic tradition and the land as subject—brings together a long history of artists working primarily with photography in the American West with that of artists using similar practices to address landscapes that have parallel histories of post-coloniality.

Any exhibition of such international scope requires the commitment and enthusiasm of many people. We are grateful to our colleagues at MOCA and at the other institutions, large and small, who contributed in myriad ways to bring this project to fruition. We would particularly like to acknowledge the Fellows of Contemporary Art (FOCA), a body that has, over the years, made a significant impact on the scholarship and history of Los Angeles art. The Fellows have long supported our mission at MOCA, including sponsoring our James Turrell exhibition in 1985. "Flight Patterns" marks FOCA's twenty-fifth anniversary, and we salute them not only for their critical support of this exhibition, but for their continuing role in the cultural life of Los Angeles. In particular we thank Chair David B. Partridge, Exhibition Liaison Diane Cornwell, Administrative Director Merry Scully, and the other board members, with whom it was a pleasure to work. We are thankful as well to the other funders of the exhibition, Audrey M. Irmas, Creative New Zealand, The MOCA Projects Council, the New Media Project, KLON-FM 88.1, and Erik and Heidi Murkoff.

MOCA's Board of Trustees is outstanding in its support of our exhibitions. In particular I would like to acknowledge Chair Audrey M. Irmas for her support of this exhibition and for her ongoing generosity and enthusiasm for the museum and its programs. President Gilbert B. Friesen has provided strong leadership and, as Program Liaison, Lenore S. Greenberg has supplied tremendous support and wisdom. I am grateful to work with such an outstanding group of individuals and patrons of the most innovative art of our time.

Finally, I thank the wonderful artists, whose works span a period of forty years, but whose thinking is rigorous and contemporary. Their work, individually and collectively, makes the debate about internationalism, globalism, and millennial culture rich, intelligent, and worth engaging.

Jeremy Strick
Director
The Museum of Contemporary Art, Los Angeles

CHAIR'S FOREWORD

Our world continues to expand and shrink at the same time, and the landscape examination of geography, politics, and culture in the Pacific Basin seems to me an ideal study to celebrate the twenty-fifth anniversary of the beginning of the Fellows of Contemporary Art. The exciting theme of "Flight Patterns" investigates the work of California and Pacific Rim artists who address important concerns of this new millennium—environment, cultural identity, internationalism, bi-cultural tensions, and globalization. This imaginative presentation of many kinds of artistic expression incorporates past, present, and future documentation through video, installation, photography, painting, drawing, and silkscreen to produce a rich and discerning tapestry of a developing new world.

The ongoing commitment of the Fellows is to nurture and support California contemporary artists. This need is growing as California has become both a major center for contemporary art and a world leader in teaching young artists and exposing their outstanding work to new horizons. This is the twenty-ninth exhibition initiated and sponsored by the Fellows in cooperation with museums throughout the state to emphasize and support emerging and mid-career California artists. Many of these exhibitions have traveled to other museums in the United States and throughout the world. Each has been thoroughly and carefully documented with a scholarly catalogue, which serves as a permanent tribute to the work of the artists whom we admire.

We are particularly pleased that this exhibition opens at The Museum of Contemporary Art, Los Angeles, as the Fellows have enjoyed presenting two previous exhibitions in cooperation with the museum. MOCA's new director, Jeremy Strick, brings enthusiastic and visionary leadership to the continuing intellectual dedication of the museum. We could not have hoped for a more cooperative and competent curator than Connie Butler, who assured the success of this challenging exhibition. We Fellows thank all of the museum staff members who contributed in so many ways to organizing and presenting this exhibition.

Several Fellows deserve special recognition. Fellow Diane Cornwell, former Chair, has been exemplary as our Board liaison for the exhibition. Our past Chair of Long Range Planning, Tina Petra and Linda Polesky, skillfully guided our committees in the selection and development of this show. Merry Scully, our Administrative Director, once again organized the myriad details that are required in completing a major exhibition.

Special appreciation goes to all of the wonderful artists whose works have expanded our horizons to the contemporary challenges of our time. Without the artists, we could not experience the landscapes that they describe so brilliantly. I am also proud of all the members of the Fellows of Contemporary Art, who give so generously their time, financial support, and passionate dedication to art in California. You enable us to spread our wings and bring life to exhibitions like "Flight Patterns."

David B. Partridge
Chair
Fellows of Contemporary Art

In the Field/On Location

Cornelia H. Butler

Perhaps one day "south" and "north" and "east" and "west" will be archaic references to a primitive, bordered world where nationalism and economic tension pitched the planet into chaos.
–Rubén Martínez [1]

In 1994, the anthropologist and travel theorist James Clifford recalled watching an earthquake scientist on television talking about working "in the field," searching for fault lines in the wake of the Landers earthquake, the epicenter of which was somewhere in the southern California desert.[2] In California, we have become accustomed to these televised experts, beaming comfort to a region at constant odds with its geology. According to Clifford, what was startling about the Landers report was that the fieldwork, the excavation, was actually a disembodied, visual survey made from the vantage point of a helicopter hovering over the land, formulating patterns from above.

This split between the very physical, lived experience on the ground in Los Angeles and the mediated view of the landscape—the "in the field/on location" of my title—is the daily reconciliation that informs all experience of this city. The filter that includes the synthesized, Hollywood version of reality, the real time of broadcast freeway chases, or the aerial view glimpsed from a plane window during the descent into the vast L.A. basin, are all part of the illegibility of life in Los Angeles. The "in the field" of anthropology implies a certain relationship to uncharted territory, the wilderness where cultural material happens. "Fieldwork is earthbound—intimately involved in the natural and social landscape.... Fieldwork would put theory to the test; it would *ground* interpretation."[3] It is this connection to the field, the grounding in the social landscape, that intrigues me about the anthropological model—the notion that if you walk the streets and inhabit the city, a cognitive order will repair our traumatized experience of cities and the land they territorialize.

In Los Angeles there are numerous public activities that occupy a space that is part docu-performance and part cultural anthropology. Running across Huell Howser of public television's *California's Gold* in Twentynine Palms, for example, you can be certain he has just come in from some corner of the desert having resurrected an obscure core sample from the marginalized vernacular of the ex-urban landscape. Drawing out the locals with his friendly awe, he endlessly mines the periphery of the greater Los Angeles area. Or there is the poet/activist Lewis MacAdams, whose activities as head of Friends of the Los Angeles River range from poetry readings to legislative confrontations with developers who seek to block construction of a greenbelt along the endangered, man-made waterway. Closer to home, artists/teachers in Los Angeles make regular pilgrimages with their students to the nearby earthworks in Arizona, New Mexico, and Nevada, both demystifying the origin of the monumental works and restoring some awareness of this particularly American strain of sculptural practice. Here, nature is both stunningly present and masterfully upstaged.

In an attempt not to order, but understand and comply with its disorder, is it possible or even interesting to attempt a specific re-reading of the city through representations of its postcolonial relationship to topography? There are several points of entry for this exhibition. The title "Flight Patterns" comes from a familiar and mediated topographic view. Often one's first introduction to a landscape is from an airplane flight plan. Whether tracking your progress while airborne on the video screen or the cockpit audio track, this in-flight mapping, with its absences and distortions, can be the initial city guide. "Flight Patterns" also refers, of course, to the migration of birds, and I am interested in the metaphor of flight, absence, and return as the way in which corporate tourism structures our first views and re-visionings.

A long-held interest in the ground of the social landscape and its particular manifestation in 1970s topographic photography is another inspiration for this project. No doubt my own empathic response to the dour, aestheticizing, black-and-white vision of the ex-urban West is somehow a generational nostalgia for a time when one could more convincingly rant against the evils of "white flight" and the anesthetizing architecture of the suburbs, which now house the majority of the population in this country. What might the current manifestations of an American topographic tradition be and how has this spatializing practice been reworked to incorporate socio-political narratives of the present? In Los Angeles, while there is strikingly little visual artwork that addresses the political volatility of life in the most culturally diverse city in the world, I would argue that the social impulse in visual art is often a spatializing one manifest in the work of photographers like Miles Coolidge, Christina Fernandez, Anthony Hernandez, and Allan Sekula, as well as in the discursive practices of recently active collectives such as the Center for Land Use Interpretation, Dispute Resolution Services, and ADOBE LA.[4] In what Norman Klein has called the "most photographed, least remembered city," these artists are involved in re-figuring Los Angeles through essentially documentary strategies grounded in a documentary or social impulse.[5]

While in New York researching the Chicago World's Columbian Exposition of 1893 during the early 1990s, I became transfixed by the notion of the frontier of westward expansion as it was then bounded by the Missouri River—one giant settlement edge running south from Chicago down the middle of the continent. Like generations of California-born artists, I migrated to the East Coast from Los Angeles after spending some formative years in Des Moines, Iowa, the insurance capital situated in virtually the middle of the country. Armed with the bad geography that those schooled in the United States inevitably carry around, I actually learned which states border Iowa, and intellectualized the extreme culture shock and claustrophobia I felt living in a landlocked place where visiting artists' studios involved long, bleary drives through corn and bean fields. I was relieved to move to New York and, over the years, successfully ignored a creeping, low-grade yearning to again live in a place with a visible horizon. The feeling became a kind of mind-body dilemma where the body yearned somehow for the ocean and desert, while the mind would only tolerate New York.

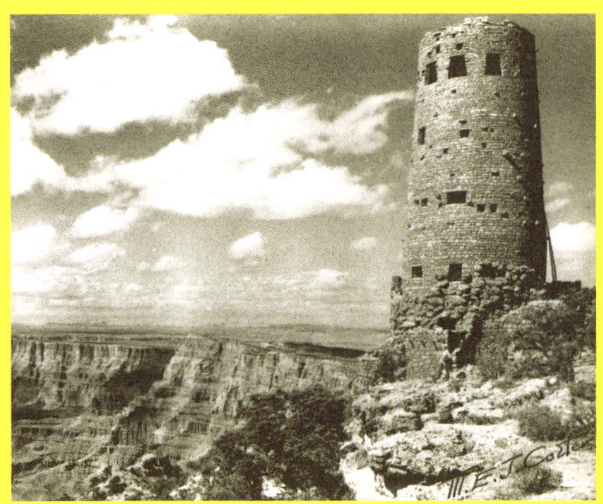

Commercial photograph of a watchtower designed by Mary Colter, Grand Canyon National Park, c. 1932
Grand Canyon National Park #17010

I mention all of this not to ground my remarks in the biographical, but to describe a kind of physical disorientation from the Los Angeles that I experienced growing up—when the strange term "back east" was how Angelenos referred to the East Coast, as though pre-visioning some inevitable, reverse migration. Always fascinated by the representation of Los Angeles from the distance of New York, I began gazing back west, allowing myself to be seduced by the hyper-mythologized Los Angeles of Mike Davis's *City of Quartz* and the exotic vastness of Lawrence Kasdan's *Grand Canyon.* And apart from Baudrillard's nostalgic and now clichéd vision of the road and desert, or the well-worn vernacular architectural terrain theorized by Robert Venturi and Denise Scott Brown in *Learning from Las Vegas*, I learned about other visions that shaped the tourist landscape of the American West and complicated its colonial history.

What about the presence of Mary Colter, "girl architect" of The Fred Harvey Company who, a century ago, designed many of the tourist sites along the Atchison, Topeka, and Santa Fe Railway from Kansas City westward, apparently often in cooperation with the Native-American peoples she encountered and whose designs she liberally appropriated? The interior architecture of Los Angeles's own Union Station, designed by Colter, is a unique mix of Mexican, Native-American, and Art Deco design. Apart from my own fantasy of somehow embodying Mary Colter—designing fabulous lookout towers or posing on the edge of the Grand Canyon, sporting knickers and walking stick—certainly the tourist landscape and the influence of the Native-American culture on the design and population of it, as well as the relationship of both to modernism in the West, is worth further study.

Not unexpectedly, the landscape of California and its persistent tourist identity as "Lotus Land" has impacted the exportation of its art to both the East Coast and the international art market. As one example, the relatively recent history of Light and Space art of the 1970s (an approach to installation making which drew its inspiration, at least in part, from the landscape, both urban and arid) has been largely unaccounted for in American contemporary art histories. Seemingly this has something to do with the way studio practice is still privileged and commodified over those that are spatially inscribed. No doubt the hippie/spiritual reading of this work's relationship to the American transcendental has something to do with the lack of historical accounting for Light and Space as well. The dreamy image of the "desert by the sea" can still be found in the current, rather dangerous tendency in the art press to frame absolutely everything produced in this supposed playground as made by upstarts frolicking in the eucalyptus-tinged, smoke-free ether. A recent *New York Times* article managed to couch a discussion of Los Angeles art schools in visions of the pastoral:

> Chris Burden began his career with a literal bang. His *Shooting Piece* required a friend to fire a bullet into his left arm from a distance of 15 feet. Perhaps that's why, when we recently met at the University of California at Los Angeles, I found it hard to imagine him patiently sitting through faculty meetings. Time does strange things. You wait long enough and even the most outrageous rebels end up grading papers and sharing career tips with students.... It was a shining afternoon, and air was fragrant with the scent of eucalyptus trees.[6]

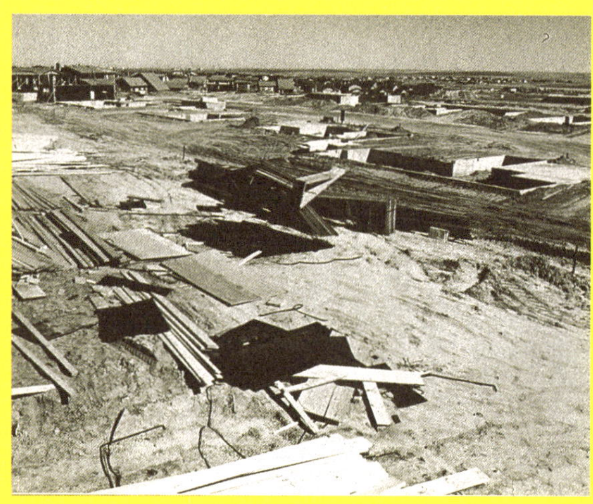

Robert Adams
Untitled, from *What We Bought: Scenes From the Denver Metropolitan Area 1970–1974,* c. 1970
Gelatin-silver print
6 x 6 inches
Courtesy Fraenkel Gallery, San Francisco

The mythologizing goes on exponentially. Back in the field, what if one looks west from Los Angeles which, in art terms, feels like trying to separate one's head from an institutional body that historically has gravitated towards New York and Europe. MOCA is situated in the geographical center of the vast region that is the "Greater Los Angeles Area," a sixty-mile circle that encompasses the counties of Los Angeles, Ventura, Orange, San Bernardino, and Riverside.[7] There is, within the city, an ongoing discourse of race and real estate; between the west and east side of the city; water versus desert; tropical, leisurely, and new, versus arid, economically edgy, and old.

Unlike New York, where patronage has determined the hierarchies and geography of visual production and institutions, one could argue that in Los Angeles, to some extent, the landscape itself has been a determining factor. Would the Getty Center have been built on a hill instead of making good adaptive reuse of a central city building if it weren't for the spectacular view? A video work by Judy Fiskin entitled *My Getty Center* (2000) wryly exploits the connection between the coincidence of the meteorological onslaught of El Niño and the opening of the Getty with dreamy imaginings of its buildings being washed out to sea in a giant flood of media frenzy and water. The Getty itself recently published *Cultural Inheritance L.A.: A Directory of Less-Visible Archives and Collections in the Los Angeles Region* (1999), which suggests that the wealth of vernacular photographic material has not been collected by museums, but is in private hands, dispersed across the city from Riverside to Venice, often in small, eccentrically organized, local archives. Indeed, in describing the L.A. art scene—from the dispersal of artists' studios across the city's illogical geography, to the flourishing of modernist domestic architecture, the citywide collection of public murals, and the art/activism around the beleaguered Los Angeles River—virtually everything can be read in topographic terms.

In some ways, my thinking about this exhibition goes back to 1989 when I first visited Australia on a cultural exchange. I was introduced to the work of Tim Johnson and Tracey Moffatt, whose stunning early film *Night Cries: A Rural Tragedy* (1989) was first screened at The New Museum of Contemporary Art. My reaction to the film mirrored my response to the vast landscape of Australia, with its desert middle and cities clinging to the continental edge. To the Western viewer arriving from the north, there is the sense of being somewhere completely familiar and disorienting at the same time—the sense that the cities and the glorious, endless water somehow camouflage the harsh and sparsely populated desert.

As is discussed elsewhere in this book, artists like Moffatt and New Zealand photographer Laurence Aberhart seek, re-present, or construct the disjunctive territory of the postcolonial landscape: a kind of suspended, nowhere space where narratives of history and representation collide, where the epic dimension of a given national story is filtered through the vernacular of the folktale.[8] Reflecting on the relationship of his photographs to topographic photography, Aberhart states that, when he "began to do the so-called minimalist abstract work of picturing architecture in relationship to the land," nobody had "managed to do the nineteenth- and early twentieth-century work, [that] I had better 'retreat' and in the absence of anyone else, start that primary stuff. Then the problem was how to do that and include/acknowledge the modern-re-examination work."[9] This dysphoric position—where the primary material, the in-the-field archival work, is morphed together with the on-location mediation of a historical present—begins to get at the project of this exhibition. In the artists' pages that follow, parallels are drawn between artists practicing in geographic regions loosely bound by the Pacific. Thinking through their works, visual material is broadly organized into thematic groupings that refer to both the history of topographic representation and to more recent thinking about the postcolonial landscape. In some ways, applying a little postcolonial work to a landscape that is simultaneously impossible to excavate and represent, yet at the same time over-represented, provides the tension at the heart of much of the work in this exhibition.

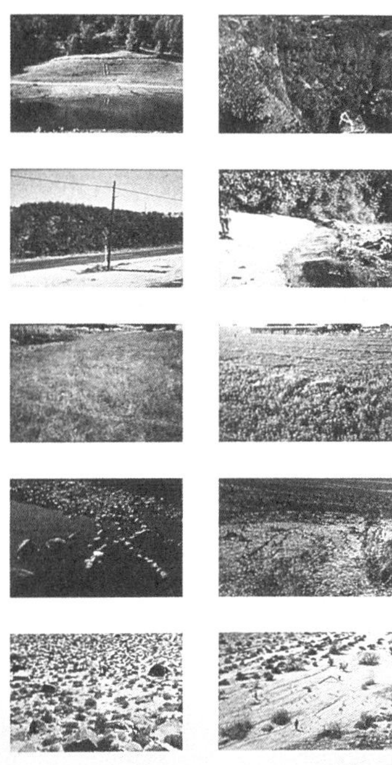

John Baldessari
California Map Project, Part 1: California, 1969, 1969
Type-R prints and typewritten sheet mounted on board
Prints 8 x 10 inches each; Text 8 1/2 x 11 inches
Courtesy of the artist

Notes

1. Rubén Martínez, "The Tense Embrace of the 'Other': Mexico & the U.S.", in *Distant Relations: Chicano Irish Mexican Art and Critical Writing* (Santa Monica, Calif.: Smart Art Press, 1995), 175.
2. James Clifford, *Routes: Travel and Translation in the Late Twentieth Century* (Cambridge, Mass.: Harvard University Press, 1997), 52. Clifford's writing and the work coming out of the History of Consciousness program at University of California, Santa Cruz, has impacted the discussion of the Pacific Rim since the mid-1980s. His insightful museological work focusing on the example of anthropology museums was specifically influential within context of multiculturalism. *See* "Of Other Peoples: Beyond the 'Salvage' Paradigm," in Hal Foster, ed. *Discussions in Contemporary Culture, no. 1* (New York: Dia Center for the Arts; and Seattle: Bay Press, 1987), 121–30. The problem of the contextualization of issues of identity in anthropological terms is ongoing, particularly as the international art market has recently embraced work from Asian cultures.
3. Clifford, 52–53.
4. In the closing issue of *World Art*, the artist Charles LaBelle talks about these artists and others who respond to the urban landscape of Los Angeles. *See* "Escape Trajectory," *World Art*, no. 20 (1999): 40–45.
5. Norman M. Klein, *The History of Forgetting: Los Angeles and the Erasure of Memory* (London: Verso, 1997), 250.
6. Deborah Solomon, "How to Succeed in Art," *The New York Times Magazine* (27 June 1999). Both the opening and closing lines of the article invoked the pastoral. Just like any female subject of a journalistic profile, who cannot escape being introduced without physical description, the art students and their teachers cannot be described without reference to the physical surroundings that must, implicitly, be affecting their production. *See* my "West of Everything," *Parkett*, no.57 (December 1999): 189–94.
7. *See* Edward Soja's discussion of the sixty-mile circle in "It All Comes Together in Los Angeles," in his *Postmodern Geographies: The Reassertion of Space in Critical Social Theory* (London: Verso, 1989), 191. Of this region he says: "one might call the sprawling urban region defined by a sixty-mile (100 kilometre) circle around the centre of the City of Los Angeles a prototopos, a paradigmatic place; or, pushing inventiveness still further, a mesocosm, an ordered world in which the micro and the macro, the idiographic and the nomothetic, the concrete and the abstract, can be seen simultaneously in an articulated and interactive combination."
8. Lynne Cooke specifically says of *Night Cries*, "the epic dimension first adumbrated in *Night Cries* remains once again filtered through the colloquial and vernacular. The result is a laconic poetic statement that, like Pasolini's, could be said not to make sense as much as to suspend sense." From an unpaginated exhibition brochure published in conjunction with "Free-Falling" (New York: Dia Center for the Arts, 1997).
9. Laurence Aberhart, e-mail to the author, 10 May 2000.

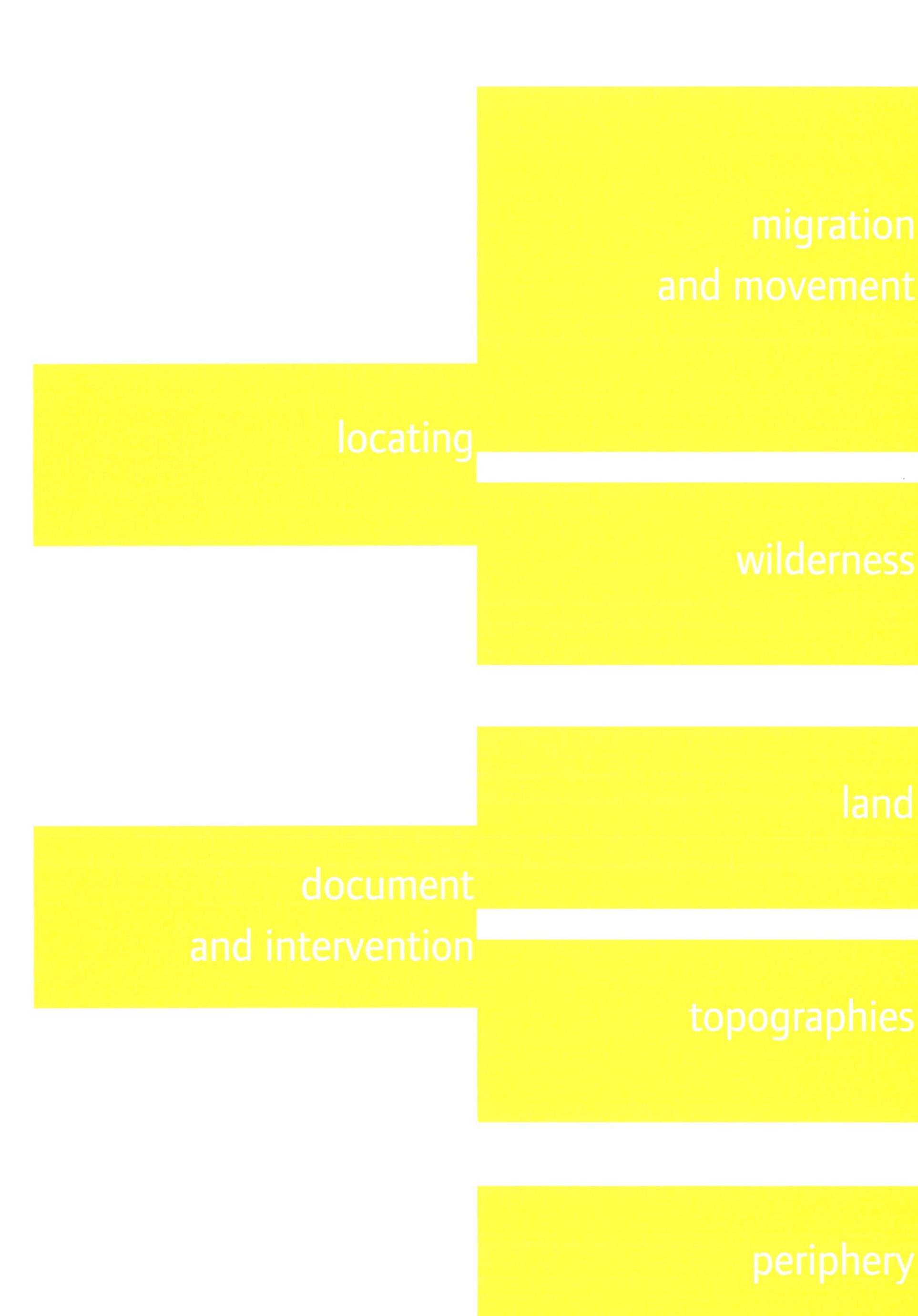
migration
and movement
locating
wilderness
land
document
and intervention
topographies
periphery

locating

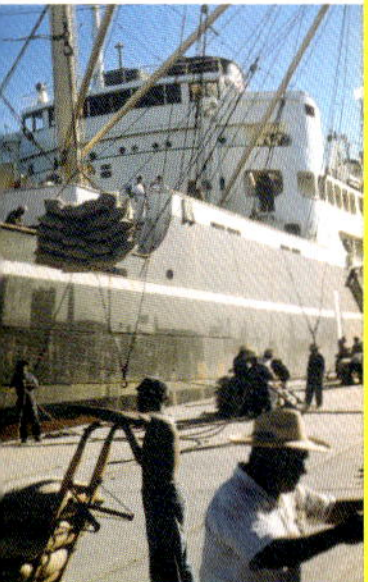
Paul Outerbridge

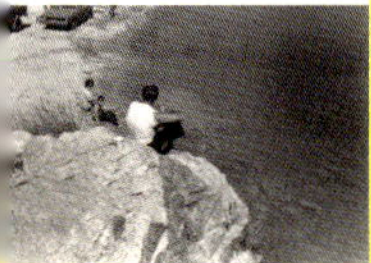
Anthony Hernandez

An unquestioned category still continues to survive: that of the West. The West is a sort of unitary category which perhaps should be further displaced and deconstructed, not so much because of the complex realities of postmodern cultures... but because, once again, it fails to undermine a politics of mere opposition and binarism.
—Annamaria Morelli [1]

In 1996, Lucy Lippard coined the phrase "The Lure of the Local." In the current discourse surrounding the global/local, notions of the ordinary, everyday, and regionally specific have been persistently invoked.[2] The North American West Coast boasts a vital history of photography and film that is closely tied to the land and the road. Whether evidenced by Edward Ruscha's seminal *Twenty-six Gasoline Stations* (1963) (not to mention his parking lots, pools, and pictorial inventory of every building on the Sunset Strip); John Baldessari's *California Map Project* (1969) and 1967–68 photo/text canvases, which pinpoint such banal locales as the "Econ-o-wash" in National City, the border town of his youth; or Jeff Wall's *Landscape Manual* (1969–70), there is a combined sense of curiosity and irreverence towards the vernacular that is part of both the reality of the artists' vision and the received myth that has helped shape the Western viewer's understanding of the West.

In the years before his death in 1958, Paul Outerbridge journeyed between California and South America taking photographs and writing travel articles for leisure publications. Though he never printed these pictures, he apparently intended to retain particular images for personal use. With their stunning color and atmospheric clarity, the work is immediately recognizable as Outerbridge's own. His photographs have an embodied, physical quality that is also characteristic of his still lifes, due in part to the dye-transfer technology used by Outerbridge but no longer commercially available. Reading across a group of the travel photographs, it is possible to trace the photographer's wandering eye as it was alternately seduced by the vernacular abstraction of a fence or empty gasoline station, and enthralled with a curbside narrative that was part of the social landscape he describes. The pictures embody a timeless, crystalline quality—they appear to occupy the present-day Tijuana of Robert Rodriguez's *El Mariachi*, as well as they might the stylized, exotic nightscape of Orson Welles's *Touch of Evil*. The clear stillness of his modernist pictures is everywhere here, from a fishing scene composed in homage to Alfred Stieglitz's *The Steerage* (1907), to the dramatic and langorous light of a hotel lobby.

Among the most intriguing aspects of this body of work, about which Outerbridge imparted clear instructions for printing finished pictures, is that it formally prefigures the minimalist focus on the architectural subject of topographic photographers, whose reductive re-visioning of the urban West came almost twenty years later.[3] In some of the pictures we see Outerbridge distracted by fragments of the built environment to the exclusion of the social narrative that is his foregrounded subject. In one image, a construction site on an ocean bluff is centrally framed in a way that anticipates the blunt formalism of Allan Sekula's *Dead Letter Office* (1997), a photographic essay that deals, in part, with the economy of the waters around the Tijuana, Mexico/California border. In another colorful abstraction, a suburban-looking house constructed from cheap colored fiberglass and cinderblock speaks to the mixed-use, temporary architecture of economically depressed, Mexican border towns. Outerbridge's flat camera angle and blank inflection immediately recall Lewis Baltz's *Park City* (1979), emptied of the "local color."

Outerbridge's legacy runs directly through to photographers such as William Current, teacher of Baltz, and to Robert Adams and Henry Wessel. But it is Outerbridge's preoccupation with the incidental, and his almost painterly rendering of everyday scenes in his travel pictures, that maintains a commitment to the documentary form. Unlike his signature modernist compositions of the 1930s and 1940s, these less composed, more narratively discursive representations attempt to fix a particular mood, a quality of light, or an almost cinematic encounter. They insist on some kind of social narrative, even if only a subdued one.

To the extent that the legacy of topographic photography is the privileging of evidence—the banal, apparently detached representation of the urban edge—Anthony Hernandez has spent a career reinvesting the reductive formalism of this kind of photography with a representation of the social. A student and contemporary of Baltz's, Hernandez's view of the city was formulated by his upbringing in East Los Angeles. Since 1986, he has been photographing, with great specificity, abandoned urban scenes: homeless sites, drug hangouts, the makeshift architecture of squatters and transients. The critic Ralph Rugoff recently described the operation of Hernandez's work in terms of evidence, observing: "His pictures ask us, in other words, to intimately inhabit spaces that we might not normally wish to occupy… suggesting the work of a wayward forensic photographer whose aesthetic sense occasionally overrides his investigatory agenda," and finds "an abiding imperative [in the pictures] to look where no one else is looking."[4]

While his color pictures depict sites deserted just long enough for any residual presence to be neutralized into abstraction, Hernandez's early black-and-white series is comparatively populated. Between 1978 and 1982 he made three studies of what one might call transitional spaces around Los Angeles: *Public Transit Areas*, *Public Use Areas*, and *Public Fishing Areas*. Hernandez manages to make what are essentially fishing holes around the city and urban plazas—those alienating, languishing public places so out of place in Los Angeles—appear entirely unlocatable and generic. The flat, white light of the *Public Fishing Areas* (1979–83), or the jarring combination of the occasional palm tree with snow-capped mountains in the distance, are perhaps our only clues to their geographic context. This series of twenty-three photographs, never previously exhibited together, documents these dusty, mixed-use locations where leisure and economic reality commingle. The work leaves us with the impression that no one else is looking at these sites, and with a feeling of unease about making any assessment of our own. They are utterly banal and yet function socially, while at the same time offer a picture of Los Angeles that is as confusing to a particular class of inhabitants as David Hockney's sexy *Mulholland Drive* (1980) might be to another. Hernandez shows us the hinterland that is just off the freeway.

Notes

1. Annamaria Morelli, in conversation with Trinh T. Minh-ha, "The Undone Interval", in Iain Chambers and Lidia Curti, eds., *The Post-Colonial Question: Common Skies, Divided Horizons* (London and New York: Routledge, 1996), 14.
2. I am thinking here of thematic, international exhibitions such as Bruce Ferguson's SITE Santa-Fe, "Longing and Belonging: From the Faraway Nearby," or the 1998 Biennale of Sydney, titled "Every Day," in which the writings of Lefebvre on the everyday, Susan Stewart "On Longing," and Fredric Jameson on "Spatiality" are referenced.
3. The Outerbridge photographs are included in the exhibition due to the efforts of curator and photography historian Graham Howe, who spoke to Outerbridge about them before his death and was given access to the negatives. According to Howe, Outerbridge considered these photographs as an extension of his travel writing and intended to print them. I am indebted to Howe for bringing these pictures to my attention in the context of a discussion about Lewis Baltz and William Current.
4. Ralph Rugoff, "Familiar Haunts: The Photography of Anthony Hernandez," *Artforum* 38, no. 5 (January 2000): 98, 100.

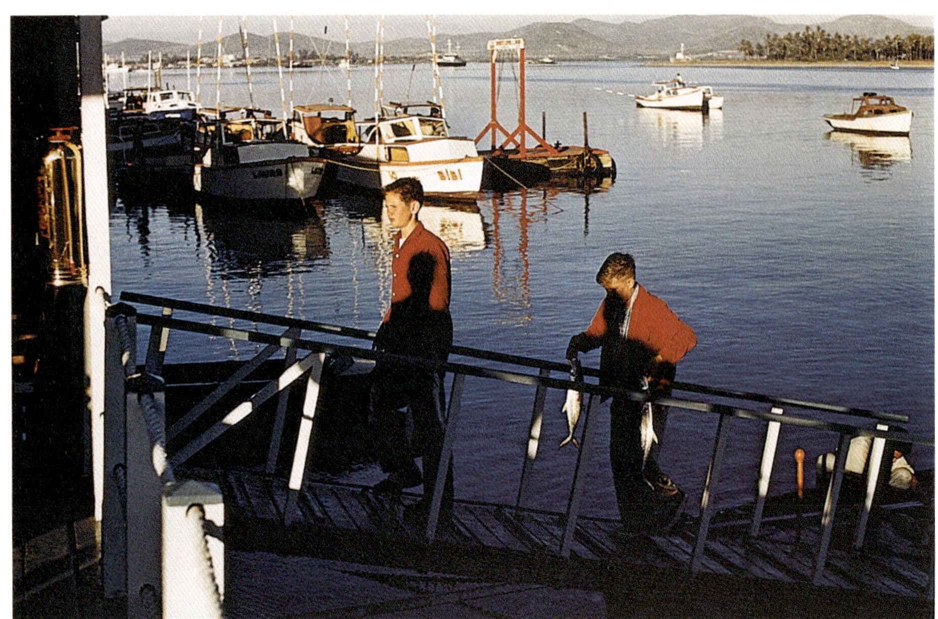

MEXICO, c. 1955

Paul Outerbridge

Outerbridge moved from New York in 1940 and spent the rest of his life in Laguna Beach, California. Taken between 1955 and 1958, these pictures were intended to accompany essays that Outerbridge published in *U.S. Camera* and other travel magazines, documenting trips he made throughout California, Mexico, and South America. Though not published during his lifetime, Outerbridge expected these pictures to be printed non-commercially as well. His hallmark crystalline color, descriptive texture, carefully considered formal composition, and suggestion of topographic narrative all anticipated the new topographic style of the 1970s.

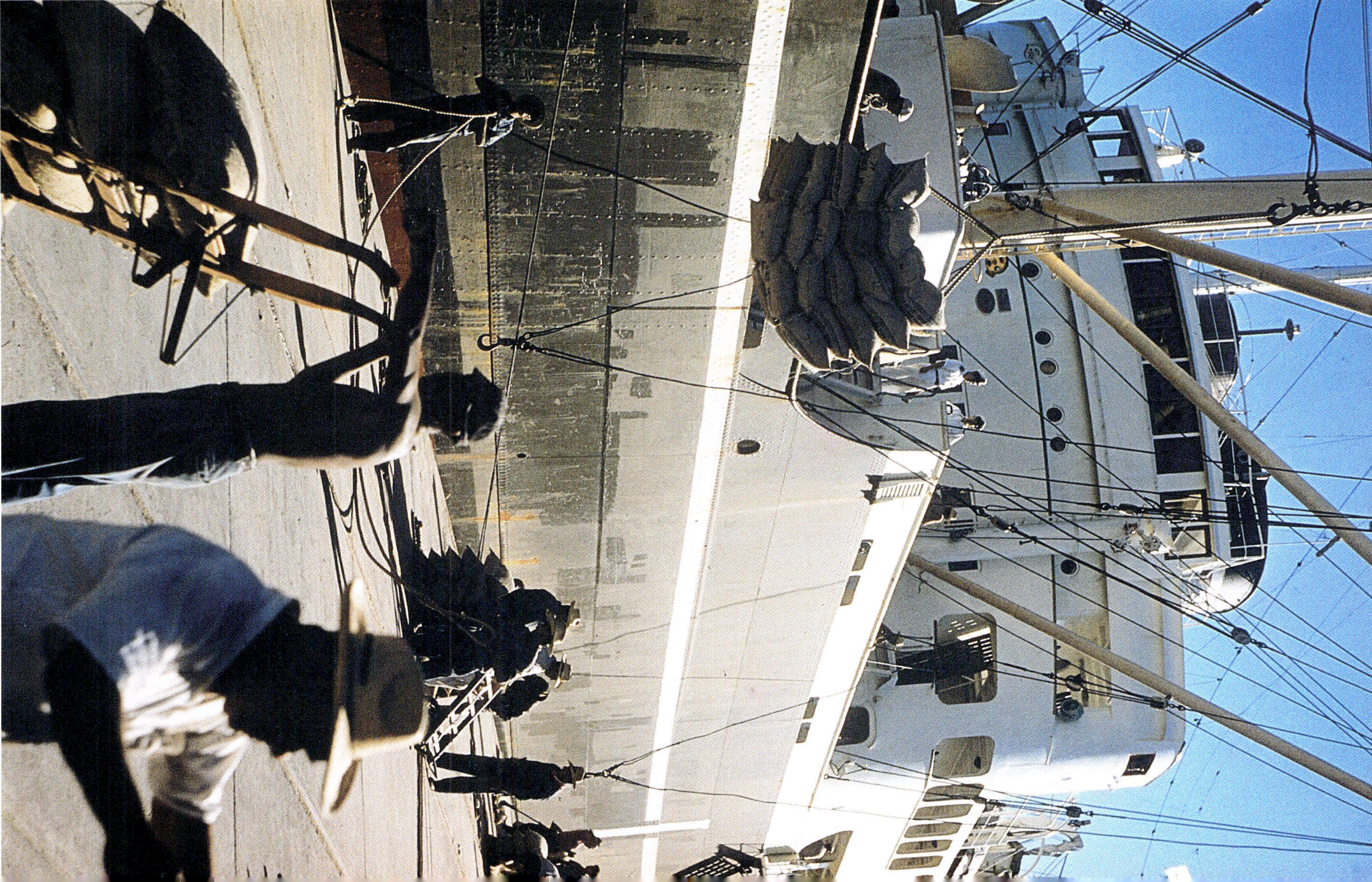

DOCKS, MEXICO, c. 1955

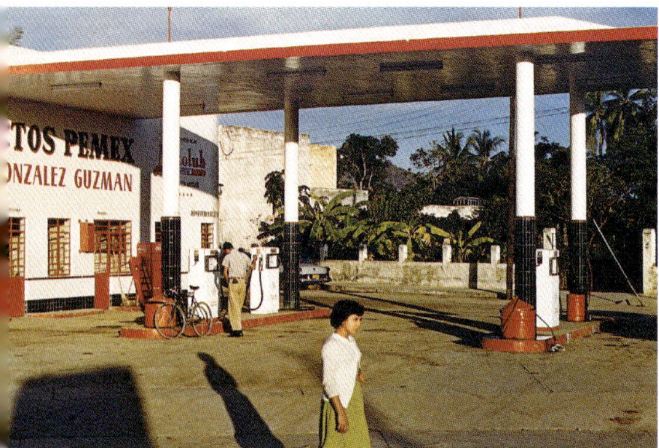

MEXICO, c. 1955

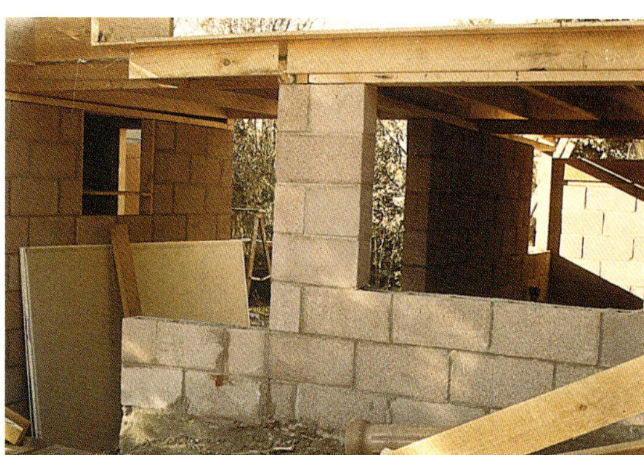

MEXICO, c. 1955

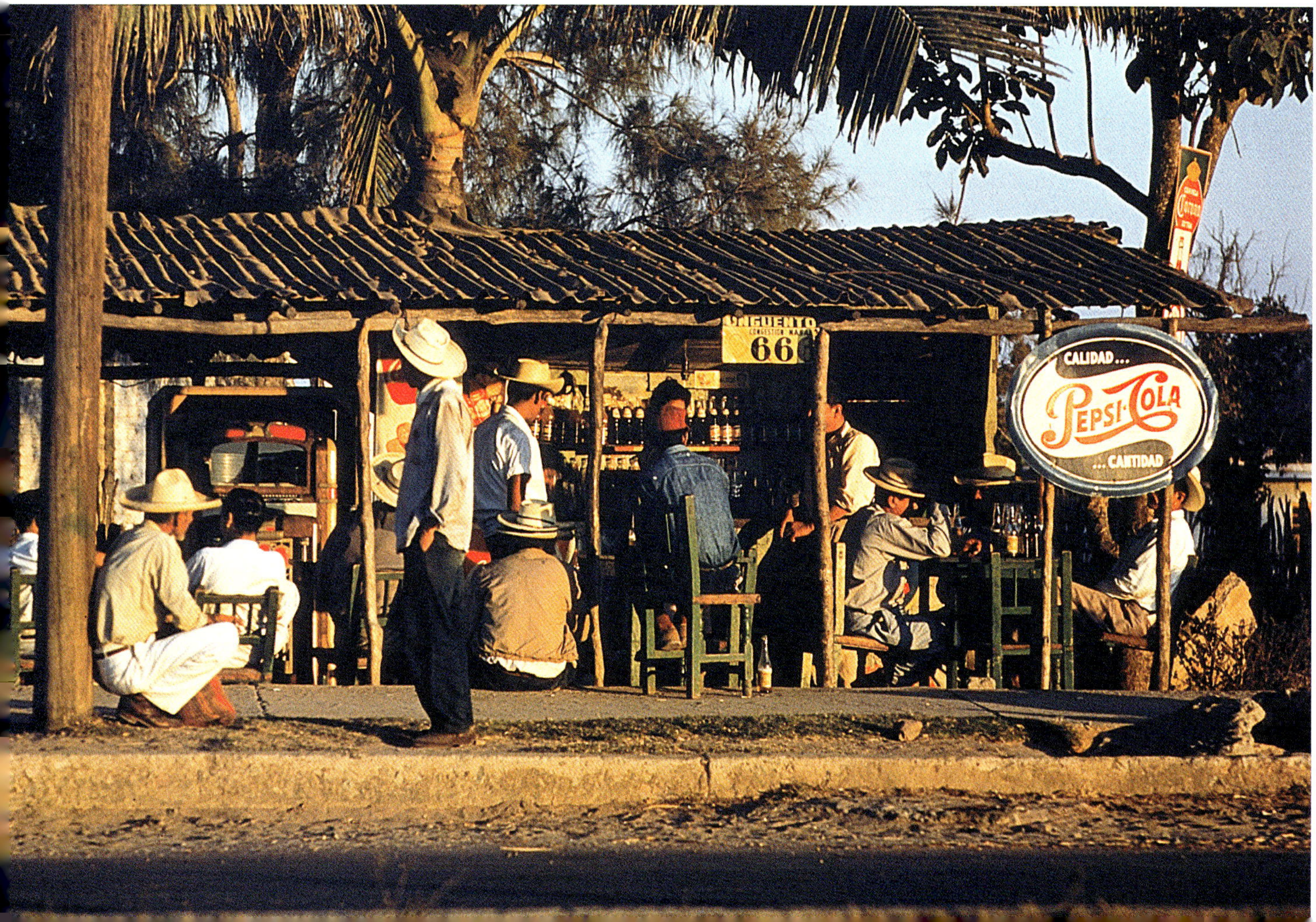

MEXICO, c. 1955

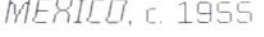

MEXICO, c. 1955

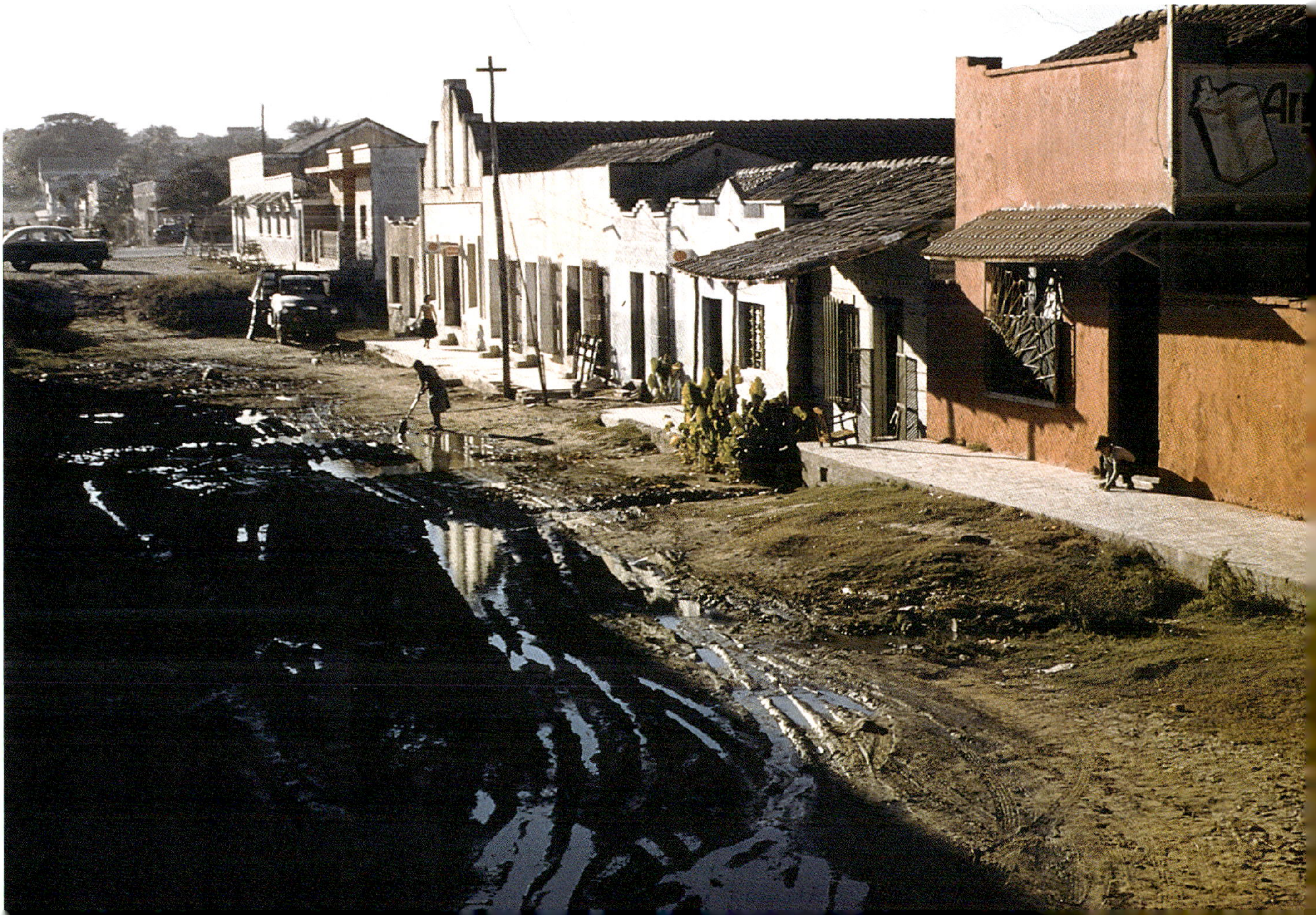

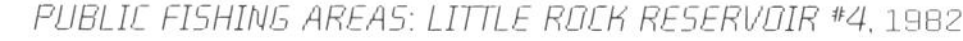

PUBLIC FISHING AREAS: LITTLE ROCK RESERVOIR #4, 1982

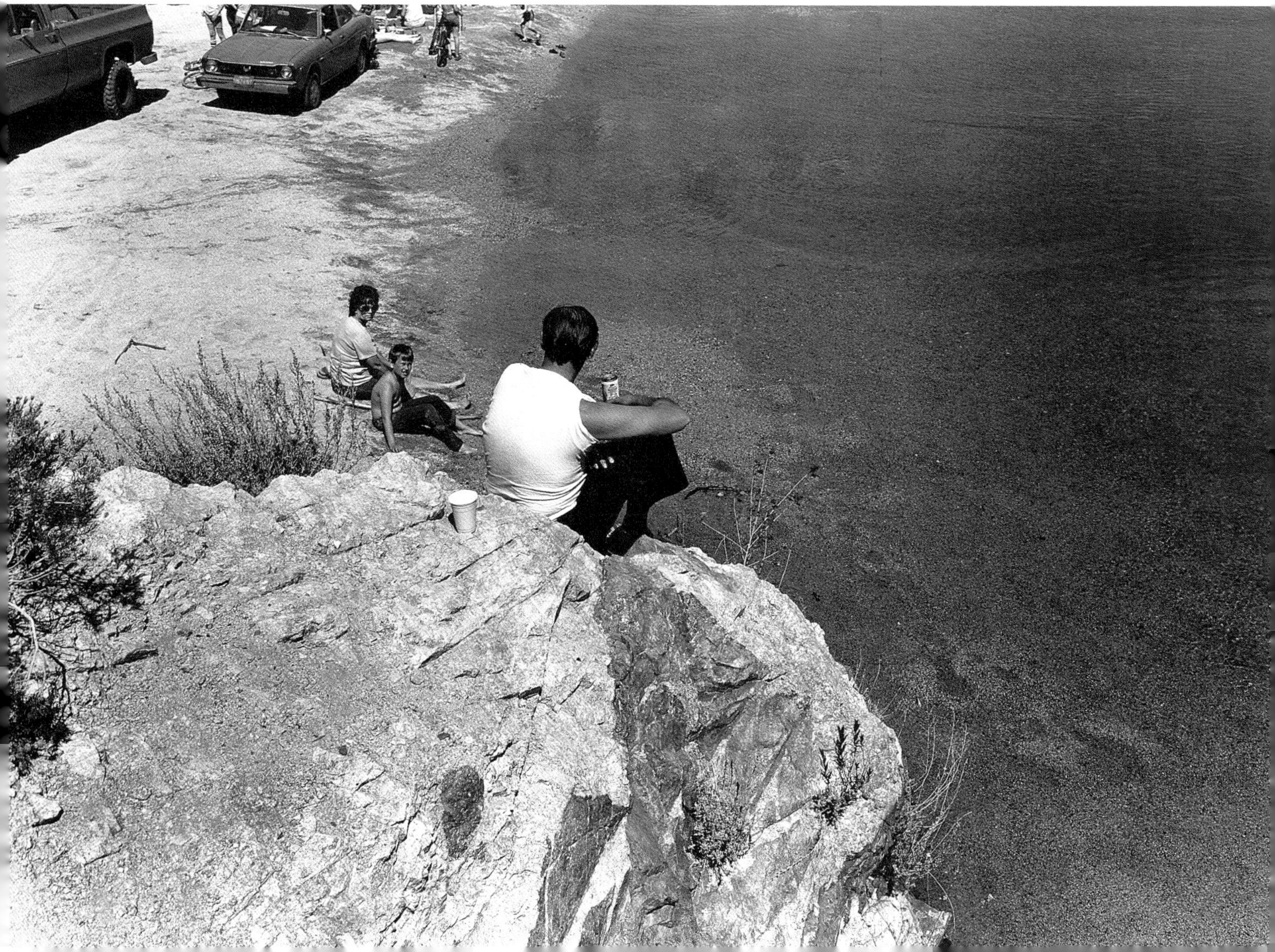

Anthony Hernandez

Between 1978 and 1982, Hernandez made three series of black-and-white pictures, *Public Transit Areas, Public Fishing Areas,* and *Public Use Areas,* that documented banal topographies of public use in and around urban Los Angeles. In *Public Fishing Areas,* watery locales—including public parks, dams, reservoirs, water conservation areas, and the Salton Sea—are represented as they are experienced in the harsh, overexposed light of Los Angeles. The surreal juxtaposition of families relaxing or men fishing for food and their environs—bodies of water that defy nature in the arid landscape, set against the snowcapped mountains or palm trees on the horizon—humanizes the topographic tradition upon which much of Hernandez's work is based.

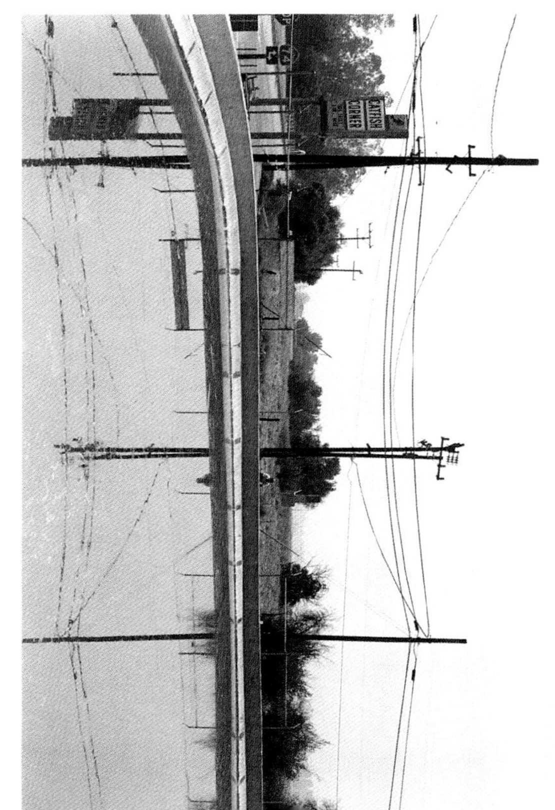

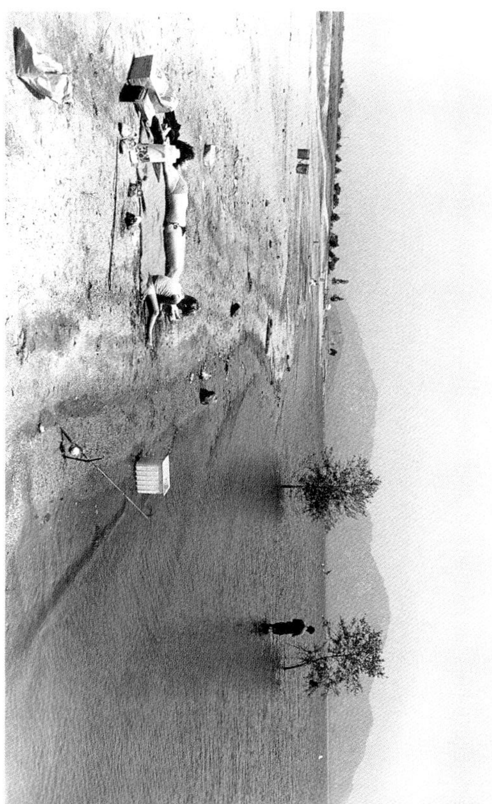

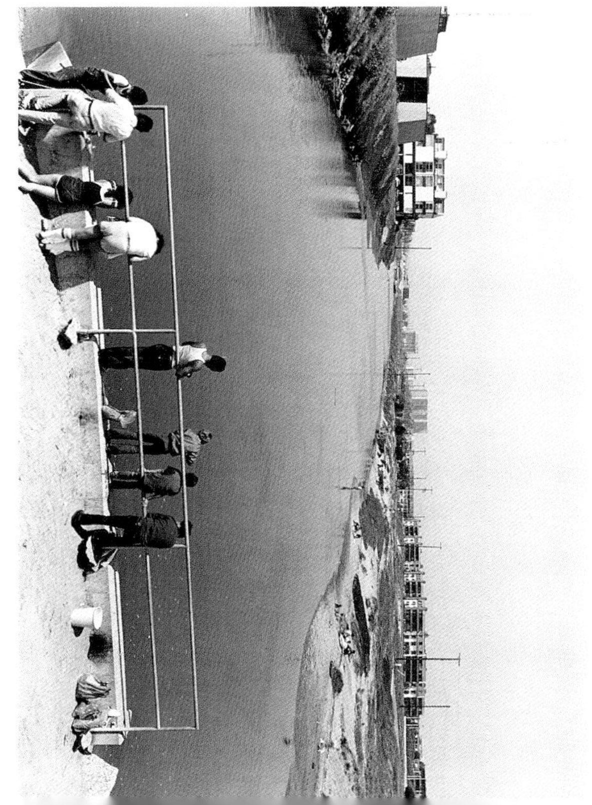

PUBLIC FISHING AREAS: CATFISH CORNER, NEAR LAKE ELSINORE, 1981
PUBLIC FISHING AREAS: HEMET LAKE, 1982
PUBLIC FISHING AREAS: MARINA DEL MAR, 1979

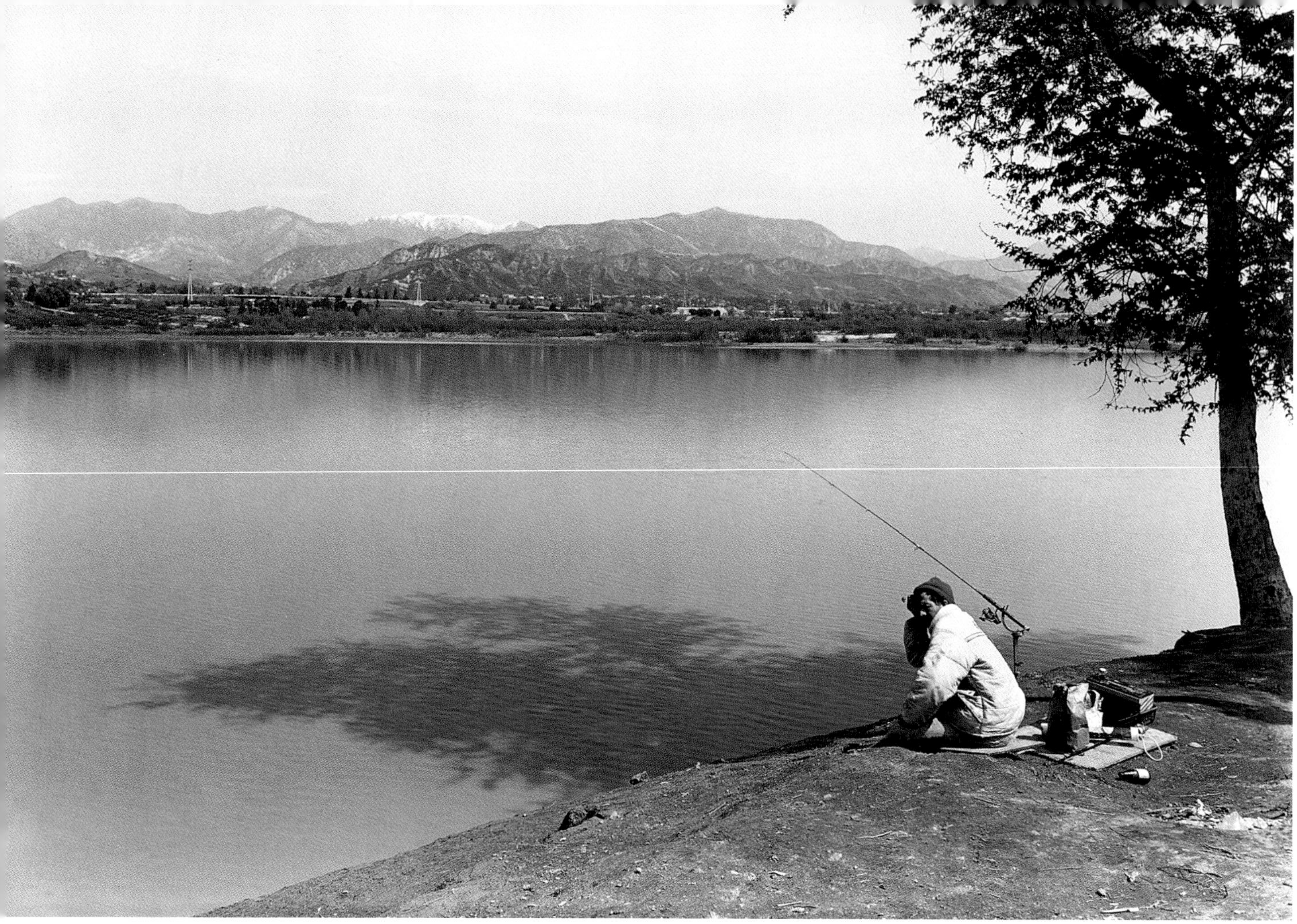

PUBLIC FISHING AREAS: HANSEN DAM #2, 1981

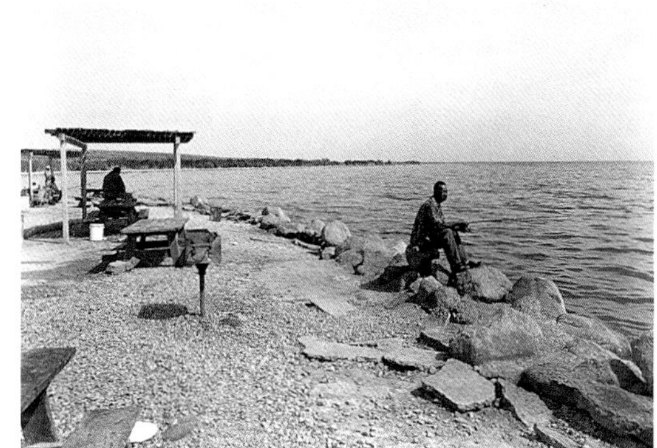

PUBLIC FISHING AREAS: SALTON SEA, 1982

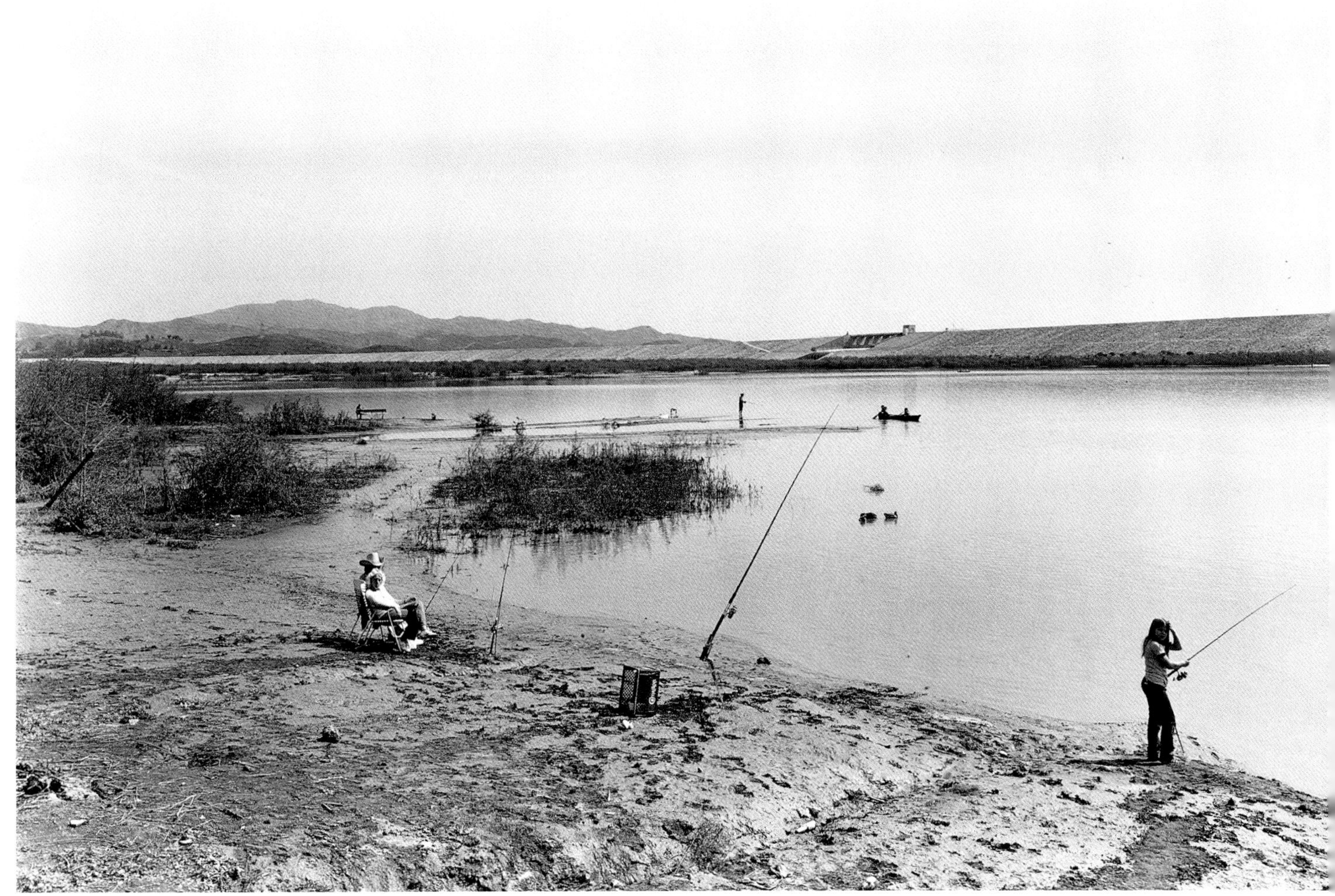

PUBLIC FISHING AREAS: HANSEN DAM #1, 1981

document and intervention

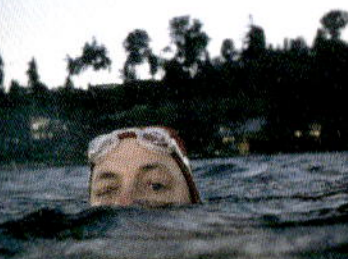
Allan Sekula

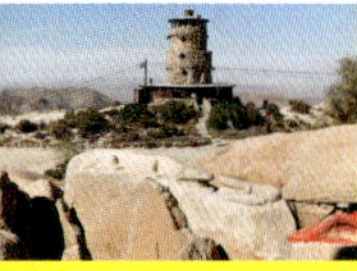
CLUI

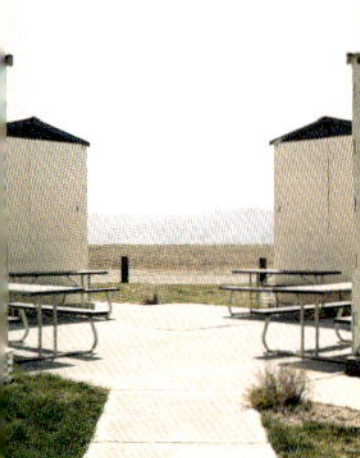
Miles Coolidge

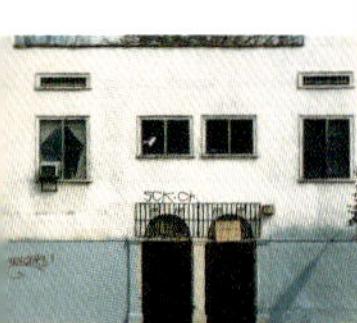
Christina Fernandez

THE SEEN/SCENE IS THAT OF A NEW GEOGRAPHY OF MODERNIZATION, AN EMERGING POSTFORDIST URBAN LANDSCAPE FILLED WITH MORE FLEXIBLE SYSTEMS OF PRODUCTION, CONSUMPTION, EXPLOITATION, SPATIALIZATION, AND SOCIAL CONTROL THAN HAVE HITHERTO MARKED THE HISTORICAL GEOGRAPHY OF CAPITALISM.

—Edward Soja [1]

Between 1983 and 1995 Allan Sekula completed a series of photographic/textual essays, titled *Fish Story*, devoted to examining what he describes as "the physical and economic transformation of ports and of the culture of the waterfront workers around the globe." Focusing his attention on port cities of the Atlantic and on South Korea, Seattle, and Tacoma as nodes in the Pacific economy, he unearths the physical changes in the urban areas surrounding these ports and in the lives of their inhabitants whose livelihood supports these economies.

Sekula's current projects *Waiting for Tear Gas* and *TITANIC's wake* (both 2000) extend his interest in global economic shifts and, by way of example, the absurdly ambitious construction projects which express a particularly American brand of hubris and often involve the economic transformation of the urban systems into which they are placed. The slide projection *Waiting for Tear Gas* comprises pictures shot at the 1999 World Trade Organization conference in Seattle and makes use of the now primitive technology of the slide projector. Using this format Sekula compiles a portrait of what he sees as a new form of political action—the new left activity around the carefully choreographed meeting of government officials and the staging of corporate media.

Seattle is, of course, also the home of Microsoft titan Bill Gates, whose many sidelines include an archival project to digitize all of the world's images of art. He has also collected such non-virtual masterworks as Winslow Homer's *Lost on the Grand Banks* (1885), an epic painting metaphorizing man's fragility in the face of nature and technology. *Dear Bill Gates* (1999) is a humorous and rather poignant triptych in which Sekula undertakes a herculean act of his own and swims the waters in front of Gates's house, futilely attempting to get an answer to his philosophical query about Gates's ownership of the painting: "The lostness depicted becomes purely metaphysical in its passage into Gates possession, he finds the painting in order to lose its specifity, the depiction of lostness stands now as the antithesis of Gates' instrumental program of total global connectedness."[2]

Part activist, part performance, part geology, and part group science project, the Center for Land Use Interpretation (CLUI) has elaborated a multi-disciplinary niche for its activities, which range from bus tours to sites through the California desert to an exhibition of postcards photographed by Merle Porter. At its headquarters, CLUI offers homespun exhibitions, currently installed in a temporary trailer, as well as a lending library of books on land, mapping, topography, and conservation. Collective members represent a range of backgrounds (including geology, architecture, and art) and insist on group identity and a strategic vagueness about the naming of their activities.

There is little irony in CLUI's agenda, which appears to be literally raising awareness about issues of the land and landscape primarily in the West but also generally in North America. Sited on a 140-acre plot leased from the Bureau of Land Management (BLM) is the Desert Research Station, a generic exhibition hall and former education space run by the BLM. The nearest town, Hinkley of *Erin Brockovich* fame, is abandoned now because of the PG&E environmental disaster that was the subject of the film. The collision not only of Hollywood as the primary image-maker of the desert landscape, but the filmic representation of people living in the desert region, is all part of the conceptual appeal of the location for CLUI.

In its day, the Desert Research Station was an interpretive center for the region complete with nature trails and a marker on the Automobile Club map. An early e-mail describes the project as "only two hours from Los Angeles but a whole other world":

> Hinkley is... remarkable for the myriad of unusual and exemplary sites... all around are huge military field test and training sites... as well as the largest open pit mine in California and many other mining sites, cultural sites, prisons off-highway recreational zones, bombing ranges, the largest solar arrays in the world, and on and on.[3]

The CLUI project intervenes in the formalism of topographic photographic strategies with a social inclination born out of humor and reconstructed frontier individualism. In a sense, they perform an inversion by populating non-sites that become the center of their activity.

The shipping container economy that now seems a relic of the late-twentieth century is the subject of a new series of pictures by Canadian-born, Los Angeles-based Miles Coolidge. Commissioned by *NEST* magazine, Coolidge made fourteen pictures of temporary, migrant-worker housing in an area called Mattawa, an orchard town just north of the Hanford nuclear fuel processing plant in eastern Washington. The economy of this fertile territory functions through the daily labor of migrant workers, many undocumented, who live locally and migrate with the crops. In many ways *Near Mattawa* extends the investigation begun in Coolidge's *Central Valley* pictures—long, horizontal scenes taken from Interstate-5, bordered by rich farm country all the way up the center of California. The tension in these earlier photographs is located in what might be called the middle landscape—the distanced, hazy view bound by the road. In *Near Mattawa* Coolidge moves literally into the field of vision, complicating our polarized understanding of the valley landscape. In documenting the architect-designed, 26 Unit Housing Authority project—named Hope—he focuses on a community of migrant farm laborers and their living spaces built out of converted shipping containers.

Made between 11:00a.m. and 1:00p.m. during one day, and shot from the same spot at each quadrant, the pictures are chillingly and insistently plain. The viewer can understand the containers simultaneously as architecture and, in the tradition of Dorothea Lange's migrant workers, can read the pictures as social artifact embodying the dilemma of the Hispanic underclass that sustains the agricultural economy in California. Uninhabited, the only information offered by the buildings is a striking statement about the residue and failure of the late modernist architectural project.

One of the most vital areas of activity for art/activist projects during the last decade is the transitional "mesocosm" of San Diego and Tijuana.[4] In recent years, photographer Christina Fernandez has made work that addresses her own conflicted relationship with the cultural border between her native Los Angeles and the country of her Chicana heritage, Mexico. Mixing references from her family history and drawing on the *mezistaje* narrative in North America, she mines the urban landscape, enacting a respatialization of what Chon Noriega has called "the linear geneology of the west."[5]

Fernandez's photo/text work titled *Manuela S-T-I-T-C-H-E-D* (1996) comprises elegant, documentary portraits of sweatshops around southern California. The transformation of the legacy of social documentary photography has benefited from the artist's resuscitation of the text as a strategy of institutional critique. Originally installed on the ground, winding as though replicating a journey or unraveled thread, Fernandez's accompanying text was culled from interviews with Latina garment workers and describes a fictional moment just after an immigration raid. The invocation of the weather, the almost biblical way the migration officers are described as a storm moving through the community of workers, is in stark contrast to the reductive building facades that are Fernandez's photographic subject. In a sobering and poignant way, the stark text and reductive pictures counter the tourist identity of southern California as a leisure destination with the concurrent reality of it as a destination for immigrants. She invests these anonymous pictures with the personal accounts of the multi-ethnic workers who inhabit them and contribute to the local economy that surrounds downtown Los Angeles, the heart of North American/Pacific Rim economy.

Notes

1. Edward Soja, "It All Comes Together in Los Angeles," in *Postmodern Geographies* (London and New York: Verso, 1989), 220.
2. From an unpublished text titled "Dismal Science: Imaginary Economies and the Late Modern System of the Arts," delivered at the Art Gallery of New South Wales, Sydney, and the Art Gallery of Western Australia, Perth, 1999.
3. Excerpted from an e-mail to the author, Wednesday, 16 February 2000, 7:22 a.m.
4. Frederic Jameson, *Postmodernism, or, The Cultural Logic of Late Capitalism* (Durham, N.C.: Duke University Press 1991). I am indebted to Miwon Kwon and her article, "Imagining an Impossible World Picture," in the *Sites and Stations: Provisional Utopias* issue of *Lusitania*, no. 7 (1995): 77–87, for this reference and for inspiring the personal tone of the introduction to this book.
5. Chon Noriega, "Many Wests," in *From the West: Chicano Narrative Photography*, exh. cat. (San Francisco: The Mexican Museum, 1995), 10. In the context of the exhibition, Noriega talks about the omission of the Chicano experience of the landscape even in revisionist works such as Jane Tompkins *West of Everything*.

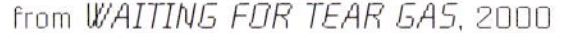

from *WAITING FOR TEAR GAS*, 2000

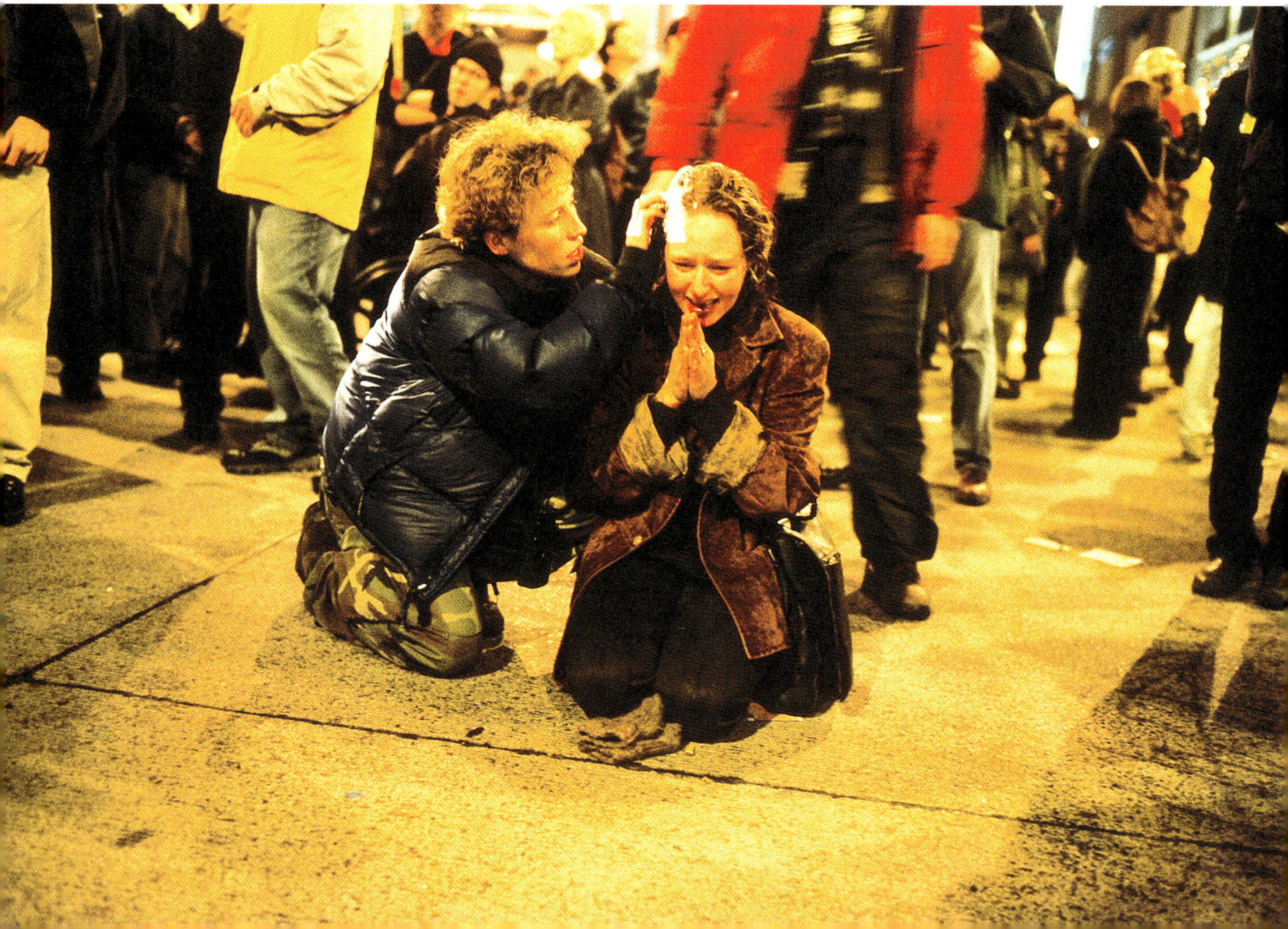

Allan Sekula

Sekula's most recent body of slide-projection works and still photographs continues his investigation of world shipping economies in pictures documenting the protests and social unrest around the World Trade Organization conference in Seattle during November/December 1999. His examination of the global capitalist transformation of maritime economies began with the extended photo-essay *Fish Story* (1989–95). The slide projection and photographic works comprising *Waiting for Tear Gas* and *TITANIC's wake* attempt to read the social narrative of new left resistance through the complex codes of the media, the official government presence, and the booming shipping and high-tech economies of the Pacific port city of Seattle.

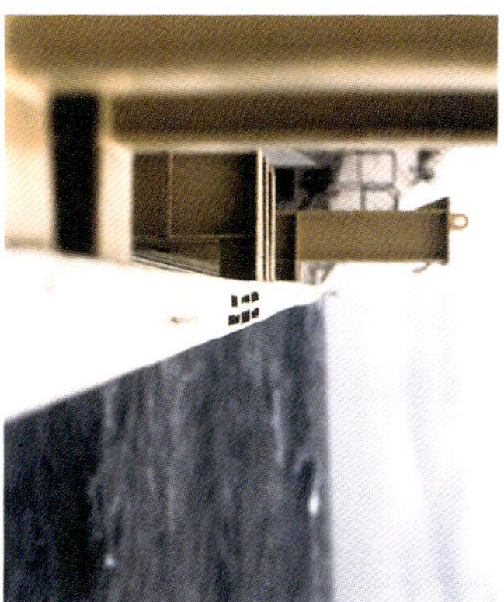
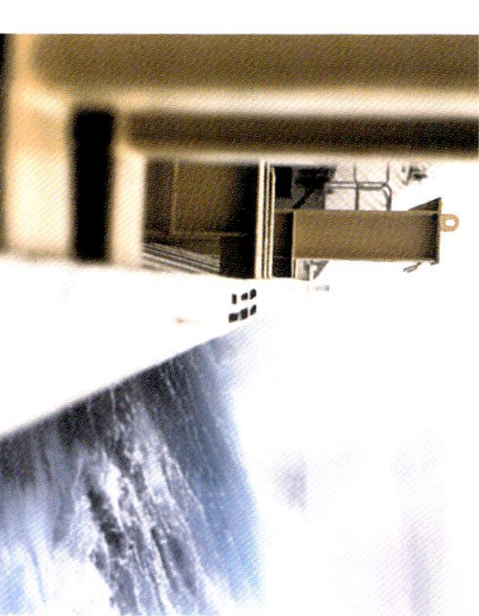

31 DECEMBER 1999, OFF THE ALBANIAN COAST (diptych), from *TITANIC's wake*, 1998–2000

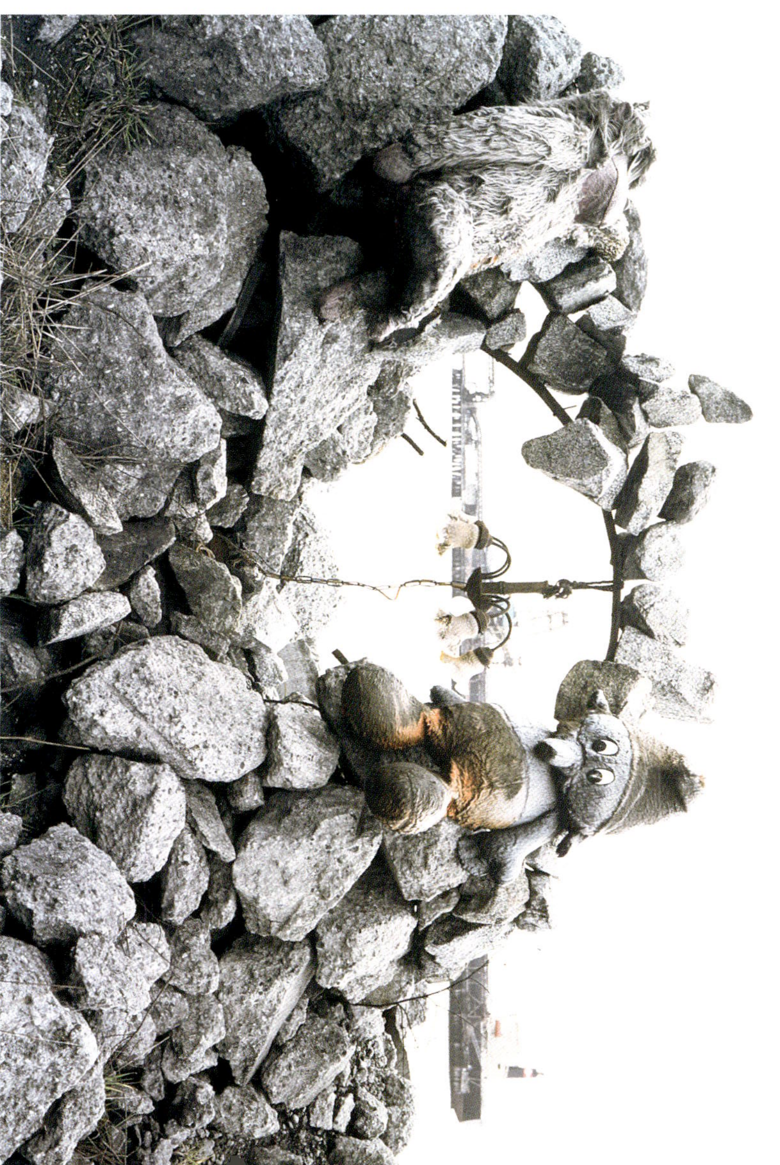

ASSEMBLAGE MADE BY COAL DOCK WORKERS, VANCOUVER, from *TITANIC's wake*, 1998–2000

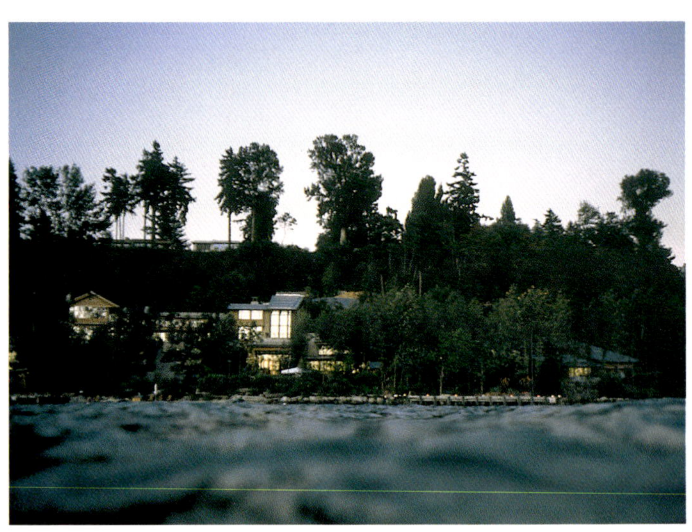

DEAR BILL GATES, 1999

November 30, 1999

Dear Bill Gates,

I swam past your dream house the other day, but didn't stop to knock. Frankly, your underwater sensors had me worried. I would have liked to take a look at Winslow Homer's Lost on the Grand Banks. It's a great painting, but, speaking as a friend and fellow citizen, at $30 million you paid too much.

HIGHEST PRICE EVER PAID FOR AN AMERICAN PAINTING!!!

So why are you so interested in a picture of two poor lost dory fishermen, momentarily high on a swell, peering into a wall of fog? They're about as high as they're ever going to be, unless the sea gets uglier. They are going to die you know, and it won't be a pretty death.

And as for you Bill, when you're on the net, are you lost? Or found?

And the rest of us--lost or found--are we on it, or in it?

Your friend

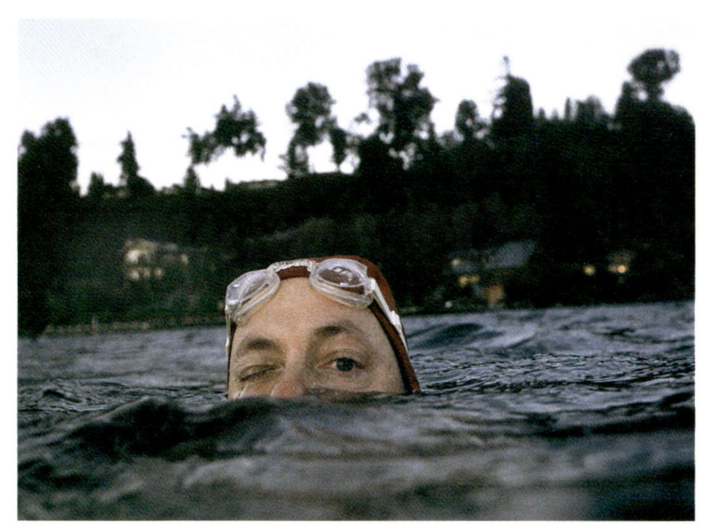

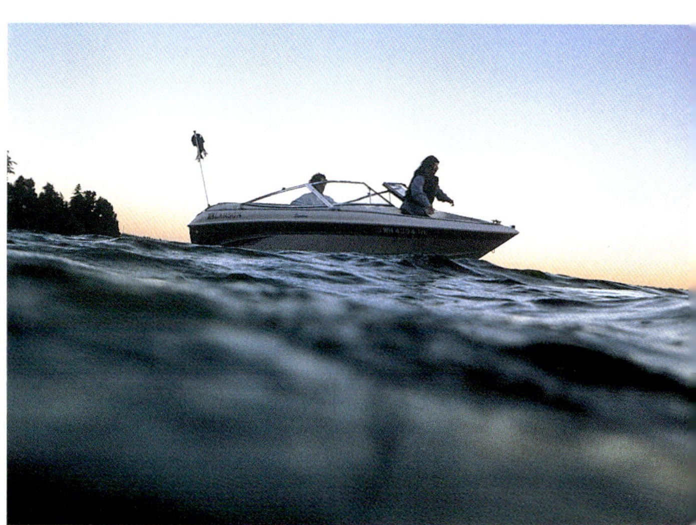

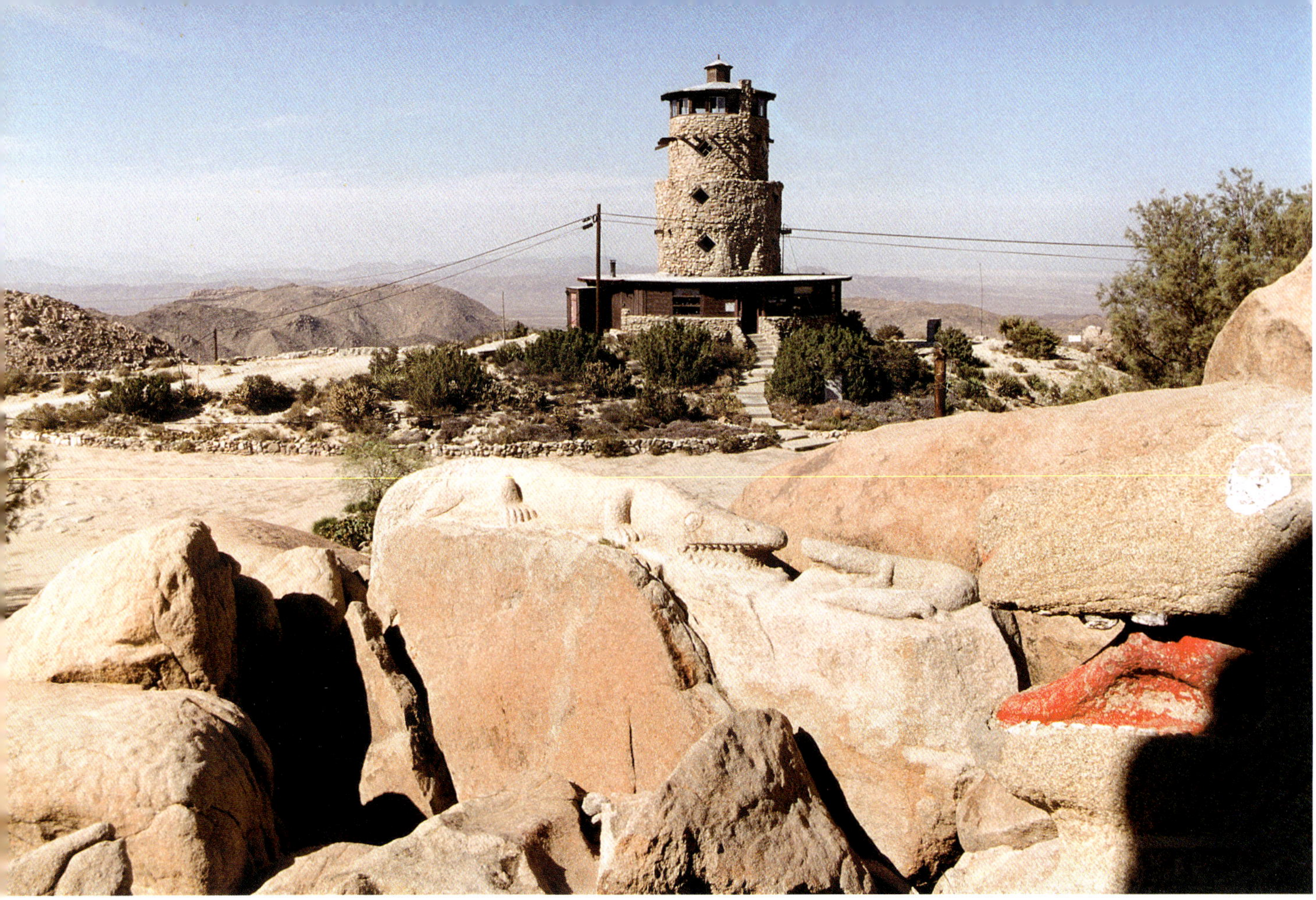

DESERT VIEW TOWER from *Hinterland: A Voyage Into Exurban Southern California*, 1997

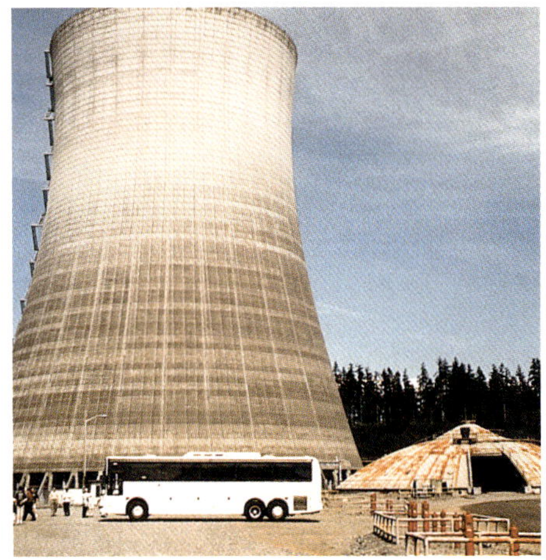

ONE HUNDRED PLACES IN WASHINGTON, 1999

CLUI

CENTER FOR LAND USE INTERPRETATION

"Dedicated to the increase and diffusion of information about how the world's lands are apportioned, utilized and perceived." For this exhibition a temporary exhibition trailer has been moved off-site from the CLUI office to The Geffen Contemporary where it functions as a trade-show-like display booth. A corresponding module, *The Desert Research Station* (2000), located in what CLUI calls the "hinterlands," the primary area of their activity located in the southern California desert south of the sixth parallel, will remain open to the public for the duration of the exhibition.

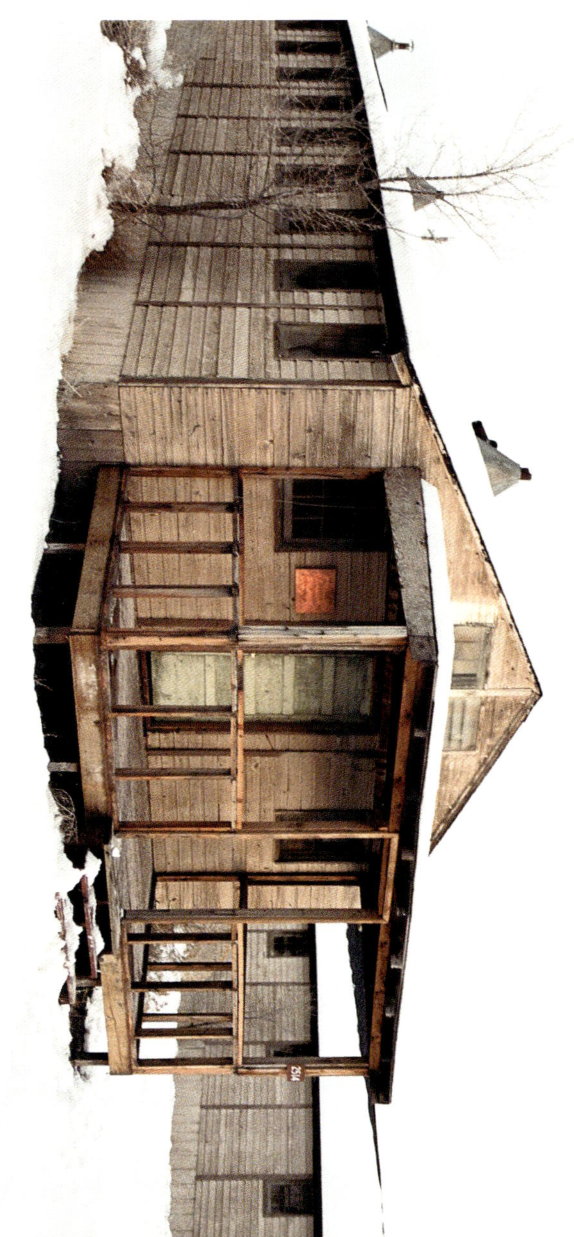

WENDOVER EXHIBIT HALL, Wendover, Utah, 1999

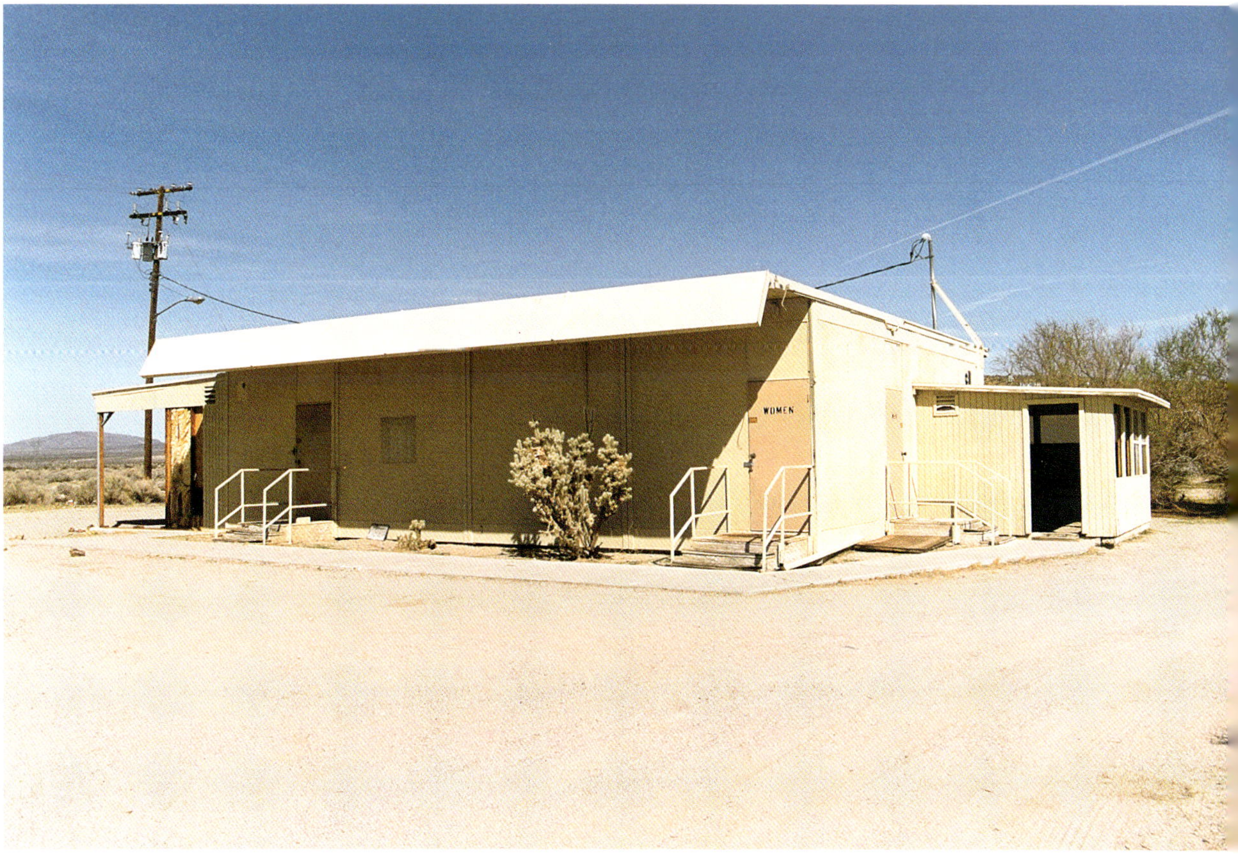

BLM RESEARCH STATION from *The Desert Research Station*, 2000

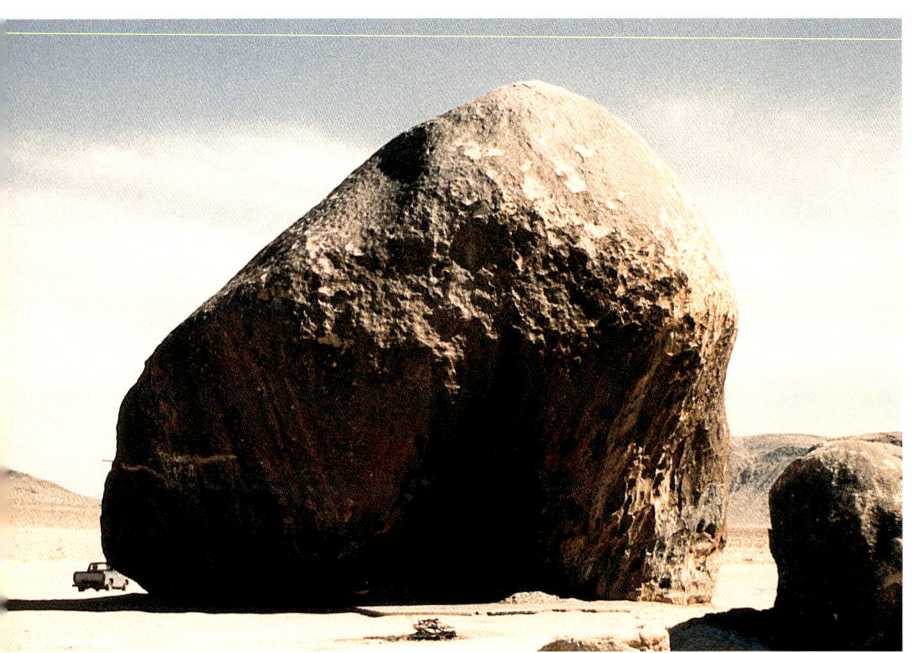

GIANT ROCK from *Hinterland: A Voyage Into Exurban Southern California*, 1997

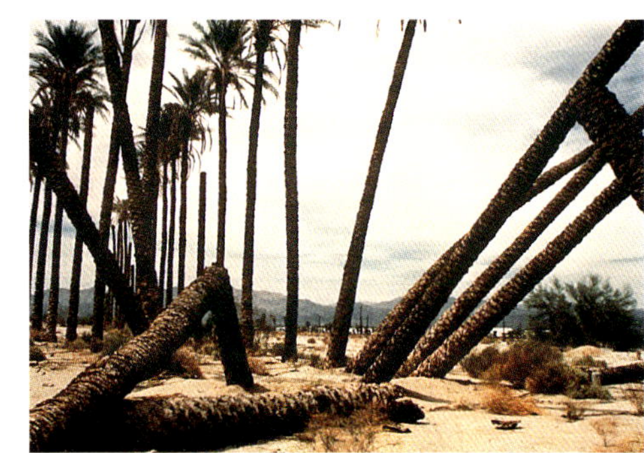

DESERT CENTER from *Hinterland: A Voyage Into Exurban Southern California*, 1997

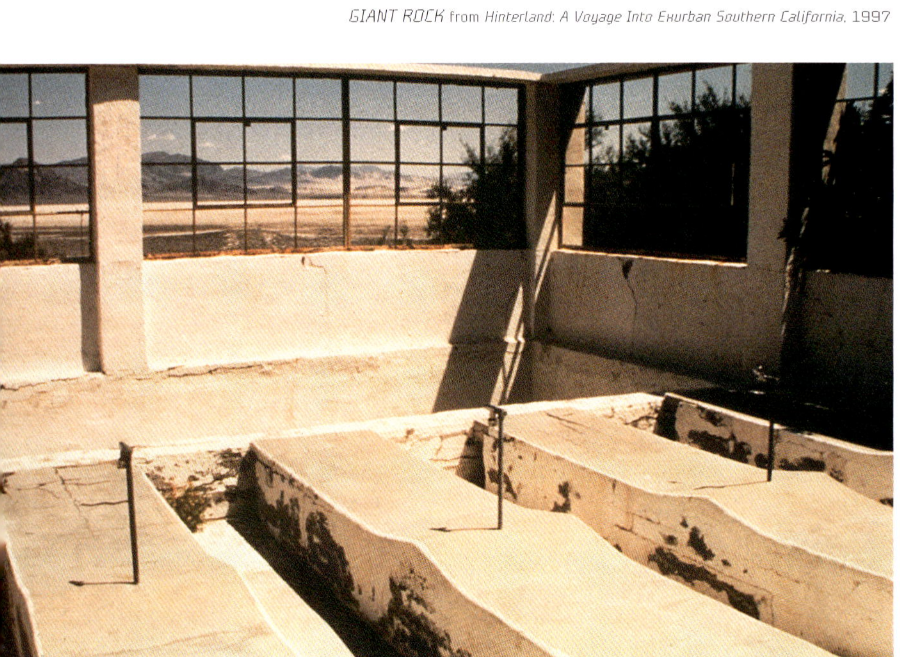

ZZYZYX from *Hinterland: A Voyage Into Exurban Southern California*, 1997

HINKLEY INTERPRETIVE TRAIL from *The Desert Research Station*, 2000

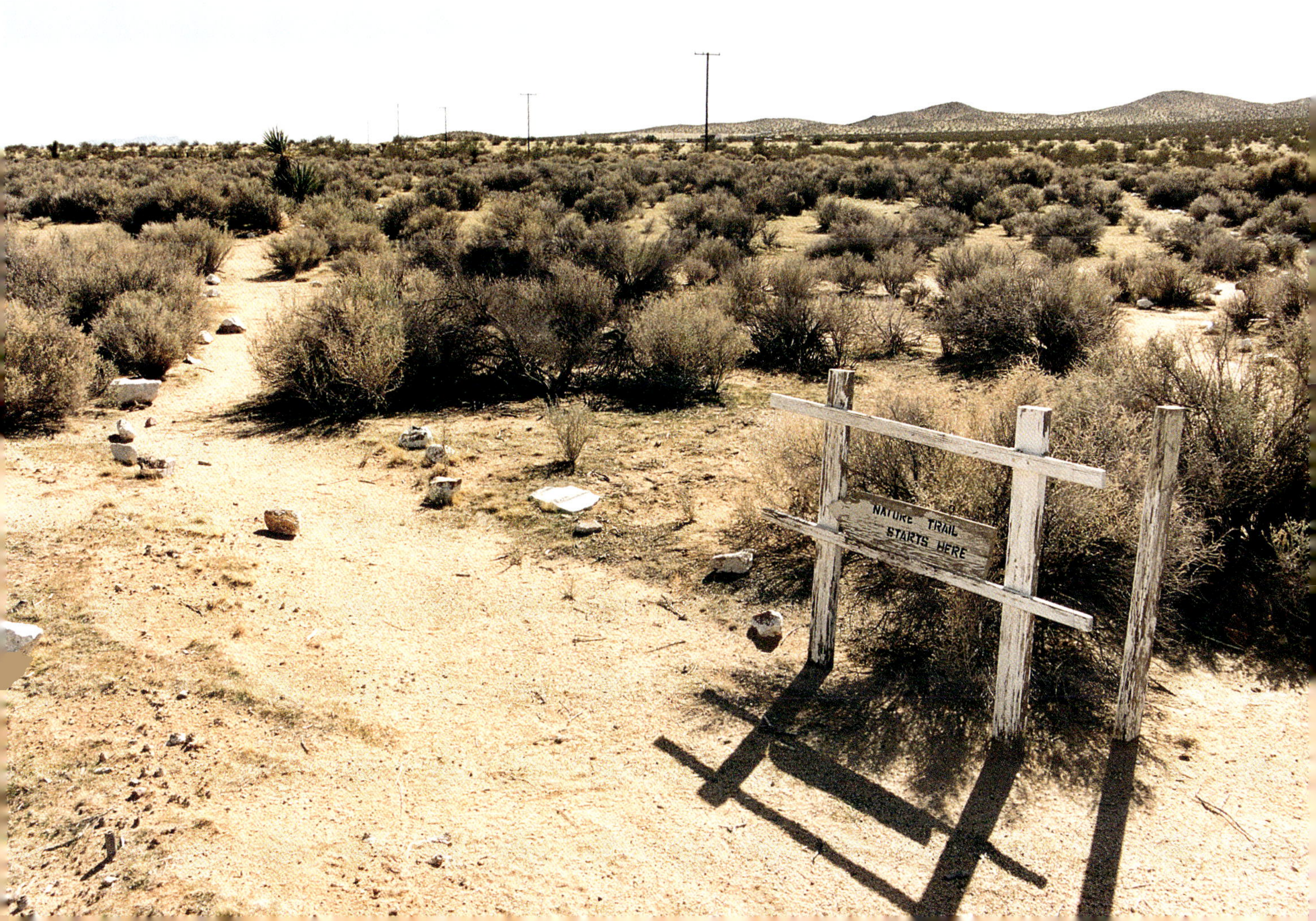

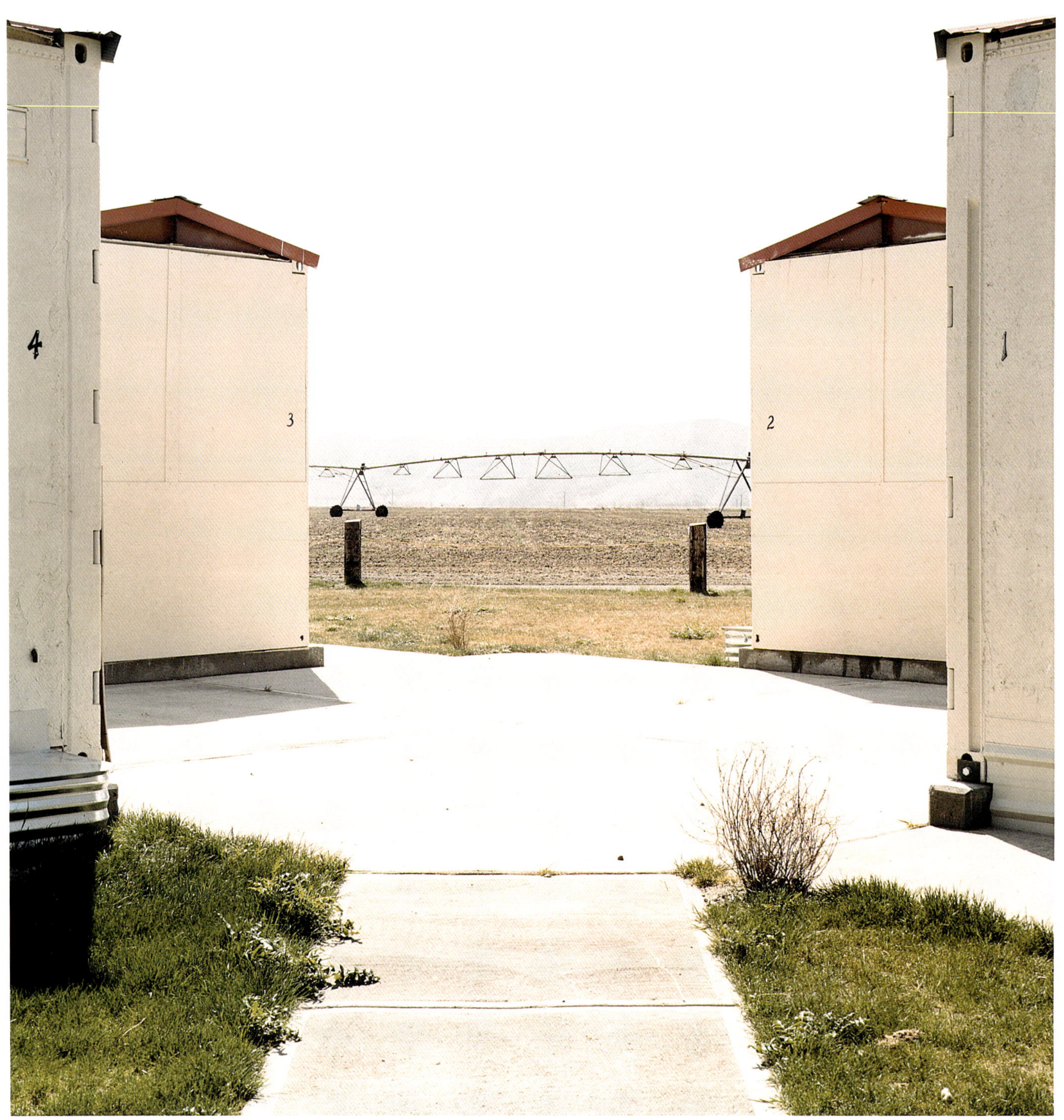

from *NEAR MATTAWA, #9*, 2000

Miles Coolidge

In this series of fourteen monumental photographs, Coolidge documents migrant workers' housing in Mattawa, Washington. The twenty-four units, made from converted shipping containers, are organized along an axis, each with a common area in the middle, and are occupied annually during the harvest months. The project was designed by an architect and the settlement is named Hope.

from *NEAR MATTAWA, #10*, 2000

from *NEAR MATTAWA*, #*12*, *13*, and *14*, 2000

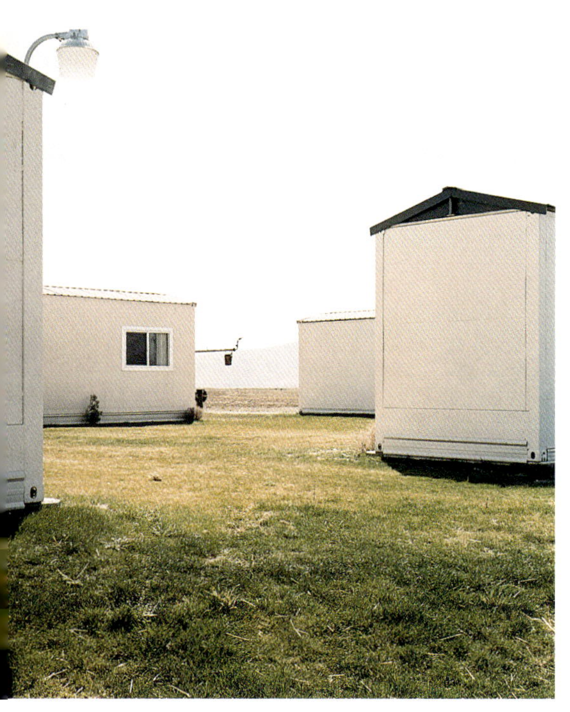

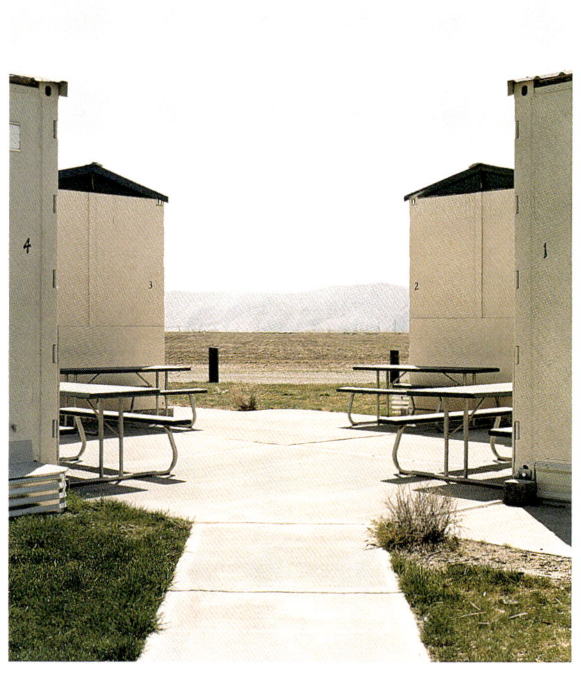

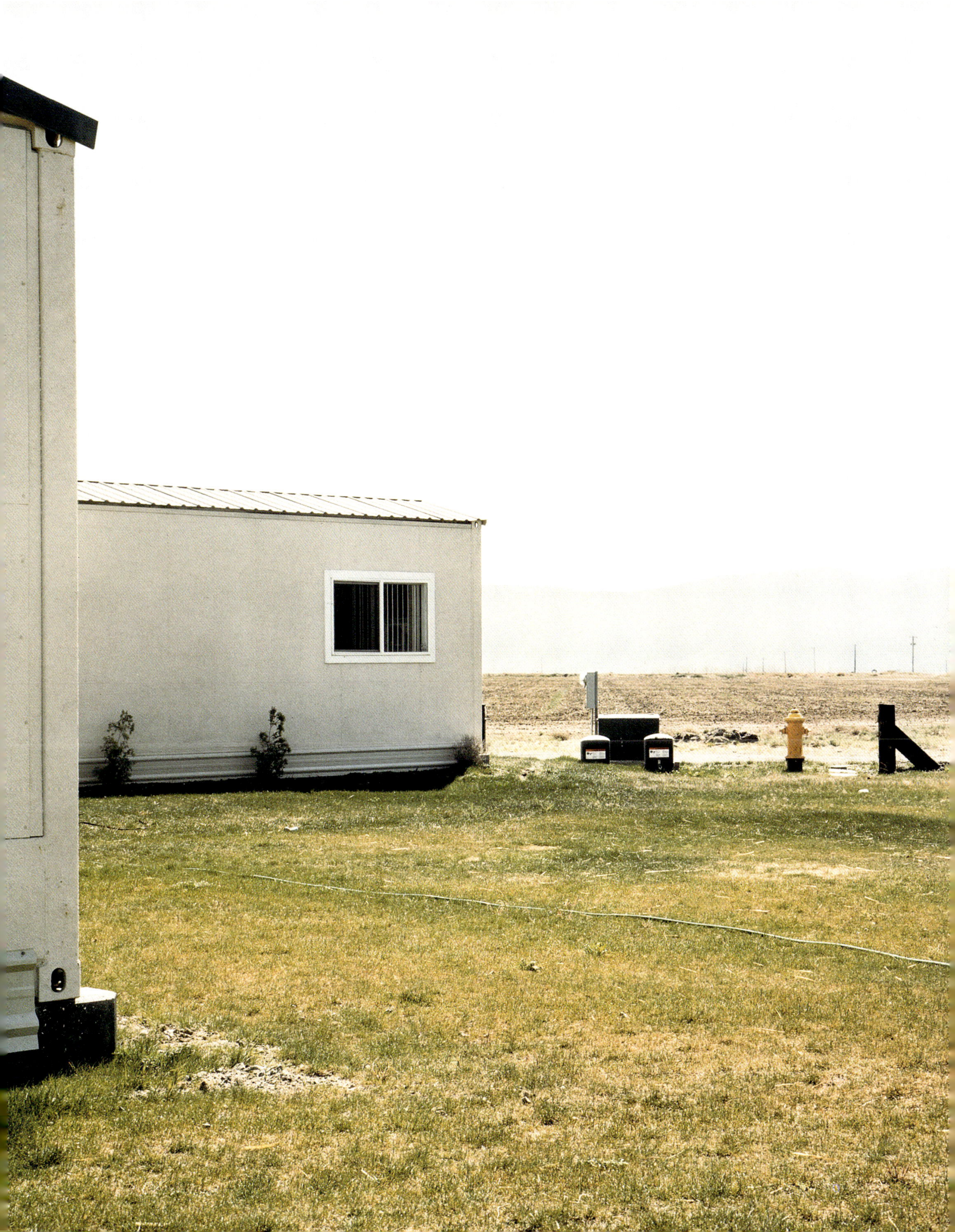

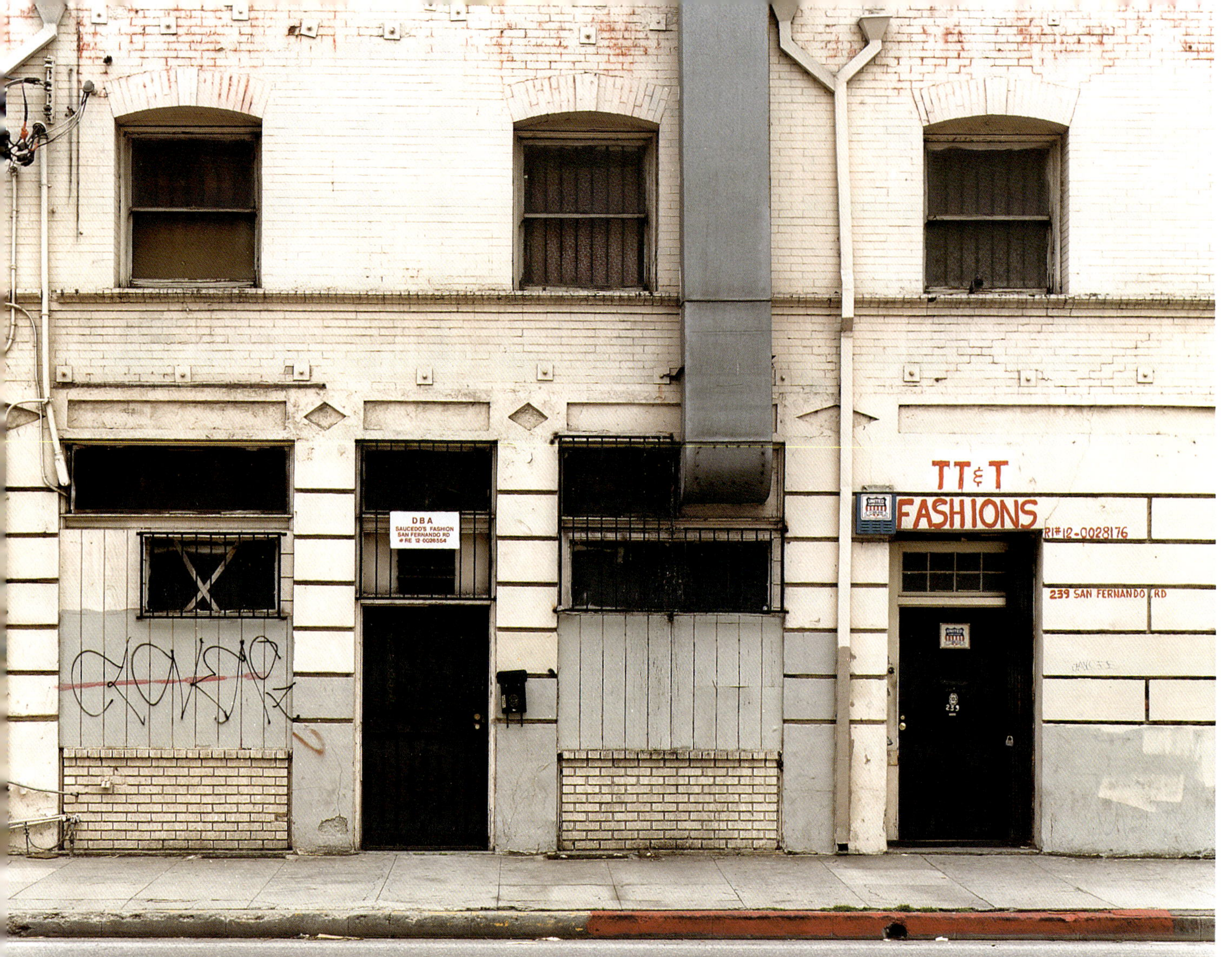

MANUELA S-T-I-T-C-H-E-D: TT&T FASHIONS, EASTERN LOS ANGELES, CA, 1996

Christina Fernandez

This series of ten photographs forms a kind of portrait of sweatshop buildings around East Los Angeles. Originally part of an installation, the photographs are accompanied by the following text excerpted from narratives of the migrant laborers who work in the factories: "Looking down she saw that her stocking had a run. *La Migra* came like a storm today. The end of black thread was caught on her heel. It trailed away winding around the corner. She pictured an empty spool and feared they would notice it and find her."

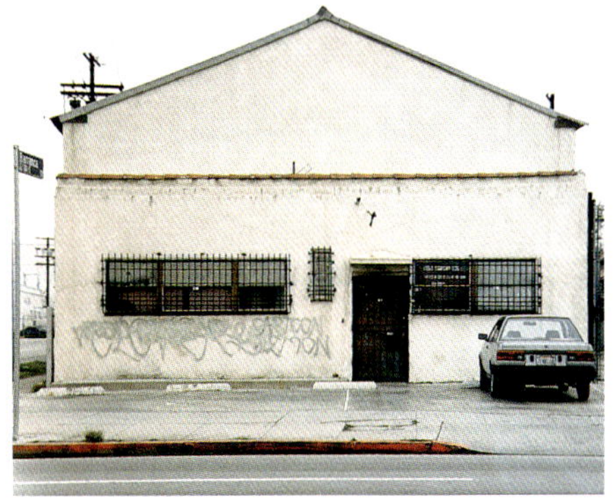

MANUELA S-T-I-T-C-H-E-D: NAPA APP. INC., EASTERN LOS ANGELES, CA, 1996

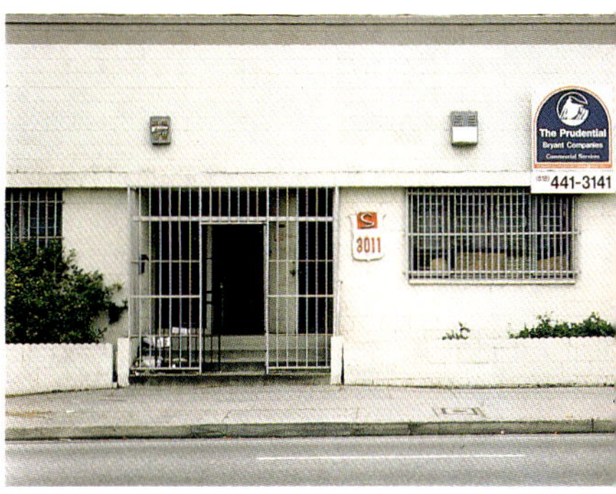

MANUELA S-T-I-T-C-H-E-D: LEO FASHION, EASTERN LOS ANGELES, CA, 1996

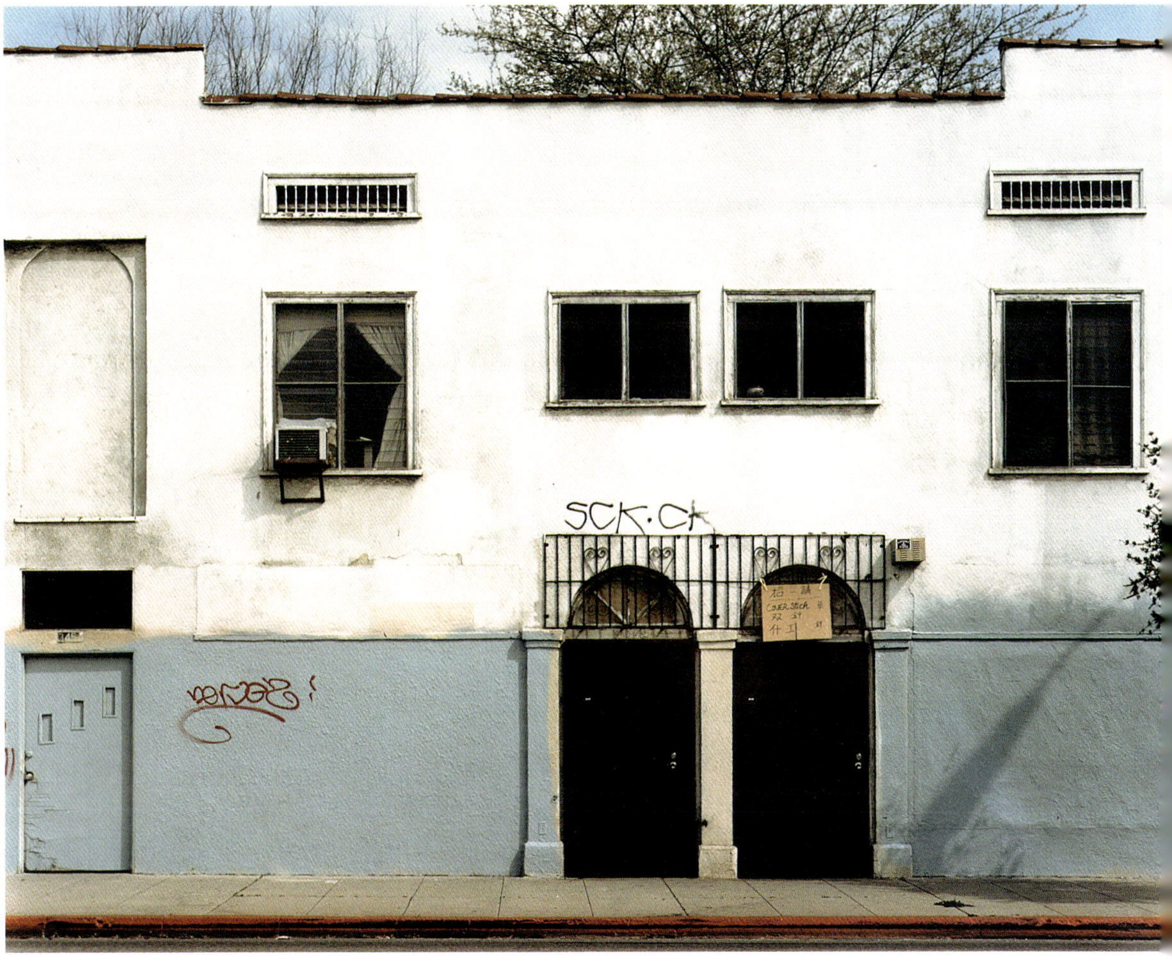

MANUELA S-T-I-T-C-H-E-D: COVERSTICH, EASTERN LOS ANGELES, CA, 1996

Roy Kiyooka

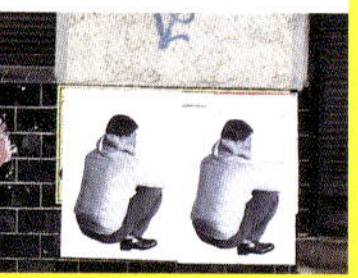
Simon Leung

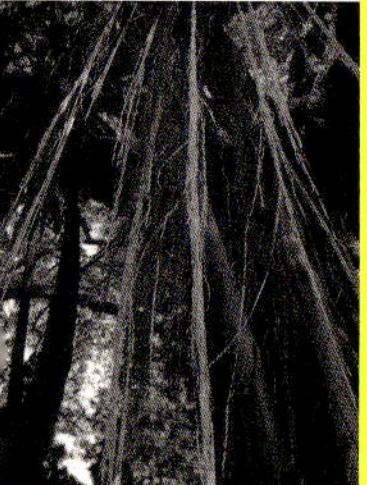
Simryn Gill

migration and movement

THE OPPOSITE OF TOURISM IS NOT "STAYING AT HOME," BUT THE INVOLUNTARY TRAVEL ASSOCIATED WITH THE PREDICAMENT OF THE IMMIGRANT. IF THE TOURIST TRAVELS, FOR THE MOST PART, BACKWARDS IN TIME, THEN THE IMMIGRANT, THE EXILE AND THE DIASPORIC TRAVEL FORWARDS WITH NO PROMISE OF A RESTORED HOME.

—Barry Curtis and Claire Pajaczkowska[1]

Art tourism, currently booming with the proliferation of international exhibitions and new museum construction, is the lens through which many of us experience the world. While not entirely benign, art travel is a sort of parallel universe—a way of immersing oneself in other landscapes. You land, learn as much as you can about the terra firma, and then, standing upon the foundation of someone else's history, you view the art and attempt to reframe your own vision for just that moment. Whenever I visit Vancouver, for example, I am struck first by the raw closeness of the wilderness—my first experience of the landscape was on an island salmon fishing with my grandfather. Initially, I gravitated toward any current manifestation of the strong landscape tradition that has dominated there—the one that the current generation of young artists is, not surprisingly, quite finished with.

A number of the works in "Flight Patterns" have to do with travel and migration, voluntary or otherwise, and the experience of a new geography. In Los Angeles, where the immigration comes primarily from the west and south, this is particularly relevant. There is also a rich history of exchange to the north—between L.A. and Canada—represented in this exhibition by the work of Japanese-Canadian Roy Kiyooka, who was active in Vancouver at the same time as Robert Smithson, Iain Baxter, and Jeff Wall, among others. In a 1971 performance titled *"Arts Canada" Afloat,* Kiyooka and three artist friends laid the pages of the provincial art magazine across a Vancouver Island beach as the tide literally washed the magazine away. Individual pages seen in pictures of the performance make reference to Canada's heroic landscape tradition. At the same time the trees at the edge of the beach have a strong physical presence, always at the edge in each of the over 100 pictures that document the washing away of a dominant and oppressive art history.

Abandoning painting for photographic practice in the 1970s, Kiyooka was influential as a poet, filmmaker, and teacher at the University of British Columbia, where he was active until a few years before his death in 1994. Many of Kiyooka's photographic projects focused on the changes in his Vancouver neighborhood resulting from government "resettlement" efforts beginning in the 1940s. Later in life he was involved with the "redress"—government compensation for displaced property. His own family had been forced to move to a remote town in northern Alberta during the early forties, and the artist's experience as an "enemy alien" provided a subtext for much of his work, reflecting "his efforts to situate himself within the historic injustices that seethe below the landscape."[2]

The fragile localism of Kiyooka's practice is reinforced by its casual format. The photographs are informally made and sequenced with a blunt lack of attention to presentation in a manner that seems cultivated, as if the performative impulse for the work dictated its spontaneous, often diaristic nature. In *Small Harbour on Nomi Island* (1984, subtitled *a small harbour on nomi island one hot afternoon in May*), this vivid but delicate description accompanies amateurish images of the artist's hands making abstract gestures near the water. The body's implied language forms a record of the artist's location—a simple gesture to mark time and place.

In 1994, Simon Leung made three posters, each featuring an image of him squatting, which were installed around the city of Berlin. Their accompanying text gave the viewer three directives: "1. Imagine a city of squatters, an entire city in which everyone created their own chairs with their own bodies. 2. When you are tired, or when you need to wait, participate in this position. 3. Observe the city again from this squatting position." One of three "squatting projects" made in Chicago, Berlin, and Vienna, this simple intervention into the urban environment is one of inscription and mapping. In a moving, personal account titled *Squatting Through Violence,* Leung recalls a memory of his younger brother describing his impulse to squat while waiting for the bus.[3] Leung articulates the translation of this gesture's meaning across time and cultures.

For *Squatting Project/Wien* (1998), Leung made 130 photographs of himself assuming—and thereby resuscitating—the degraded squatting position at sites around the city owned by the Generali Foundation, the host of the exhibition for which the work was made. By bringing this work home to Los Angeles, where Leung has lived on and off since the early nineties, the work territorializes another landscape, both physical and institutional. As both the subject and originator of this subdued documentary expose, Leung assigns cultural ownership to himself both as an exoticized, global transient, and as an artist in a fixed relationship with the institution. Artists are finding themselves in increasingly complicated positions vis-à-vis the museum when they travel to assume the role of the performing subject. Invited to respond to the institution, Leung participated by institutionalizing his own critique. In what Julie Carson has called Leung's "socio-minimalist" style, there are references both to Hans Haacke's political strategies and, more to the point of this exhibition, to Lewis Baltz's mute landscapes, which foreshadow the global capitalism that has irrevocably altered the ex-urban landscape of the North American West.

The localism of the "global/local" argued in Lee Weng Choy's text elsewhere in this volume, and articulated by James Clifford as "localism and worldliness,"[4] exists as a symptom of transnational travel and its byproduct, cultural translation. The slippage of memory and its connection to place explored in Simon Leung's poignant, performative photo-document is also one locus of meaning in Simryn Gill's sculptural and photographic works. Like Kiyooka, Gill's practice is loosely configured but resonates with a deep complexity and subtle sense of humor derived from the artist's insistently light touch and the work's ability to simultaneously occupy several different zones.[5] Through a kind of cultivated sense of futility and ineptitude of materials, the artist attempts the simplest interventions without yielding to the simplistic.

Though primarily large in scale, Gill's photographs are not monumentally conceived or produced. They are installed unframed, pinned to the wall, and exist residually in terms of the performance or site intervention she has made. The fourteen photographs comprising *Forest* (1996–98) extend the artist's investigation into cultural translation. The pictures self-consciously reference botanical and ethnographic photographs of the turn of the century. They record places in two colonial gardens in the artist's homeland of Malaysia where she has gently grafted text onto the existing density of vegetation. The texts are all colonial, representing the kind of culture of received knowledge in which the artist was educated. In fact, the presence of the text—the text literally becoming the landscape—metaphorizes the way cultural narratives become truth for all "natives" who live as transplants from a homeland.

Notes

1. Barry Curtis and Claire Pajaczkowska, "'Getting There': Travel, Time and Narrative", in George Robertson, Melinda Mash, Lisa Tickner, Jon Bird, Barry Curtis and Tim Putnam, eds., *Travellers' Tales: Narratives of Home and Displacement* (London: Routledge, 1994), 202–203.
2. Sharla Sava, "Roy Kiyooka: Photographing the Local from the Inside Out," *C International Contemporary Art*, no. 60 (November 1998–January 1999): 32. For a brief discussion of Kiyooka's connection to the literary scene in Vancouver, *see* Robert Linsley's "Roy Kiyooka's Yonville," *Art/Text*, no. 64 (February–April 1999): 70–75.
3. Leung in *The Making Of*, exh. cat. (Vienna: Generali Foundation, 1998), 106; and Leung, "Squatting through Violence," *Documents* (Spring/Summer 1995): 92.
4. I first came across this term of Clifford's in an essay by Okwui Enwezor titled "Between Localism and Worldliness," in *Cross/ing: Time. Space. Movement*, exh. cat. (Tampa, Fla.: Contemporary Art Museum, University of South Florida, 1997), 62.
5. In a wonderful essay on Gill's photographic work, Yao Souchou explores the aspect of humor and the impossibility of separating our experience of nature—specifically the landscape of tropical Malaysia—from what he calls the "hangover of European Romanticism." See "Procrastination; Or How I Relearn the Pleasure of the Tropics," *parallax* 5, no. 1 (1999): 76–78.

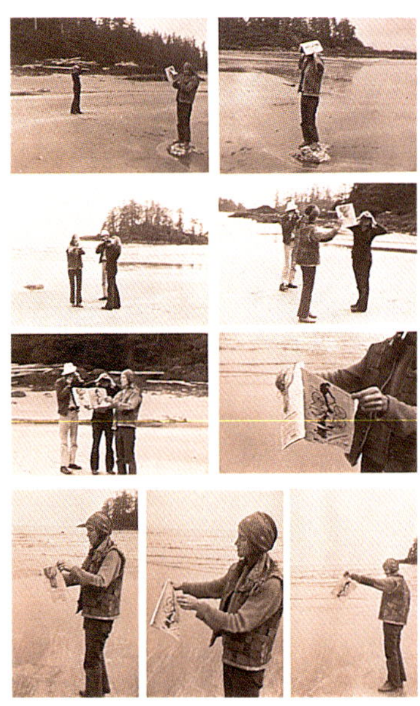

"ARTS CANADA" AFLOAT (detail), 1971-74

SMALL HARBOUR ON NOMI ISLAND (detail), 1984

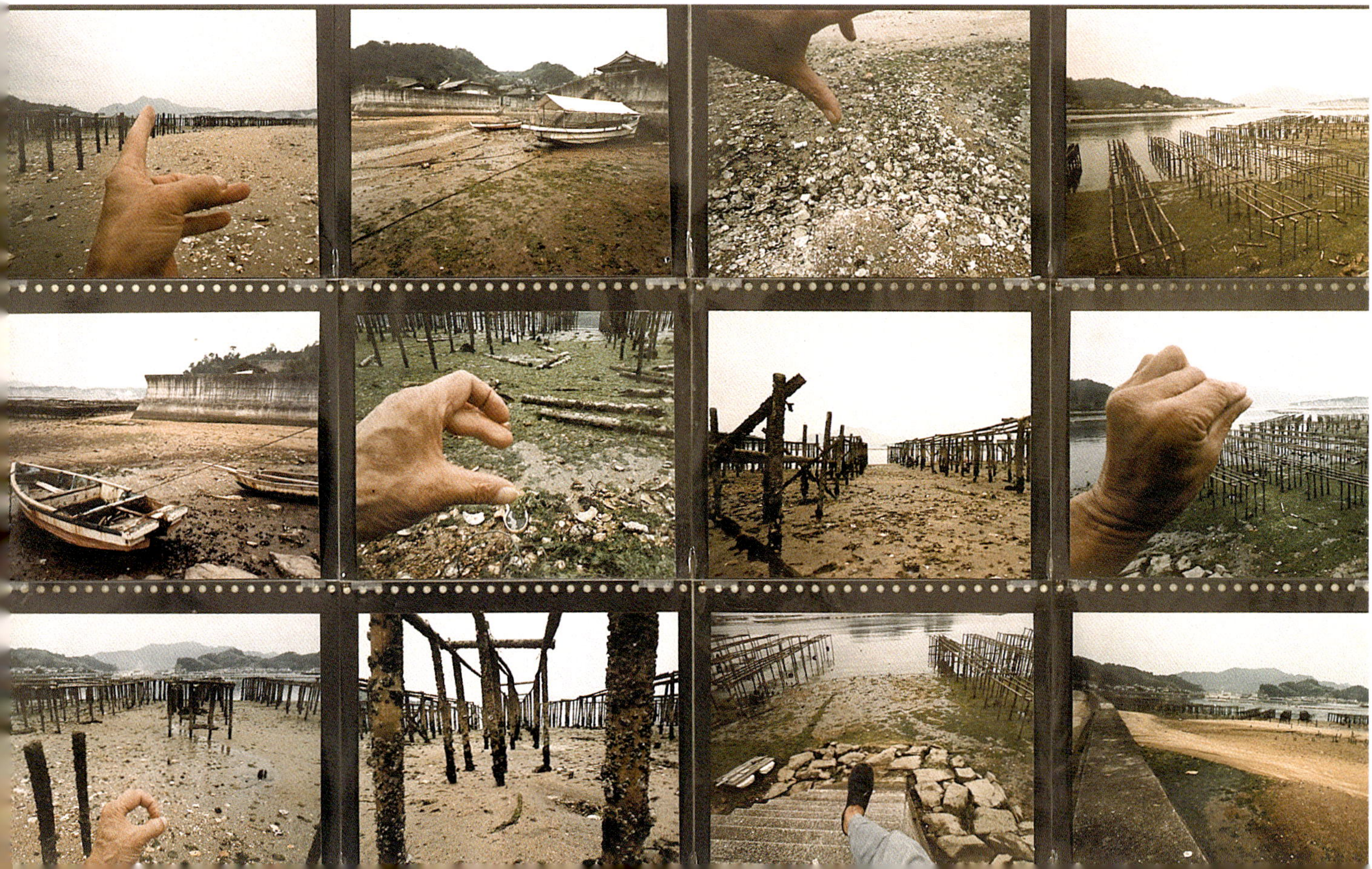

Roy Kiyooka

Roy Kiyooka immigrated to Vancouver, Canada, from Japan in 1960. Trained as a painter, Kiyooka began writing poetry and making films and conceptual photo projects in the late 1960s. Influenced by the modernist poets in San Francisco and the Vancouver poetry movement "Tish", Kiyooka was prominent as a teacher and his discursive photo works often dealt with themes of localism and displacement. *"Arts Canada" Afloat* is a monumental photo work documenting a performance in which Kiyooka and friends floated pages of the Canadian art magazine into the sea. Visible on one page is an article celebrating Emily Carr, the most prominent member of Canada's dominant school of landscape painting.

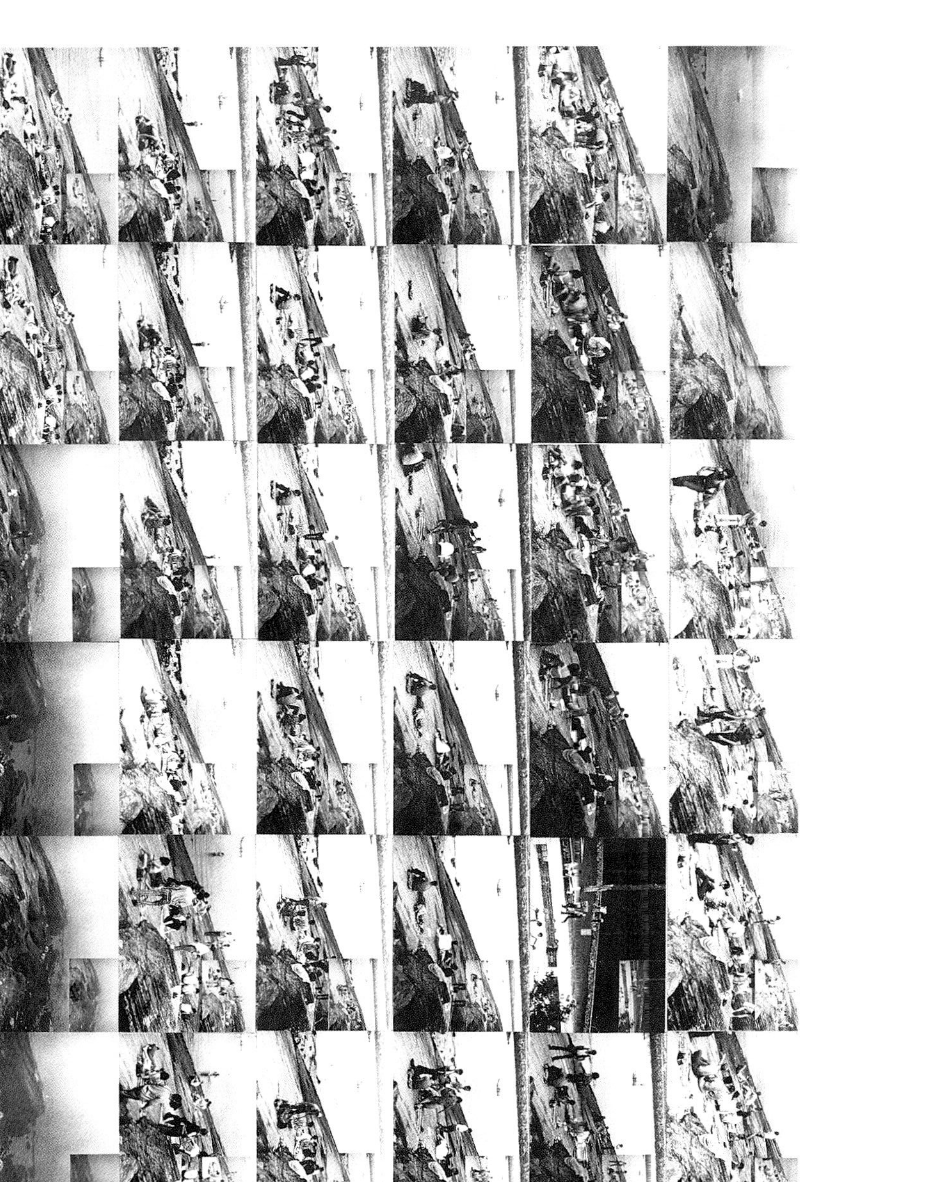

HALIFAX SEA AND ROCK, 1971

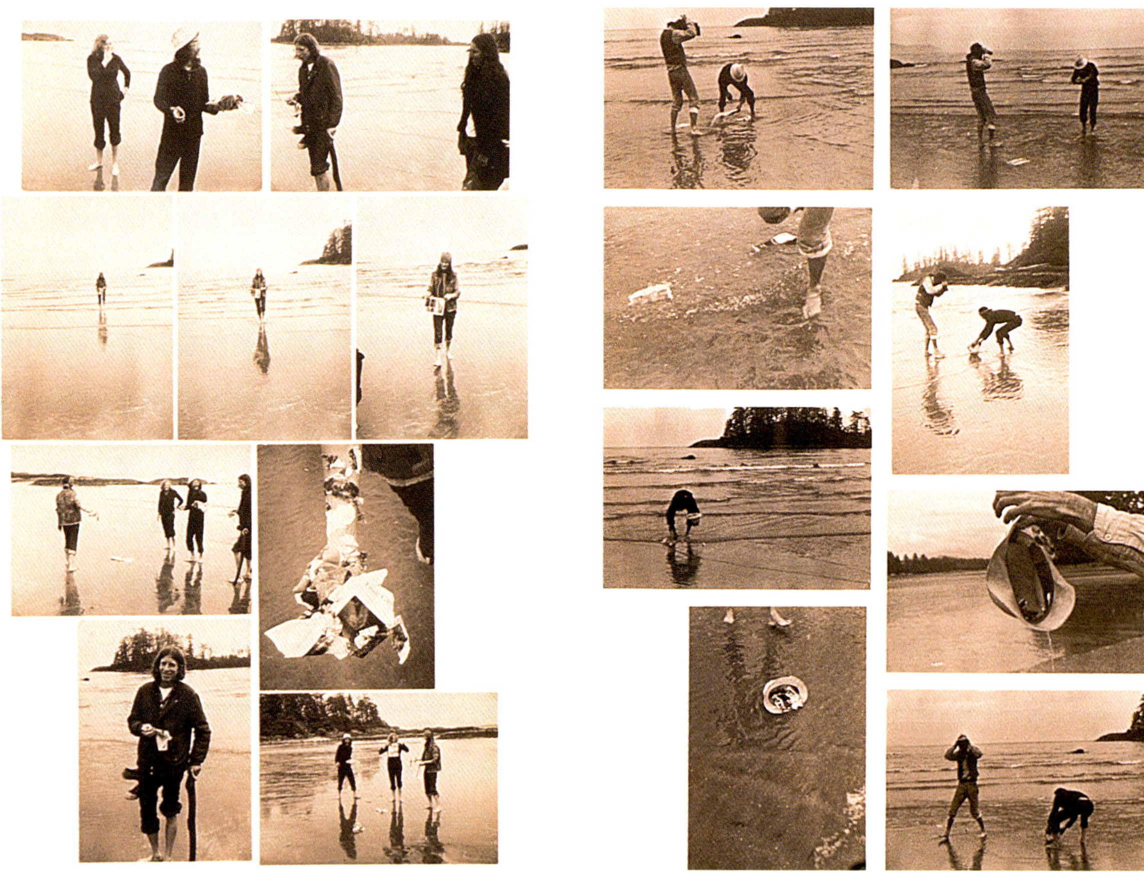

"ARTS CANADA" AFLOAT (detail), 1971-74

"ARTS CANADA" AFLOAT (detail), 1971-74

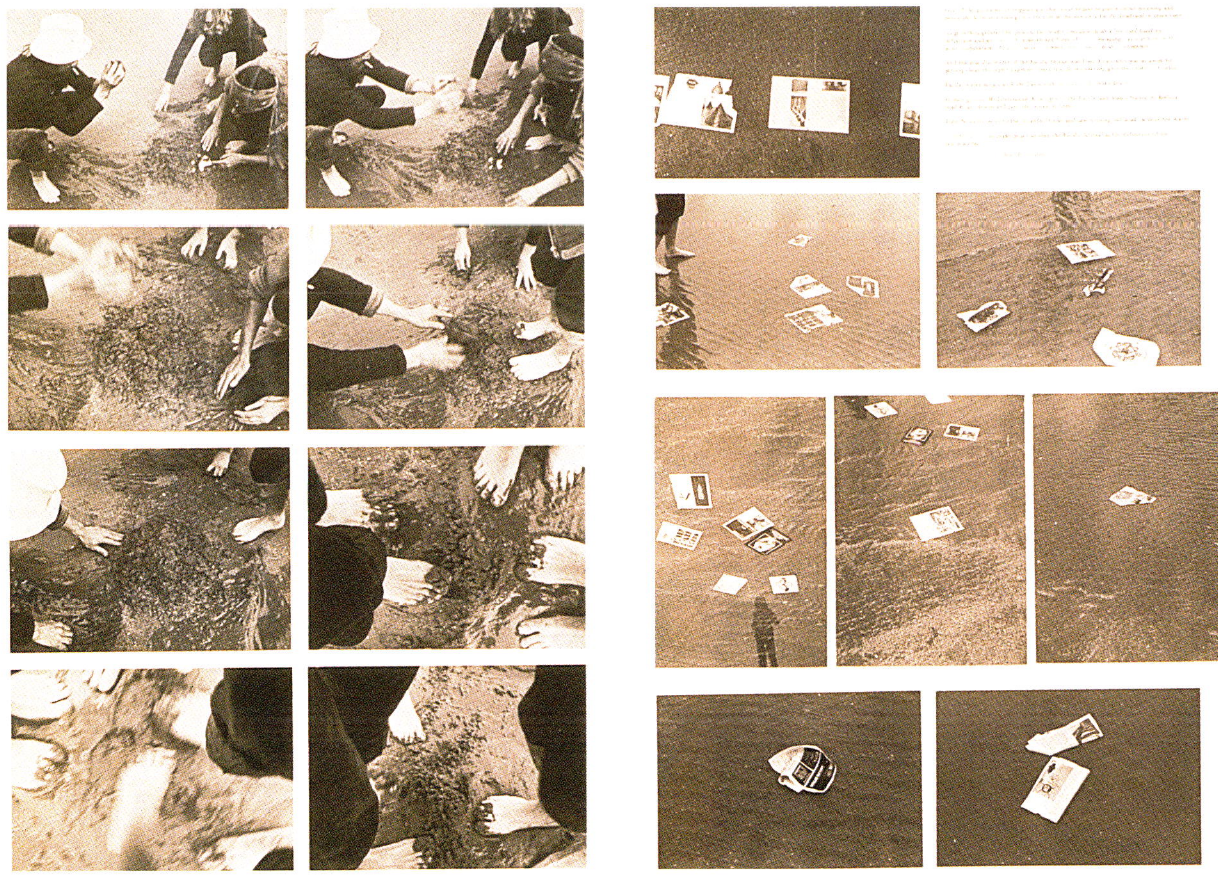

"ARTS CANADA" AFLOAT (detail), 1971-74

"ARTS CANADA" AFLOAT (detail), 1971-74

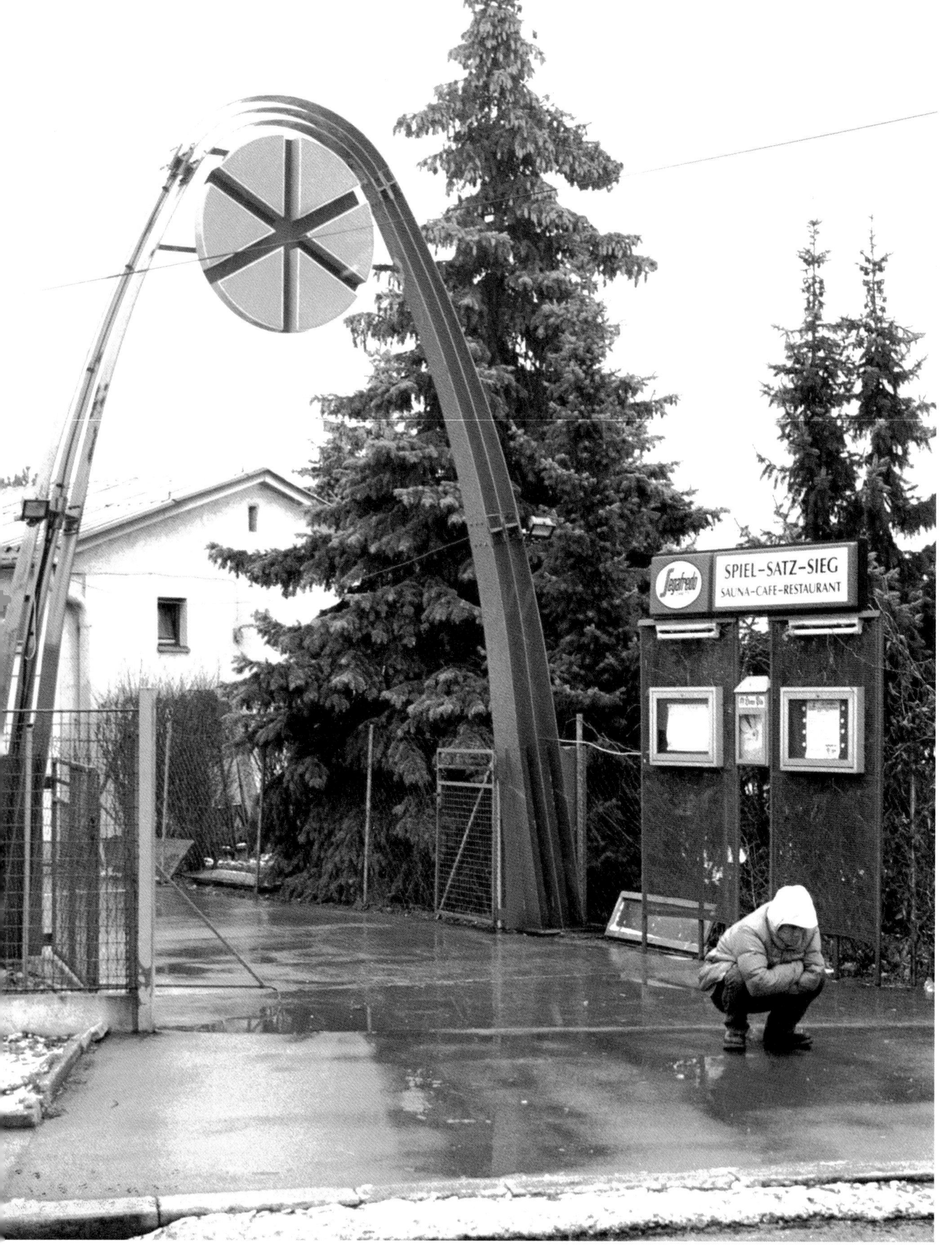

SQUATTING PROJECT/WIEN 1998, 1998

Simon Leung

Squatting Project/Wien (1998) is part of a series of works on the subject of the residual space of the Vietnam War. A black-and-white series of 130 photographs records the artist squatting in front of all the real estate owned by Generali Foundation in Vienna. The degraded act of squatting—an at-rest position in Asian cultures—becomes a transgressive act marking a space of resistance in the urban environment.

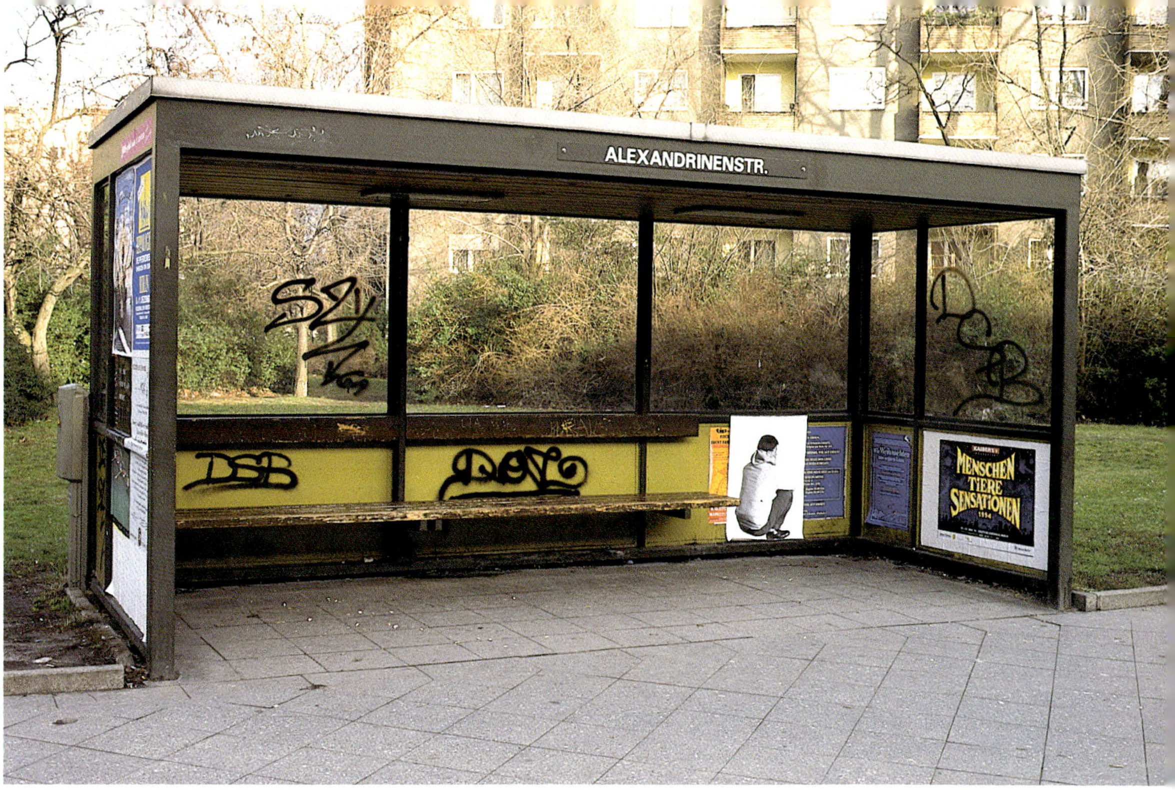

SQUATTING PROJECT/BERLIN, installation view, 1994

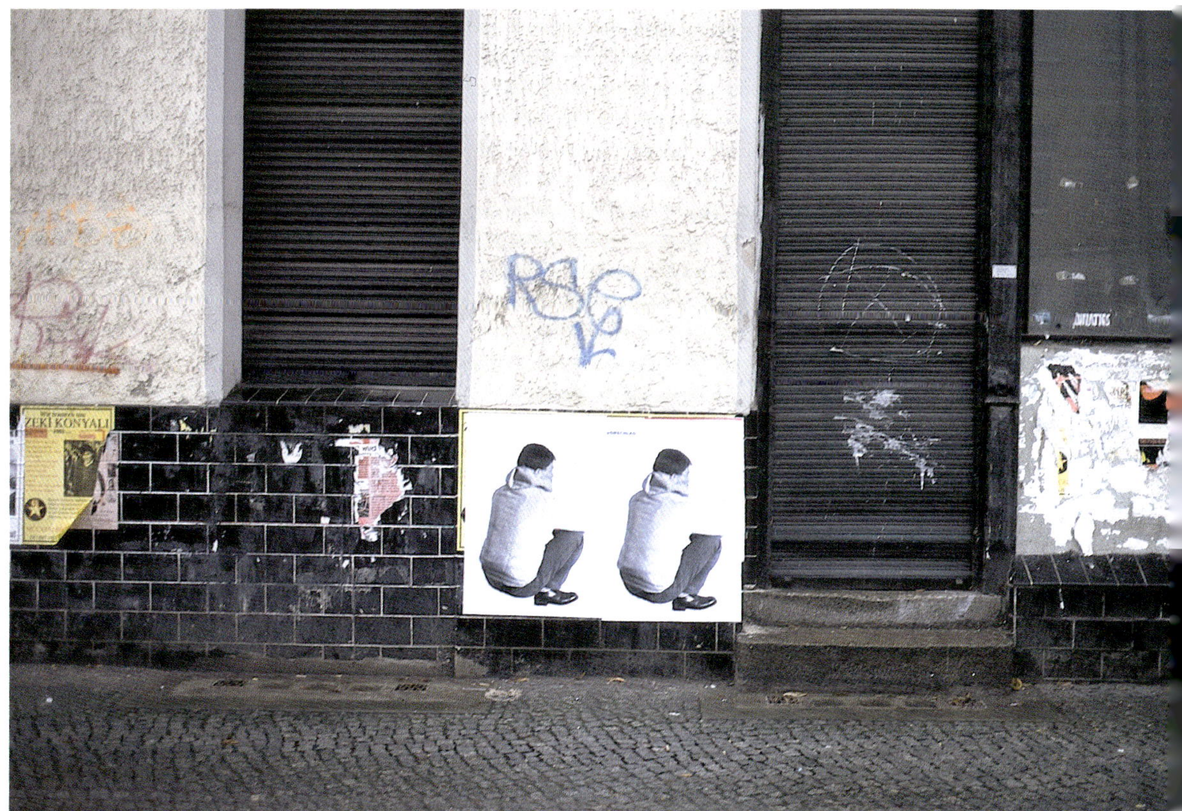

SQUATTING PROJECT/BERLIN, installation view, 1994

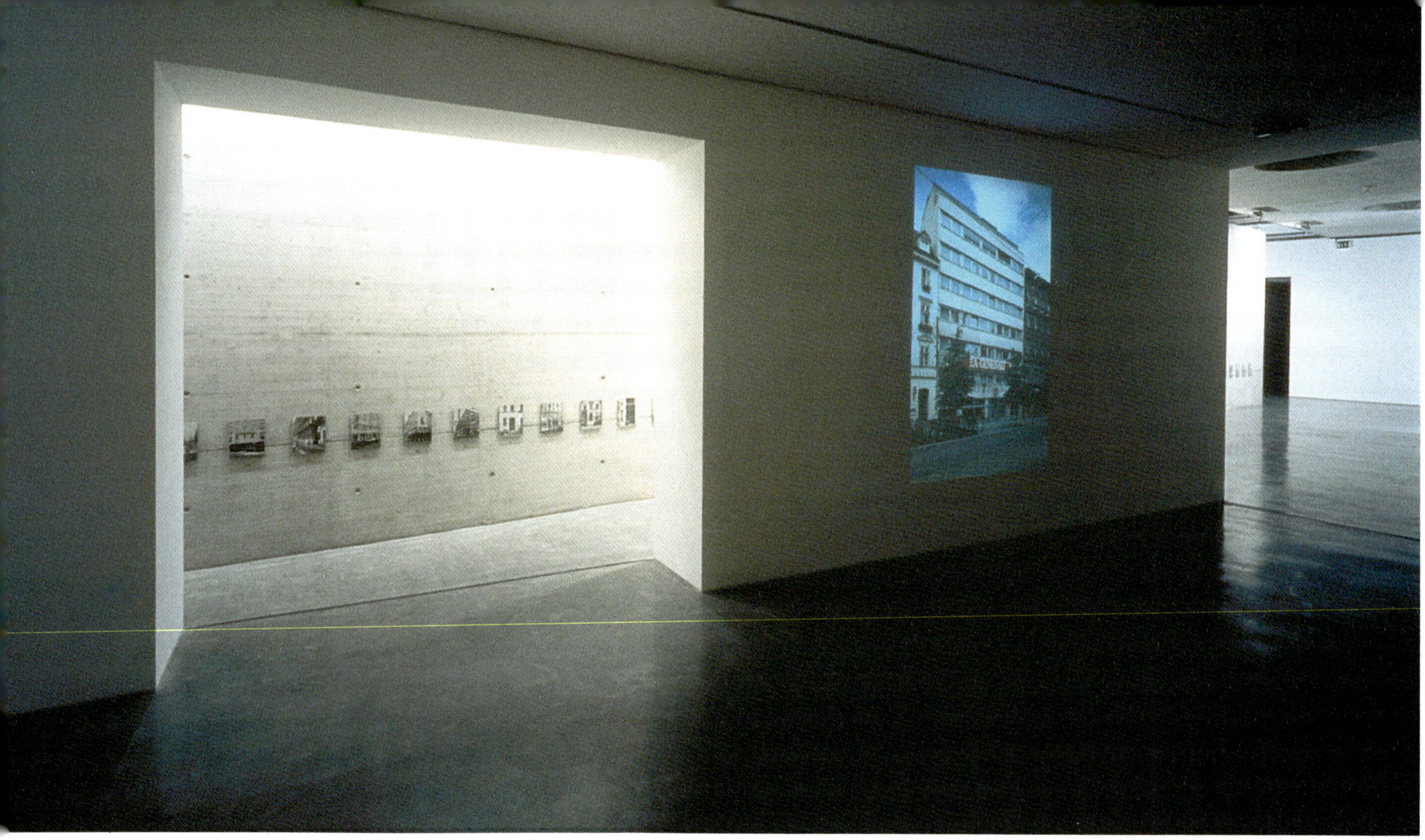

SQUATTING PROJECT/WIEN 1998, installation view, 1998

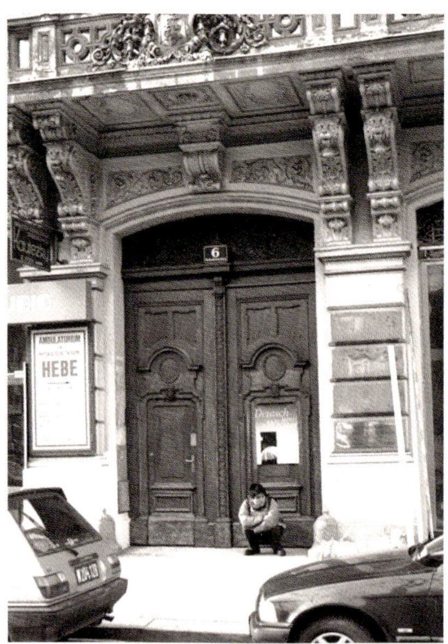

SQUATTING PROJECT/WIEN, 1998, (detail), 1998

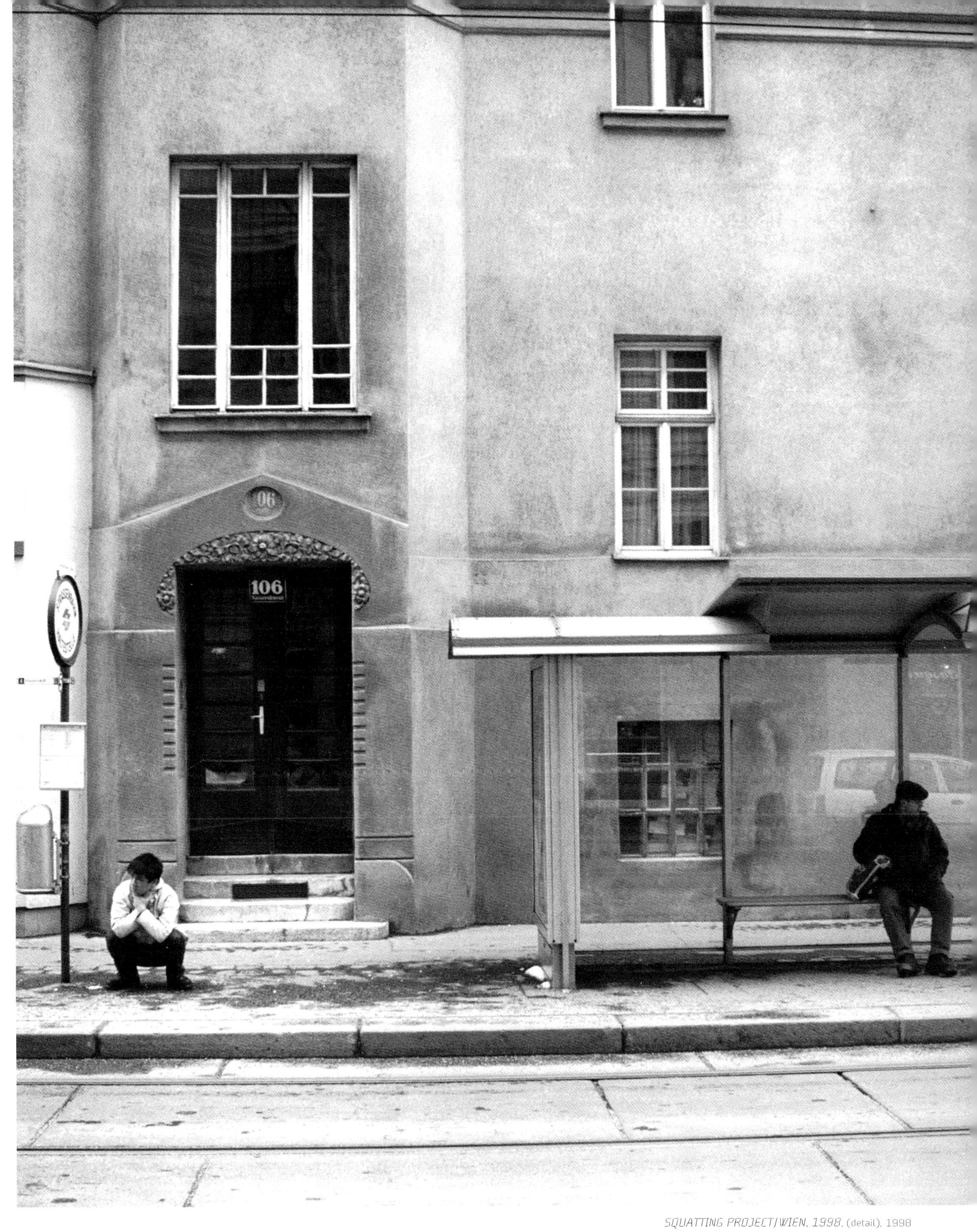

SQUATTING PROJECT/WIEN, 1998, (detail), 1998

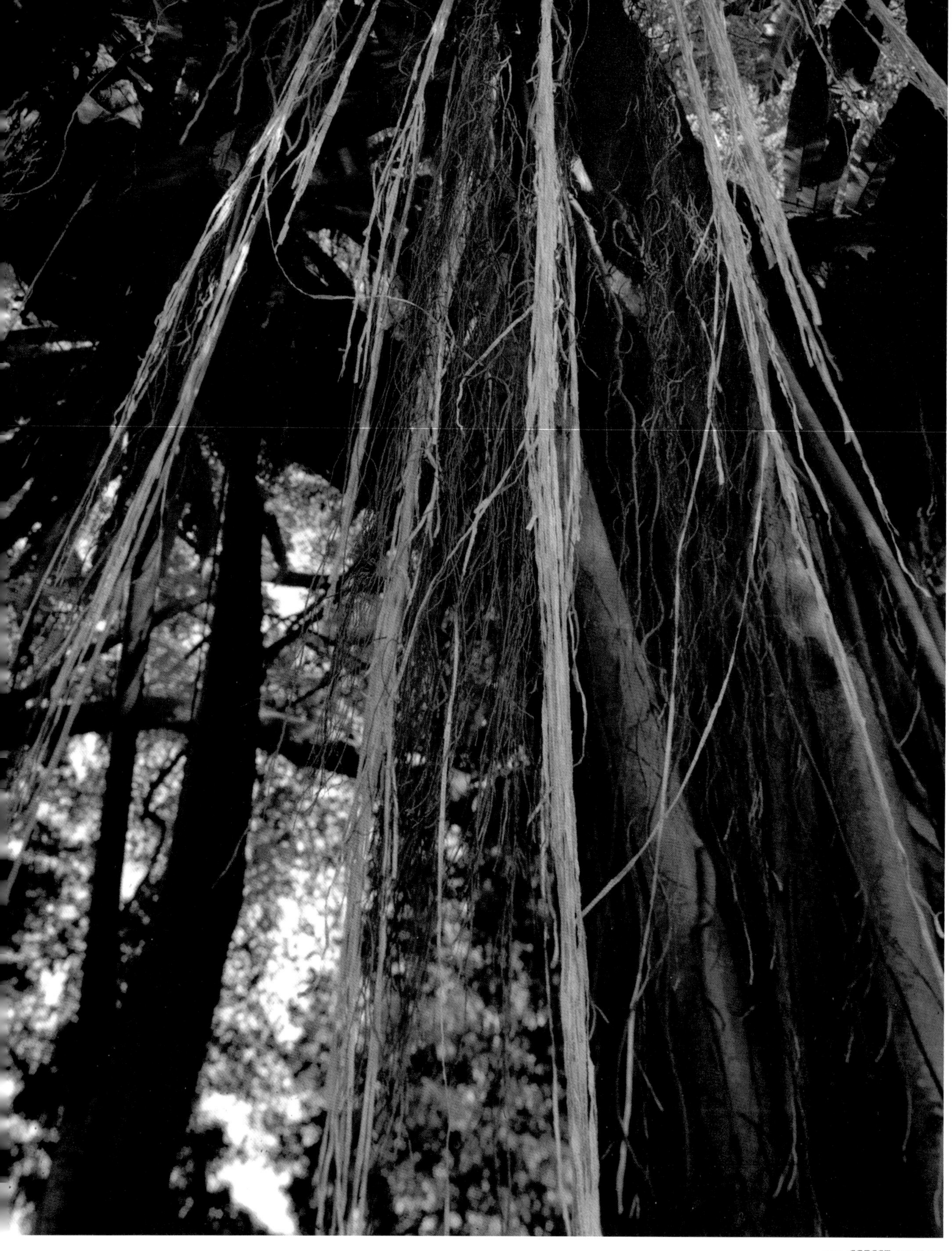

from *FOREST*, 1996-98

Simryn Gill

Forest is the title of a series of black-and-white photographs Gill made between 1996 and 1998. In these monumental pictures, delicate strips of text have been literally lifted from pages of books and attached to living plants, which were then placed back in nature and returned to living matter. Like Gill's more recent projects *Rampant* (1999) and *Self-Seeds* (1998), this body of work makes poetic metaphors of vegetation and writing to address issues of cultural transplantation. Originally commissioned for a permanent installation in a bus terminal in Yokohama City, Japan, where commuters would experience moments of nature in passing, these photographs record the process of decay and entropy in sites ranging from the personal (in the artist's parent's backyard in Port Dickson, Malaysia) to the political (in a British colonial garden in Singapore).

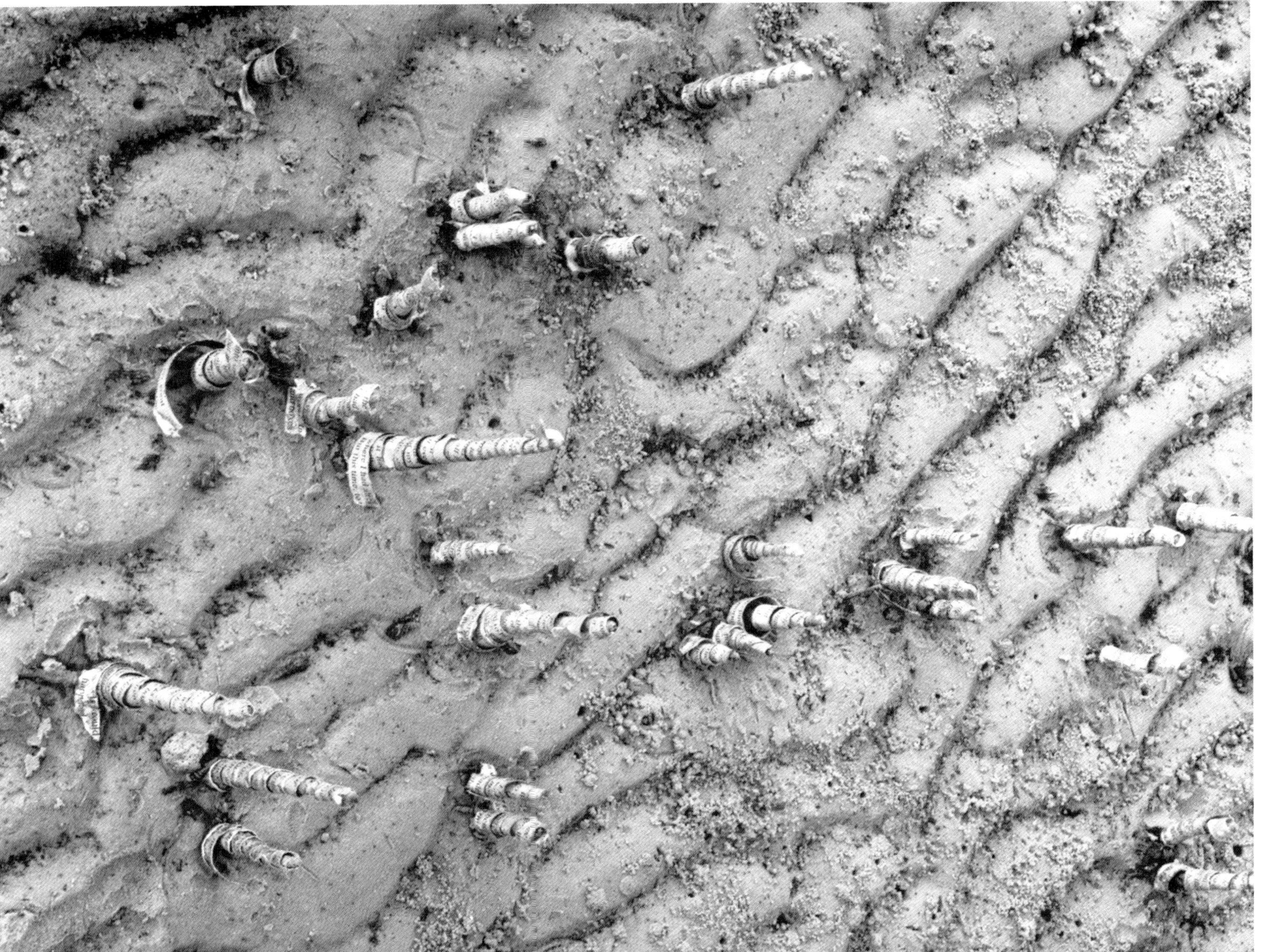

from *FOREST*, 1996-98

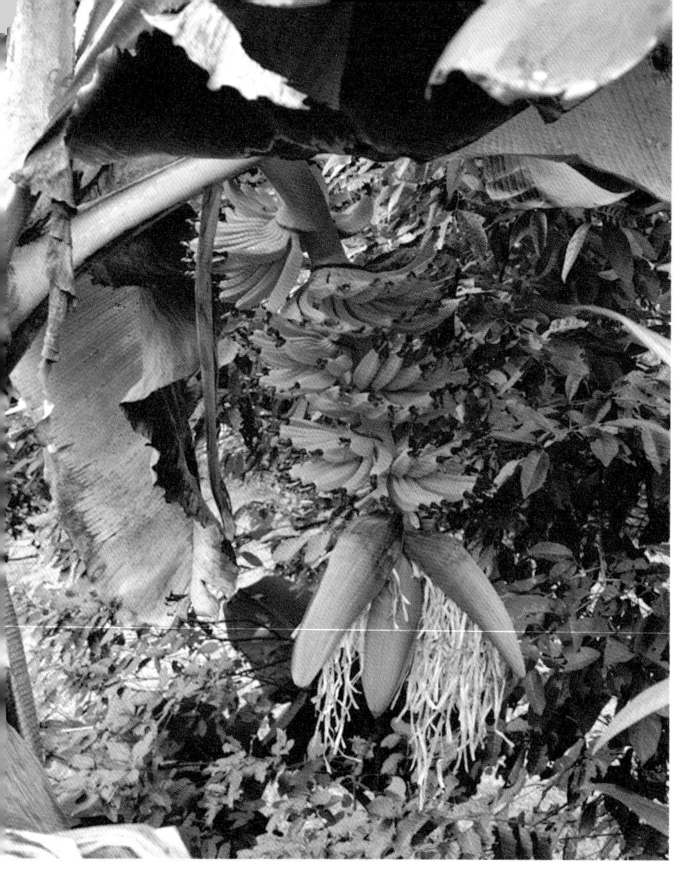

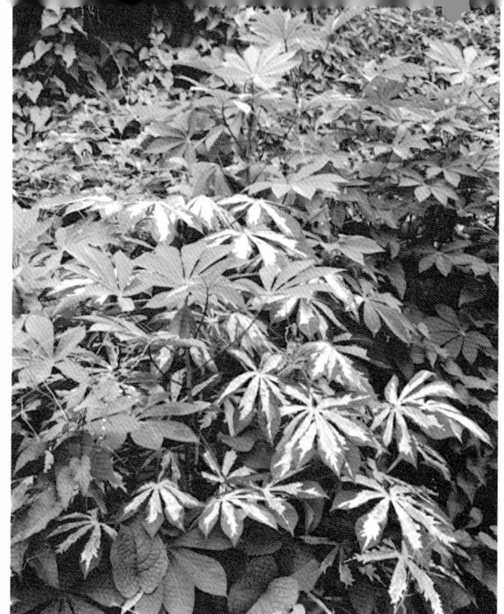

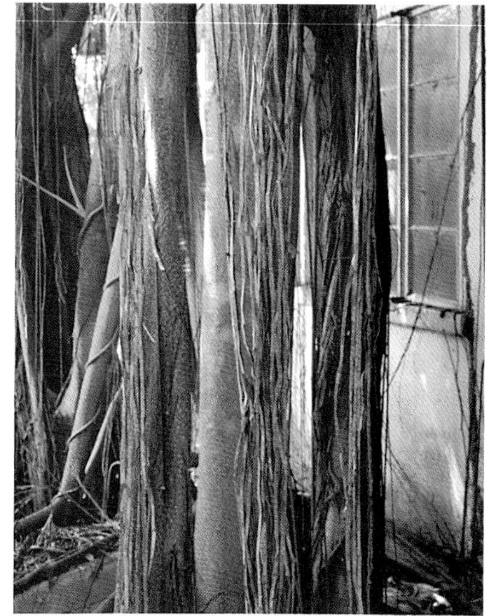

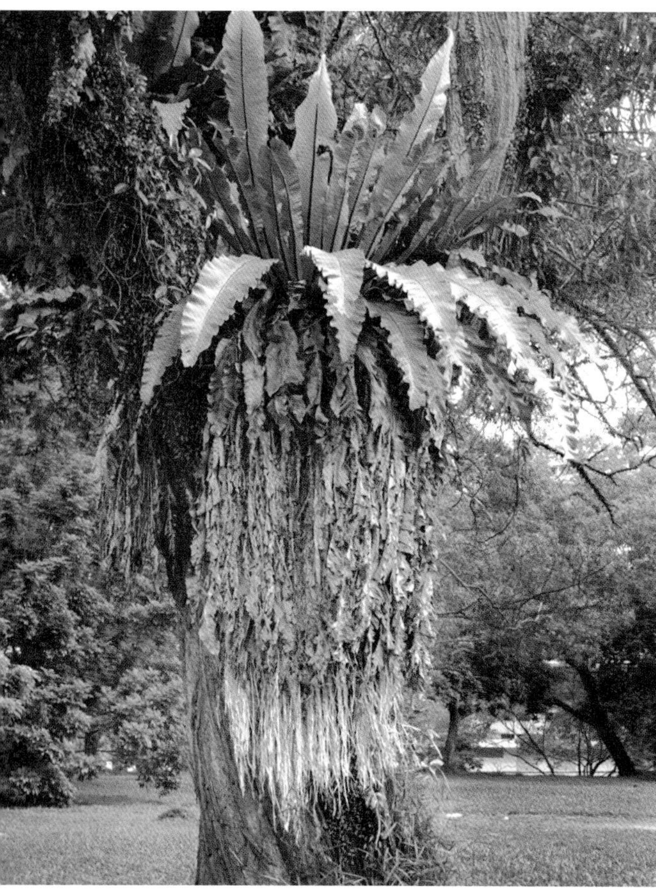

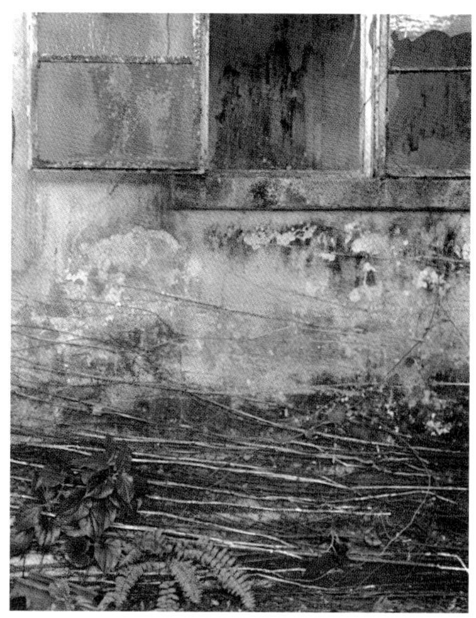

all from *FOREST*, 1996–98

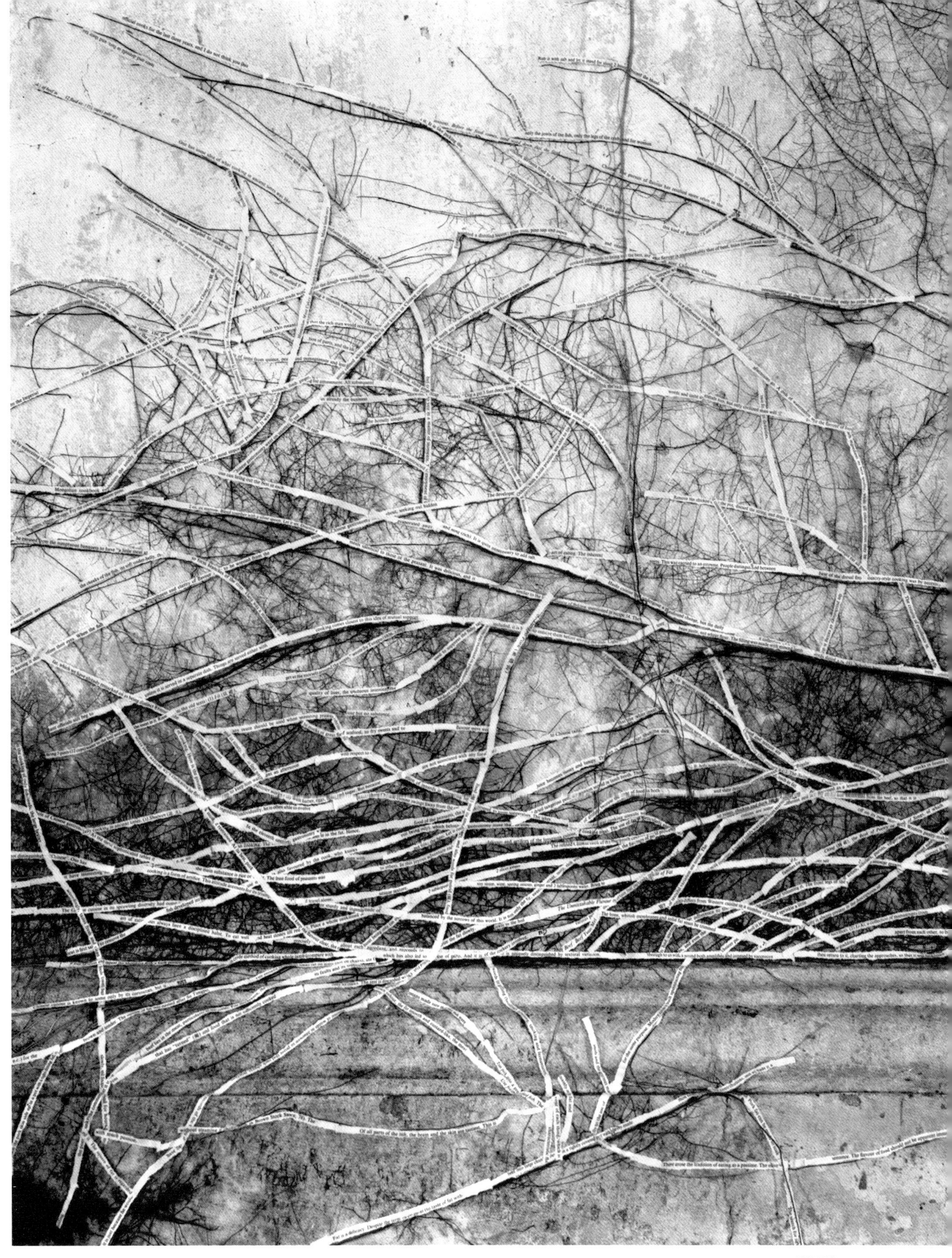

from *FOREST*, 1996–98

wilderness

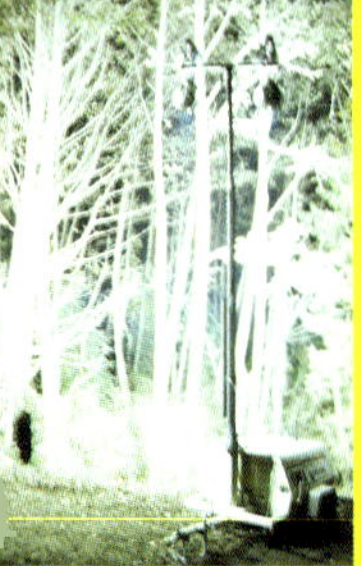
Rodney Graham

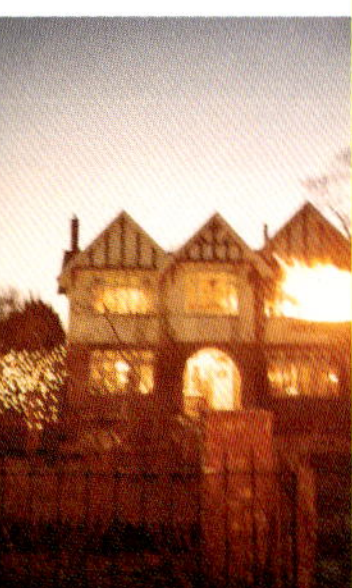
Gavin Hipkins

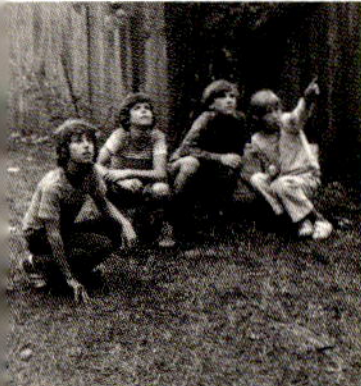
Rachel Khedoori

THE WILDERNESS, AFTER ALL, DOES NOT LOCATE ITSELF, DOES NOT NAME ITSELF.
—Simon Schama[1]

The profound presence of the raw wilderness is, by now, a cliché of existence in Canada. In Vancouver, there is no part of the city from which the water and mountains are not visible and looming. Made more surreal by the intense "off-shore," waterfront development of the last decade, the juxtaposition of snow-capped peaks, Pacific waters, glass towers, and tourist totem poles (signifiers of the marginalized native presence), and the overwhelming reality of the land have always been visual facts to be reconciled. Artists such as Jeff Wall, Roy Arden, and Stan Douglas have made complex photographic works that address the signification of the landscape as a contested territory ravaged by changes wrought by the Pacific economy. Within the context of the internationalist language of modernism, the work of these artists serves as the gateway to art practice in Canada. Curator Scott Watson describes the wilderness in Canada as "a vast emptiness.... *Nature, natural, wilderness,* and *emptiness* are all familiar terms in Canada's cultural production where they are usually deployed to describe something essential about the country and the psyche of its citizens."[2]

Canadian Rodney Graham investigates nature through a highly personal conversation on the pastoral. Beginning in 1976, Graham made a series of "illumination" works interrogating the relationship of film to nature: *75 Polaroids* (1976), seventy-five flash photographs of nature at night; *Illuminated Ravine* (1979), a staged illumination of a ravine; a 35mm film titled *Two Generators* (1984–92); and *Edge of a Wood* (1999), which now exists as a video projection. Utilizing primitive filmmaking techniques, Graham recorded unremarkable natural occurrences—a ravine, a rushing river, and a forest's edge—all staged at night. Initially made as notational works, not easily resolved for exhibition, each of these has become a seminal work for Graham.

Edge of a Wood is in some ways the most poetic of the four. Jeff Wall's description of *Illuminated Ravine* anticipates Graham's illumination of the woods:

> an agitated, transient model of our real relation to parklands and nature reserves: it recognized them as stage-sets, isolated objects of alienated contemplation. The work built upon its audience's growing awareness of environmental abuse to make perceptible the neurotic aestheticism inherent in the contemplation of special parts of nature dissociated from the labouring totality.[3]

In pitch-blackness, a helicopter approaches the forest and, a few minutes later, begins panning the trees with its searchlight. The shaky light and the tall trees are both majestic and spooky; sentinel-like, they form a massive thicket that the encroaching surveyor cannot penetrate.

For First Nations People, the margin of settlement between the edges of forest and water is a spiritual and sacred space. In historical photographs of *potlatch* ceremonial gatherings, this territory is often delineated with grand totems facing out towards the sea. At night, the trees assume this pose, appearing both forbidding and mystical. In Graham's seven-minute loop, as the helicopter retreats, we are left both with the memory of their haunting mass and density and the reality of the legislated territory they occupy. Graham's pastoral view signals an unresolved interrogation of the landscape. Again Watson states, "In a global economy, all difference is leveled by the commodity form, everything is of equal gravity in the flow of the green river: owls, sequoias, real estate developers and the lumber lobby."[4]

In New Zealand, the land is perhaps the most charged symbol of contestation, and the notion of wilderness the most pervasive embodiment of the tourist imagination and national identity. Like Australia, New Zealand/Aerteroa is understood as a vast wilderness, a tamed paradise floating in the Pacific. New Zealand's two islands officially became bicultural in 1990; Maori and Pakeha societies seem to exist in a kind of productive, semi-colonial tolerance of each other, although the question of colonial status is still a point of rigorous debate among those who feel that the colonialization is complete. Gavin Hipkins is a young artist who lives in Wellington, a cultural center at the southern tip of the North Island. In his archival photographic project entitled *The Homely* (1998–2000), Hipkins documented sites of the colonial landscape, confronting definitions of nativeness and homeland.

> Many of the photographs in *The Homely* have their place of origin in domestic settings. But the [subject] also ventures away from the home's safety and moves between the actual landscape and (diorama) depictions of landscape. This blurring of the real and the simulation of the real belongs to a denatured space: the postmodern sublime. Although New Zealand has an international reputation for being "clean, green and beautiful"… it is the treatment and conquest of nature as an adventure playground that interests me with this project.[5]

Hipkins interrogates sites of crisis in the culture—where modernity meets its demise. An embedded narrative within *The Homely* deals with the parallel notions of the wilderness and the landscape, the appropriated and the cultivated, the indigenous and the subsumed. Like the colonial cultures of New Zealand and Australia, whose unruly co-existence of indigenous and settler culture fosters whole academic disciplines such as "settlement studies" that are rare in the United States, the pictures hover in an uneasy territory between cozy folklore and residual violence.

In Los Angeles, where cultural hybridity characterizes the everyday but the dominant culture is Hollywood, the idea of the wilderness is both constructed and real. There are, for example, unusually long stretches of uninhabited beachfront and the untamed environment preserved in the Channel Islands. Naturally ignited fires fueled by the Santa Ana winds annually burn parts of Malibu and the surrounding hills. Within the city, the experience of the wilderness is mediated too, and areas like Griffith Park are the simulacrum of themselves as parkland.

In her film installations and video works, Australian-born Rachel Khedoori exploits all sides of her chosen vistas. In the 1996 16mm-film installation titled *Griffith Park,* she combines a staged pan of the park landscape and the overtly displayed apparatus of the film machinery itself, including its sound and physical presence in the gallery, with photographs of children at play. The source photographs were snapshots taken by Khedoori's uncle, an amateur landscape photographer in Sydney, where the artist grew up. In this installation, the photographs are reproduced as posters, stacked on the floor for the visitor to take home—a bit of point-and-shoot memorabilia of a day in the park. In the context of the slow, creeping film pan and the flat walls of the stage set, photographs of children playing an innocent game of "cops and robbers" appear to be gruesomely excerpted from a horror film set in the Griffith Park familiar to us through film noir. The haunting landscape is both banal with its picnic tables and visible low-tech production, and reinformed by the volatile pictures of the boys on the verge of adolescence, playing at violence.

Like Rodney Graham, Khedoori's fascination with the mediated presence of nature within the urban context is always located through film. In all her installations she creates a situation in the gallery where the viewer is self-consciously aware of the process of viewing. An earlier work, *105 Westchester* (1998), consisted of a slow pan, a moving inventory, of all the buildings on the street where she lived while a student. As a portrait of a transitional neighborhood near the Los Angeles airport, it also slyly acknowledges the bizarre mix of architectural styles characteristic of many strips in the city. The lazy, crawling pace of Khedoori's footage lulls the viewer into a re-framed relationship with the banal urban terrain.

Notes

1. Simon Schama, *Landscape and Memory* (New York: Alfred A. Knopf, Inc., 1995), 7.
2. Scott Watson, "Disfigured Nature: The Origins of the Modern Canadian Landscape," in *Eye of Nature* (Banff, Canada: Walter Phillips Gallery, 1991), 103. Watson's remarks are within the context of a discussion about the "Group of 7," a group of landscape painters whose work in the 1920s profoundly shaped the image of the Canadian West in the popular consciousness.
3. Jeff Wall, "Into the Forest," in *Rodney Graham*, exh. cat. (Vancouver: Vancouver Art Gallery, 1988), 33. Wall's text and a comprehensive listing of Graham's "Illuminations" are published in *Rodney Graham Works from 1976–1994*, exh. cat. (Toronto: Art Gallery of York University, 1994).
4. Watson, 127.
5. From a letter to the author from the artist, 22 November 1999.

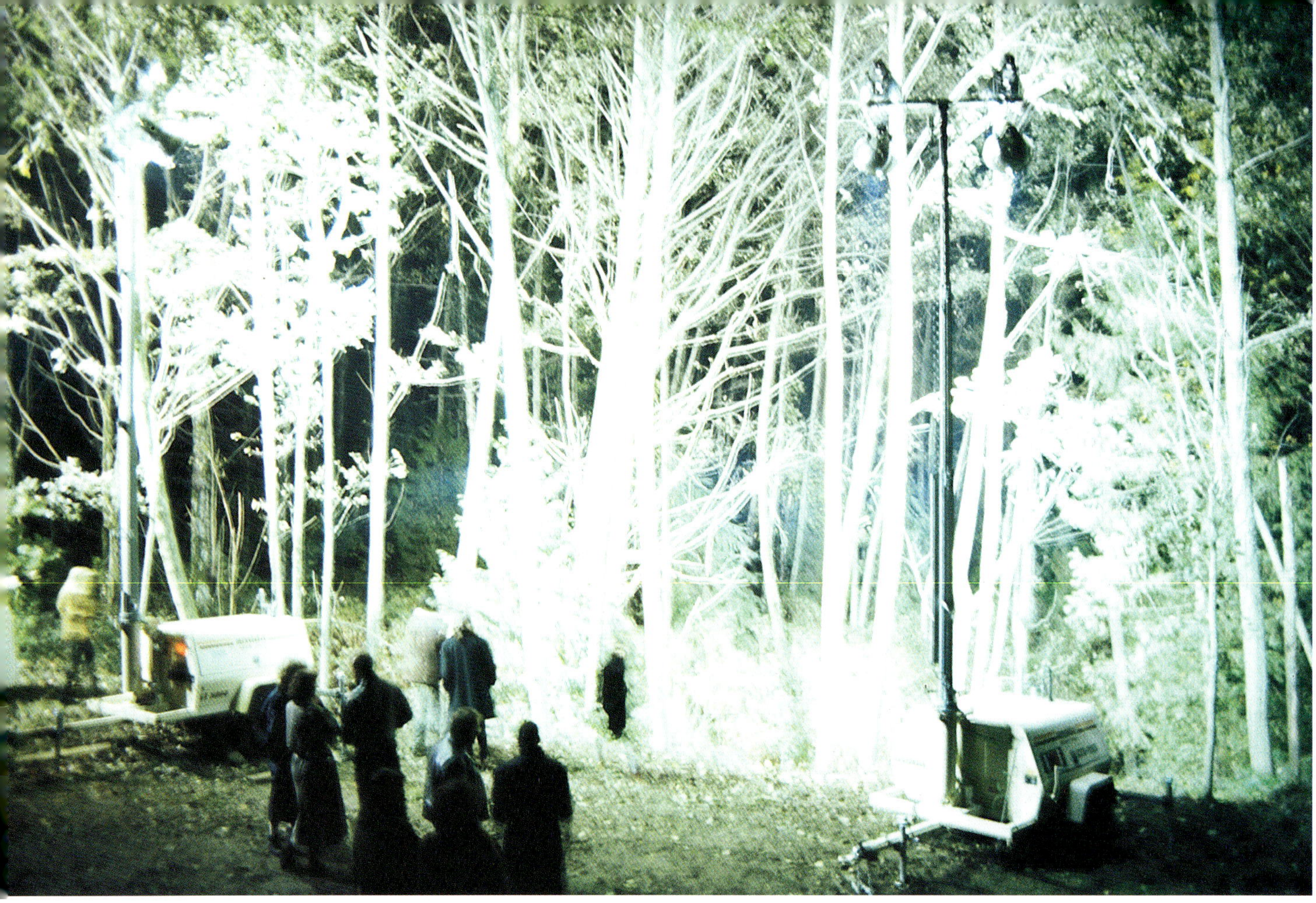

ILLUMINATED RAVINE, 1979/1991

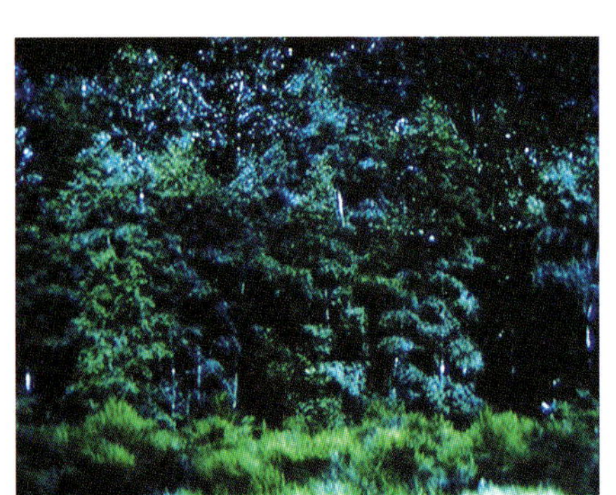

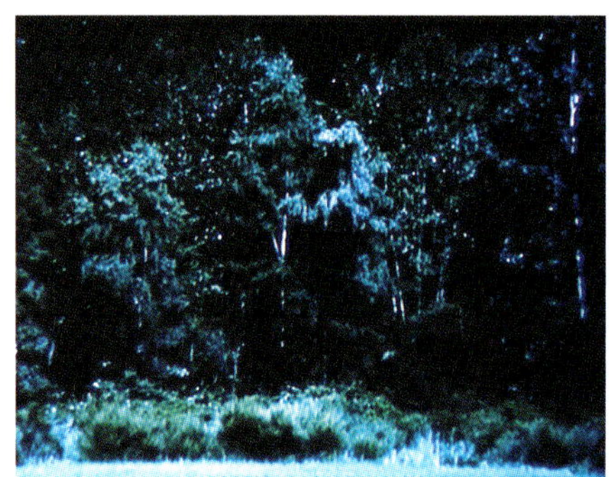

EDGE OF A WOOD, 1999

Rodney Graham

In 1979 Graham made *Illuminated Ravine*, the first of three illumination works that include *Two Generators* (1984) and *Edge of a Wood* (1999). The framing of nature is an ongoing subject for Graham, and in each of these works sound, light, and duration enhance the physical experience of the film. *Edge of a Wood* was shot with two cameras and is displayed as a double video projection. The work begins in complete darkness and silence, until the viewer hears an approaching helicopter that hovers and pans the forest edge with its searchlight. Simultaneously harsh and strangely poignant, the film embodies the raw stature of the forest and its mythic presence within the landscape of Canada.

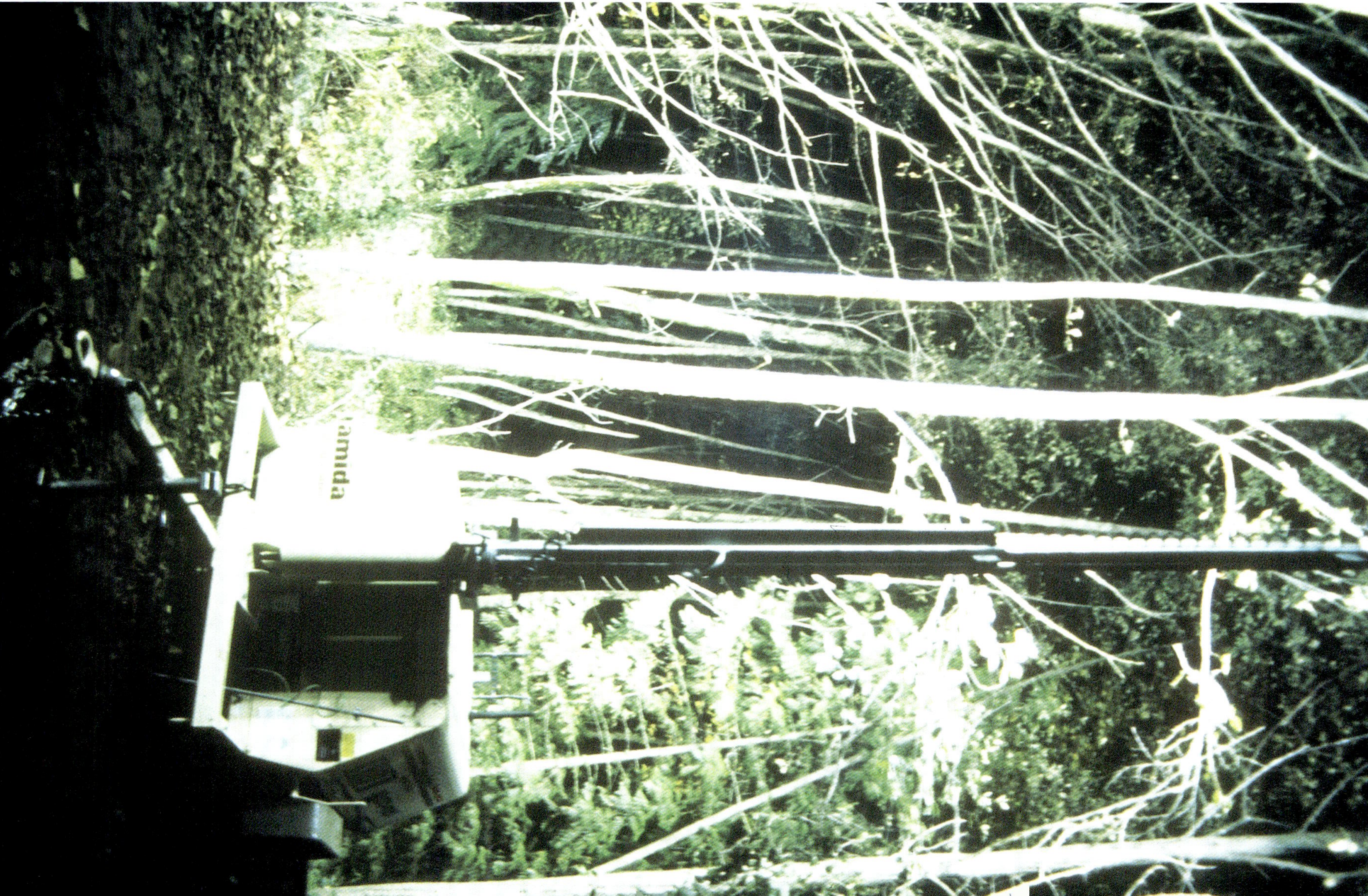

ILLUMINATED RAVINE, 1979/1991

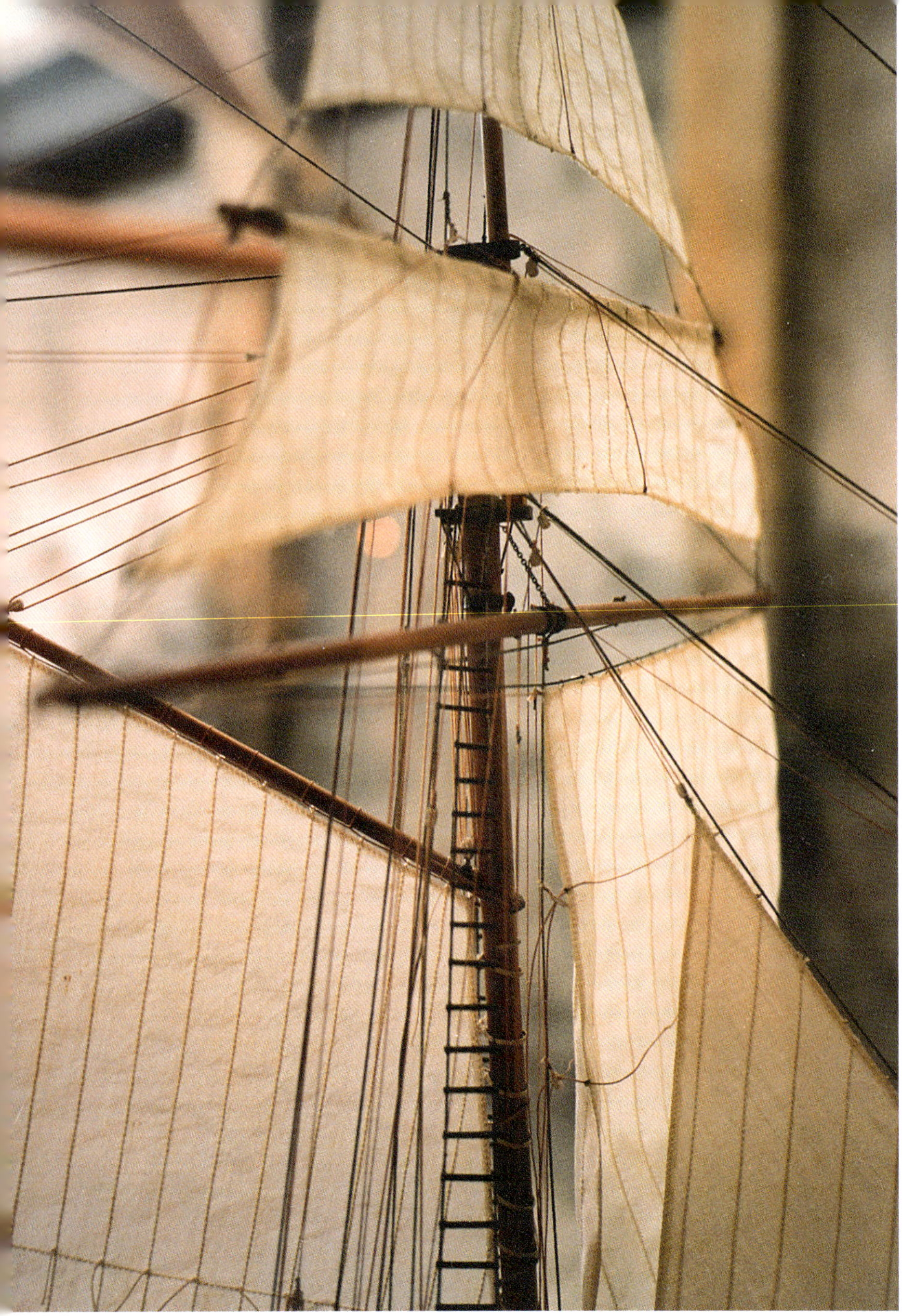

THE HOMELY: AUCKLAND (MODEL), 1998

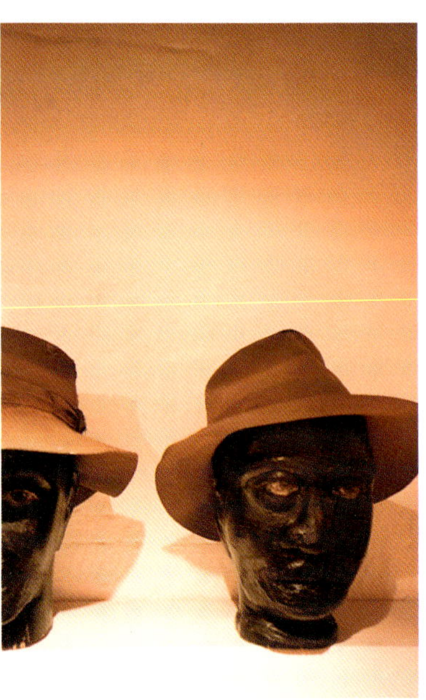

THE HOMELY: SYDNEY (HEADS), 1998

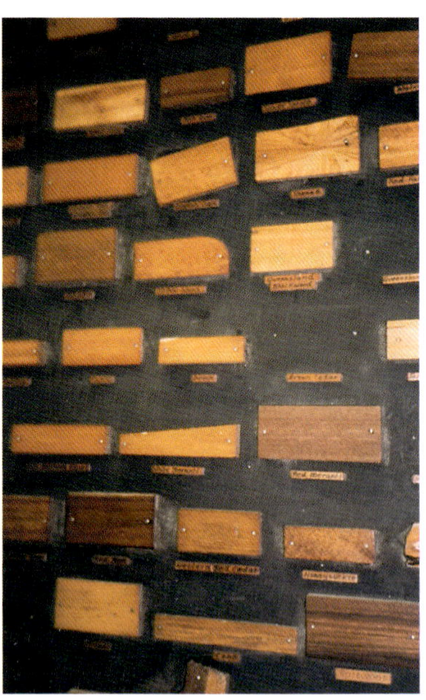

THE HOMELY: MELBOURNE (WOOD), 1999

Gavin Hipkins

Taken from Freud's essay on the uncanny, *unheimlich* or homely, the notion of the "other" is embodied in Hipkins's beautiful and somber pictures that document the bicultural landscape of New Zealand. Hipkins continues his exploration of the legacies of modernist utopianism by excavating icons of (post)coloniality. Highlighting the cultural construction of landscape and its representation, this selection of thirty pictures is drawn from a larger series of 160 images that the artist calls a "postcolonial Gothic novel." *The Homely* cites a history of New Zealand and Australia by representing elements that have been used to define nationhood and historic folklore.

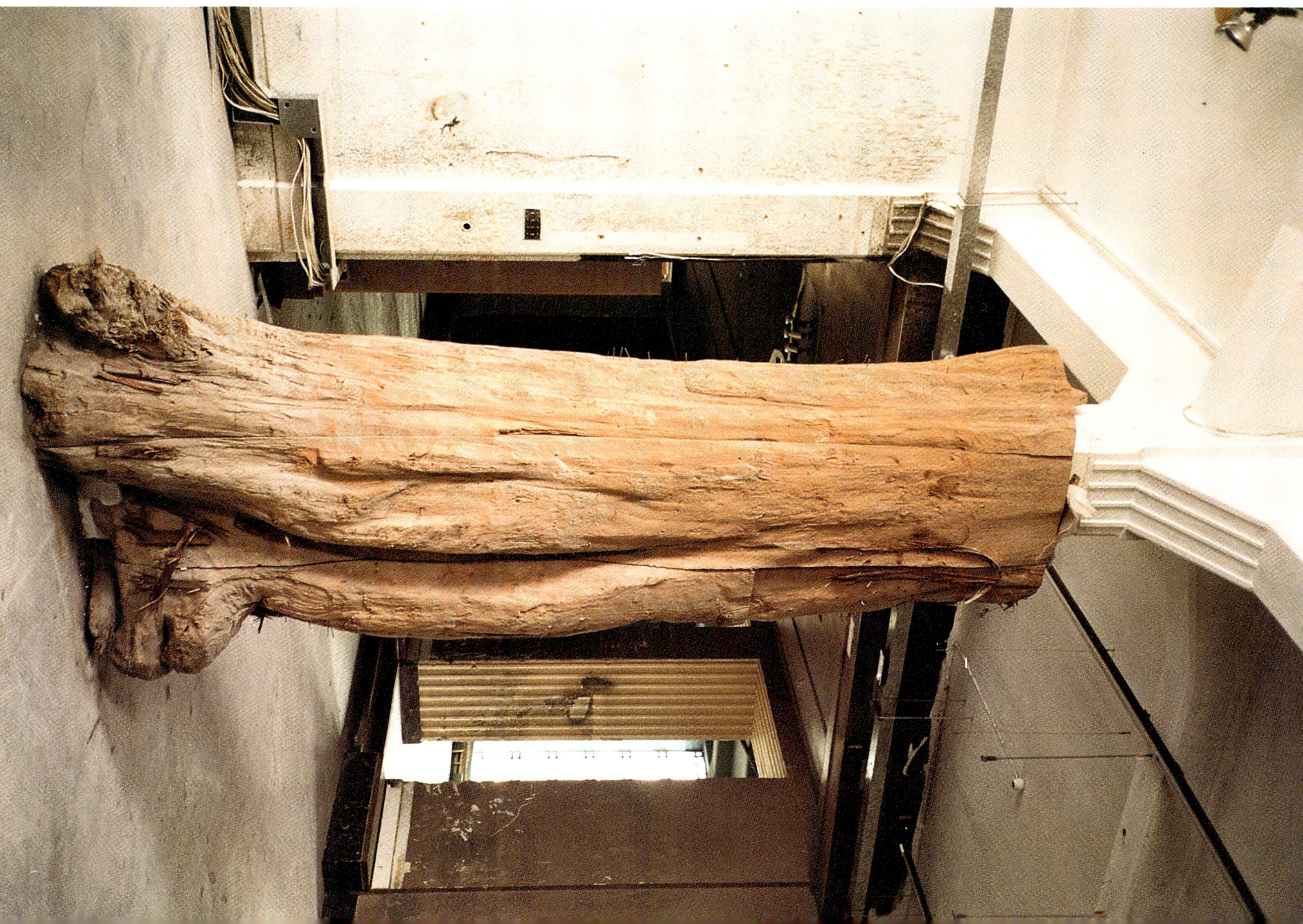

THE HOMELY: WELLINGTON (MUSEUM), 1998

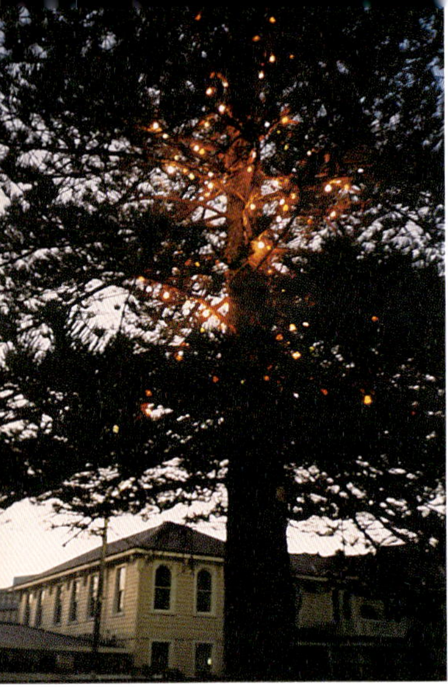

THE HOMELY: NAPIER (TREE), 1999

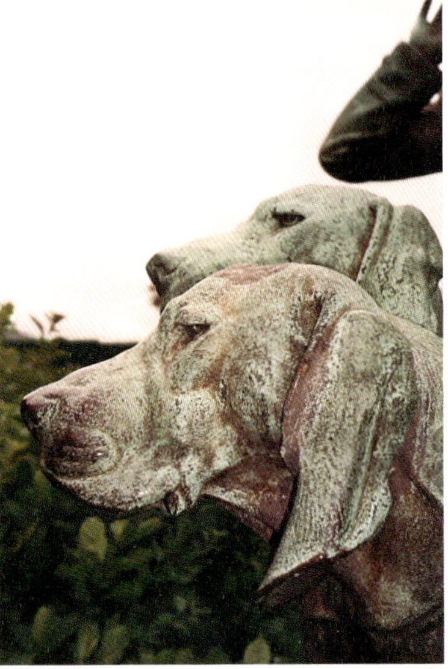

THE HOMELY: SYDNEY (DOGS), 1998

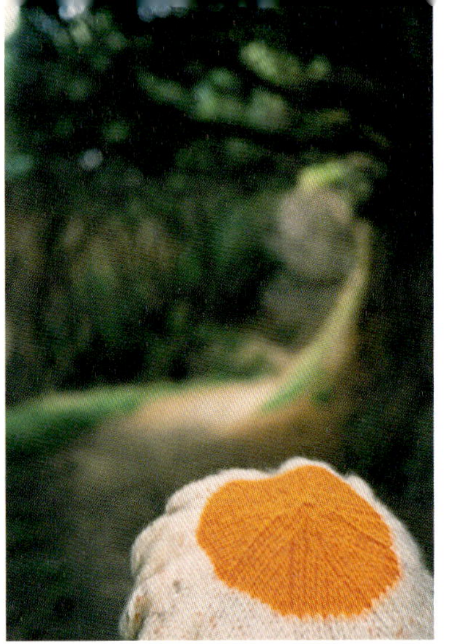

THE HOMELY: WELLINGTON (PATH), 1999

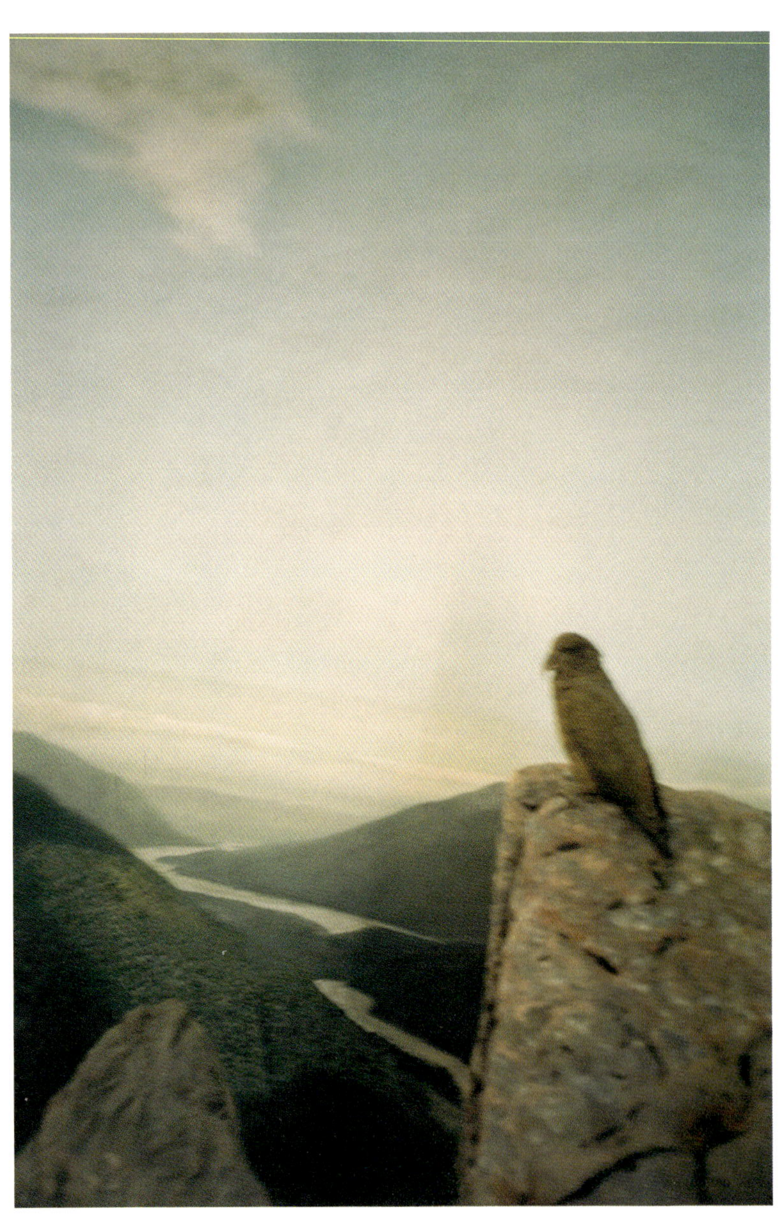

THE HOMELY: CHRISTCHURCH (MUSEUM), 1998

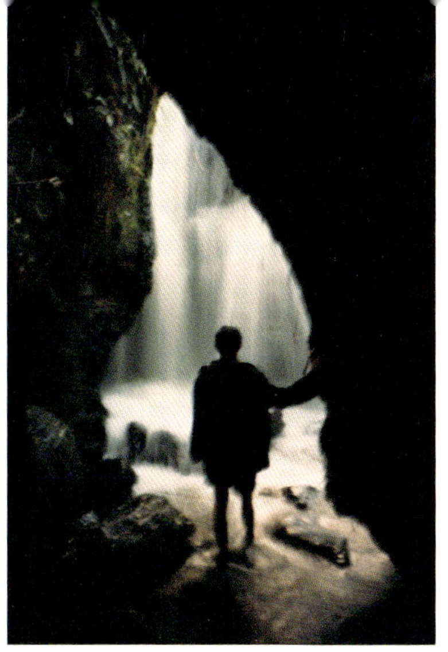

THE HOMELY: TE WAIROA (FALLS), 1999

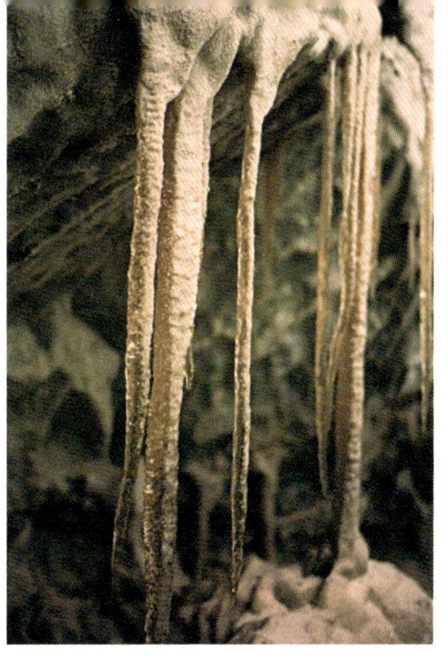

THE HOMELY: CHRISTCHURCH (ICICLES), 1998

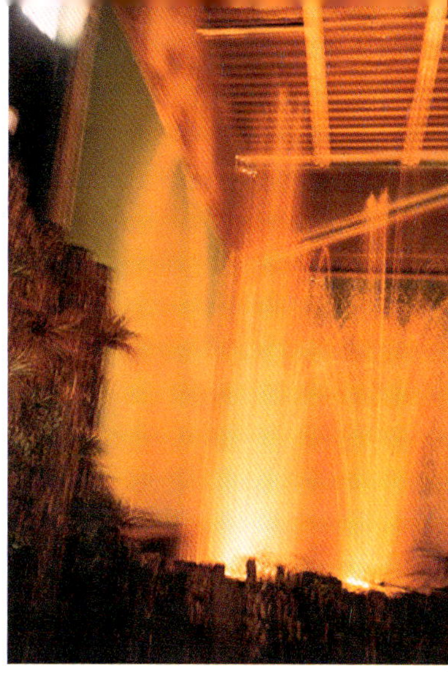

THE HOMELY: ROTURUA (FOUNTAIN), 1999

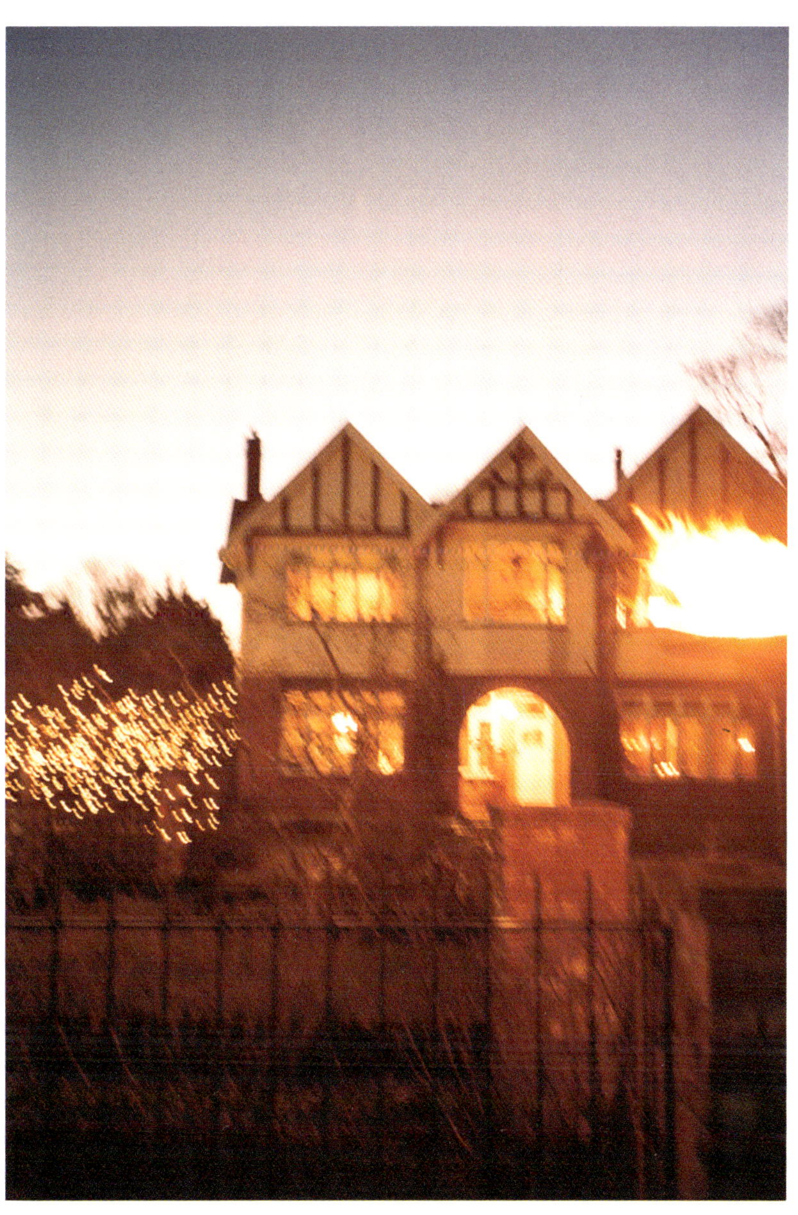

THE HOMELY: SOUTH ISLAND (HOUSE), 1999

from *GRIFFITH PARK*, 1996

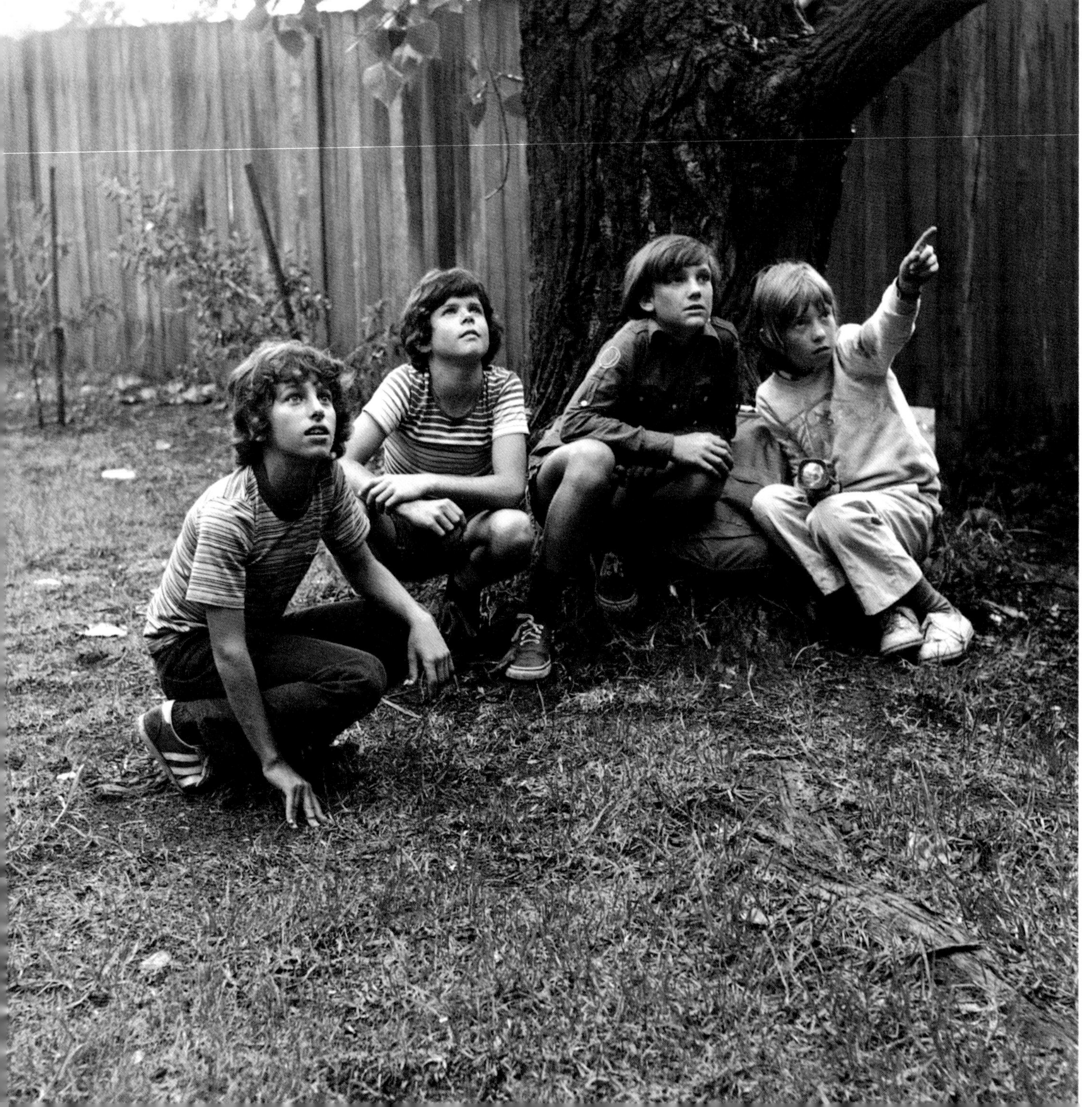

Rachel Khedoori

Based on the landscape of Griffith Park, this installation includes a looped film shot from a car window, panning the empty park in early morning, and posters depicting a group of boys enacting noirish film scenarios they choreographed themselves. Originally photographed in Sydney in 1977 by a landscape photographer, the children in the pictures are caught at the moment between theatrical adolescence and adulthood, and their drama recalls the kind of films that inform our understanding of the landscape of Hollywood's Griffith Park. The sound and presence of the 16mm-film projector enhance the physicality of the installation.

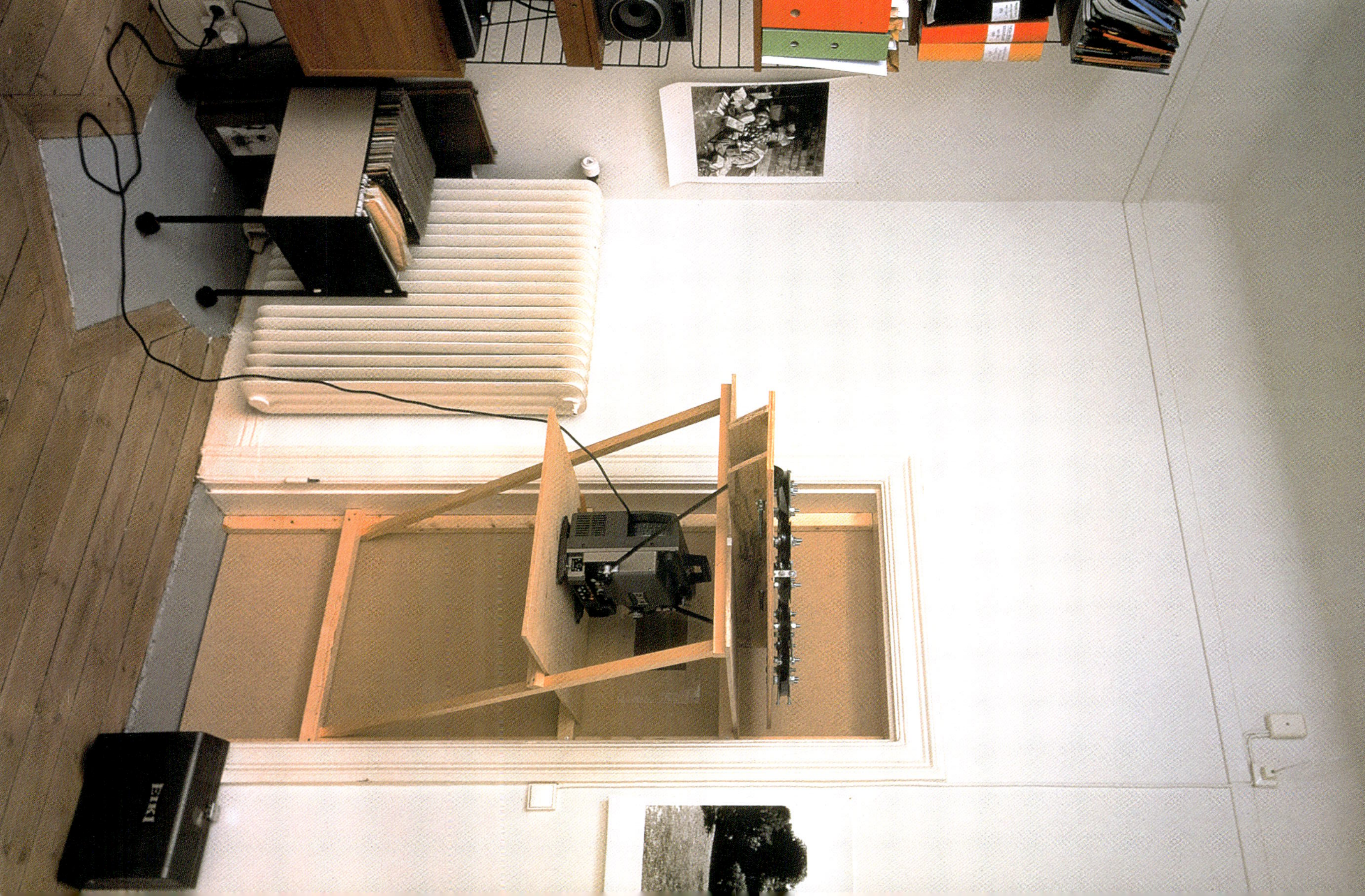

GRIFFITH PARK, installation view, 1996

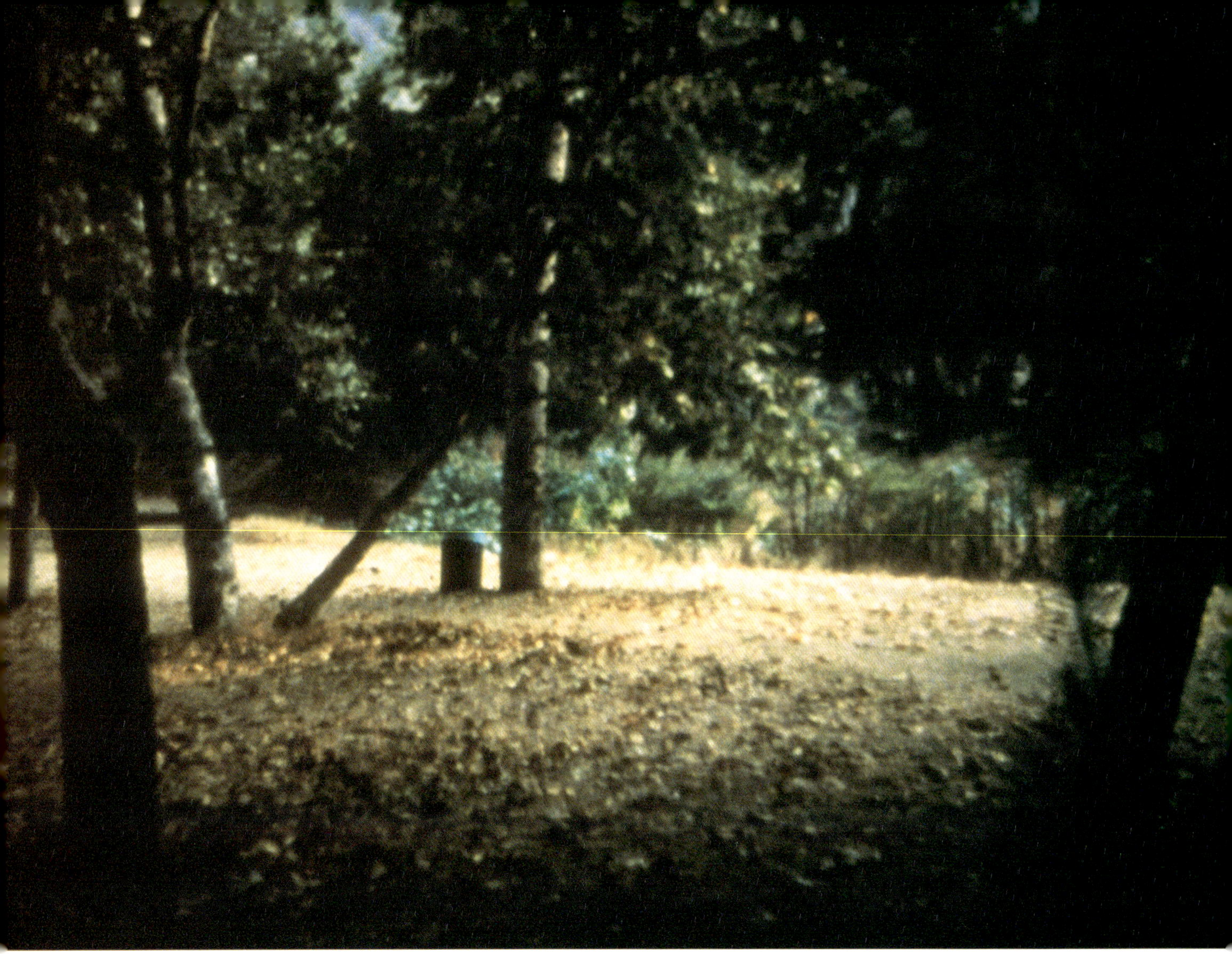

from *GRIFFITH PARK*, 1996

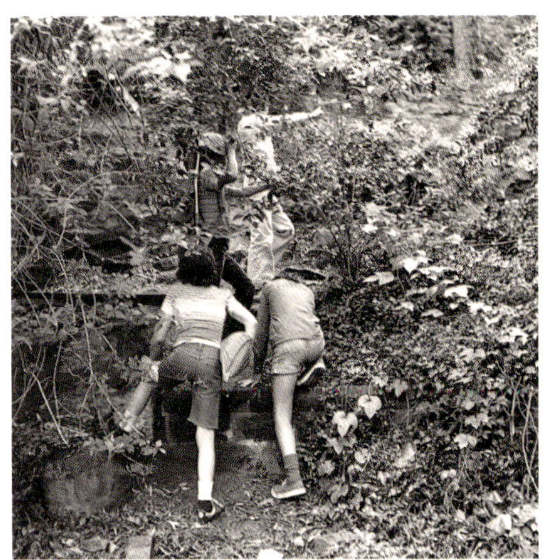

from *GRIFFITH PARK*, 1996

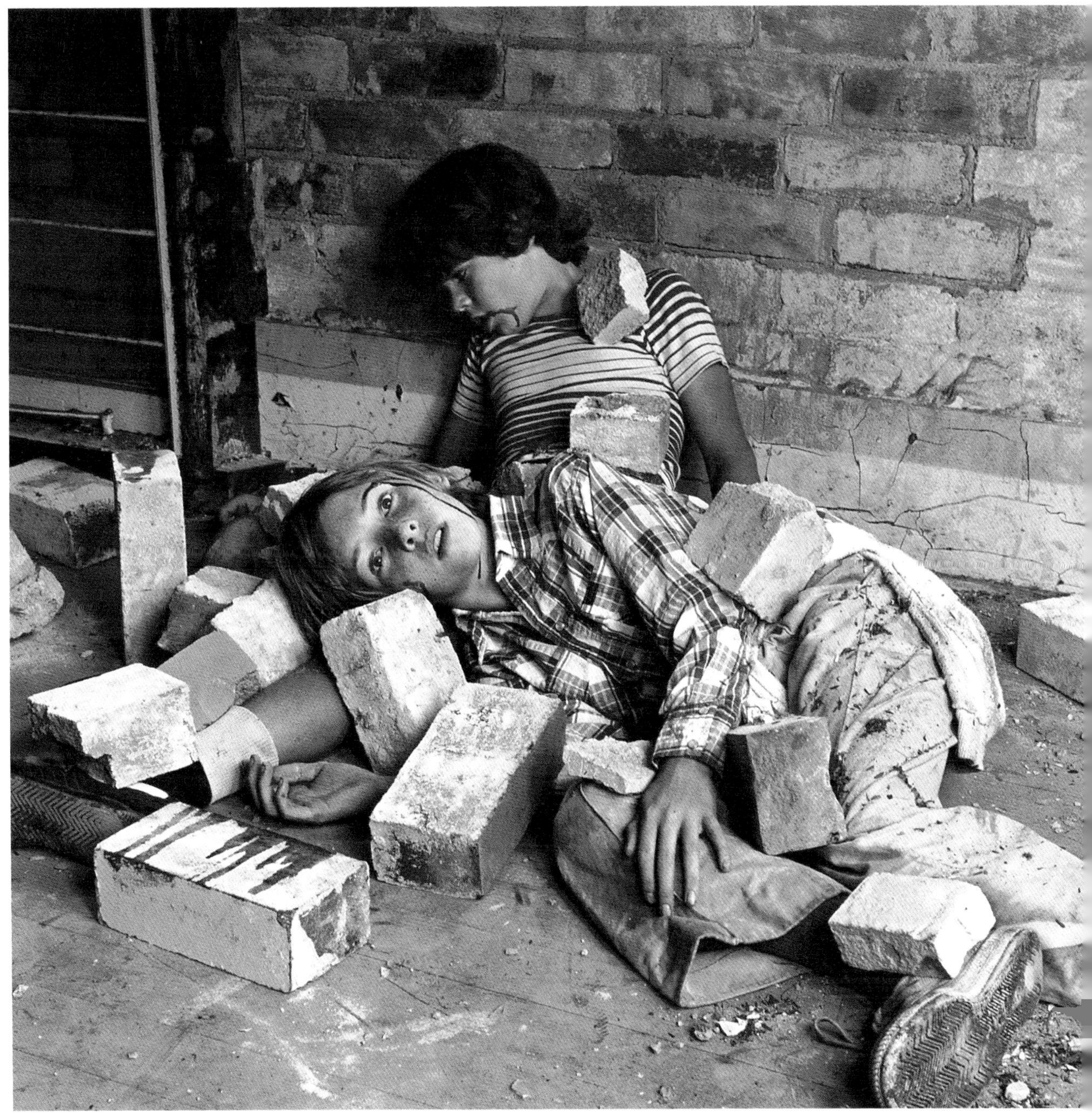

from *GRIFFITH PARK*, 1996

land

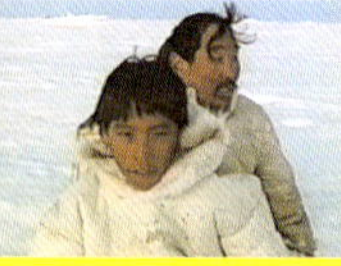
Igloolik Isuma Productions

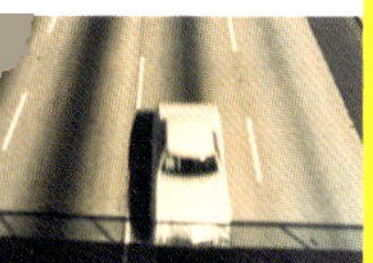
David Lamelas

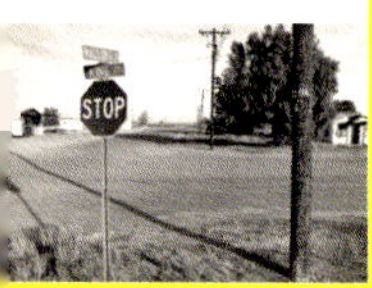

Glen Wilson

Inherent to any discussion of the landscape in the North American West is the narrative of settlement and its relationship to questions of identity. Between 1974 and 1986, Argentinean-born David Lamelas lived in Los Angeles and made experimental films exploring narrative structure and spectatorship. As an outsider choosing to move his artistic production to Hollywood, the heart of simulation culture, Lamelas was interested in the spectacle of film. Partly mining his own culture shock, Lamelas made his first professionally produced film in 1974, titled *The Desert People*, which was for the artist a study of American movie-making.

Conflating the narrative structures of the road movie with the documentary, the drama moves between five characters who detail their experiences on an Indian reservation through monologues that push the limits of viewer attention and problematize the motivation of the characters. A slightly haughty anthropologist talks about the socio-political structure of life on the reservation; a feminist magazine journalist investigates the role of women in Indian culture; a hippie college student is only interested in her own personal experience of the exotic on the reservation; a voyeuristic swinger is just as interested in the social dynamics of this strange group as he is the Papago Indians; and Manny, a Papago Indian. These are the talking heads that lead us, in uncomfortably extended shots, through the narrative of their trip to the reservation. The narrative shifts when Manny, who appears isolated in a solitary desert or beach landscape, starts to talk about the extinction of his people. Moving from staged documentary to a sobering monologue in which Manny moves from English to Spanish to his native Papago language, the narrative culminates in the film's shocking ending as the group meets its demise in a spectacular veer over an ocean cliff.

What is fascinating is how the reading of this film functions differently for today's audience. The characters' dialogue is punctuated with endless driving scenes on a freeway that seemingly leads nowhere, ambiguously taking place either before or after their visit to the reservation. Lamelas problematizes time and duration both as structural elements, and in terms of the viewer's experience. What becomes a hovering presence in the film, and the source of some anxiety for this viewer, is that the reservation itself never appears on-screen. It is the negative space around which the narrative cycles until the aggressive ending literally steers the film in another direction. The anthropological/filmic experiment ends when the voyeur character drives the car violently and, apparently for no reason, off a sheer cliff and into the ocean. This nihilistic end in the vast Pacific follows a pivotal encounter with the only character in the film who is not a caricature. When Manny shifts languages, we realize that only at that moment have we encountered some degree of authenticity, albeit a staged one. According to Benjamin H.D. Buchloh, "the principle of permutation is now transferred to a rather different concept that has itself by now come under considerable pressure, if not dispersal, namely that of identity. Permutation in Lamelas's film examines identity as *representation*, as linguistically, culturally and historically constructed."[1]

The role of film in the enactment and representation of colonialism is profound. In the nomadic community of Igloolik, located in the northeastern region of Canada, the nation's first peoples were not introduced to television until 1982. The Inuit filmmaker Zacharias Kunuk, formerly a carver by trade, has been making films for the past ten years, recently as part of the collective Igloolik Isuma Productions.[2] All set historically, the films purport to document a history never previously recorded. Often intentionally jarring, political references to such events as the rise of Hitler or the bombing of Pearl Harbor provide the historical context against which the Igloolik cast performs the staged stories of their everyday existence.

Set against these events, the blunt real-time of Kunuk's daily narratives offers a striking resituation of the way indigenous peoples register the passage of time. Like Lamelas's adoption of a pseudo-documentary mode, Kunuk's re-appropriation of the *National Geographic* photographic style turns on its head the heroicizing impulse of a particular brand of documentary. Critiquing such emblematic films as Robert Flaherty's *Nanook of the North* (1922) (for decades the only other film to record Eskimo life), Kunuk pictures his Inuit contemporaries engaging in the banal activities of nomadic existence not as an anthropologist monumentalizing and projecting onto his subjects, but as one with a place in their community. "In these tapes we see the old life as if it still existed, when everyone wore skin clothing, traveled by dogteam, lived in igloos and skin tents, ate only what could be killed by the men or gathered by the women and children."[3]

The parallel frames of geologic and astronomical progression which govern Inuit life, and the culturally constructed timelines of historical events, co-exist in Kunuk's film with a bizarre humor in a mix of document and drama. No doubt, for viewers not living in "the North," the attraction to Kunuk's raw landscape is due in part to the seductive powers of the exotic. When his family spends a day (or longer, who can tell?) on the construction of a porch out of ice blocks, the correlation the non-indigenous viewer unavoidably makes is to the Earth projects of Robert Smithson. The use of entropic materials, and the grounding of activity somehow in the vital resource of the land, is mystical and also utterly elementary for the Inuit. The presence of the landscape returns the colonizing gaze of the viewer—it is at once a view seemingly unmediated until the point-of-contact, and it situates the viewer at that point of contact. This is precisely Kunuk's point and the locus of the irony or a kind of knowing humor in the work. Each of these films functions as primary, ethnographic material, but with a keen awareness of their own remote, exotic appeal. How do we understand our own intense response to a landscape so strangely luminous and "other"?

Glen Wilson's video and photographic work also wrestles with the documentary legacy and its relationship to the representation of cultural identity. In his travels through the Southwestern desert, Wilson befriended an old, African-American farm worker named Elijah, who had migrated to the California/Arizona border region in the 1940s to work in the cotton fields. Struck by the unusual presence of this man and his family in this otherwise Hispanic area, Wilson was interested in the common experiences of transplants whose history is embedded in unexpected areas of the Southwest. In Wilson's own neighborhoods, first San Diego and now Venice, California, his investigations focus on the lives of longtime residents, his photographic interventions operating as a kind of mapping of the socio-geography of place.

Titled *Desert Fishing*, the video and photographic project about Elijah explores Wilson's and our expectations about a certain official history of the landscape and its economic and social reality. Again, the topography is the mute subject here. The project's three other subjects are a woman who has lived in the artist's Venice neighborhood for years and guards its history, and a Japanese friend's parents who were interned in California during the 1940s. The story of Wilson's neighborhood highlights our own (mis)readings of a now-blighted area known for its gang activity, which was settled primarily by African Americans. How each person navigates their relationship to place becomes the subject of Wilson's investigation, and he knowingly walks the line between sentimentality and documentary to make a space for the subjects to speak for themselves.

Notes

1. Benjamin H.D. Buchloh, "Structure, Sign and Reference in the Work of David Lamelas," in *David Lamelas: A New Refutation of Time*, exh. cat. (Munich: Kunstverein München; and Rotterdam: Witte de With, Center for Contemporary Art, 1997), 142.
2. Film and video historian Peggy Gale was generous in sharing with me her unpublished text on Kunuk and Igloolik Isuma Productions titled "OUT (T)Here... Video in Igloolik" (1999). She has written extensively on their films.
3. *Ibid.*, 1.

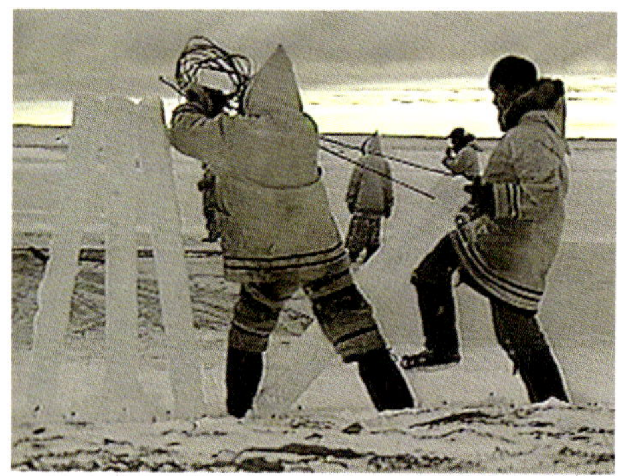

both from *TUGALIAQ (ICE BLOCKS)*, 1995

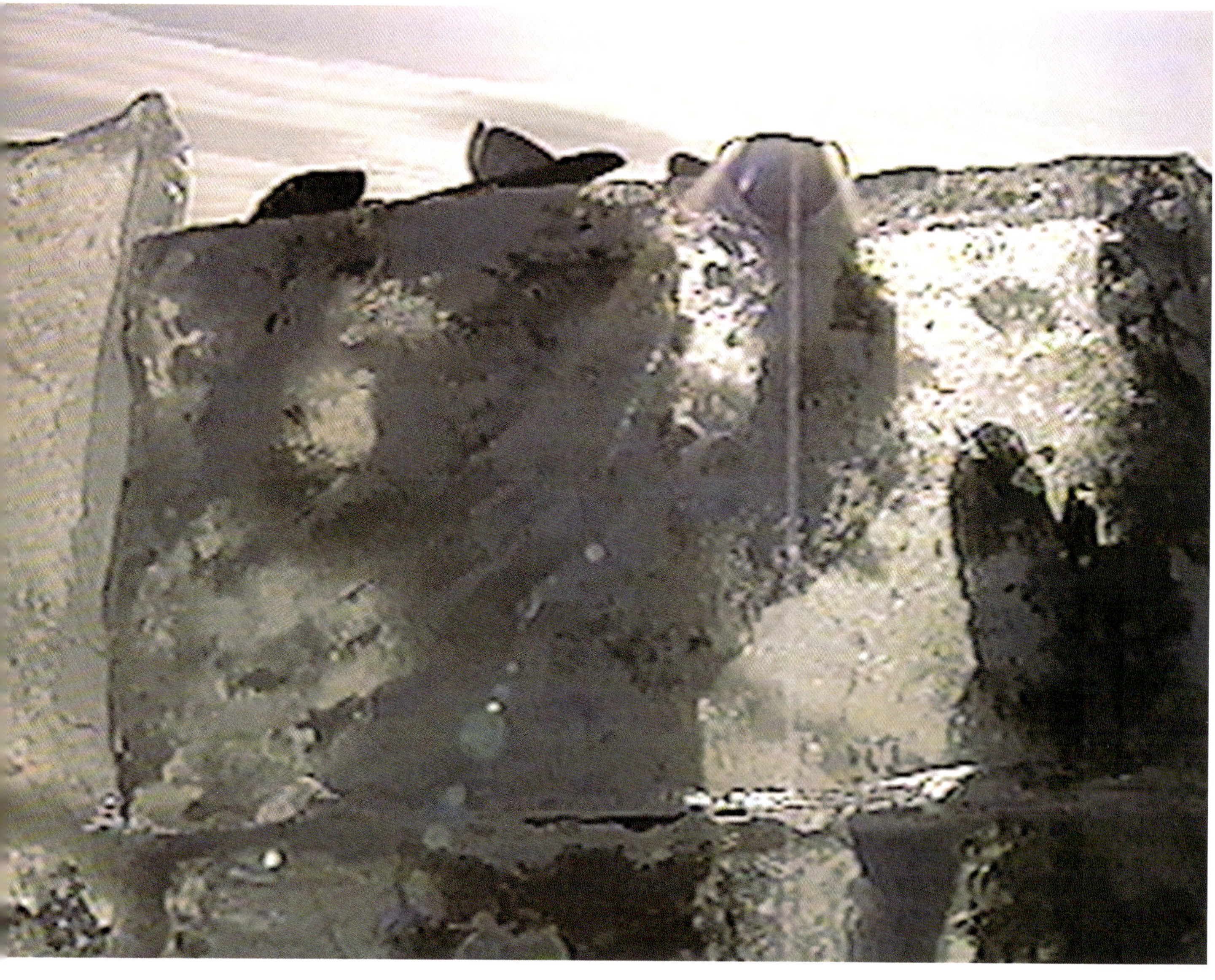

Igloolik Isuma Productions

In 1985, Zacharias Kunuk began making faux-documentary style films about the Isuma people living in the settlement of Igloolik in northeastern Canada, and is now part of a collective calling itself Igloolik Isuma Productions. The real-time films record, through narrative reenactment, the nomadic life and daily activities and traditions of the Isuma which are otherwise undocumented and unknown to an outside audience. The films *Qimuksik (Dog Team)* and *Tugaliaq (Ice Blocks)* are from an episodic series titled *Nunavut (Our Land)*.

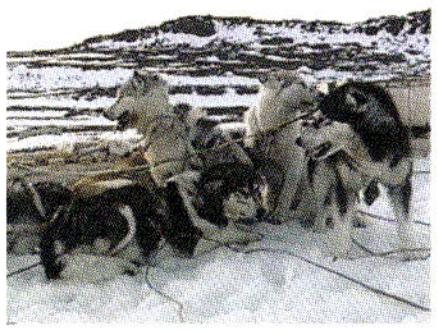

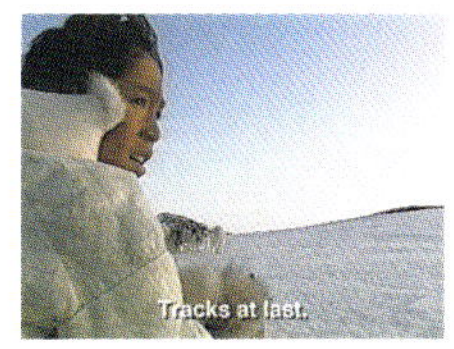

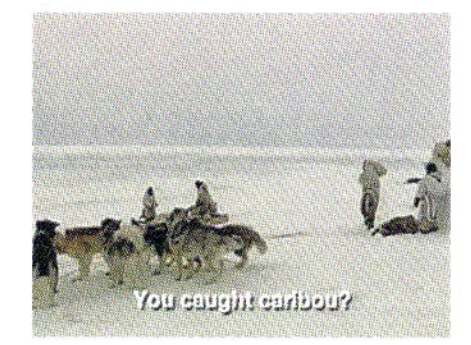

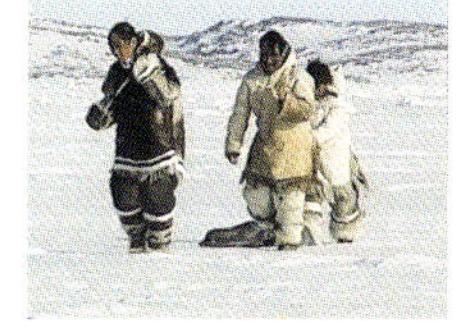

all from *QIMUKSIK (DOG TEAM)*, 1995

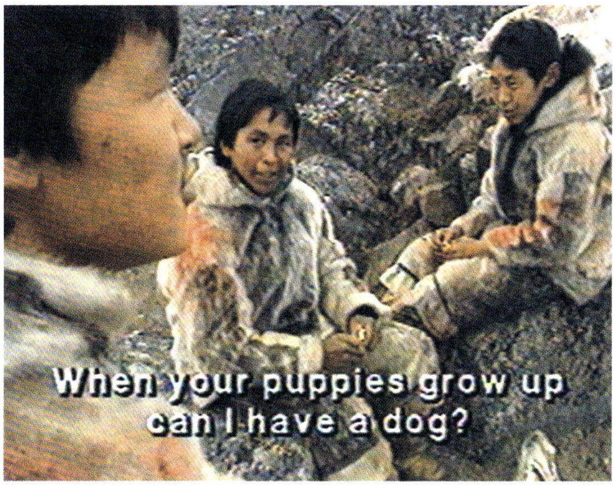

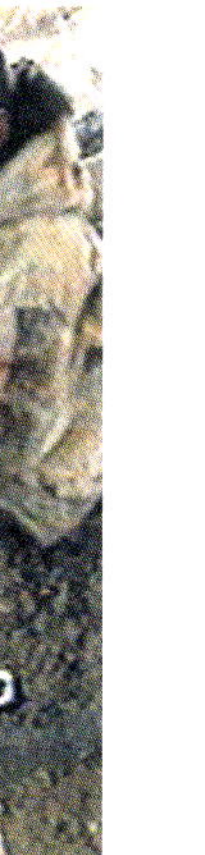

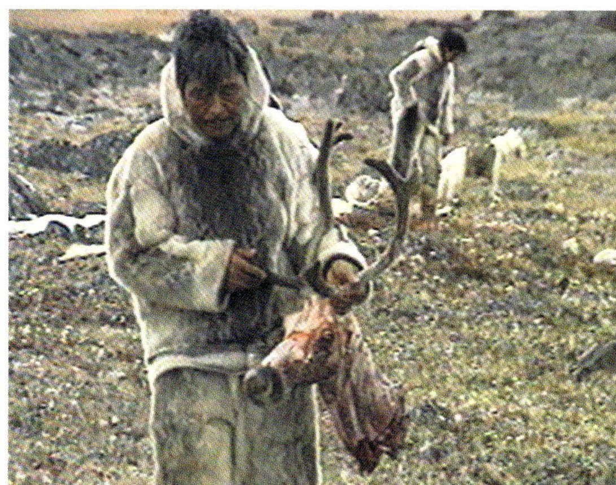

from *NUNAQPA (GOING INLAND)*, 1991

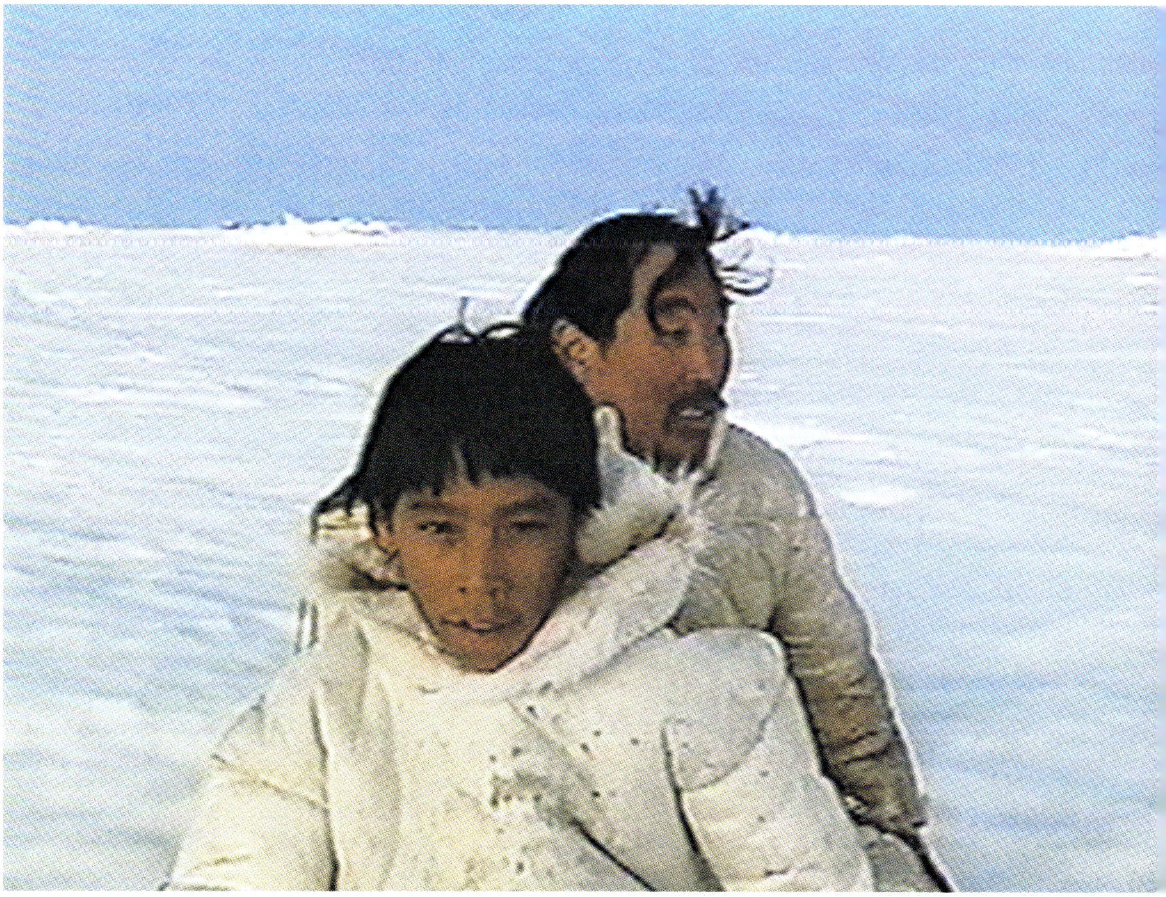

from *QIMUKSIK (DOG TEAM)*, 1995

all from *THE DESERT PEOPLE*, 1974

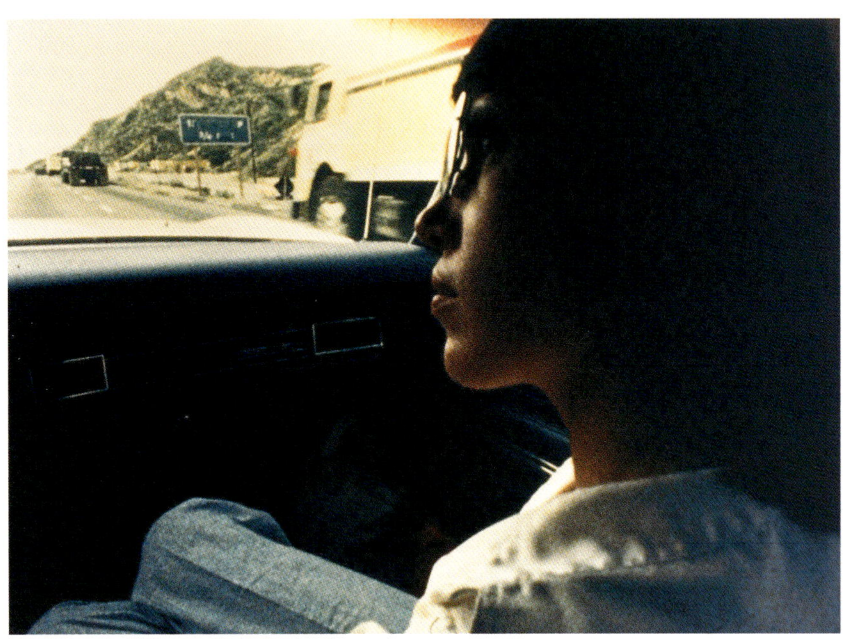

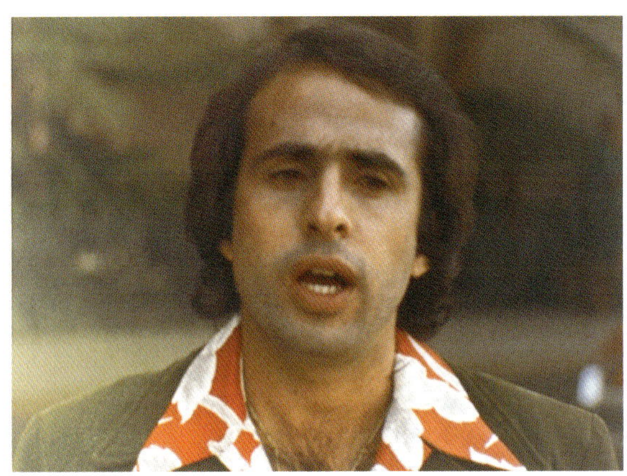

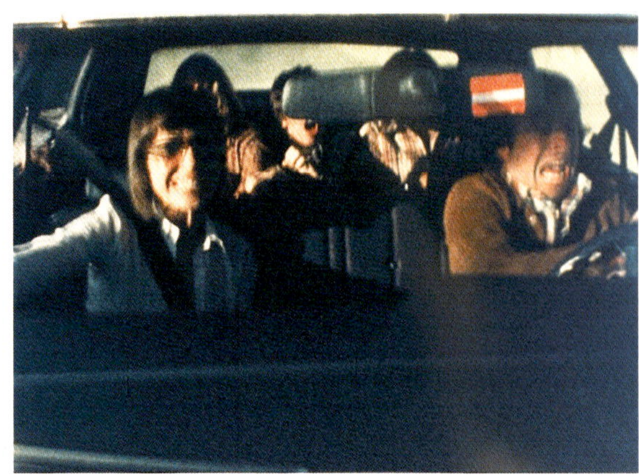

David Lamelas

The Desert People is Lamelas's first professionally produced film and marks his departure from conceptual art. The film adheres to the dictates of late 1960s structuralism, but introduces a narrative about representation and memory. In dispersed monologues directed at the camera, five characters reflect on their experience visiting the reservation of the Papago Indians. These talking heads are interspersed with long scenes of the group driving on the freeways around Los Angeles apparently on their way to or from the reservation, which never ultimately materializes.

from *THE DESERT PEOPLE*, 1974

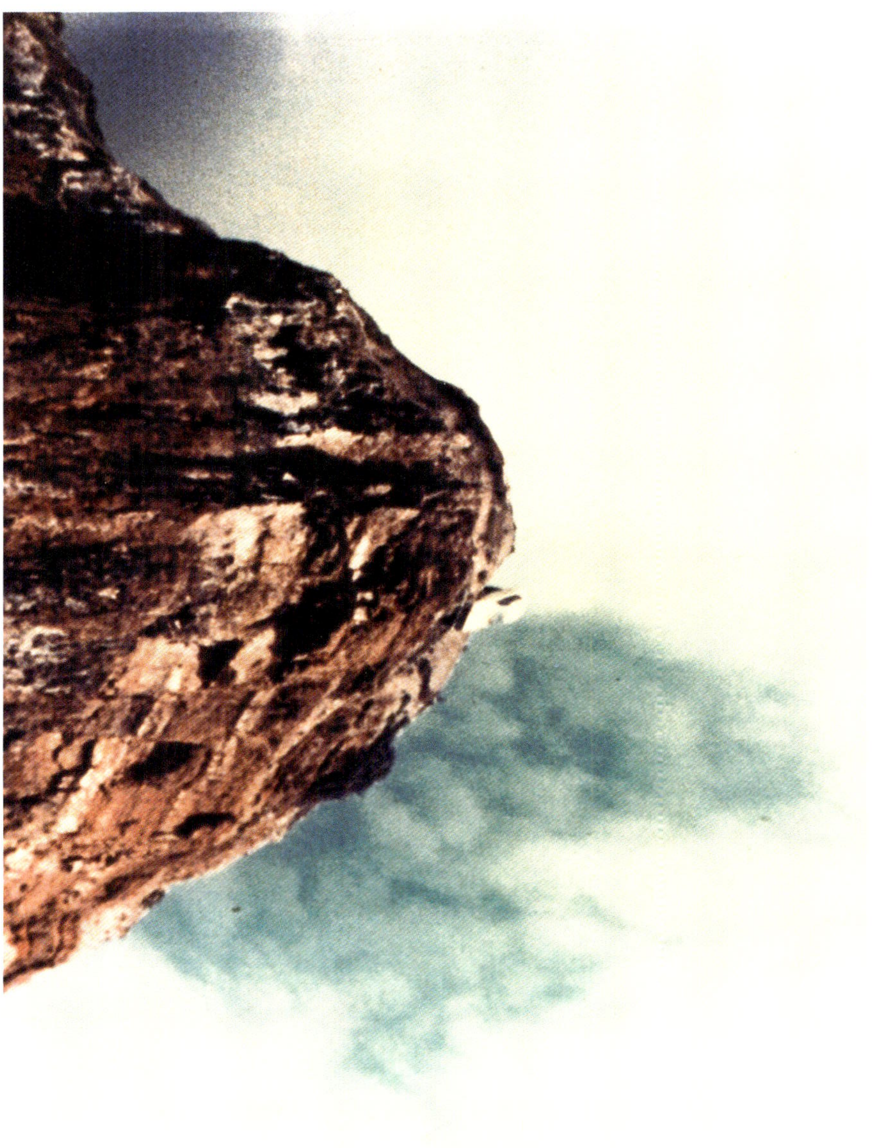

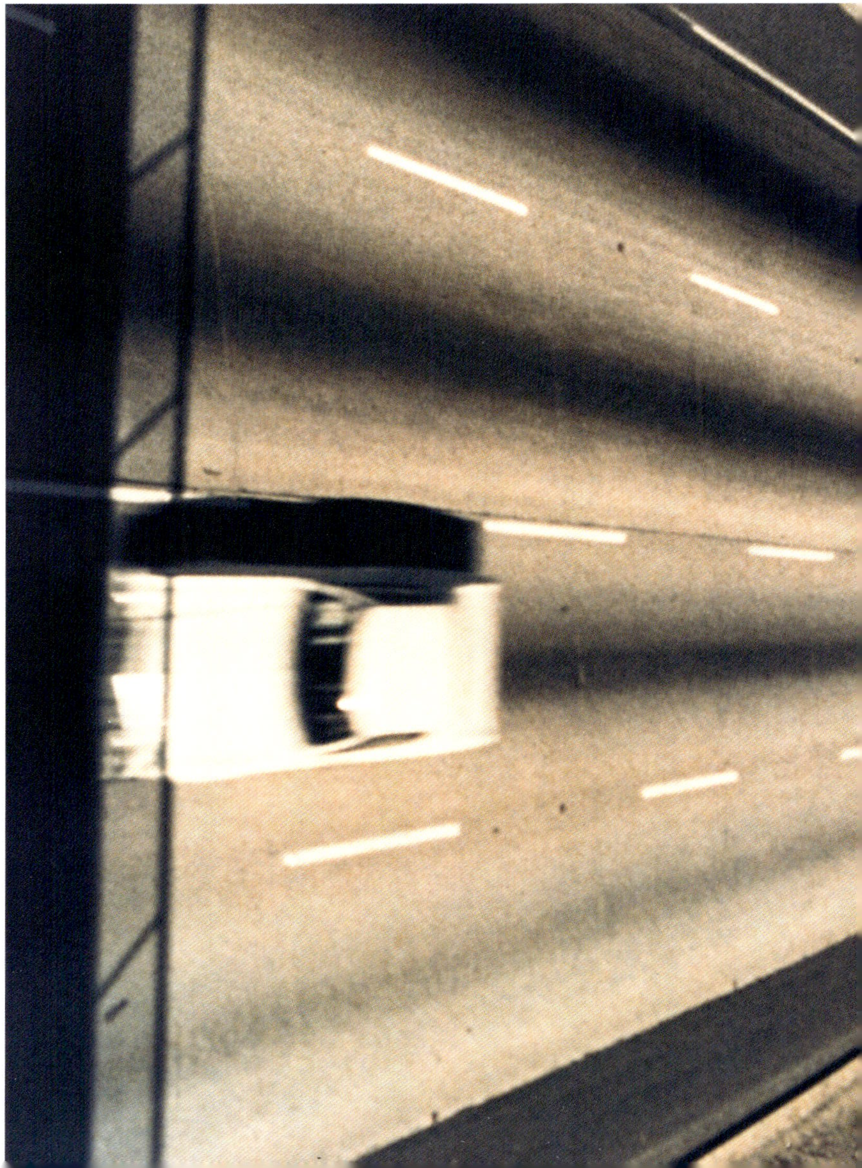

from *THE DESERT PEOPLE*, 1974

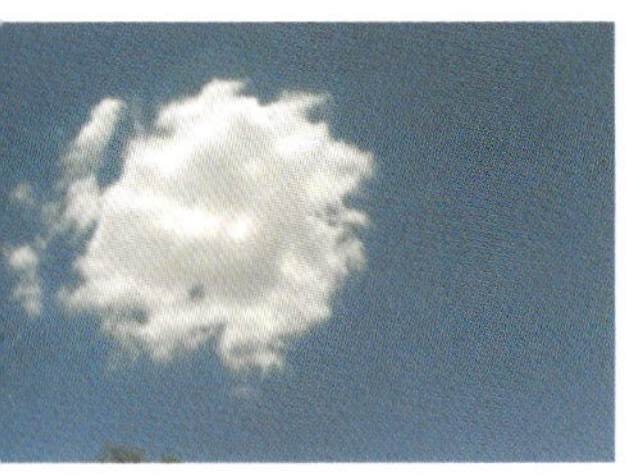

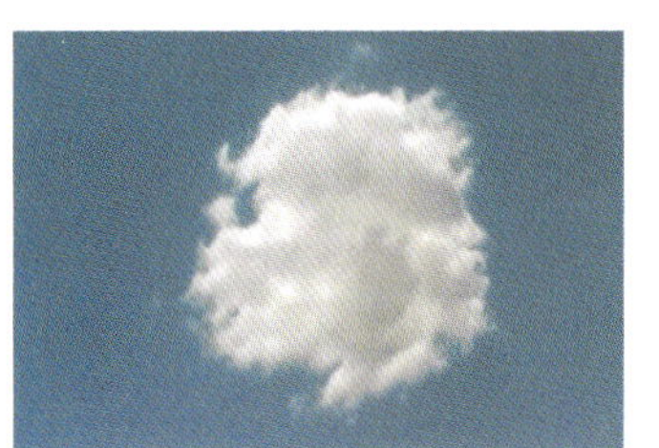

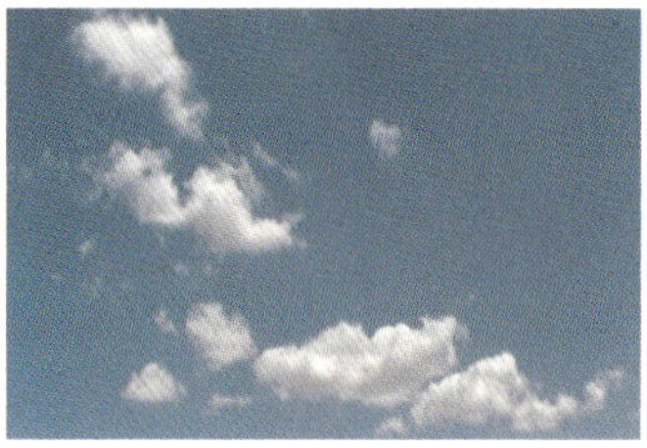

all from *DESERT FISHING*, 2000

INTERSECTION OF MALCOM X ST. AND KING ST., RANDOLPH, ARIZONA from *Desert Fishing*, 2000

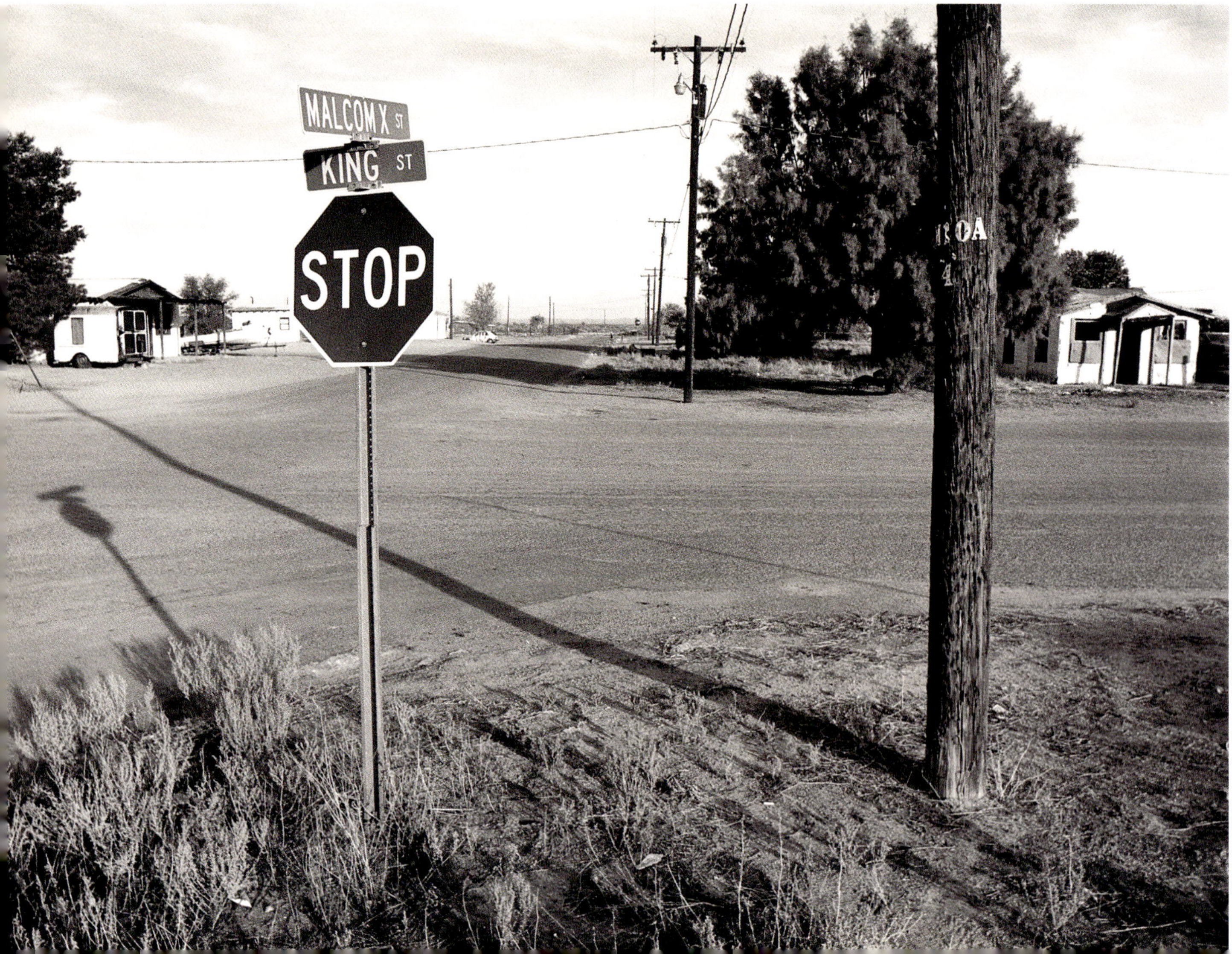

Glen Wilson

In a 1996 installation entitled *Drum*, Wilson displayed a group of color photographs of a black farm worker named Elijah. He has since returned to the town of Eloy where Elijah lives to record him in his community talking about his past as a farmer in Arkansas and his migration in the 1940s to the border region of Arizona and California to work the cotton fields. The project explores a lesser-known narrative of this landscape and, through Wilson's very personal engagement with his subject, re-maps the terrain through the identity of his subject.

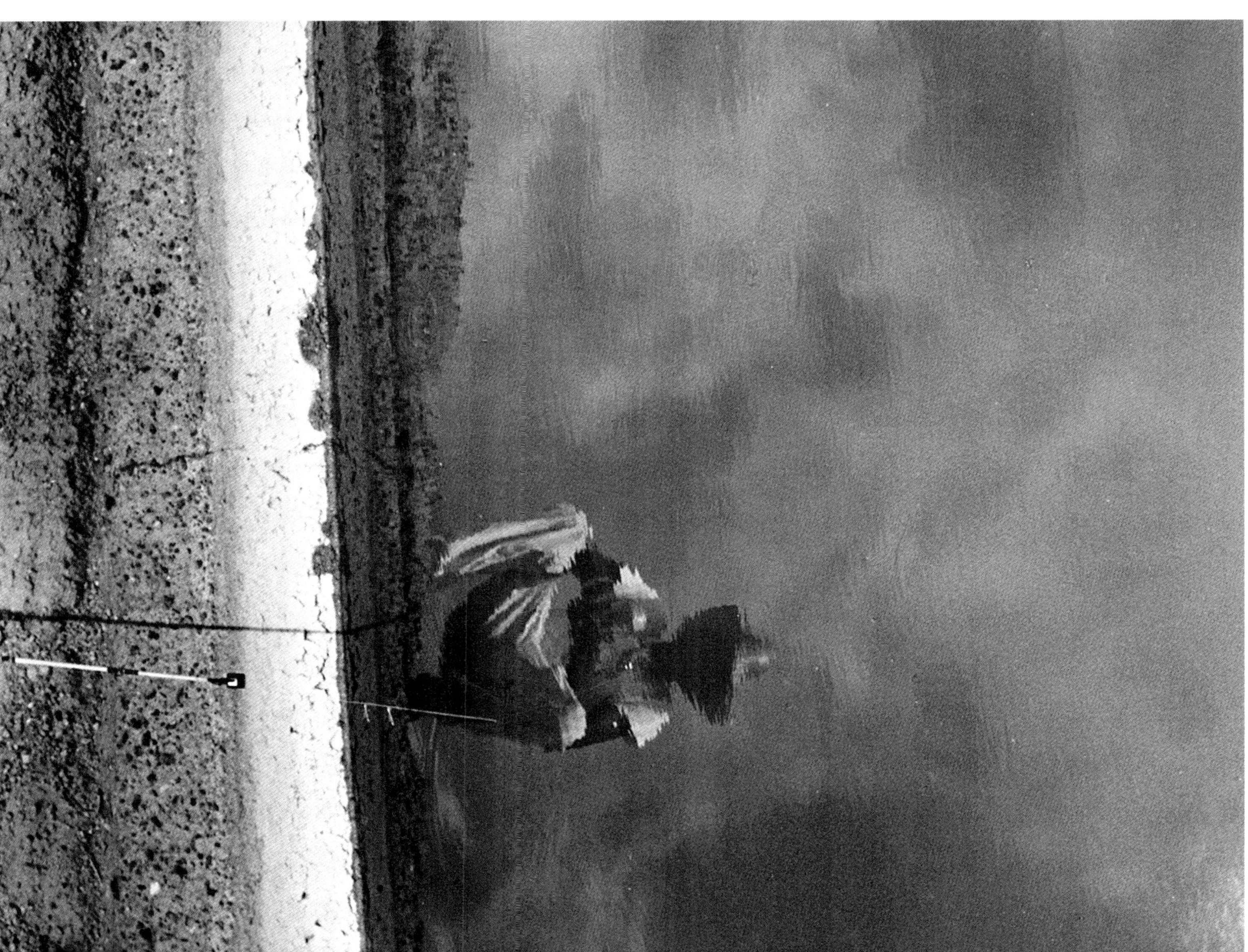

ELIJAH WHITE'S REFLECTION IN AN IRRIGATION DITCH from *Desert Fishing*, 1995

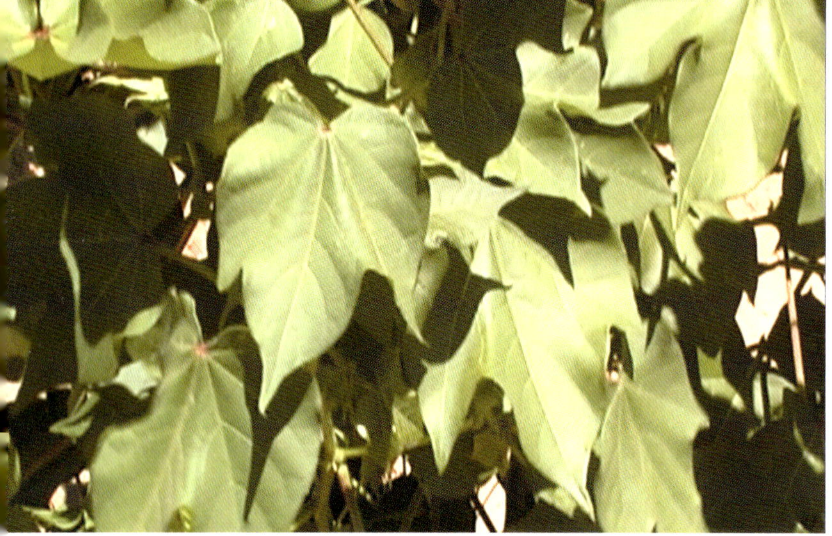

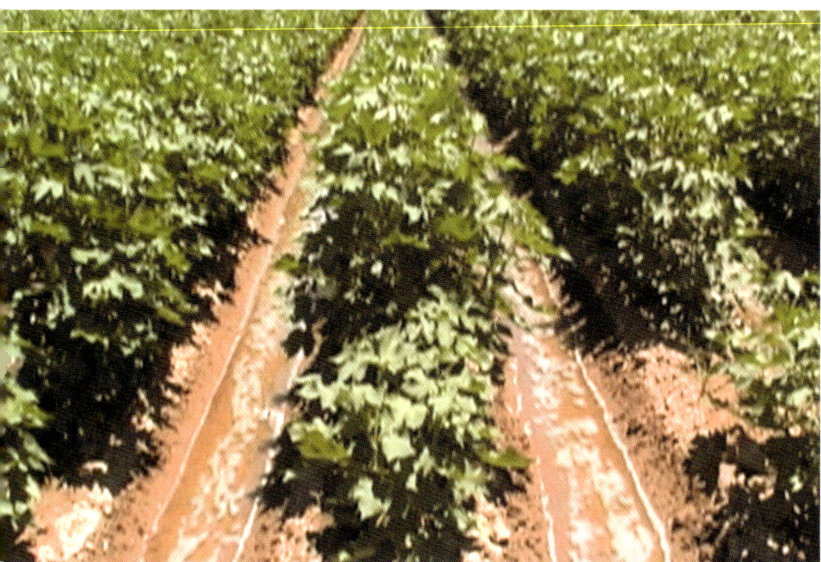

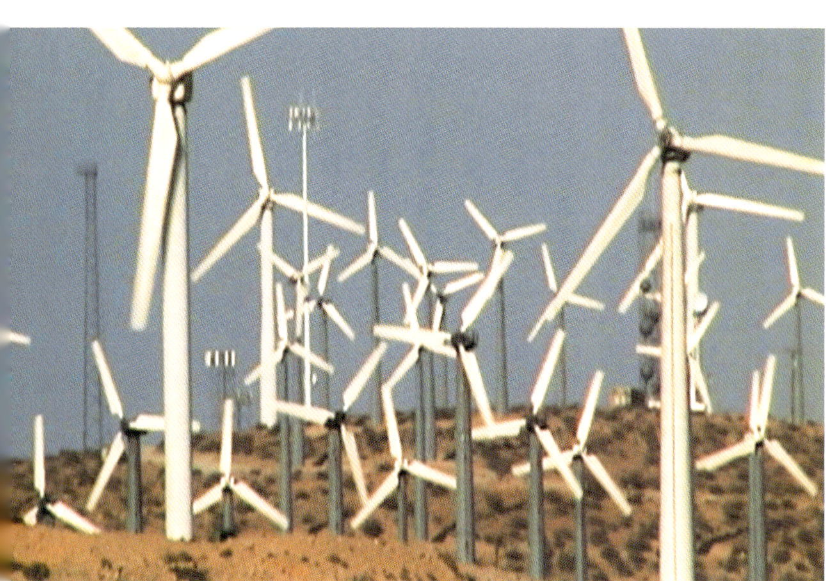

all from *DESERT FISHING*, 2000

ELIJAH WHITE from *Desert Fishing*, 2000

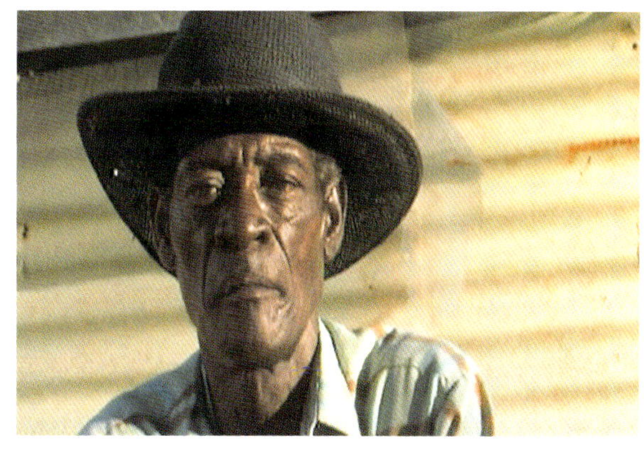

ELIJAH WHITE from *Desert Fishing*, 2000

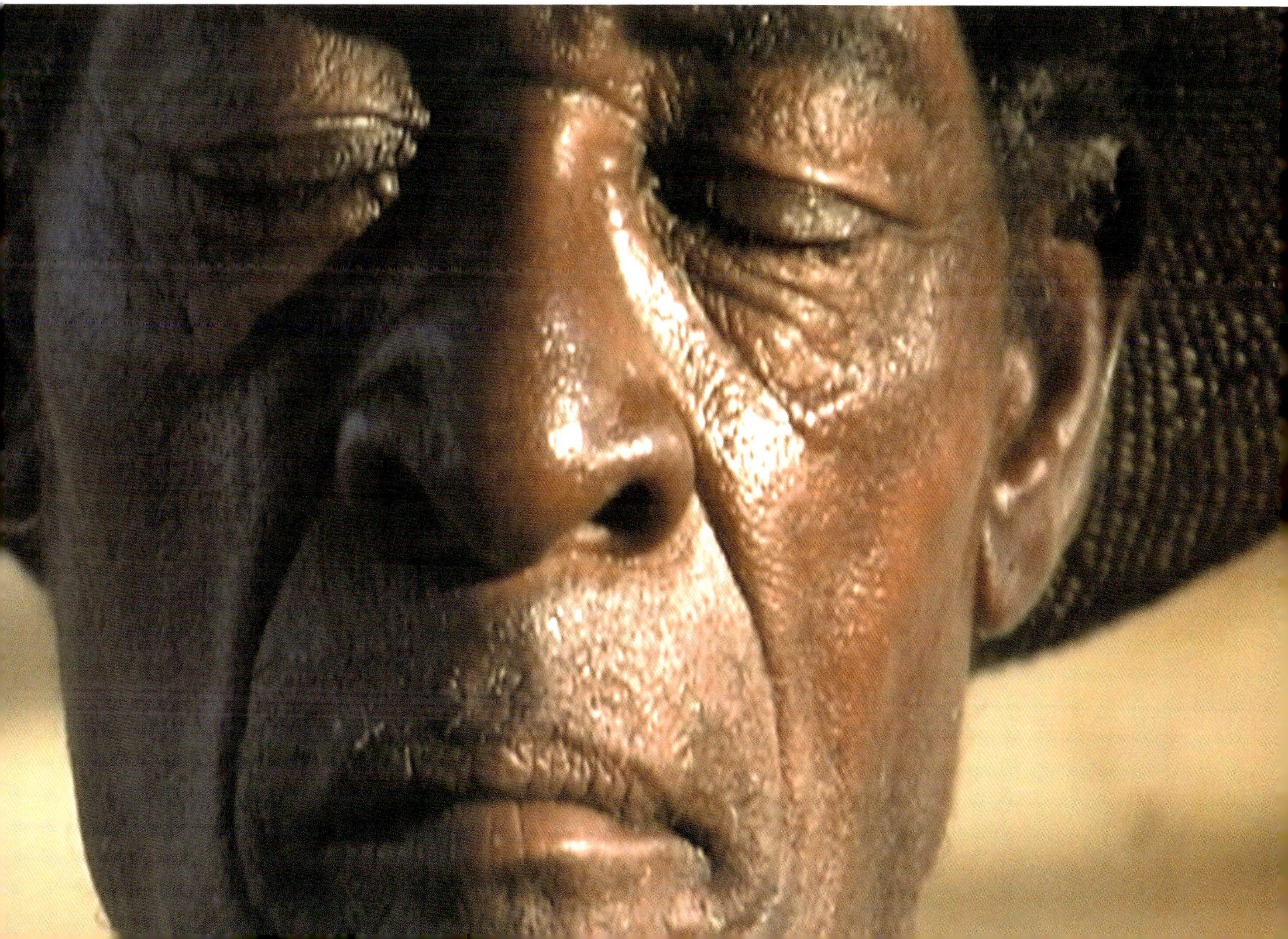

topographies

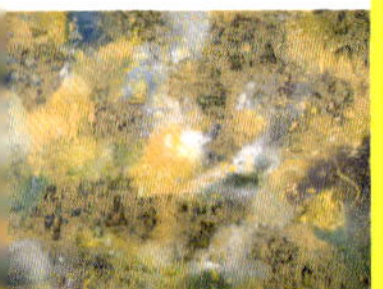

Tim Johnson

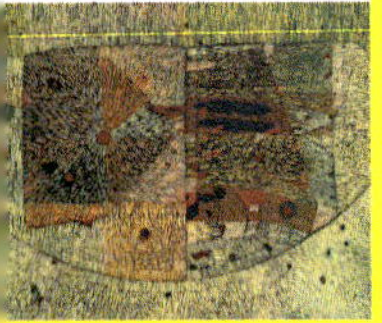

Lee Mullican

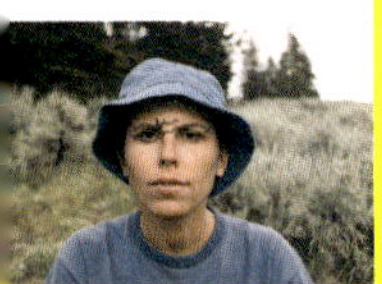

Caryl Davis

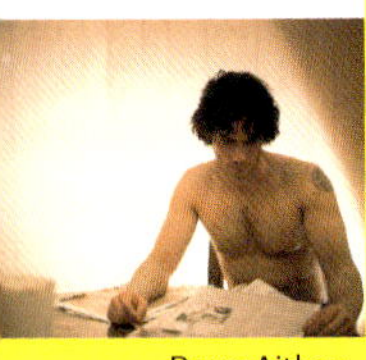

Doug Aitken

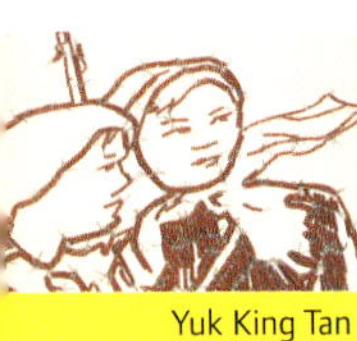

Yuk King Tan

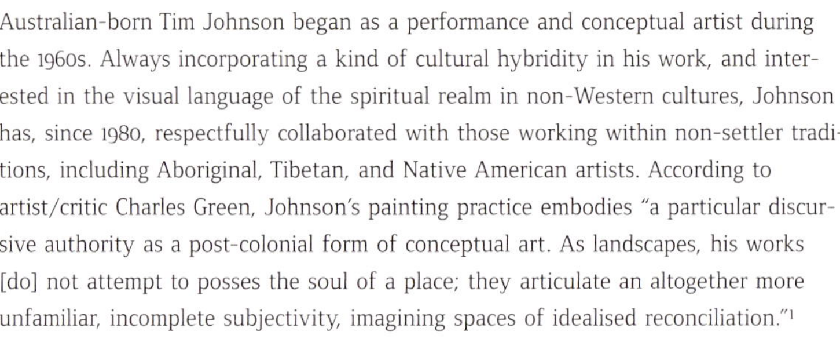

Australian-born Tim Johnson began as a performance and conceptual artist during the 1960s. Always incorporating a kind of cultural hybridity in his work, and interested in the visual language of the spiritual realm in non-Western cultures, Johnson has, since 1980, respectfully collaborated with those working within non-settler traditions, including Aboriginal, Tibetan, and Native American artists. According to artist/critic Charles Green, Johnson's painting practice embodies "a particular discursive authority as a post-colonial form of conceptual art. As landscapes, his works [do] not attempt to posses the soul of a place; they articulate an altogether more unfamiliar, incomplete subjectivity, imagining spaces of idealised reconciliation."[1]

Johnson has pursued the position of artist/interlocutor since 1980, when he visited Alice Springs in the Australian Western Desert region. Painting has been introduced to the region's population within the last thirty years, and an ongoing debate rages about the commercialization of work by Aboriginal painters and the West's understanding of the relative authenticity of the "Dreamings" or *Tjukurrpa* (ancestral stories) that these painters use as the basis for their transcendent abstraction. Johnson studied and observed the artists of the "Dreamings," or Papunya Tula painters who live in the region, and was an early collector and translator of their works. Early paintings of Johnson's such as *Papunya* (1983–85), the name of their community, represent the figures of Aboriginal artists working on the ground in their characteristic dotted style. Their paintings narrate the desert and maintain a tradition of storytelling without divulging the mystic iconography of their traditions. After developing a relationship of trust with the native artists, Johnson began appropriating their style and transforming it, using imagery from his own constellation of Buddhist, East Indian, and imagined symbols.

About his process Johnson has said, "My own 'western' culture teaches 'endtime,' 'judgment' and the annihilation and dematerialisation of life on this planet. Non-'western' cultures have a field of ideas, imagery and representation that I can relate to, where less of the past is lost."[2] He has, most recently, embraced the virtual space of the Internet as a site of intra-perceptual travel and randomized architecture of information analogous to the landscapes of his paintings. Certainly on some level, Johnson's paintings, and now CD-ROM projects, retain some of the playful quality of the pseudo-spirituality of 1960s counterculture from which he emerged as an artist. The political act of translation, or what we might now call the downloading of cultural symbols other than one's own, engenders a kind of lazy slippage that functions in extending the discourse of post-identity politics.

In the early 1950s, the American painter Lee Mullican was looking at the native painters of the Southwestern United States. Mullican joined with his contemporaries Gordon Onslow Ford and Wolfgang Paalen to form the Dynaton group, whose rhetoric and idealism was fueled by the forces of nature, chaos, and automatism, and a surrealist interest in the explosive formal and emotional potential of abstraction. Particularly in his paintings of 1950–53, Mullican's own semi-abstract language was informed as well by his army training in map making. His interest in the landscape of the West and in indigenous topographic practices, such as Navajo sand painting, yielded a palette and vocabulary that was closely interpretive of the California and New Mexico desert where Mullican spent considerable time throughout his career until his death in 1998.

In paintings such as *Section From the Burlap Plain* (1951), there are distinctive structural elements that refer to the land. The sloping hemisphere that divides and anchors the picture frequently appears in Mullican's paintings of this period. Mullican's use of the word "section" in the title invokes a military or scientific topographic understanding of the landscape and perhaps the artist's imaginary aerial view from above. Works such as *Asia Minor* (1953) name a location using its official, yet rather abstract or continental description. The vertiginous feeling of these abstractions is perhaps a metaphor for the dreamy overview, the simultaneous positions of "in the field" and "from above." Mullican seems to be interested in fixing his own tectonic position in these paintings—his location and the setting of his location. Perhaps out of an interest in the Native American relationship to the land which, like that of the Aboriginal Australian is both physical and supernatural, Mullican tried to enact this sense of bodily engagement with the landscape.

The location of the body, experienced from within and from above, phenomenologically and from the bird's-eye view, is the position from which Caryl Davis's series *How Light Becomes Me* (1996–2000) operates. Disembodied and fully embodied at the same time, we are situated between the artist and her subject, in a space that is collapsed *en abyme*. We experience the uncanny sense of both looking at the landscape, and mimicking the artist looking at the landscape, which returns both her and our gaze through the drawn representation of the viewed scene on her forehead. Recalling John Baldessari's *California Map Project, Part I: California* (1969), for which the artist embedded map text in the exact physical locations that similar text appears on a map of California, Davis attempts to fix a specific geography to her own physical experience—she wears the simulation of what she sees.

In an earlier series titled *Past Pants* (1996), Davis photographed the space between her legs. From a low vantagepoint, the viewer spies a lovely landscape vista framed by the abstracted outline of Davis's inner thighs and calves. The transmutation performed in these pictures is actually a superimposition of her monumentalized body onto the glorified vistas of nature as a sort of feminized Manifest Destiny. *How Light Becomes Me* is in some ways a less aggressively feminist work, but the transgression that occurs—the slippage between the artist's self-presentation and her presence in nature—is more explicit. Reminiscent of the nature performances of Mary Beth Edelson, or the earth-based works of Michelle Stuart, Davis offers explicit evidence of her own essentializing view of nature in the form of drawings and snapshots.

The video work of Doug Aitken almost always touches on his own very personal and physical relationship with the drama of nature and, in recent works such as the stunning *Electric Earth* (1999), the urban landscape. Though his installations are usually a hallucinatory combination of video and an architectural manipulation of a space, Aitken shoots his work on film to capture the quality of transparency and luminescence of light as it interacts with film.

Aitken's engagement with the geographic landscape has permeated his work since the mid-1990s. As part of the conceptualizing and production of films such as *Monsoon* (1995), shot at the abandoned site of the Jonestown tragedy in Guyana; or *Diamond Sea* (1997), made in the Diamond Areas in Namibia, Aitken exploits his own impulse to corporeally occupy these forbidden, entropic territories in order to understand and map their complicated terrain. Repeatedly he has sought landscapes where time and space are warped by nature's logic or radically altered by the randomness of social or political intervention. In order to produce *Monsoon*, for example, Aitken traveled to Guyana, the site of the Jim Jones People's Temple mass suicide, and waited for a monsoon. This performative frame imposed on a site, where nature has reclaimed a human drama and neutralized its emotional impact, is characteristic of Aitken's strange voyeurism. Often exterior elements such as the monsoon, or the fragments of abandoned architecture in *Electric Earth*, initiate and propel the narrative. Aitken's presence in the films is a part of their texture, whether through the often hand-held camera or the sensation of breath that frequently permeates a haunting soundtrack that functions as an insistent physical ambience beneath the imagery.

Aitken seeks to represent what he calls a hybrid landscape where hierarchies of time and space dissolve. In previous works, his selected landscapes are timeless or suspended. In the current work *blow debris* (2000), Aitken explodes this notion of suspension by making a landscape that is immersive—experienced differently and constantly with each encounter in the gallery. He creates a kind of filmic architecture for the absorption of information and the transmission of the language of dystopia. In *blow debris*, Aitken for the first time employs structuralist techniques such as the vertical role and continuous vertical narrative. The narrative begins in apparent reality and, as in *Electric Earth*, (de)evolves into a situation of primordial transformation.

In his treatment for *blow debris*, Aitken talks about the late twentieth-century alienation from the body—an entropic view that encompasses the crisis of distance we experience from the natural environment and elements from which we are made. The morphing of the body of the character in *Electric Earth* with the pulsing technology of the car wash or surveillance camera, or the watery landscape of *Monsoon*, can be read in terms of the "postinidividual fish/cyborg" body of Pacific Rim discourse.[3]

New Zealand artist Yuk King Tan also explores this watery realm of the Pacific in a lyrical series of works called *The Picturesque* (1997/2000). The reading of the Pacific as the "American Lake" in expansionist language of the later nineteenth and early twentieth century is well documented.[4] For this series, Tan made drawings with firecrackers, exploring the thematic of the ocean and the discourses of time and motion. Of these works she says:

> The fuse works and the firecracker works are narrative trails, they record their own journeys and counteract the gesture of performance with the residue of time and place. The "sea" recurring motive [sic] in the fireworks have a relationship with a metaphysical property (Chinese energy meridians) and the evocation of a romantic tradition... *The Picturesque* was an installation investigating pictorial aesthetic[s]. I saw it as a[n] anarchic playful mix of landscape/painting/modernism with a climax of explosive performance reversing the act of construction.[5]

While Tan has avoided specifically making identity-based work, she is interested in how her own cultural heritage straddles traditions that include, by her own description, Malaysian/Chinese, New Asian, and European. The subtext of her work responds to the cultural climate in New Zealand where, in addition to the ongoing dynamics of biculturalism, there are tensions resulting from new Asian immigration in the largely white suburbs of Auckland.

The instability of Tan's reliefs beautifully metaphorizes the ambivalence of her own transcultural position. Initiated by a transgressive act within the gallery context, the fireworks-cum-drawings intervene in conventions of art viewing. The *sfumato* of the residual ashes which comprise parts of the drawing (not all of the crackers are expired) and mark its own explosive performance look somehow more familiar, like some kind of contour or brushy Chinese landscape. In *The Picturesque* Tan co-opts well-worn landscape painting tropes from both Asian traditions and the European topographic tradition framed on the land of her native New Zealand's settler culture. "The haze that results from the exploding crackers mimics the obscuring veils cast over formerly essential cultural values: truth, beauty, order, judgement, permanence, assuredness. The effect of the interventions made possible by Tan's work and its interaction with the gallery... is to parade the very anxieties that accrue from a decline in tangible and intangible certainties."[6]

Notes

1. Charles Green, "Postcolonial Art and Peripheral Vision," in Green, *Peripheral Vision: Contemporary Australian Art 1970–1994* (New South Wales: Craftsman House, 1995), 130–132.
2. Tim Johnson, "Translating Other Cultures," in *Beyond the Future: The Third Asia-Pacific Triennial of Contemporary Art*, exh. cat. (South Brisbane, Australia: Queensland Art Gallery, 1999), 184.
3. *See* Christopher L. Connery, "The Oceanic Feeling and The Regional Imaginary," in Rob Wilson and Wimal Dissanayake, eds., *Global/Local: Cultural Production and the Transnational Imaginary* (Durham and London: Duke University Press, 1996), 304.
4. *Ibid.*, 300.
5. From a letter to the author, 7 April 2000.
6. Peter Shand, "A Sense of Smoke," in *The Picturesque*, exh. cat. (New Plymouth, New Zealand: Govett-Brewster Art Gallery, 1999), unpaginated.

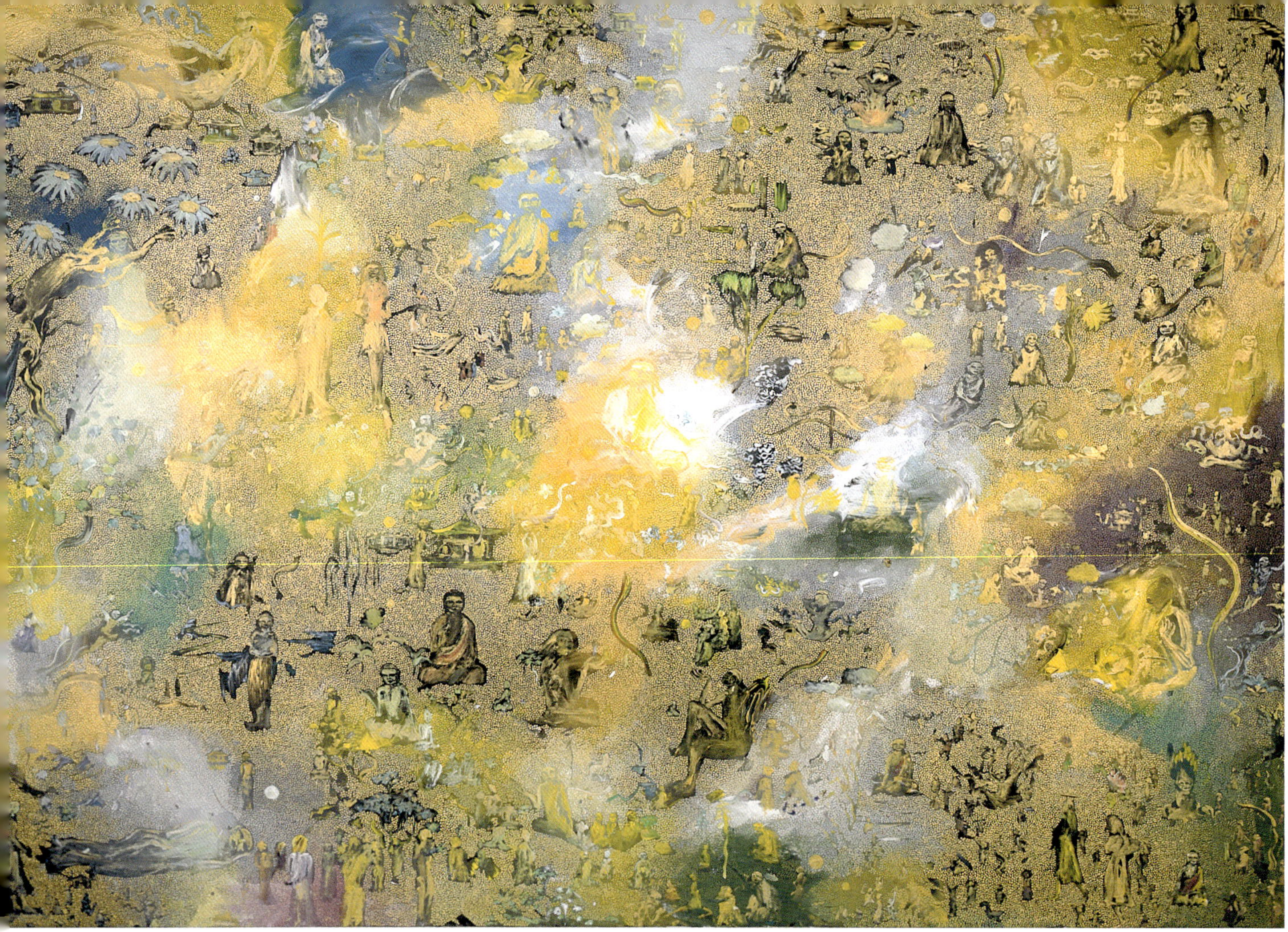

THE SUN, 1994

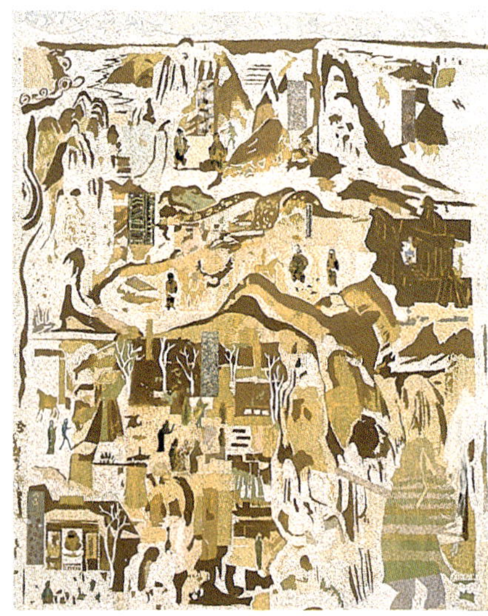

ILLUSORY CITY, 1983-85

Tim Johnson

After an early career as a conceptual artist, Johnson now makes conceptually informed paintings that conflate the Western traditions of painting with the imagery and iconography of the aboriginal "dreamings" painters and imagery from Buddhist and East Indian traditions. Beginning in the early 1980s, Johnson collaborated with the aboriginal artists who make paintings that narrate their complex, nomadic relationship to the land of the western Australian desert. Early works show the Papunya painters working in the desert and more recent works abstract their dot-making technique into hallucinatory, spiritual topographies.

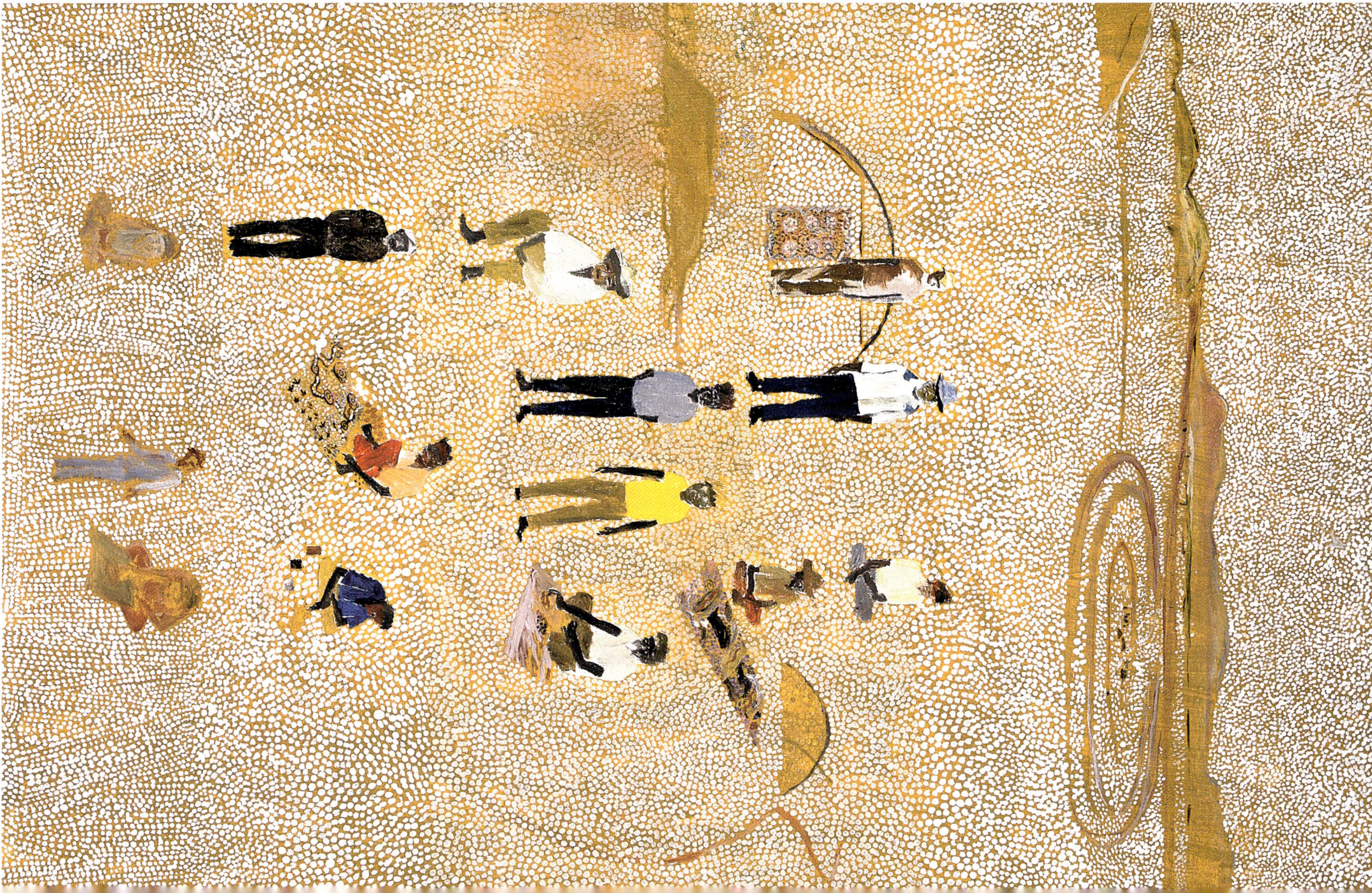

PAPUNYA, 1983-85

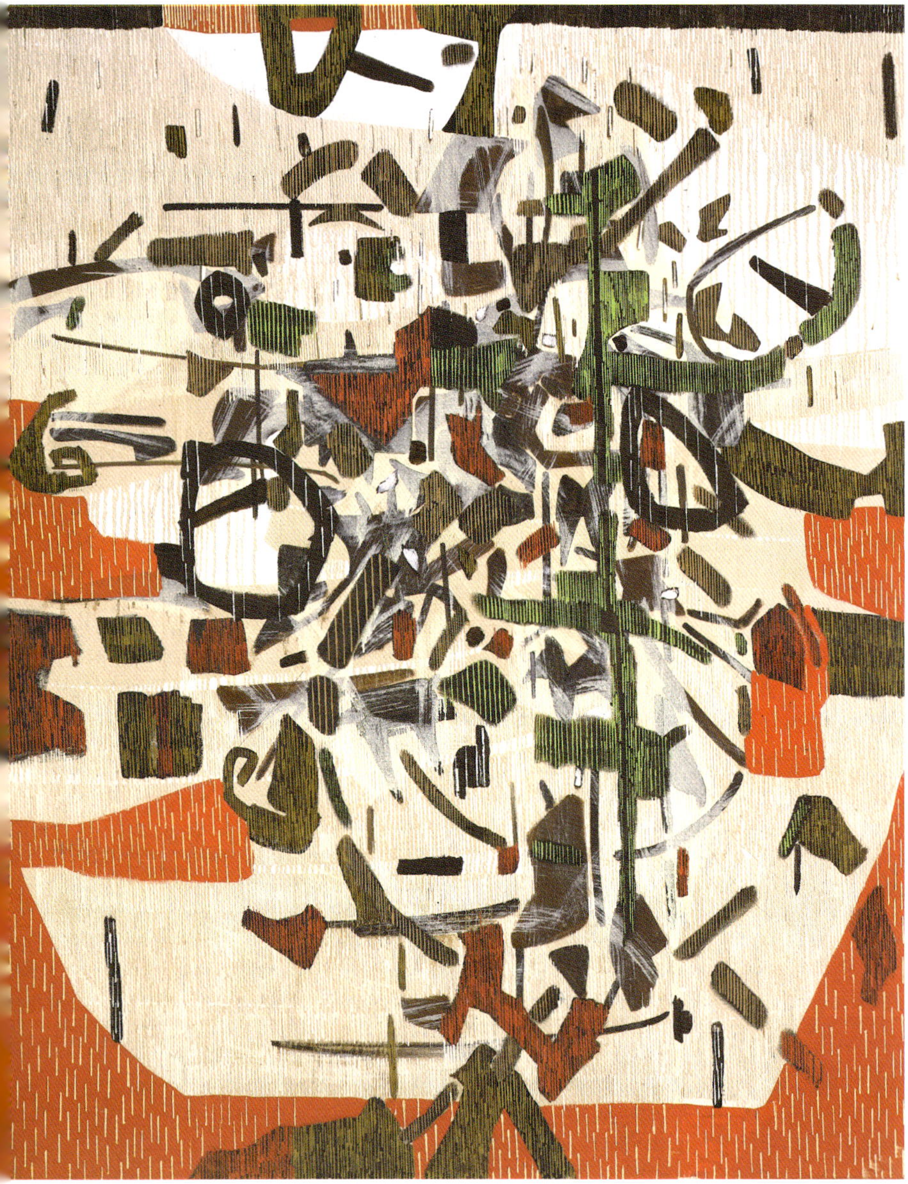

DRUM BAZAAR, 1953

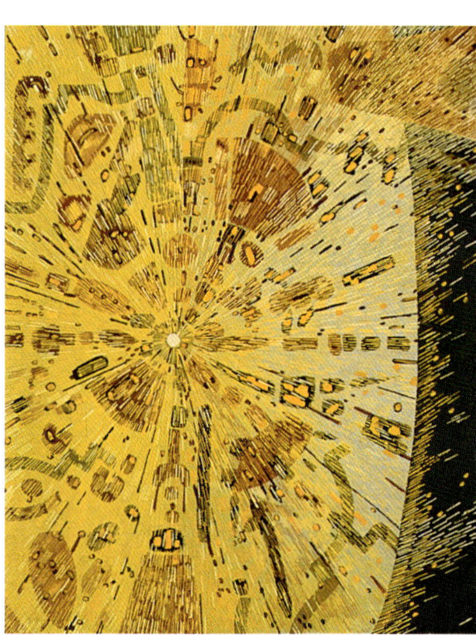

AGAWAM, 1950

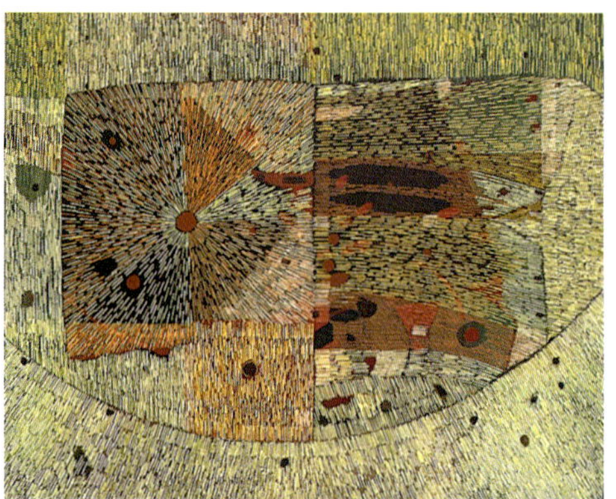

SECTION FROM THE BURLAP PLAIN, 1951

Lee Mullican

In the early 1950s, Mullican made a group of paintings dealing with topography and mapping. Enrolled in the army's Topographic School, as well as stationed in the California desert, Hawaii, and Japan in the early 1940s, Mullican combines his interest in mapping and landscape in these luscious abstractions. Working in the San Francisco Bay Area during the 1950s, Mullican was part of the Dynaton group and drew on influences including surrealism, northwest painters such as Mark Tobey, and Native-American sand paintings.

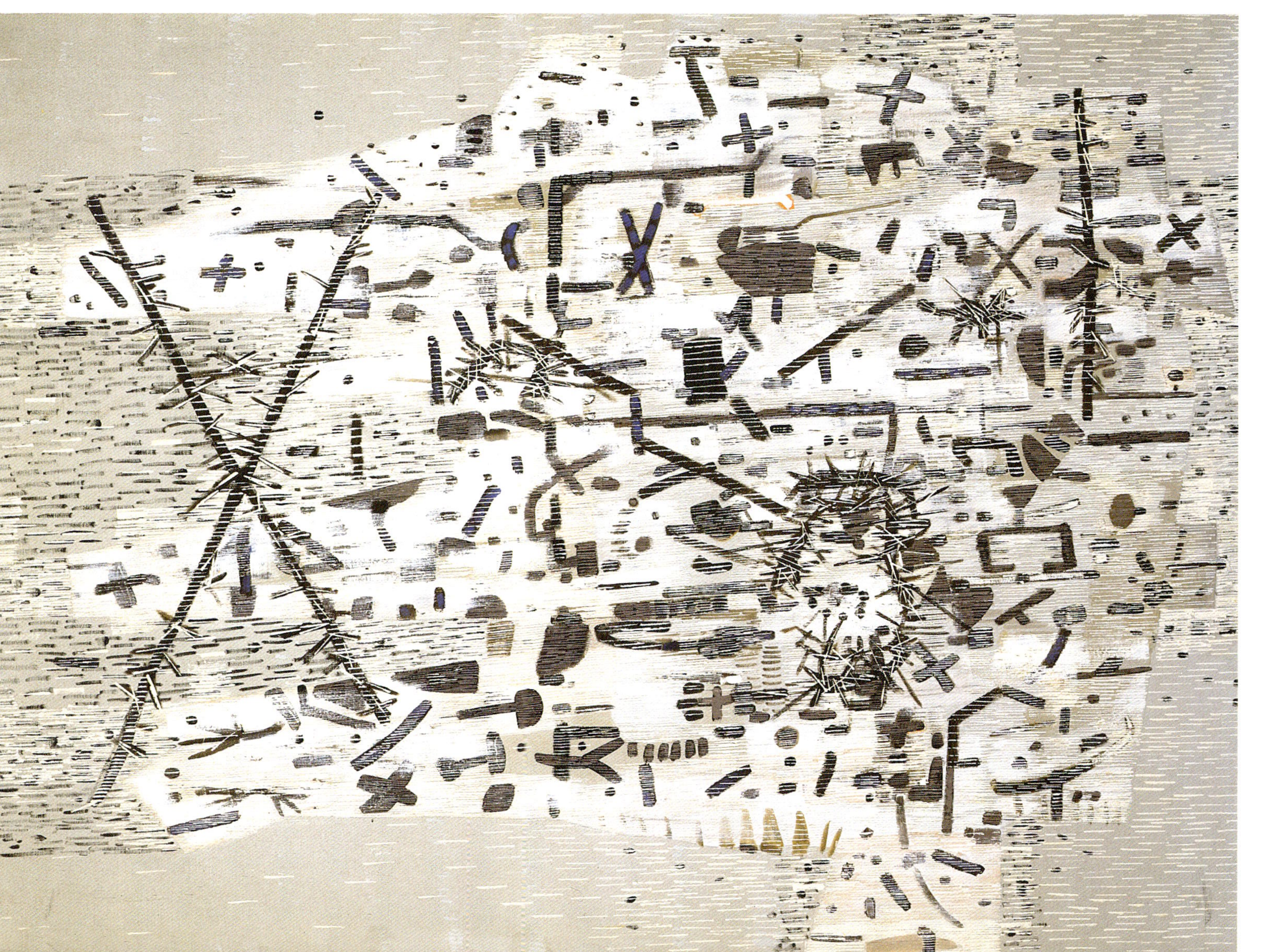

PASSAGE FACTOR, 1953

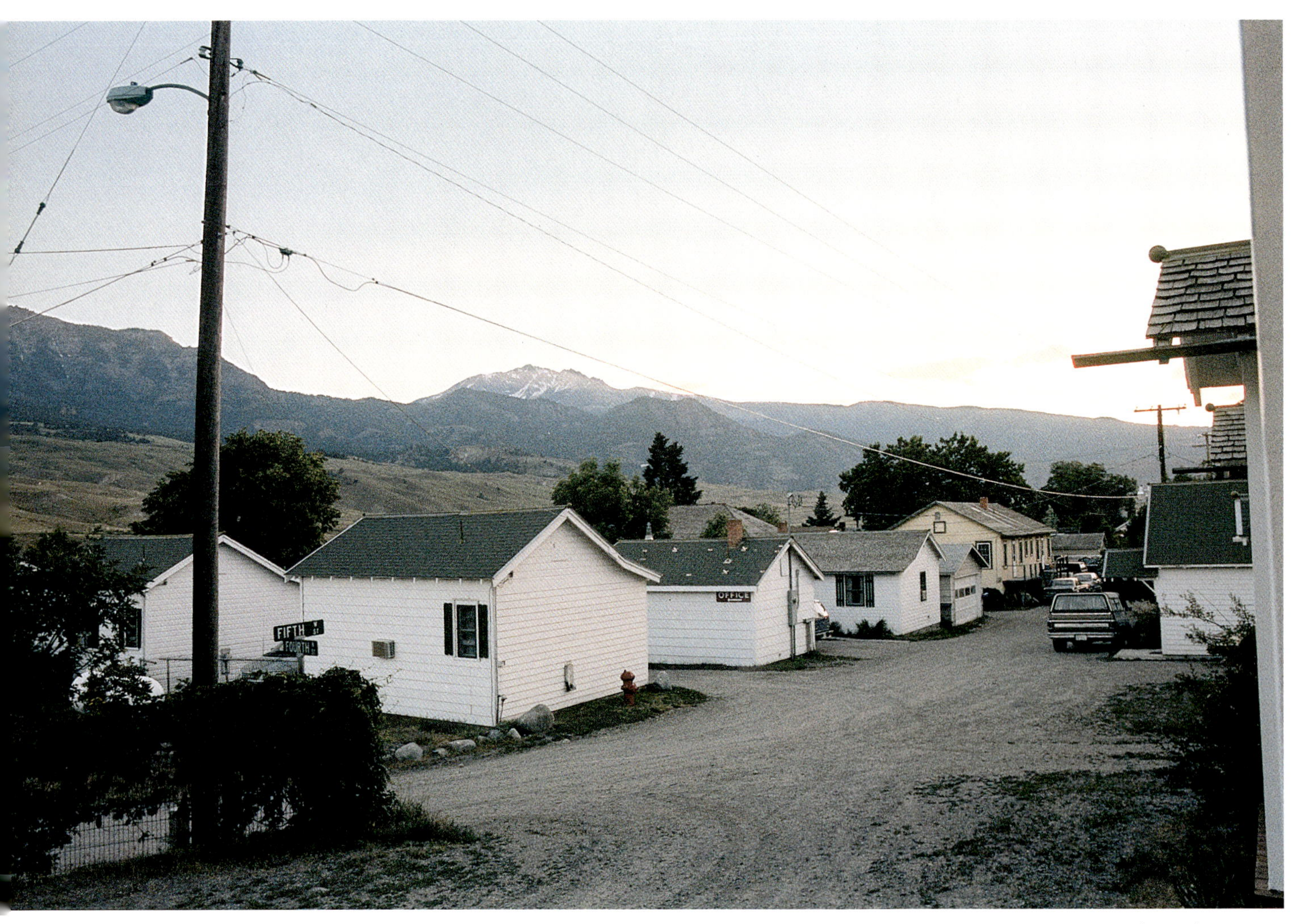

HOW LIGHT BECOMES ME (PORCH), 1996-2000

Caryl Davis

In her recent photographic works Davis explores the phenomenological relationship of her body to the (en)visioned landscape. In six pairs of photographs, the artist juxtaposes snapshots of the landscape facing her with images of herself. Replicating the most elementary of academic exercises—drawing the landscape *in situ*—she draws the viewed landscape on her face in an attempt to conflate the essentially unrepresentable space of nature with its likeness.

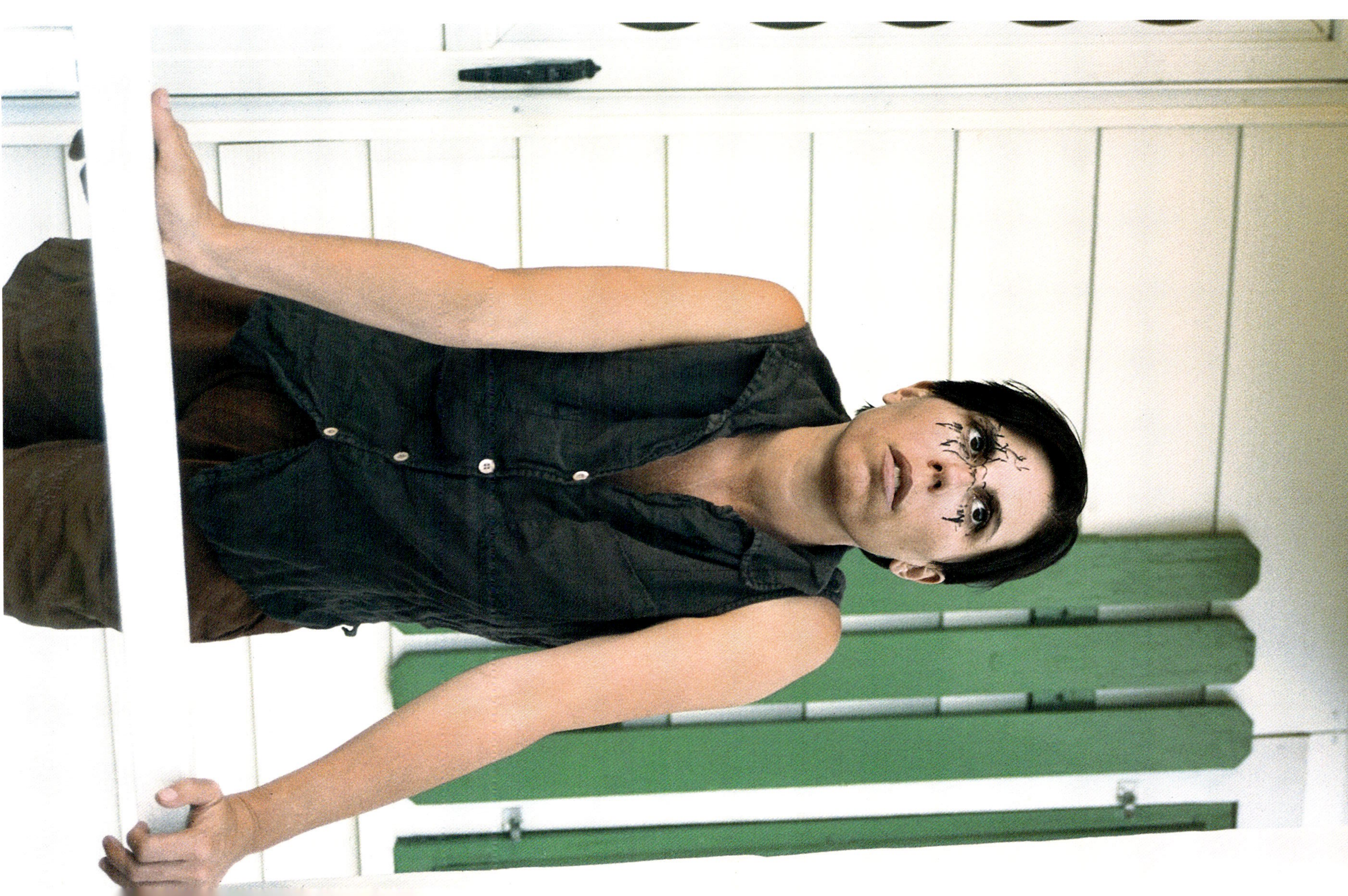

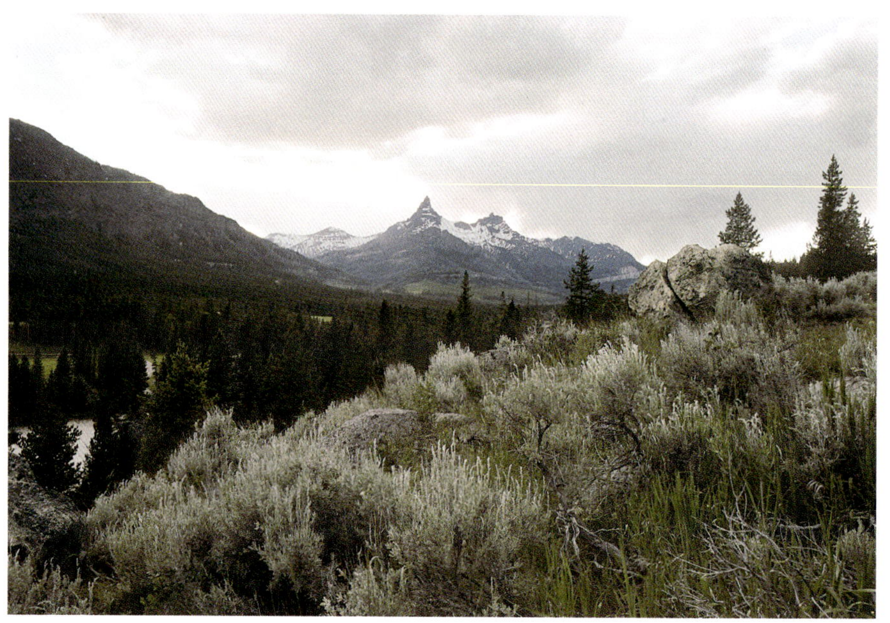

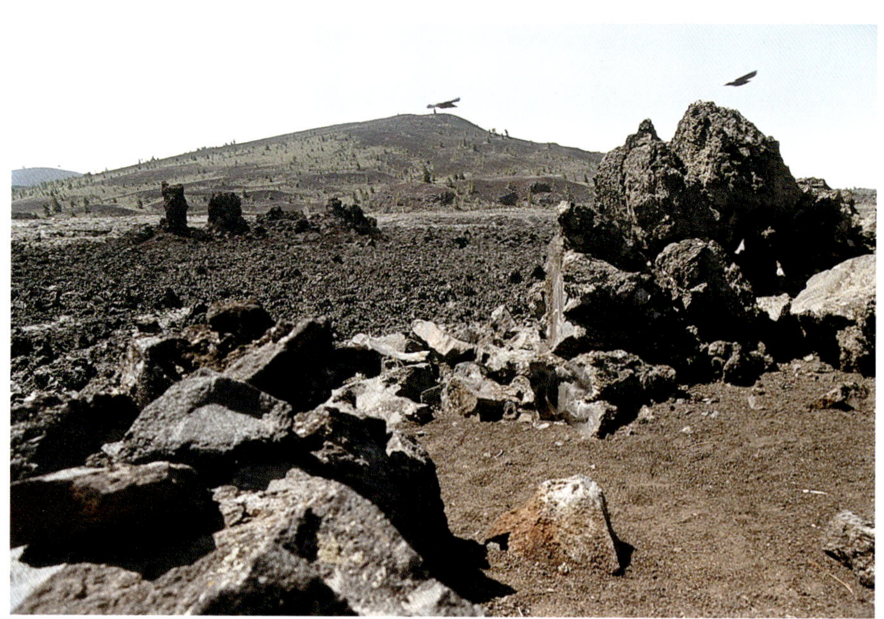

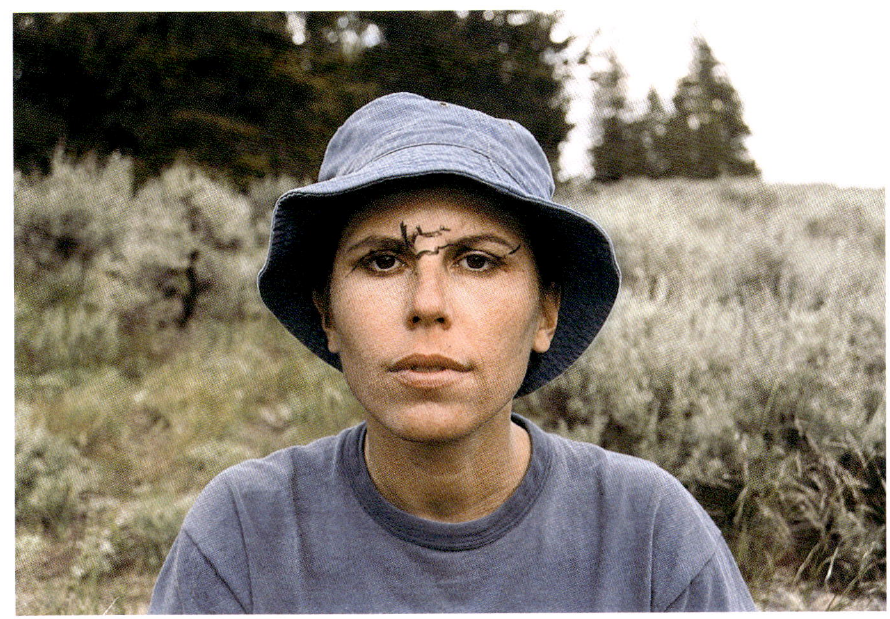

HOW LIGHT BECOMES ME (PEAK), 1996-2000

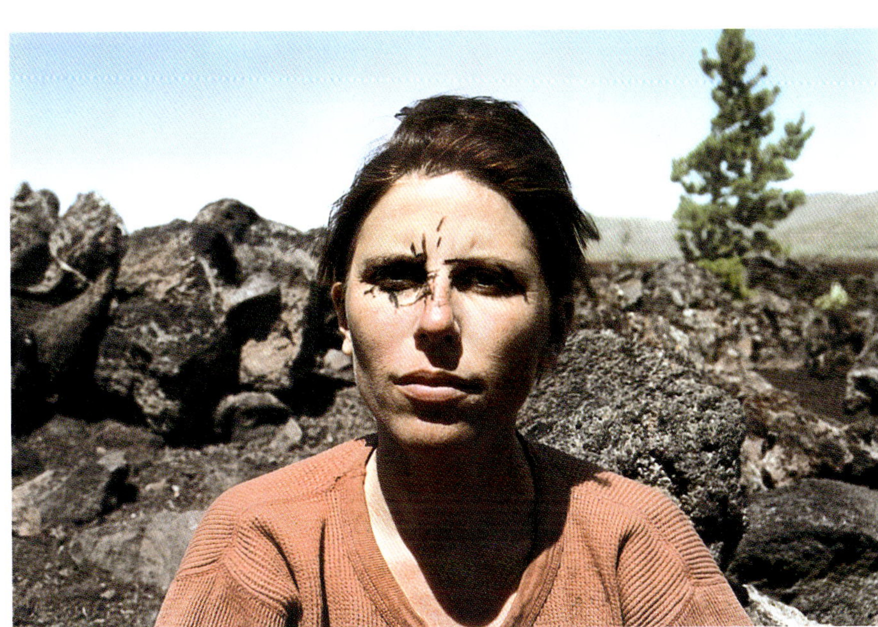

HOW LIGHT BECOMES ME (LAVA), 1996-2000

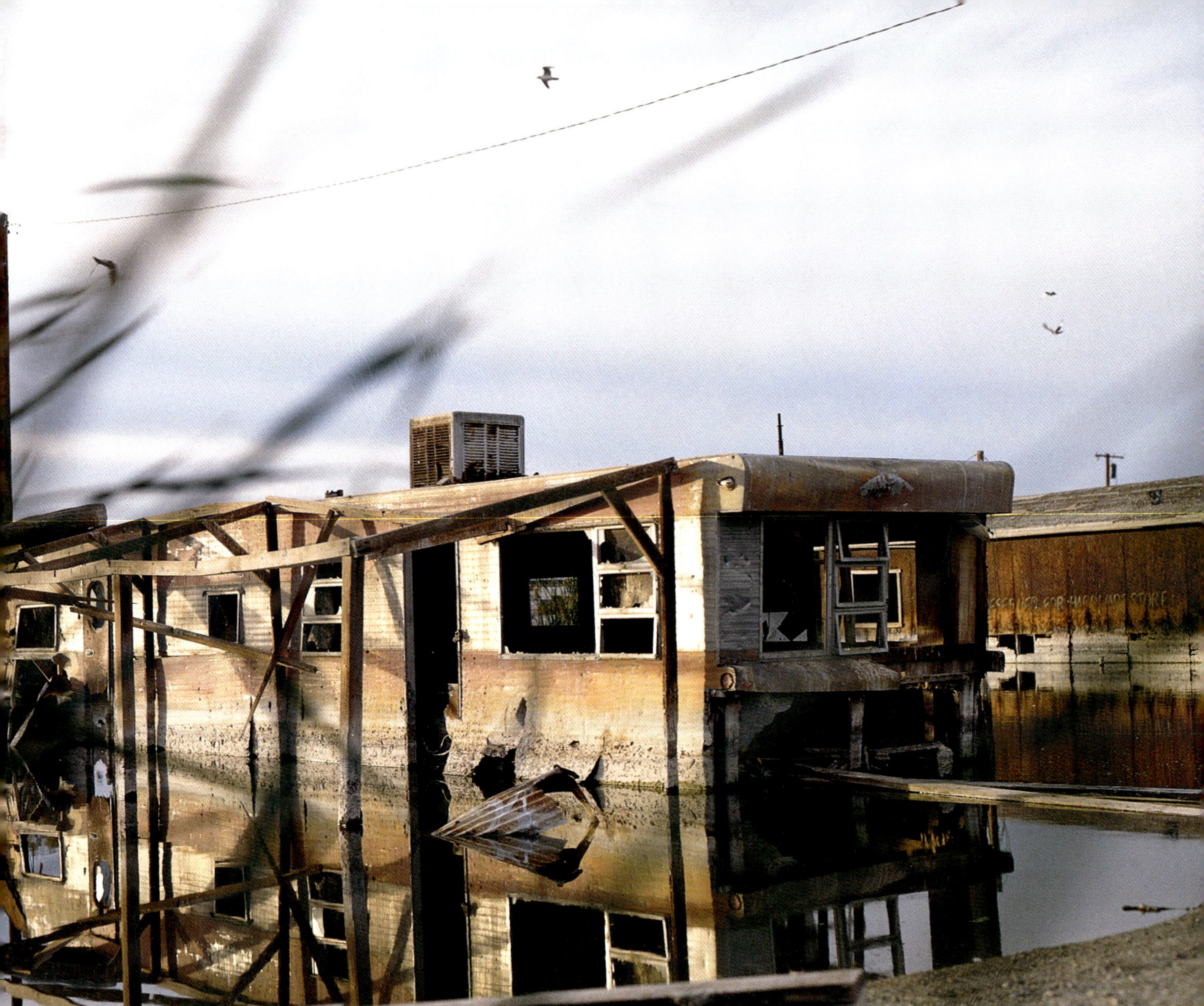

from *BLOW DEBRIS*, 2000

Doug Aitken

In his new, multi-screen video installation *blow debris*, Aitken explores the desert landscape of southern California. Aitken is interested in the subject of time and its relationship to the landscape. The human body serves as a vehicle for the processes of nature, and time provides the metaphorical structure for Aitken's hallucinatory narrative, which undulates and pulses through the landscape. Focusing on remnants of human presence such as abandoned architecture, Aitken introduces the notion of memory into the otherwise bleak and harsh terrain.

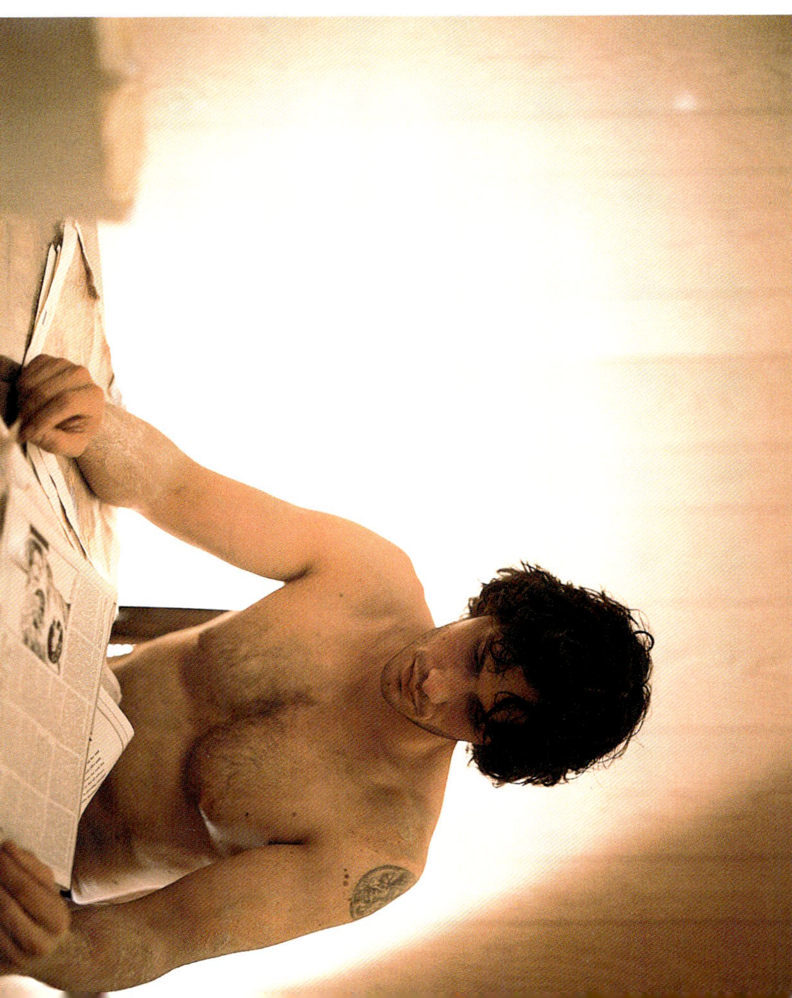

from *BLOW DEBRIS*, 2000

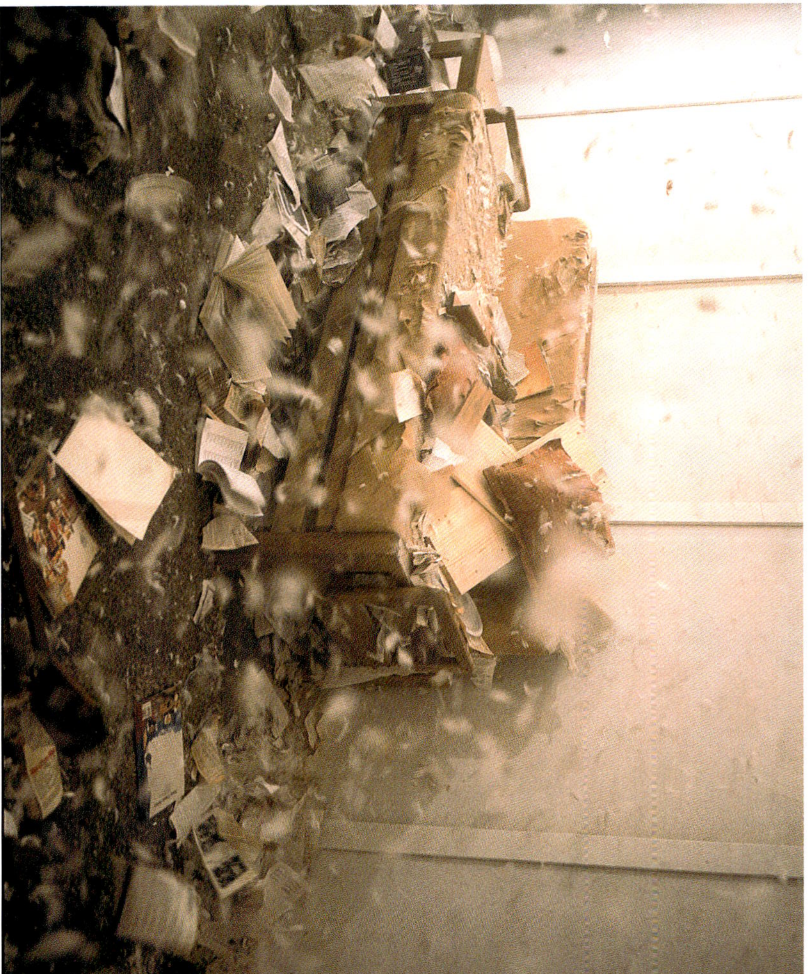

from *BLOW DEBRIS*, 2000

all from *BLOW DEBRIS*, 2000

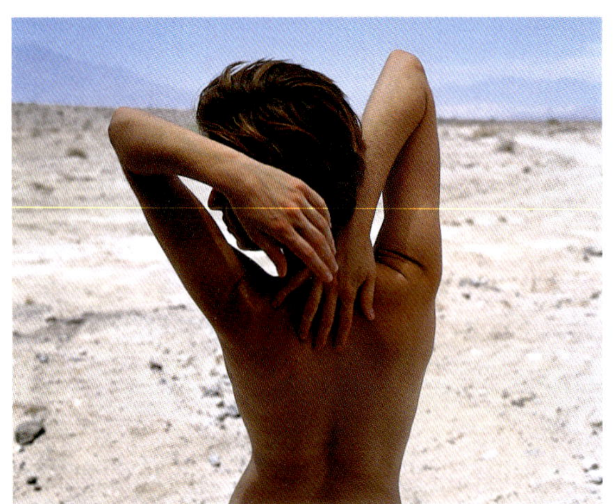

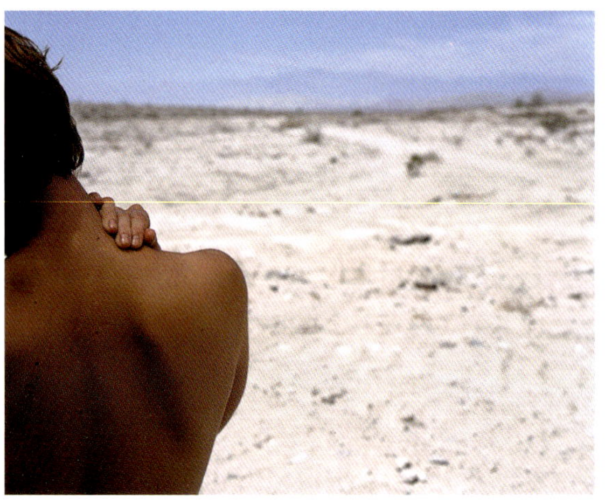

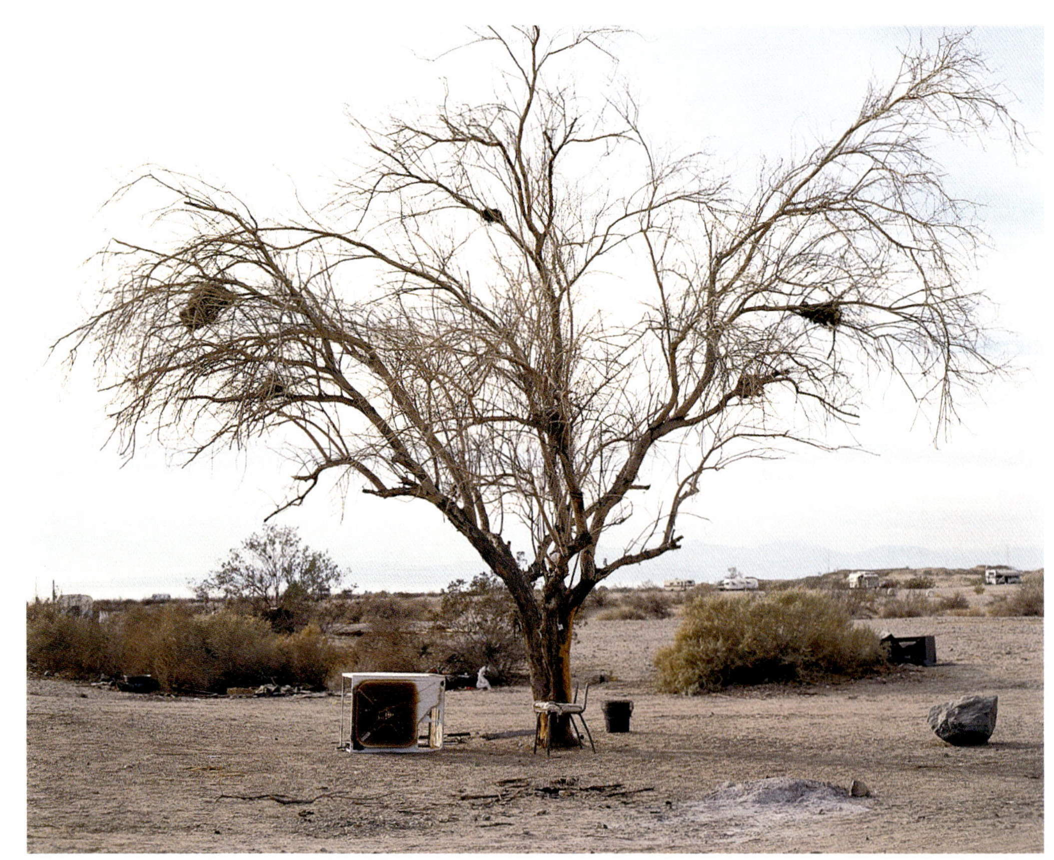

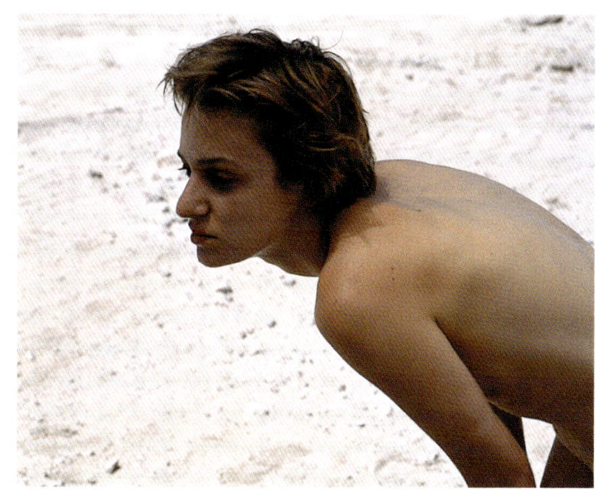

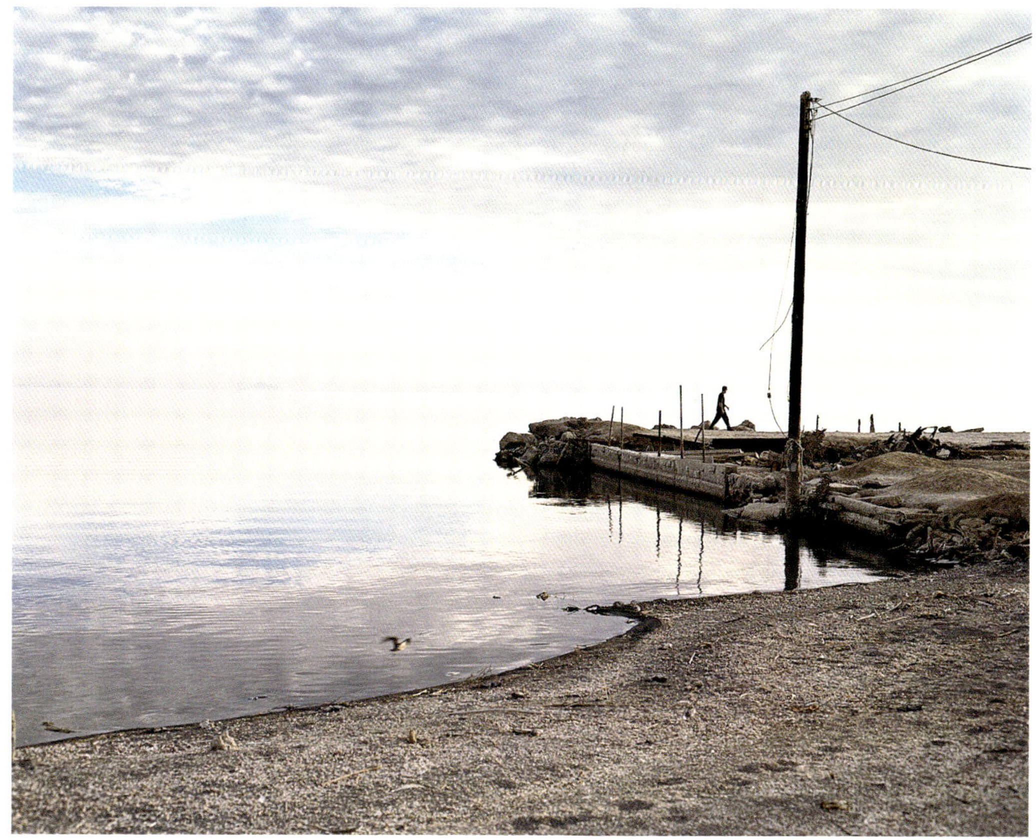

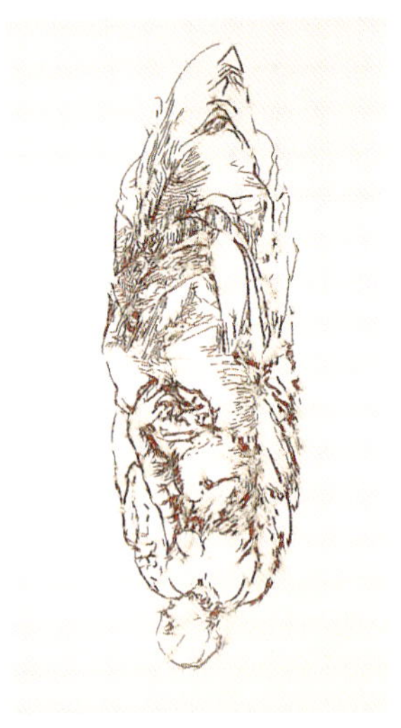

all from *THE PICTURESQUE* (details), 1997/2000

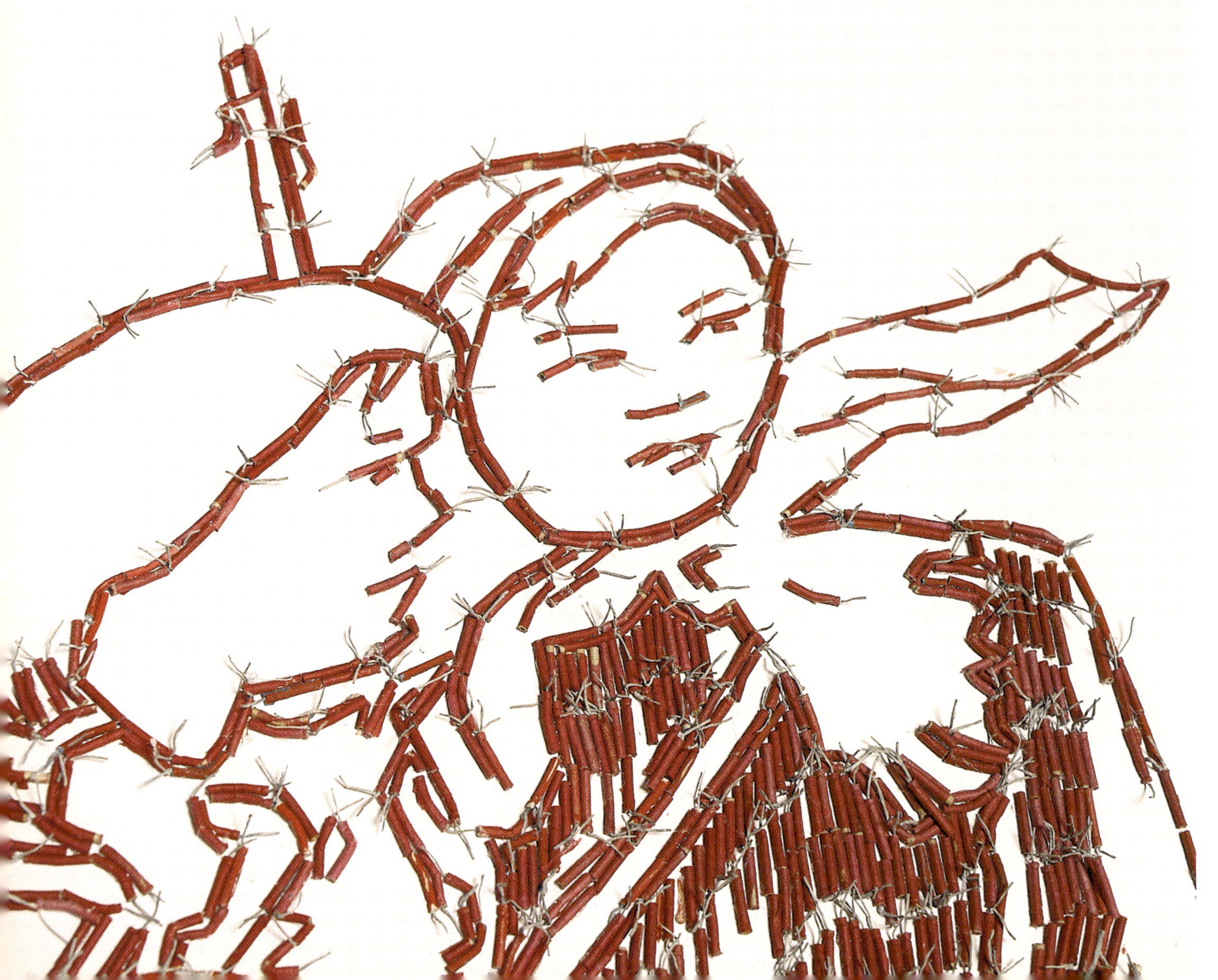

Yuk King Tan

In these works Tan makes sculptural drawings on the wall from the residue of burned firecrackers. Self-consciously adapting the traditional Chinese toys used in public festivals and celebrations, Tan references the tourist identities of Asian culture to explore the traditions of her heritage. In a series called *The Picturesque* she draws on the conventions of Chinese landscape painting to address the tropes and myths of the representation of nature in the Pacific region.

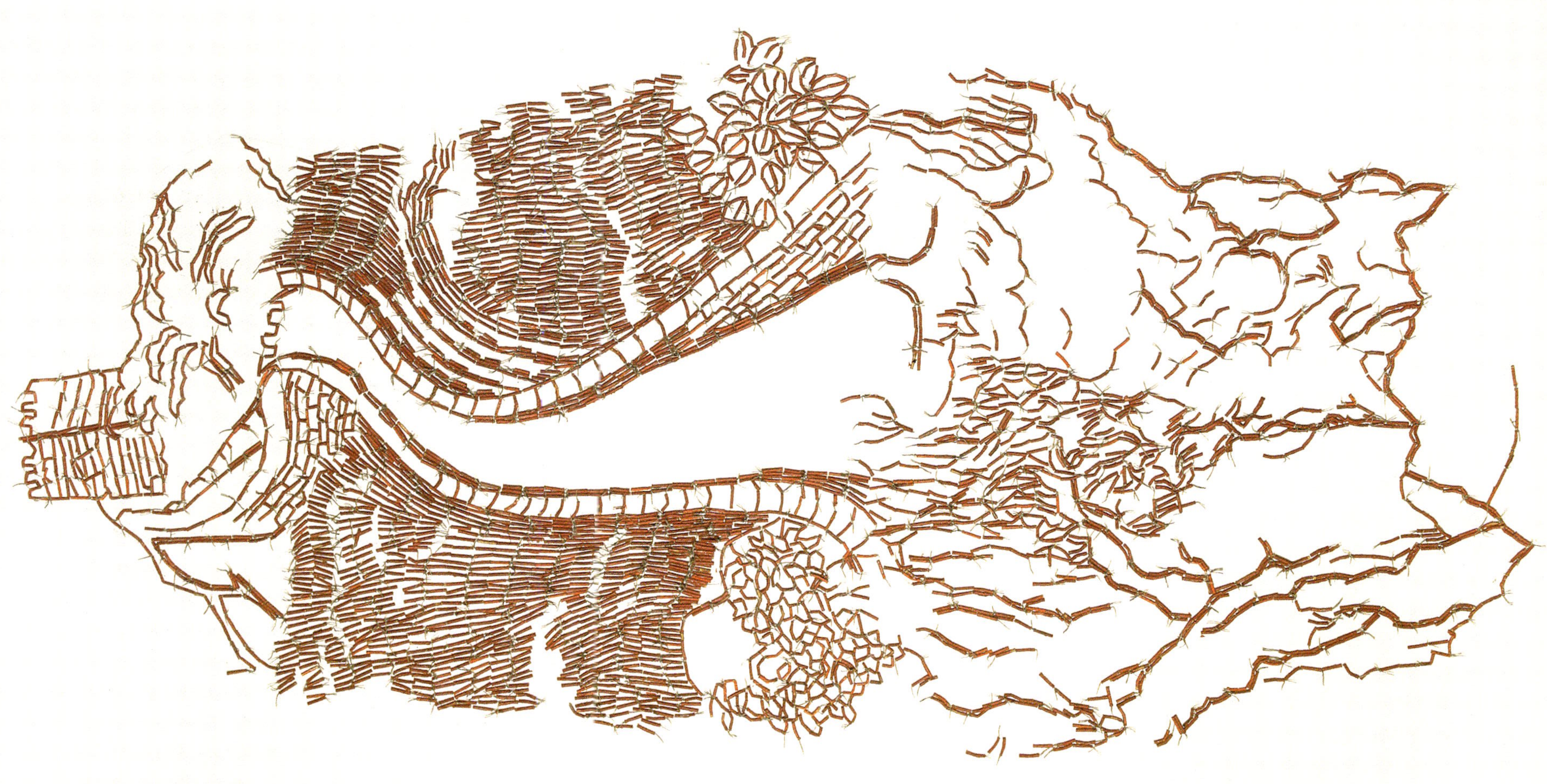

periphery

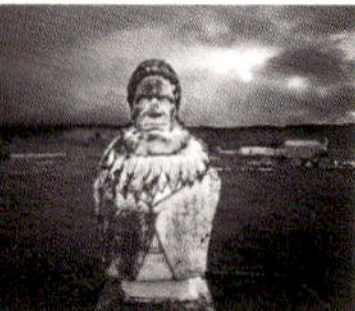

Laurence Aberhart

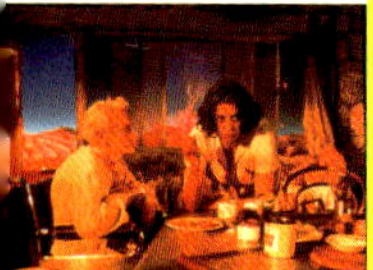

Tracey Moffatt

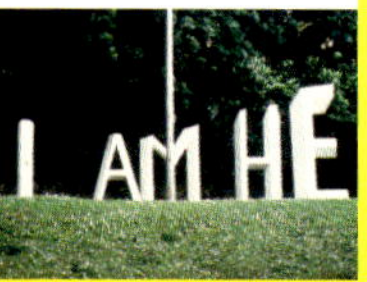

Michael Parekowhai

I AM AFRAID OF CITIES. BUT YOU MUSN'T LEAVE THEM. IF YOU GO TOO FAR YOU COME UP AGAINST THE VEGETATION BELT. VEGETATION HAS CRAWLED FOR MILES TOWARDS THE CITIES. ONCE THE CITY IS DEAD THE VEGETATION WILL COVER IT, WILL CLIMB OVER THE STONES, GRIP THEM, SEARCH THEM, MAKE THEM BURST WITH ITS LONG BLACK PINCERS... YOU MUST STAY IN THE CITES AS LONG AS YOU ARE ALIVE, YOU MUST NEVER PENETRATE ALONE THIS GREAT MASS OF HAIR WHICH LIES AT THE GATES.

—Jean-Paul Sartre[1]

When I was a child, I was taken on a trip to Tahiti as a substitute for my best friend's sister. On the interminable plane ride home, crossing distances now taken for granted, we were rerouted via the Pacific island of Samoa. After a disorienting layover in the sweaty, provincial airport, my friend's father confidently ushered us onto a plane he thought was departing for Oakland, California—everything he could do to hurry us safely back to the proper hemisphere. We ended up in Auckland (New Zealand) rather than Oakland (California)—a doppelganger of language or, rather, a confusion of dialect. In any location where two cultures meet, a collision not only of space but of language is practiced. One hears Mexican teenagers in Los Angeles say things twice to each other in a vernacular slang, in which English and Spanish flip back and forth in seamlessly compounded words and sentences. In

Auckland, Pakeha teenagers wear feathers in their hair, effortlessly embracing the body decoration of the Maori with a gesture that is both fashion statement and active symbol of biculturalism.

James Clifford speaks about "travelling-in-dwelling" and "dwelling-in-travelling," and the cultural simultaneity which discursively maps most international cities through which we pass.[2] The theorizing of the periphery in post-colonial discourse has profoundly impacted how international exhibitions are organized. Issues of the global and local are debated with an increasing sense of urgency and exhaustion. The so-called periphery, whether practiced in terms of identity or space, is increasingly seductive to an art-viewing public weary of work created from the same position of a fully internationalized, European modernism.

The work of Laurence Aberhart, Tracey Moffatt, and Michael Parekowhai, grouped here within this notion of the periphery, shares a quality of surreal beauty and compelling strangeness. Together these artists represent three generations and three very different artistic strategies. As I mentioned in the introduction to these artists' pages, Aberhart and Moffatt share an interest in describing, and perhaps exaggerating, a space of nowhere that permeates the imaginary of a particular kind of settled, touristic landscape, where centuries-old traditions simmer close to the surface, like the clinging vines that encroach upon Sartre's romanticized cityscape. Aberhart and Moffatt locate their pictures in an intentionally disturbed and re-exoticized space they choose to understand as the edge of civilization and consciousness.

Aberhart's pictorial practice records New Zealand's postcolonial landscape through a process of archival tracking. Taken as a whole, the body of work, which spans three decades, never builds momentum nor resolves particularly. This sense of narrative disorientation or distance perhaps reflects the ongoing bicultural evolution amidst which he lives and works. The pictures have a timeless quality, and are for the most part unpeopled. But what makes them different from, say, Lewis Baltz's uninhabited suburban tract-house compositions, or Robert Adams's bleak pictures of suburbs in the American west, is their almost complete lack of irony or critique. The masonic temples, Christian churches, Maori meeting houses and cemeteries, and Maori and Pakeha war memorials accumulate as evidence. As with Moffatt's pictures, it is difficult to know where the artist stands in relationship to his subject. The view camera Aberhart employs, and his use of fashion-printing techniques, make the otherwise conventional views deeply unsettling and atmospheric, almost erotic in their intensity. The low camera angle, used in horror films to track or embody an uncanny and lurking presence, renders the trees and sky particularly distorted and enervated. In rare photographs where figures do appear, as in *Lesley, Kamala, and Charlotte, South Springston, Canterbury, 1980* (1980), they are ethereal and orphaned of all civilizing presence.

Aberhart makes his way through the homeland much like Zacharias Kunuk approaches the documentary project of "discovering" the Igloolik community in which he lives. There is the sense that Aberhart's views of the historical present are first views—that the landscape as it appears, Maori meeting houses occupying the land with cemeteries and masonic temples, has always been the same. The modern retrospection on this complicated past lies precisely in the timeless, unmediated quality of the pictures.

Tracey Moffatt forces a sense of vertigo into her pictures by blatantly forcing certain filmic devices and references. In her *Up in the Sky* pictures (1997), the camera seems to circle overhead like a vulture surveying its prey, reminiscent of John Woo's dangling stunt camera used to make slow-motion, fighting bodies appear almost liquified and distorted. Moffatt stages the Outback: "the sere, sparsely populated Outback on the fringe of Australia's hot desert landscape, where Aborigines and poor white people live together on the edge of civilization... The underlying theme is the hard struggle for survival, the internal and external threats it poses, its rituals and the often obsessive yearnings it engenders, but also the primal experience of nature and existence."[3]

In her most recent body of work, titled *Invocations,* Moffatt returns to the imagery of her 1989 film, *Night Cries: A Rural Tragedy*. The hyper-synthetic style which characterizes all of her work is established in the lurid color of the painted-landscape backdrops framing the narrative, one that is literally crammed within. The characters are oppressed and blinded by the expressionistic mountains and sparse trees. Lynne Cooke has described Moffatt's use of the landscape as part of the artist's critique of ethnographic films and the history of postwar Australian landscape painting.[4]

The sparse melodrama of *Night Cries* is loosely autobiographical. A young woman of Aboriginal descent tends to her ailing white mother and, over the course of one hallucinatory night in a barren shack in the desert, comes to terms with her eventual death. Until recently it was common for Aboriginal children to be taken for adoption by white parents, and the relationship between these white parents and Aboriginal children is often emotionally charged and politically burdened.

Invocations fills in an earlier, perhaps imagined chapter of the Aboriginal woman's history. Depicted in a series of wildly atmospheric hand-colored prints, a little girl is enveloped by an animated forest wilderness and struggles against nature on the open land. The little girl appears to inhabit a folktale, turn-of-the-century, colonial landscape. Moffatt disorders our reading of the scene by rendering it in full "Grimm's Fairy Tale" color and detail. The little girl moves through a landscape that might have been read to her in stories told by her adoptive, white family. As the girl begins to appear older in the pictures, she is tormented by the landscape, her face and identity literally obliterated as she wrestles with the demons of her dreams. This older girl is dressed like the Aboriginal woman of *Night Cries*, or of Moffatt's other recent series, *Laudanum* (1998). Wandering around the thick desert atmosphere, the woman and the land are erotically linked somehow, trapped in a centuries-old struggle.

Michael Parekowhai gets a little wistful when describing his monumental sculpture, *The Indefinite Article* (1990). Parekowhai indulges in the agility of ready-made text in his highly fabricated riffs on the cultural signs of his native New Zealand. The sculpture spells out the pronoun sentence "I AM HE," writ in giant white letters that loom overhead, forming a kind of two-and-a-half-meter-high thicket across the floor. The "I AM" is well known to New Zealanders as the phrase painted by Colin McCahon, the near mythic painter revered as the greatest artist in the modern history of the country. McCahon, who died in 1987, persists as a shadow under which all artists work and whose most interesting resuscitation is coming from a generation of emerging artists who choose to rework or simply go around the legend.

For Parekowhai, who added the "HE" to the legendary "I AM," what resonates is that McCahon likened the experience of his moody paintings to a walk in the landscape. "He" is also Maori for "wrong," and the cluster of all three pronouns imply a scrambling of the artist's first name. Wrong place, wrong time, wrong artist—this is the identity that Parekowhai embraces and lovingly mucks around in. He has fashioned an identity that is both friendly "native" and sardonic, a cultural critique on par with his show-stealing *Ten Guitars* (1999) made for Artspace in Auckland and part of the recent Asia-Pacific Triennial in Brisbane. Charming his audience like a regular-guy Sinatra with a song, the most common form of expression in modern Maori culture, he remixes Engelbert Humperdinck's folksy "Ten Guitars." Interestingly, in Moffatt's *Night Cries*, scenes of the old/young woman character are intercut with images of a popular Aboriginal entertainer from the 1950s.

In Maori, the indigenous language of New Zealand, the word "maori" means ordinary, regular, everyday. There is, of course, nothing at all ordinary about being a young Maori artist, working in a society made officially bicultural in 1990, doing McCahon via Duchamp. Parekowhai has staked out a wide and hybrid territory in which his work functions beyond the local, and yet is deeply committed to it. The work is poignant, gorgeously fabricated, a bit cocky, and located in an exotic and, in Western terms, exoticizing cultural position. This is what makes it provocative.

Notes

1. Jean-Paul Sartre, *Nausea*, trans. Lloyd Alexander (New York: New Directions, 1959), 208–209. As quoted in Maureen P. Sherlock, "The Accidental Tourist," in *Eye of Nature* (Banff, Canada: Walter Phillips Gallery, 1991), 123–24.
2. James Clifford, *Routes: Travel and Translation in the Late Twentieth Century* (Cambridge, Mass.: Harvard University Press, 1997), 54.
3. Brigitte Reinhardt, "Creating One's Own Reality," in *Tracey Moffatt: Laudanum*, exh. cat. (Ostfildern, Germany: Hatje Cantz, 1999), 22.
4. Lynne Cooke, "Free Falling," exh. brochure (New York: Dia Center for the Arts, 1999), unpaginated.

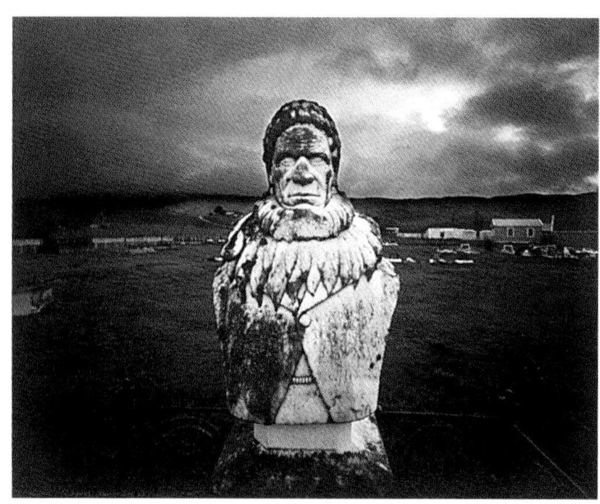

TE HAPUKU, TE HAUKE, HAWKES BAY, 17 JUNE 1982, 1982

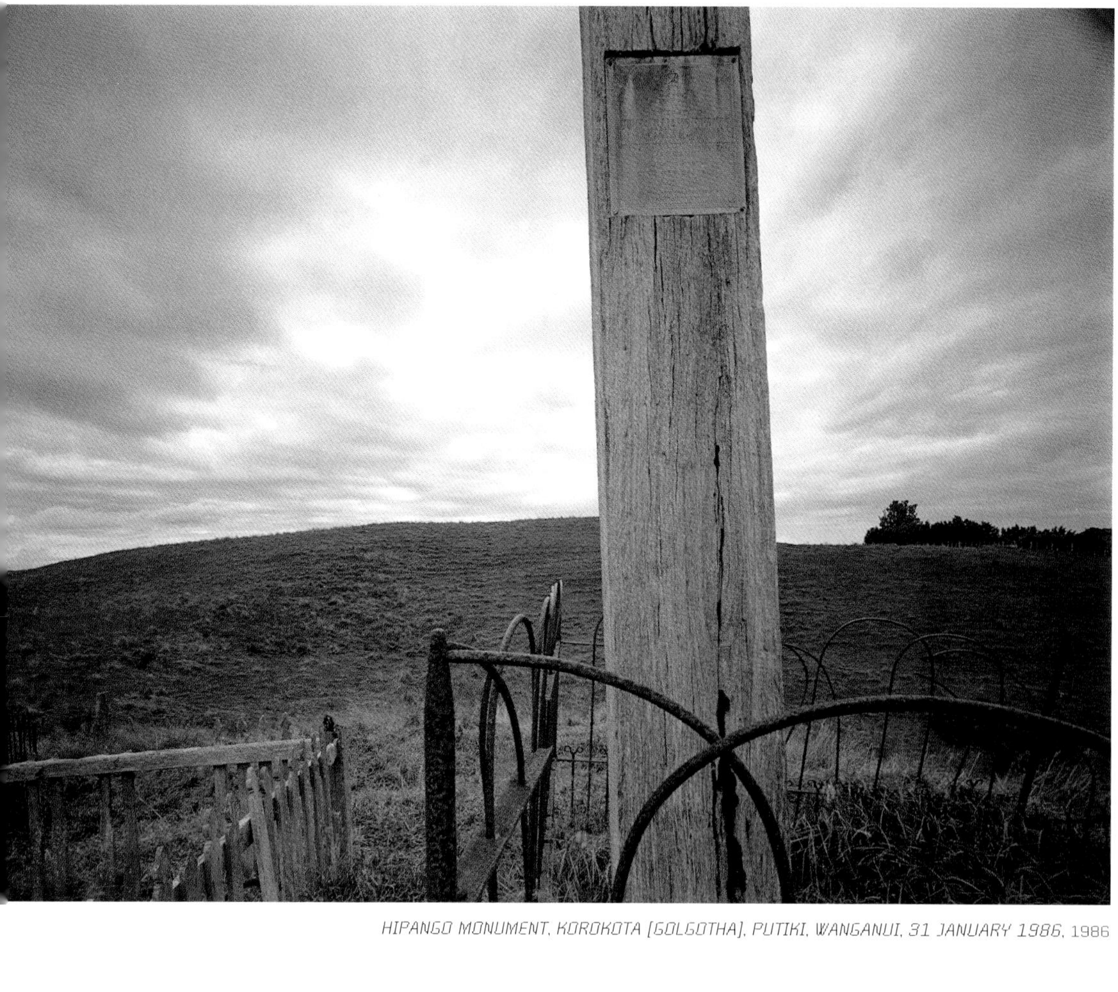

HIPANGO MONUMENT, KOROKOTA [GOLGOTHA], PUTIKI, WANGANUI, 31 JANUARY 1986, 1986

Laurence Aberhart

Over his thirty-year career as a photographer, Laurence Aberhart has created a visual archive of New Zealand's public spaces. In haunting, black-and-white photographs made with an 8x10-inch view camera, he archives the postcolonial landscapes primarily of New Zealand and Australia. Thematic groupings, including masonic lodges, war memorials, cemeteries (both Maori [indigenous] and Pakeha [white]), derelict buildings, and dramatic, cloudy skies, reoccur throughout his production, complicating any chronological understanding of the pictures and enhancing its eerie, timeless quality of the bicultural present.

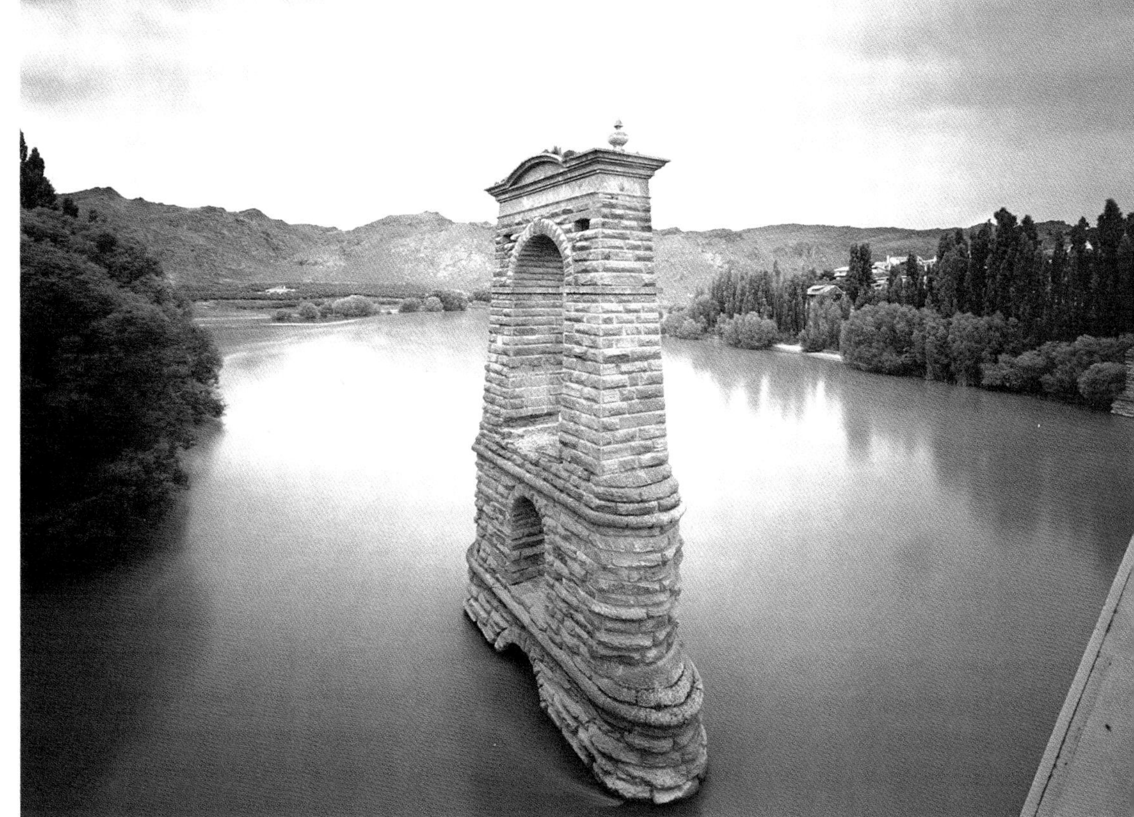

OLD BRIDGE STRUCTURE FROM NEW BRIDGE, CLUTHA RIVER, ALEXANDRA, DECEMBER 1980, 1980

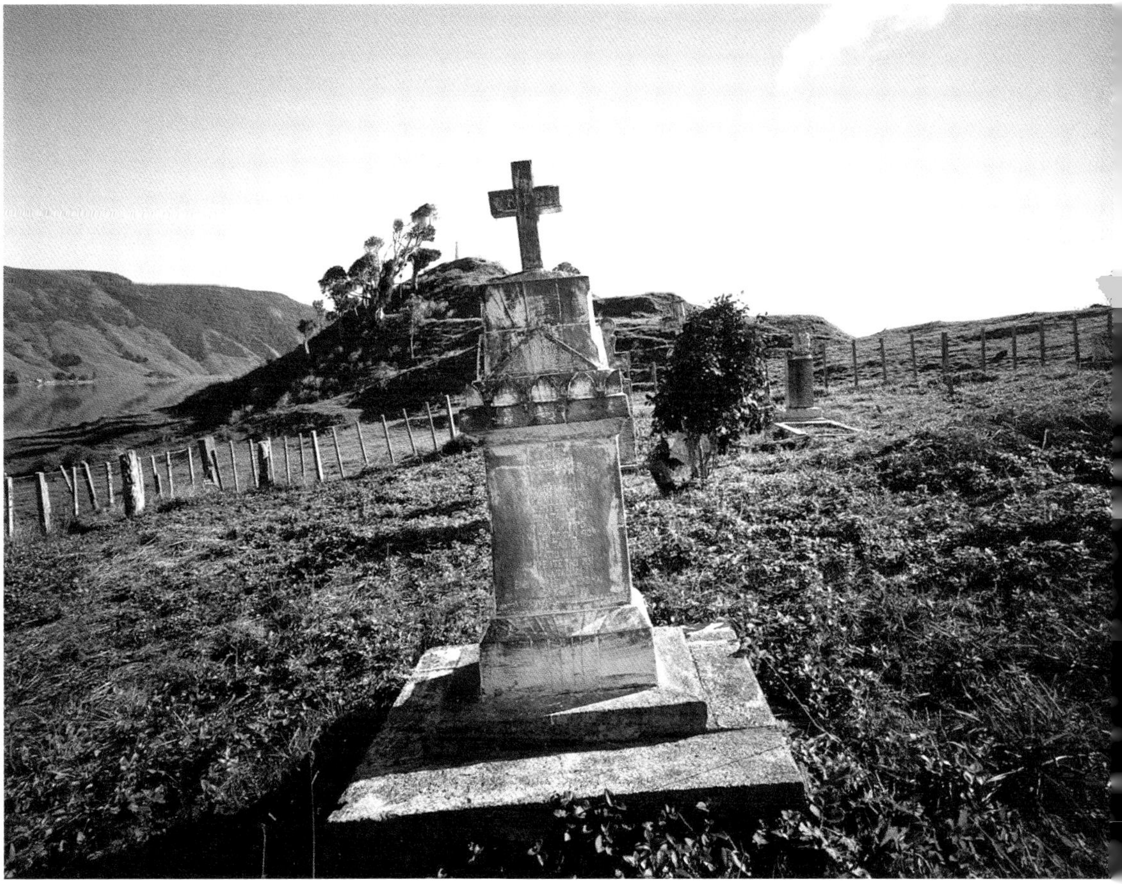

CARVED HEADBOARD #2, PAWARENGO, WHANGAPE HARBOUR, NORTHLAND, 10 MAY 1982, 1982/83

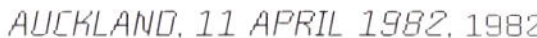

AUCKLAND, 11 APRIL 1982, 1982

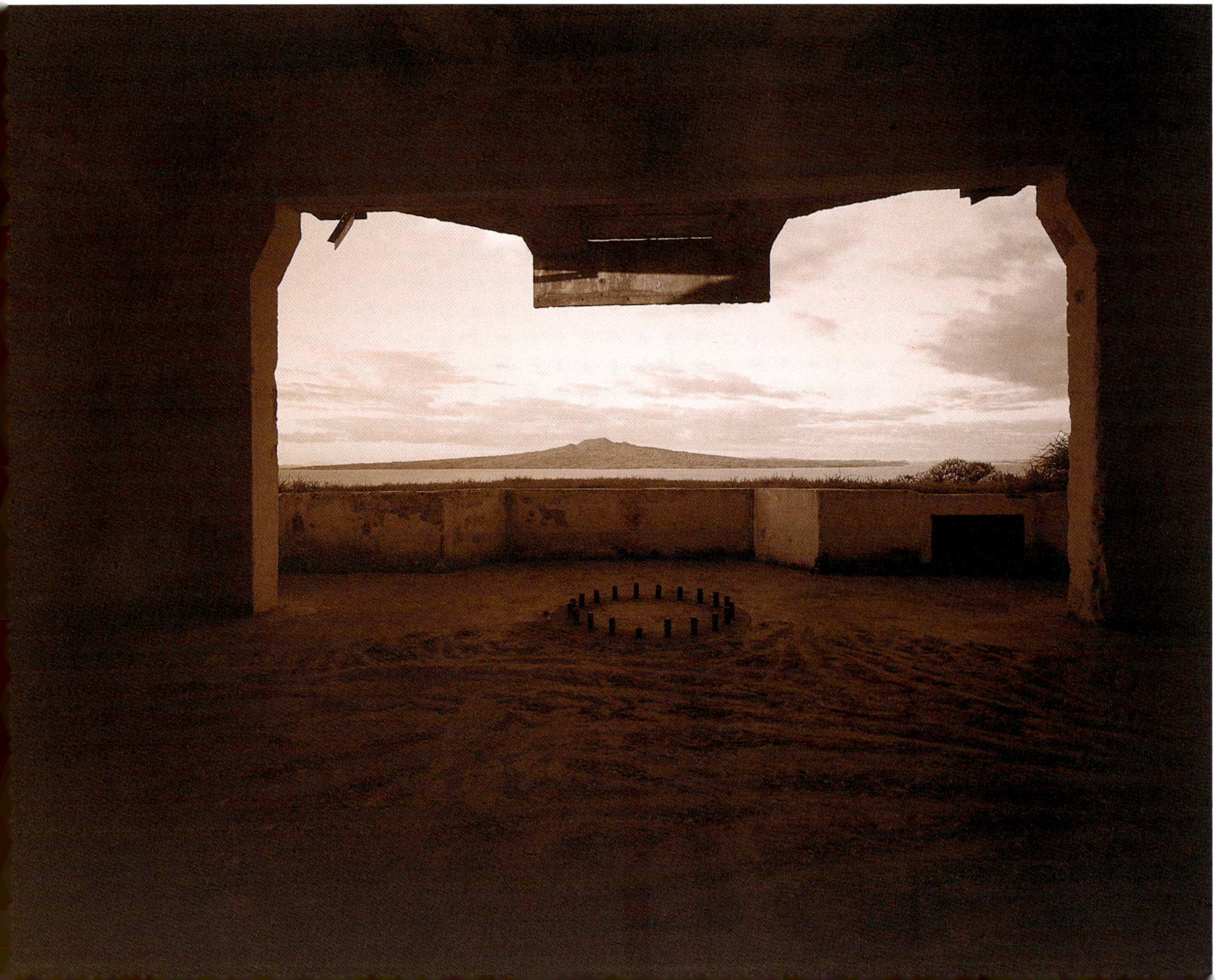

LESLEY, KAMALA, AND CHARLOTTE, SOUTH SPRINGSTON, CANTERBURY, 1980, 1980

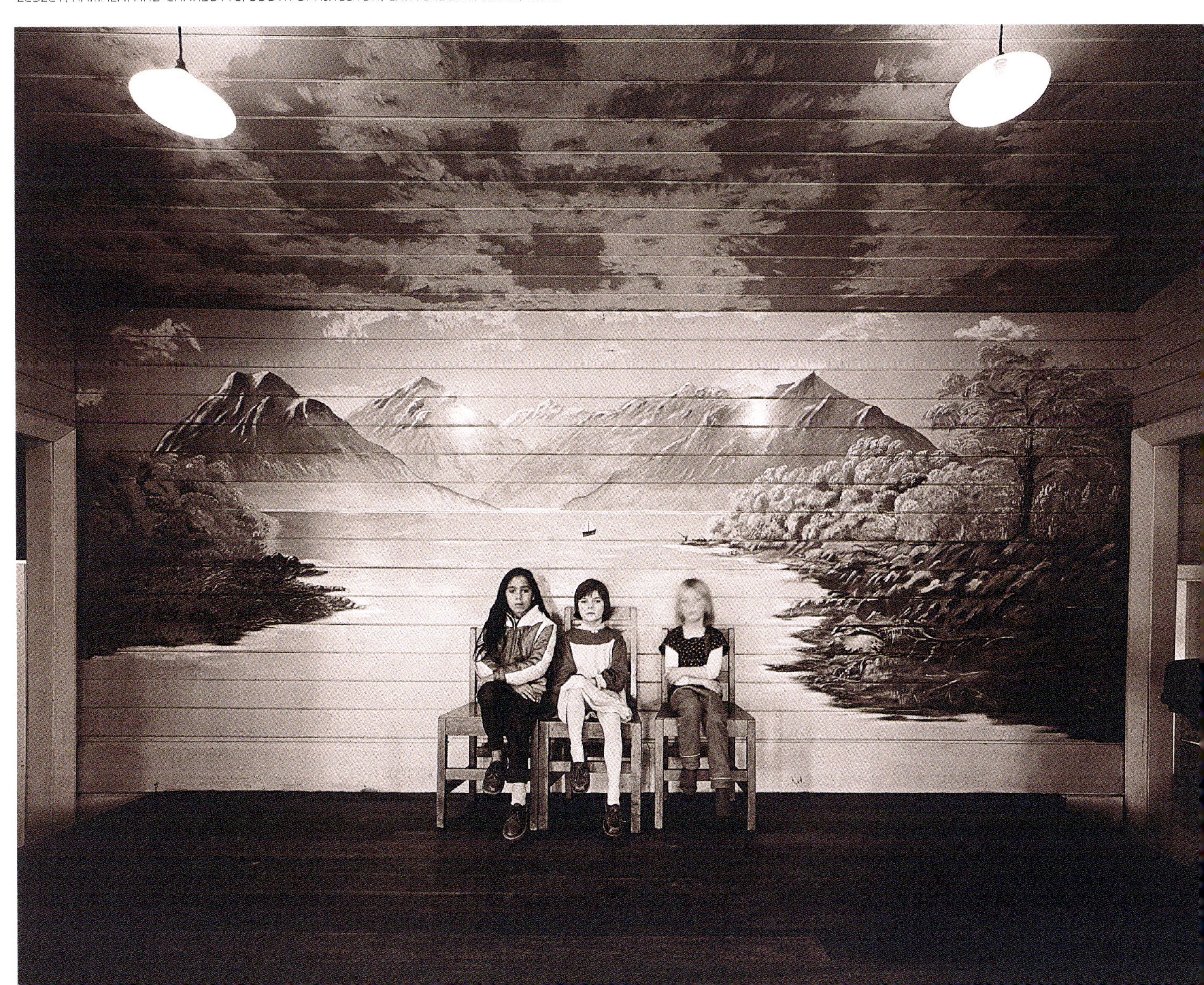

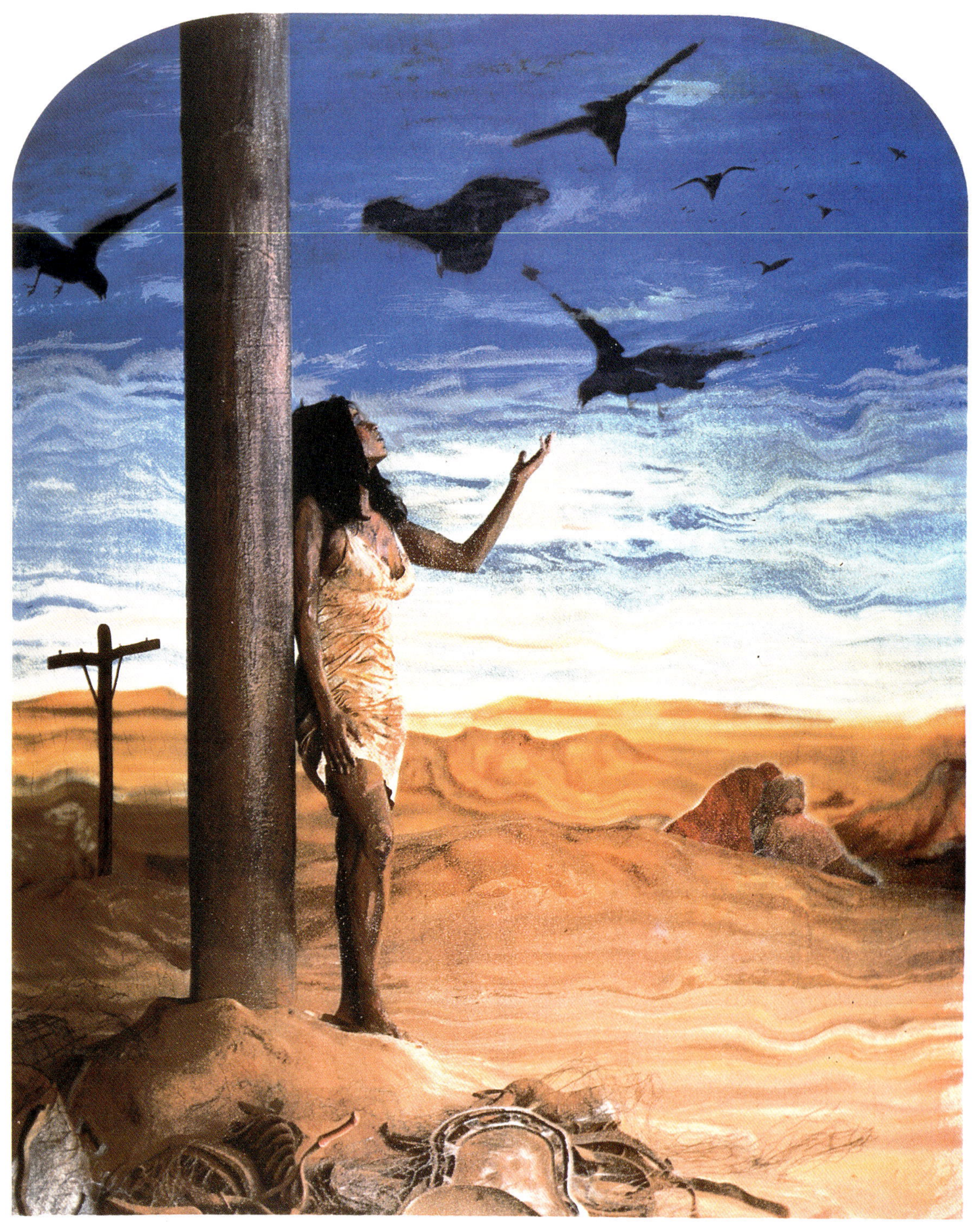

INVOCATIONS (2), 2000

Tracey Moffatt

In her early film *Night Cries: A Rural Tragedy,* Moffatt introduces an aboriginal female character who continues to appear in her work up to the present. In the film, the woman cares for her ailing white mother in a luridly colored set made to resemble the Australian desert of colonial landscape paintings. In recent photographs and photo-silkscreens, an aboriginal woman again is haunted in a stark, desert dreamscape by fantastic visions of her childhood and by strange demons of the night.

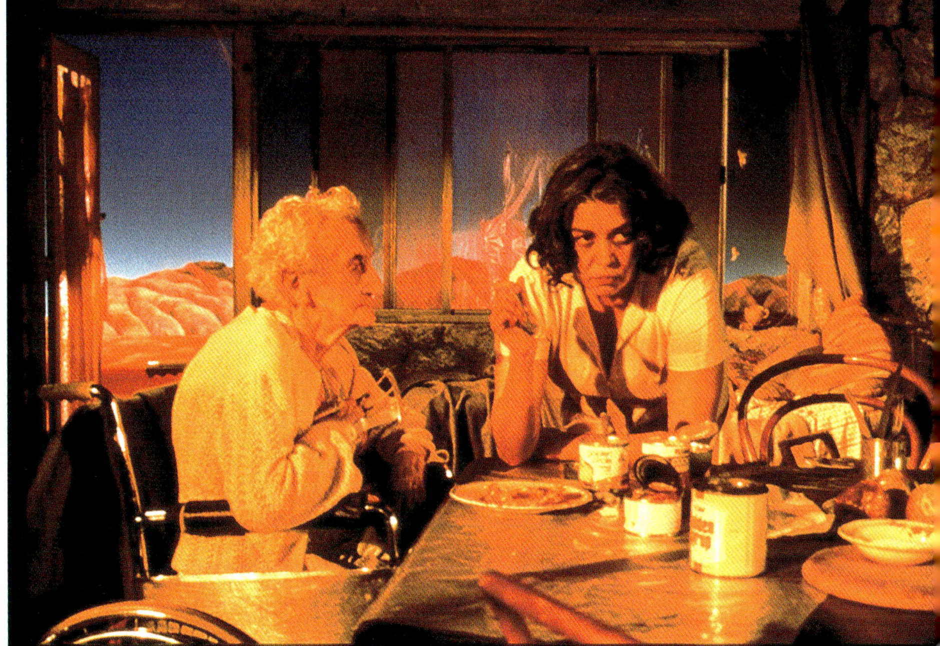

from *NIGHT CRIES: A RURAL TRAGEDY*, 1989

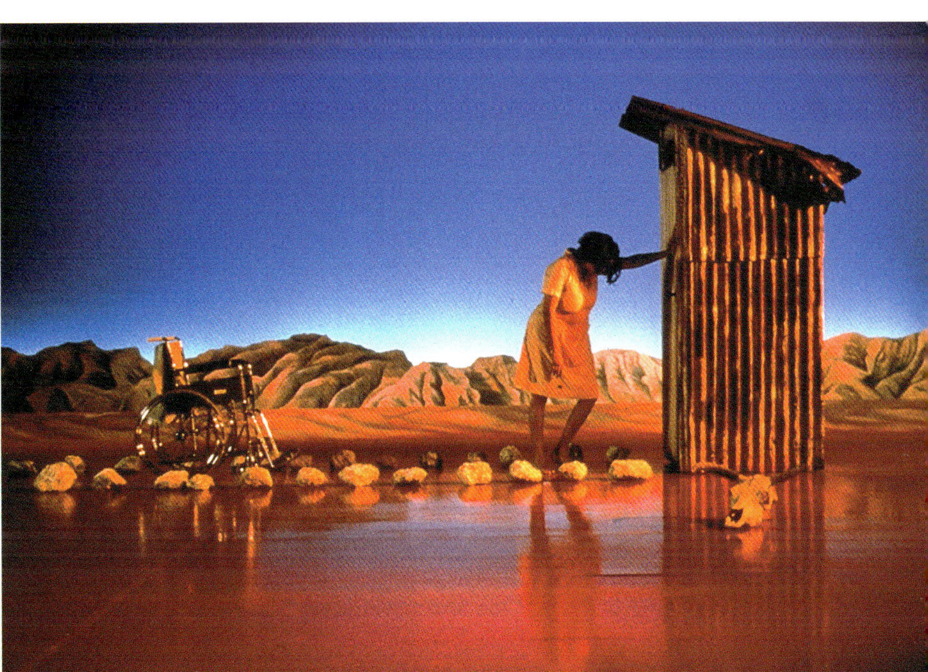

from *NIGHT CRIES: A RURAL TRAGEDY*, 1989

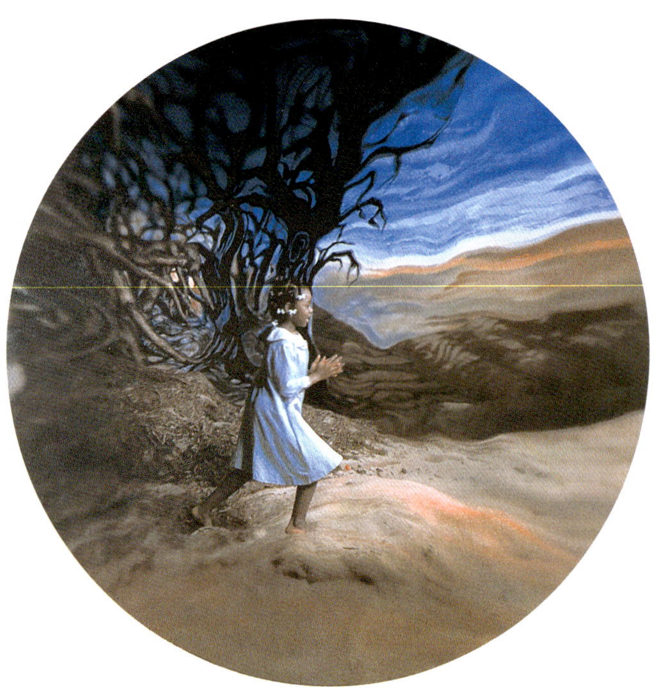

INVOCATIONS (10), 2000

INVOCATIONS (11), 2000

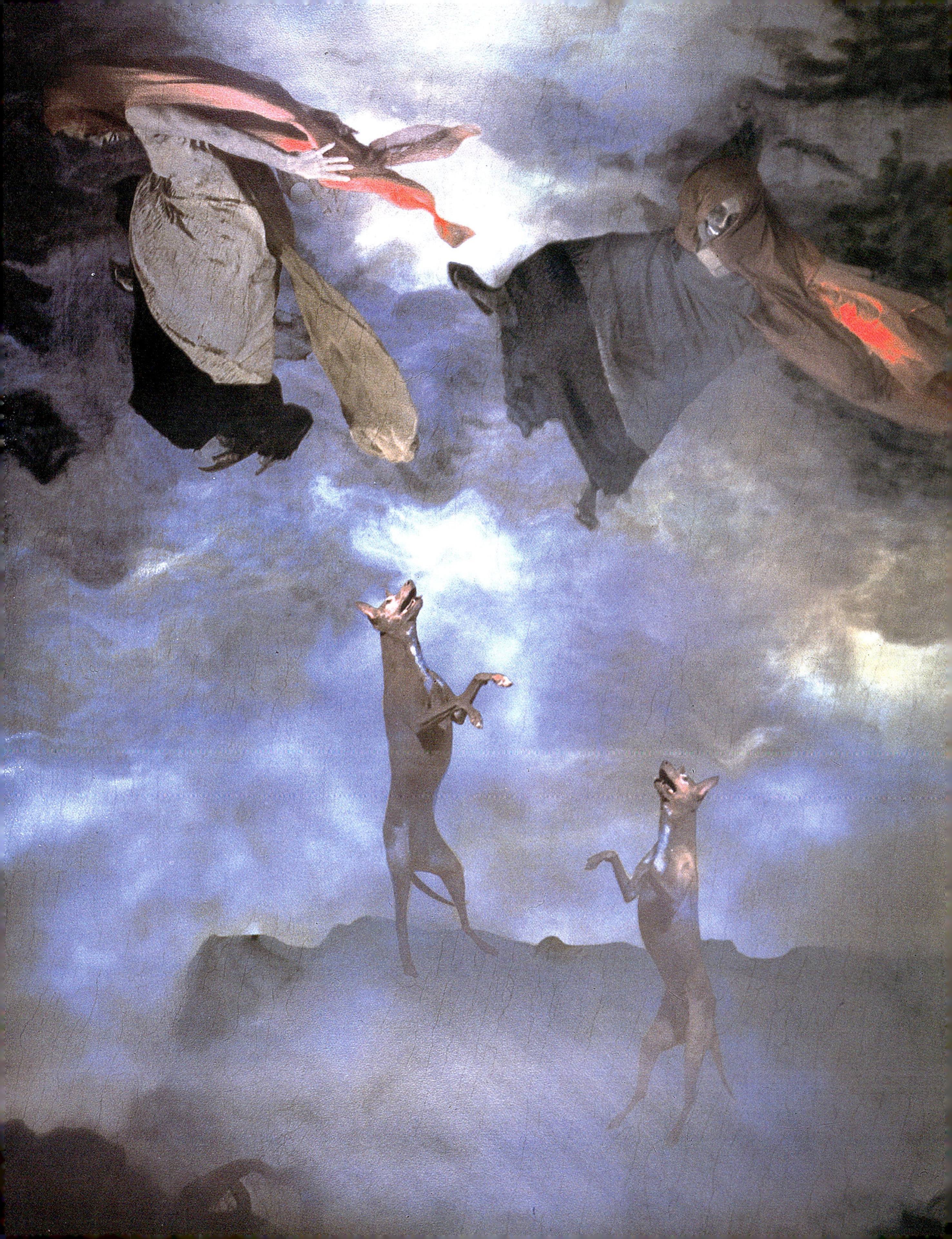

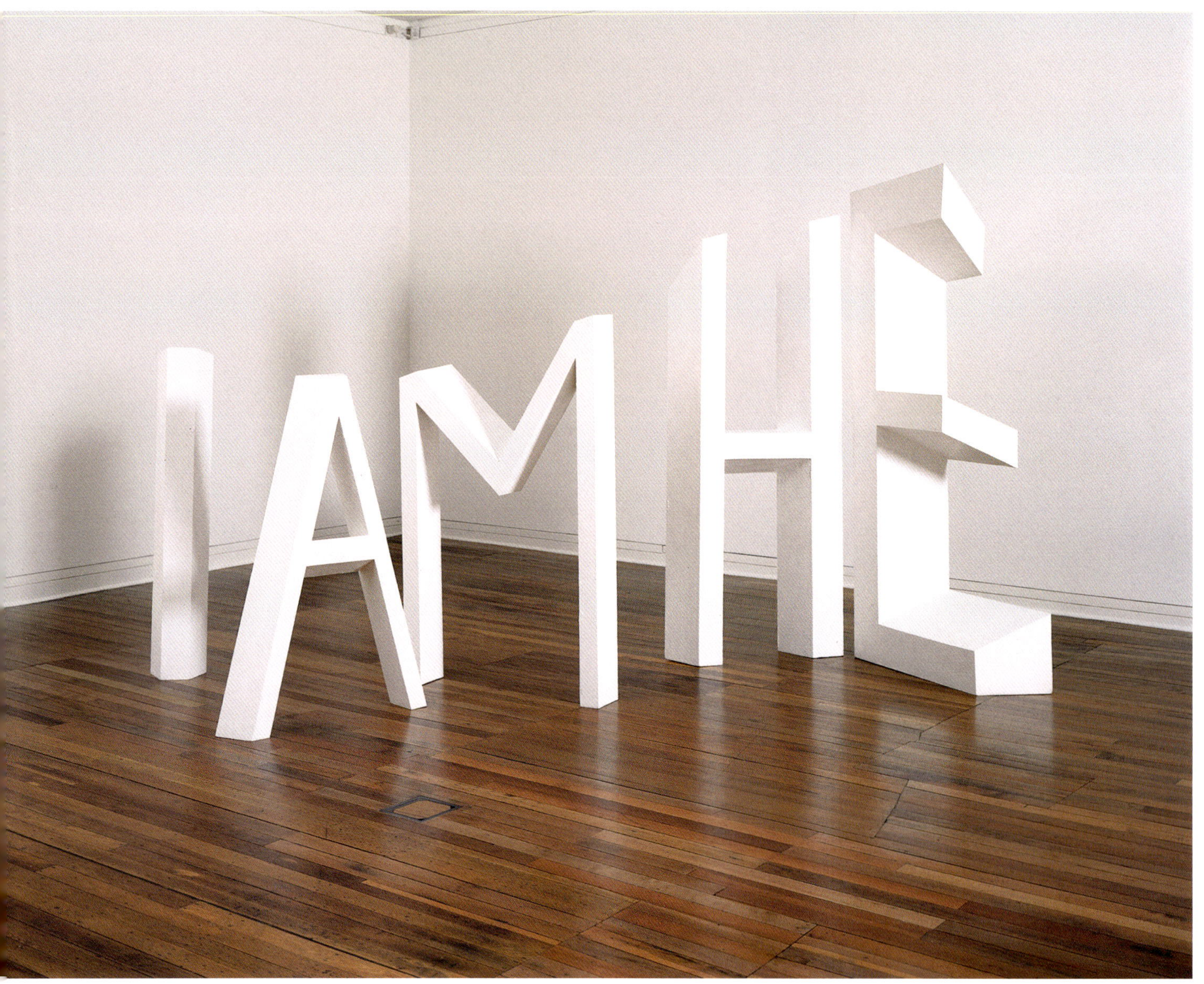

THE INDEFINITE ARTICLE, 1990

Michael Parekowhai

In highly fabricated, narrative sculptures, Parekowhai visually puns and manipulates linguistic fragments from his Maori heritage. *The Indefinite Article* is an homage to a famous painting by New Zealand's most celebrated landscape painter, Colin McCahon, who often incorporated Christian text into his paintings. The thicket of three-dimensional letters refers to the contested space of the homeland in postcolonial New Zealand.

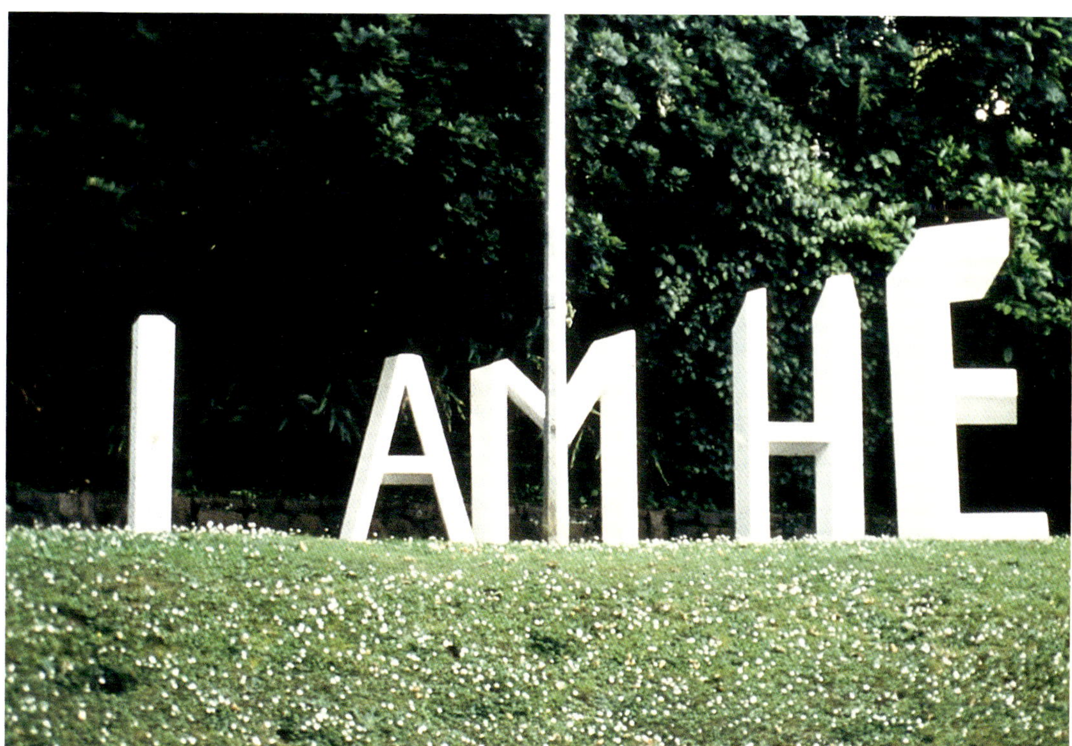

THE INDEFINITE ARTICLE, 1990

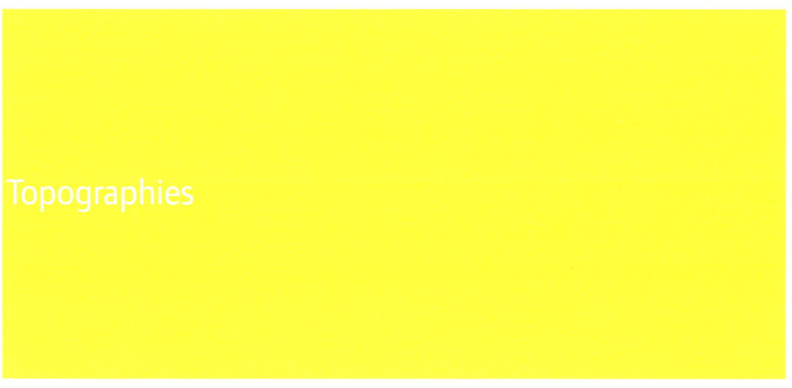

Francis Pound

Just What Is It that Makes the Term Global-Local So Widely Cited, Yet So Annoying?

Lee Weng Choy

Checklist of the Exhibition

Exhibition Histories

Topographies

Francis Pound

It is one of the most persistent patterns of New Zealand's Nationalist[1] high culture to speak of a flight from England—the place of captivity—towards the Promised Land. A key painting of that pattern, and one whose title actually spells out the flight trope, is Colin McCahon's *The Flight from Egypt* (1980). McCahon inscribes *The Flight* with its title on each panel, followed by the additional inscriptions, one per panel: "WHEN DO WE START"; "the Desert"; "a big tree offers shade"; "WHEN DO WE GET THERE"; "I AM TIRED"; and, gazing uncertainly through the last airplane window,[2] out to the ochreous desert, "arrival: is THIS the PROMISED LAND—." It is a flight, it seems, which must perpetually be renewed—a flight after an elusive goal; a flight on which one may become exhausted and fail; an interminable, inextricable flight, whose end is uncertain; a flight even now not properly begun.

More than thirty years before, McCahon had proclaimed the flight's success in *The Promised Land* (1948). Here the painter gazes at us from the foreground left, prophetically to announce New Zealand as the place promised. There is a lighted candle, sign of divine vision, and a jug of water, sign of holy purity.[3] An annunciatory angel, the only being as yet who shares the painter's vision, stares from the sky. Near its head are the words: "The Promised Land." So the painter's vision is made a promise divinely vouchsafed, and his work miraculously authenticated—proved by angelic announcement, and by the signs of divine purity and light.

Or, if the flight is over, and its landing long ago achieved, the question may fall, as if in melancholy and uncertain retrospection, into the past tense, as in the title of a McCahon landscape of 1962, *Was This The Promised Land?*[4] Or the wilderness through which the Promised Land is sought may seem so boundless, and so perpetual, that the only hope left is that in the dark of the wilderness itself there may be some shaft of grace. Since we must die in the wilderness, such redeeming grace will come, therefore, not as that light-suffused and bounteous end of the flight, the Promised Land, but—in the words of the McCahon series title—as the Necessary Protection only, granted from above. As McCahon writes: "Moses was not permitted by God to reach the Promised Land—this is the place where the painter never arrives."[5] There is, for the painter-prophet, only the wilderness on the way.

Or the country of the Promised Land may come to be envisaged as never to exist in the world at all—which would be not just another kind of failure of the Nationalist flight, but rather its total breakdown and its abandonment. This might seem to be the conclusion McCahon reaches by the time of *A Letter to Hebrews* (1979). Here McCahon writes that: "By Faith, Abraham obeyed the call to go out to a land destined for himself and his heirs and left home without knowing where he was to go. By Faith he settled as an alien in the land promised him, living in tents as did Isaac and Jacob, who were heirs to the same promise."

Reading these painted words, one might think of the first waves of European colonists who left England, Ireland, Scotland, and Wales, hardly knowing what was to come of their vast journey to settle as aliens, living in merely temporary habitation in the land promised. But, so the inscription goes on to tell, Abraham "was looking forward to the city with Firm foundations whos [sic] architect and builder is GOD." Does this mean that the Just City may yet be achieved in New Zealand, with God's help—or is such a city only to be found outside of this world?

The inscription continues, speaking of Abel, Noah, Isaac, Jacob, Sarah, and Abraham as precursors for we who still await the Promised Land. "ALL THESE PERSONS DIED IN FAITH. THEY WERE NOT YET IN POSSESSION OF THE THINGS PROMISED, BUT HAD SEEN THEM FAR AHEAD AND HAILED THEM AND CONFESSED THEMSELVES NO MORE THAN STRANGERS OR PASSING TRAVELERS ON THE EARTH." This sounds like a confession of failure. Here, perhaps, having come to see the justice and power of the prior Maori claim to the country, McCahon now saw as "aliens" and "strangers" and mere "passing travelers" those Pakeha[6] like himself who had once sought to create the Promised Land. Yet, though the New Zealand landscape of so many Nationalist hopes is gone, entirely blackened out, the concern with country remains in the words of the painted text.

"Those who use such language show plainly that they are looking for a country of their own," so the next lines say, and "they could have found the opportunity to return" to "the country they had left. Instead we find them longing for a better country." It might seem that this "better country" is in some sense still New Zealand, and that those who could have returned yet did not are the immigrant "aliens" from Britain. But, the inscribed lines go on to say of the "better country": "I mean the heavenly one," as if the only hope left now is in the geography of the heavens.

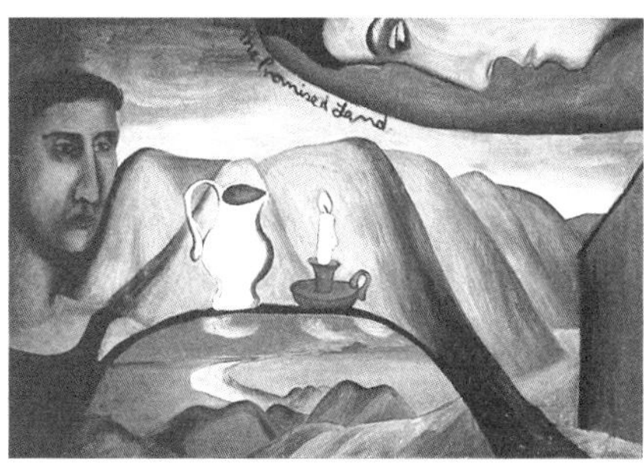

Colin McCahon
The Promised Land, 1948
Oil on canvas
35 7/8 x 53 1/2 inches
Presented by the McCahon Family, 1988. Courtesy of the McCahon Research and Publication Trust

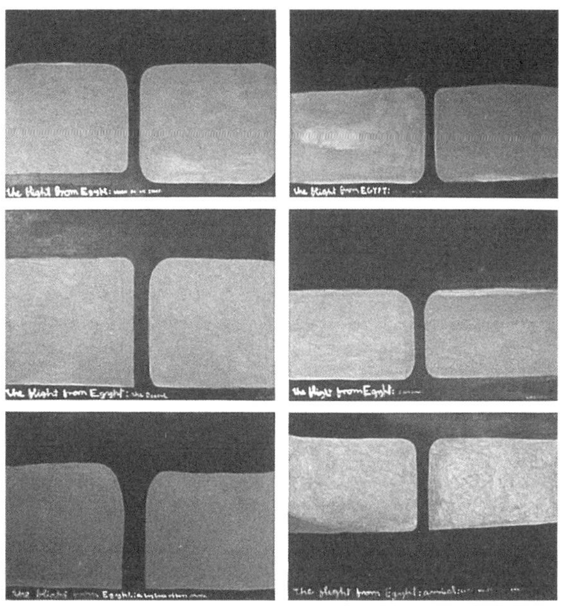

Colin McCahon
The Flight From Egypt, 1980
Acrylic on six sheets of paper
28 1/2 x 34 inches each
Courtesy of the McCahon Research and Publication Trust

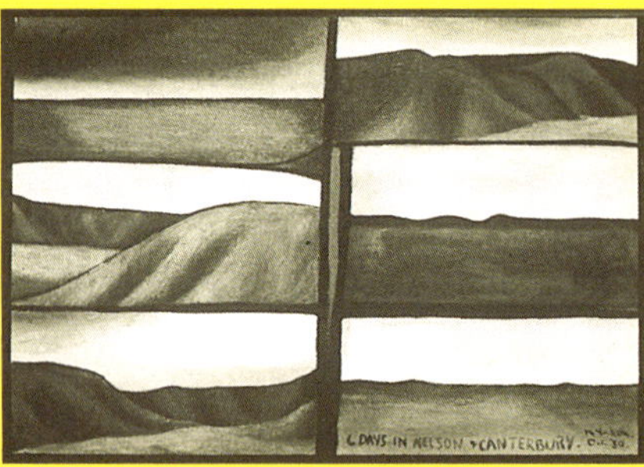

Colin McCahon
Six Days in Nelson and Canterbury, 1950
Oil on canvas
34 1/2 x 45 1/2 inches
Presented by the artist, per the Friends of the Auckland City Art Gallery, 1978. Courtesy of the McCahon Research and Publication Trust

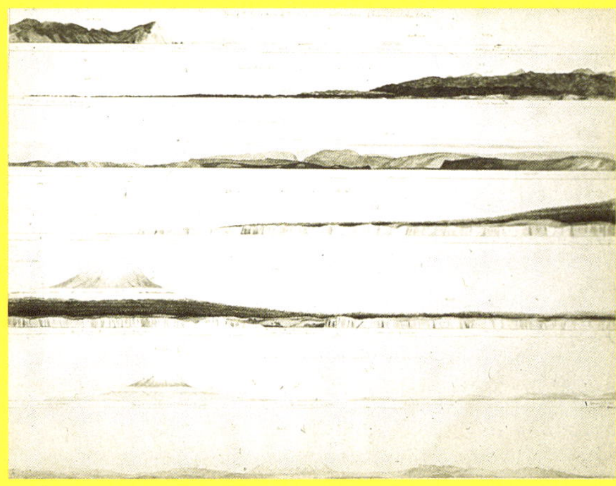

Charles Heaphy
View of the Rocks Laying Off Point Jackson—North Entrance of Queen Charlotte's Sound, c. 1842
Watercolor
15 1/8 x 19 1/2 inches
Courtesy of the Alexander Turnbull Library, Wellington, New Zealand

All that can be promised, then, to those on the flight, is not the Promised Land of tomorrow, not a future Promised Land, "but one," as in Jacques Derrida's words, "whose concept is linked to the to-come, to the experience of a promise engaged, that is always an endless promise."[7] "Endless because it can never be declared fulfilled,"[8] it remains and always will remain in the future tense, a future which—and such is its structural function—nevertheless "makes the most imperative demands" on Nationalist actions in the present.[9] In their every painting or poem, in their every utterance on the perpetual flight, Nationalist artists are burdened with a responsibility towards this Promised Land to come.

In much New Zealand Nationalist discourse, it is as if New Zealand is so far just a conspiracy of cartographers, not yet truly known to the mind. "We are the unmapped frontier."[10] "We were mapping the coasts of mind."[11] "A kind of exploration in a country of the mind."[12] A "charting of this often neglected country."[13] "A country physically measured by the cartographer," but "still little known as a human inspiration."[14] Poet and painter alike claim to be "making a new discovery of their country."[15]

All this talk of cartography, of charting, of discovery, of exploration, of mind, irresistibly recalls McCahon's *Six Days in Nelson and Canterbury* (1950). This painting, where blood spills down the central frame as if from a wound, is in many ways the summary of the early Nationalist endeavor. Six days: the six days of God's creation of the world—and six days of the painter's creation of a country. The blood: Christ's sacrificial blood—and the artist's.

Six Days in Nelson and Canterbury is a map of McCahon's and Nationalist concerns—and it is a map of memories. The way the landscapes are stacked one above the other is reminiscent, too, of the seventeenth-, eighteenth-, and nineteenth-century charts of coastal profiles made as navigational aids in exploratory voyages in the Pacific, and for the further mapping of coasts once they were settled. But, with McCahon, the stacked strips of landscape become something more than description or memory, and the journey something more than a physical one. They are charts of a country to be found and formed in a flight of the mind.

Again, when the six panels of *The Flight from Egypt* are hung, as they almost invariably are, in two stacked groups of three, the painting seems to allude to the same maritime charting tradition as does *Six Days.* With such references to the earlier exploratory prototype of the stacked profile, McCahon's claim—and indeed the whole Nationalist claim—is established in paint of making now a new, more properly *spiritual* discovery of New Zealand. This is the discovery the poet and theorist of regionalism Allen Curnow requires, when he calls for "a new discovery" of New Zealand, with the artist as "spiritual colonist."[16] For, as Curnow would have it: "The nineteenth-century colonists achieved their migration bodily, but not in spirit."[17]

It is no accident then, nor mere matter of form, but rather a major source of its resonance, that the solitary foreground figure of McCahon's *The Listener (Head)* (1947) should repeat the gazing over the land of the innumerable foreground spectator figures in colonial and proto-colonial New Zealand topographical paintings—figures which might be said to incarnate the colonial gaze.[18] The gaze of *The Listener*, in rehearsing the gaze of that colonial prototype, is enacting Curnow's "new discovery" of New Zealand.

"And how many generations does that take?"[19] "That promised land it will not be ours to enter, and we shall die in the wilderness."[20] It is a country in the process of a perpetual *deferment*—it may only be saluted from afar. At most there are always, it seems, as in the essayist M. H. Holcroft's claim, only "the *beginnings* of a journey which might be traveled in a search for truth as it exists for New Zealanders... in the silences of the land that received their fathers."[21] As Curnow has it: "We have begun, but only begun."[22] Always, New Zealand remains "still little known as a *human* inspiration. In this sense it is still the enigma *Terra Australis Incognito*, the elusive southern land."[23]

For Maori, Aotearoa (New Zealand) is hardly elusive—they have lived here since the sixteenth century. Aotearoa is a land that needs not so much to be *found* as to be *returned*. It is interesting, then, that the most recent use of the topographical, stacked-landscape convention of the "explorers" and "colonists" should be that of the Maori artist Jacqueline Fraser.

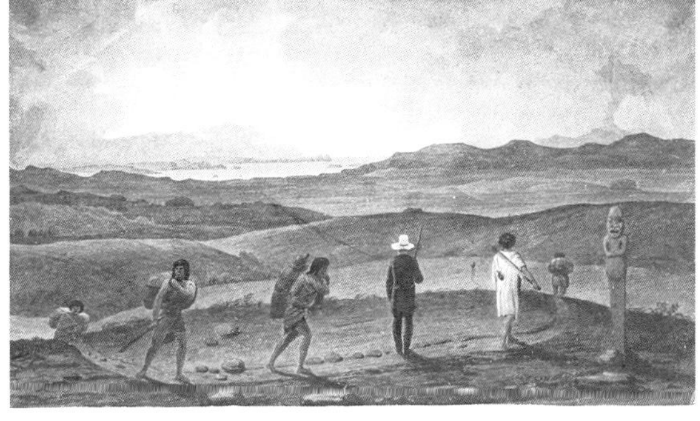

Augustus Earle
Distant View of the Bay of Islands, New Zealand, c. 1827
Watercolor
10 1/8 x 17 1/4 inches
Rex Nan Kivell Collection; NK12/70.T108. By permission of the National Library of Australia

In her installation *The Long Persecution of the Dear Blessed Vision (With Three Sure Acts of Victory)* (1999), Fraser puts the stacked profile to a new political use. In alluding to works like McCahon's *Six Days in Nelson and Canterbury*, and to the European drafting tradition of the stacked profile to which McCahon himself referred, Fraser might seem simply to place herself within the same tradition. However, drawn, twisted, and knotted as her profiles are with colored electric wires, and curtained or veiled as they sometimes are with translucent shot silk, they also recall the weaving patterns and techniques that were the traditional preserve of Maori women. Fraser, while recalling a colonialist tradition, declares herself to be speaking from *somewhere else*.

With these topographical-landscape profiles, each attentively subtitled with its own place name, Fraser celebrates the Crown's return of lands to her tribe under the terms of the 1997 *Ngai Tahu* Treaty of Waitangi settlement. She depicts not the new Nature of the exploring and colonial draftsmen, but the intimately known ("dear darling," she calls them)[24] places appropriated by the colonizer and, now, after more than a century of Maori mourning and quest, returned. This is the "Victory" of Fraser's title.

Maori intimacy with place is further marked by the veiled self-portrait face in each panel, gazing at each returned place ("We love it more than a diamond tiara"),[25] and by the way various self-portrait figures—each splendidly dressed for the occasion—hold stacks of profiled hills, lakes, and islands in their hands. The land that McCahon and his Nationalist peers had declared as empty, without history, and silent ("The Great Silence"),[26] is now shown to be a land with a bitter history, echoing with anguished voice.[27] These works, then, are something like the exact opposite of the triumphal celebrations by colonial topography of newly confiscated land. Topography—always colonialist—is here turned against itself.

God seems largely absent from the post-Nationalist landscape. One might claim, perhaps, as some sign of God-in-Nature the churches and Masonic lodges that so repeatedly appear in Laurence Aberhart's photographs. Yet his work permits no biblical inscriptions, angels, and such to appear, except those the human eye might plausibly see in the contemporary world. The clearest signs of the presence of the old *topos* of God-in-Nature are those churches and such inscriptions as are conveniently to be found on them, and such stone angels as occur in their cemeteries.

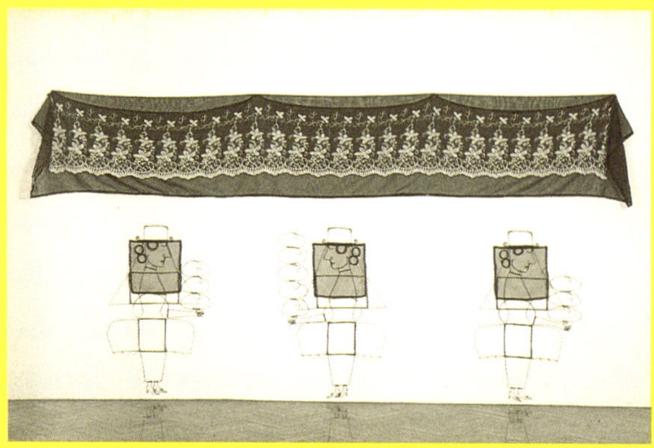

Jacqueline Fraser
The Long Persecution of the Dear Blessed Vision (With Three Sure Acts of Victory): No. 11, 1999
Wall installation: pins, electrical wire, Portuguese lace, organza
13 1/8 x 6 1/2 feet
Courtesy of the artist and Sue Crockford Gallery, Auckland, New Zealand

"Show me an angel and I'll paint one," the nineteenth-century realist painter Gustave Courbet is said to have declared. Aberhart, without breaking the realist rule, does manage to find angels, and to photograph them, in his repeated depictions of cemetery statuary. Or—inside one of his derelict churches, most likely—he finds a "Holy Picture" of the Mother of Sorrows. In the photograph he makes of it, *Mater Dolorosa* (1986), the state of the worn, stained, and insect-ravaged card adds its own poignance to the sacred image it bears—an anonymous oleograph which, were it whole, might well strike us as kitsch.[28] Two tears slide down its face. It is as if decay were the final sorrow.

Certainly found in a church, since it is pictured there, is Aberhart's St. Joseph holding the Christ Child. The saint stands amidst the silent flow of light from two windows to the sides. The holy pair are not, as they might be with McCahon, an apparition in the New Zealand landscape. Rather, their status as "real" is clearly given as representation in the second degree—as a plaster statue, of a debased Baroque, which has happened to survive in an abandoned-looking church, and to be photographed there. Or rather, if this pair *is* an apparition, it is its very unexpectedness in this deserted space that makes it so. If God and His saints exist, they do so now only in desolation or in these moments of small surprise.

Aberhart's depictions of churches, lodges, and tangible angels might, however, be read not as signs of the divine, but as simply historical records. They might seem to do no more than mark a European and Christian colonization, its traces left on the land by a merely human endeavor. Perhaps, as Alexa Johnson puts it, they "tell the story of *other* people's beliefs and hopes,"[29] and perhaps those people are irreparably confined to the past. After all, most of Aberhart's churchgoers are in their graves; and even those graves are falling into ruin. Nor will the wall built of hay bales around the vernacular Gothic church in an empty field be sufficient defense against a final ruination. It may be significant, in this respect, that Aberhart has described himself as no more than "an eclectic collector of cultural debris as it washes up, and before it disappears."[30]

McCahon once said, "I saw an angel in this land."[31] Aberhart can only say: "I saw a funerary statue of an angel." This manner of speaking the sacred is absolutely different from McCahon's. It is to say: here is where the sacred is placed in this society, such have been its actual conditions of use. This mode might serve, then, as no more than a parody, or as a nostalgia for a lost or decaying sense of the sacred, or as an anthropology, a sociology, a history. It proffers a view of the sacred only from the *outside*.

Consider Aberhart's *Taranaki (The Heavens Declare the Glory of God), New Plymouth, 14 May 1986*. Its domed observatory pointing up, like Mt. Taranaki/Egmont behind it, into the radiant emptiness, spells the period notion out: "THE GLORY OF GOD." Even science, Aberhart shows us, was once inextricable from Christianity. Significantly, however, in another Aberhart photograph, one letter of a variant of this inscription has been effaced, so that it reads: "THE GORY OF GOD." God is now a fragile concept, subject to vandalism and loss; His high claim can at any moment disintegrate into a derisory pun.[32]

The text lettered on the gate of *Maori Cemetery, Waimate, South Canterbury, 25 April 1999*, reads "Sacred Ground." While the word "Sacred" is still easily legible, the word "Ground" has faded nearly away, and that is precisely it: the sacred seems to have lost its ground, to be ungrounded now. And yet, in another sense, everything here *is* grounded—in this history, in this place. The fact alone of the Maori word "Waimate" in the title, compounded by the *tiki* figure painted on the apex of the gate, and the *kowhaiwhai* (rafter pattern) to its sides, means this cemetery can be found nowhere else but New Zealand.

And the glow of the sky over Aberhart's other country cemeteries; the bend of the black macracapa; the sweep of the dry, untended grass; the corrugated iron and red oxide; the wood and white lead of a Colonial Gothic; the broken marble of a Victorian faith and sentiment; the desolation of rust and peeling paint: all this is posed—in Curnow's words—as if it had been "marked or molded everywhere by peculiar pressures"—those "pressures arising" at once from the "isolation," the "physical character" and the "history" of place.[33] *Every* sign becomes signature—the "signature of a region."[34]

Aberhart's exactitude in naming his Maori cemetery photographs, giving not only the site, but also the town or area and the province, echoes the practice of the nineteenth-century topographers. In its surface inscriptions the topographic painting

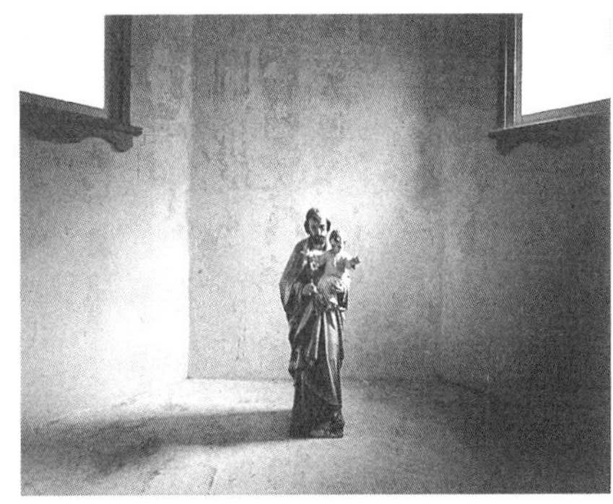

Laurence Aberhart
Interior [Joseph & Jesus], Lower Waihou, Hokianga Harbour, Northland, 3 May 1982, 1982
Gelatin-silver print
8 x 10 inches
Courtesy of Sue Crockford Gallery, Auckland, New Zealand

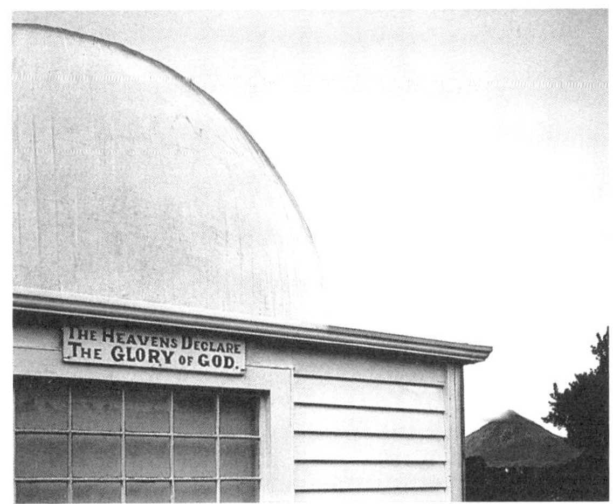

Laurence Aberhart
Taranaki (The Heavens Declare the Glory of God), New Plymouth, 14 May 1986, 1986
Silver contact print, gold and selenium toned
8 x 10 inches
Courtesy of Sue Crockford Gallery, Auckland, New Zealand

could properly record such details as the place of its making and its viewing point, and even its latitude and longitude and height above sea level. However, such inscriptions would be out of place on the surface of the grand machines of the Ideal and the Sublime, or on the face of the Picturesque. Sometimes, as was the nineteenth-century topographic photographer's habit, Aberhart writes his title directly on the photograph's surface.[35] Aberhart's art is topography: literally, in its etymology, a writing or graving of place.

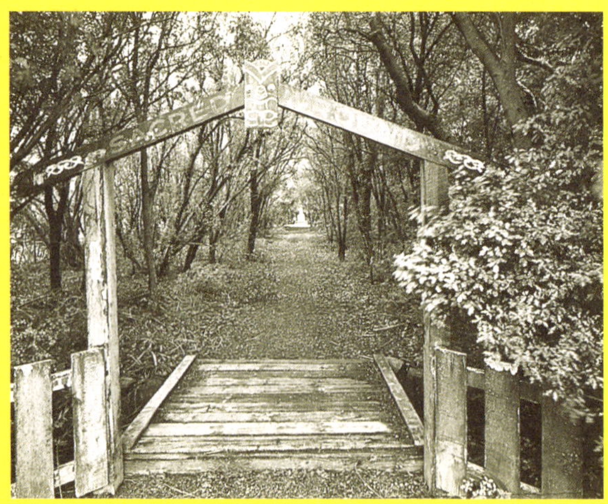

Laurence Aberhart
Maori Cemetery, Waimate, South Canterbury, 25 April 1999, 1999
Silver contact print, gold and selenium toned
8 x 10 inches
Courtesy of Sue Crockford Gallery, Auckland, New Zealand

Just as McCahon and his painter peers took up the conventions of colonial topographic painting, including the inscription of place names, Aberhart takes up the large 8 x 10-inch view camera of the colonial photographers. As always, a given technology is a shaper of style. The large-plate camera, whether used by nineteenth-century photographers or by Aberhart, requires very long exposures (up to one hour by day or twelve by night)—exposures which necessitate an entirely still subject, or one almost entirely still.[36]

Occasionally, Aberhart's photographs seem so close in subject and style to the landscapes of the colonial photographers that they might be distinguishable only by experts.[37] That he sometimes presents them with a curved top edge, or afloat in an aureole of darkness or light, or in the antique tones of sepia or platinum prints, makes them seem all the more akin to the works of some colonial albums.[38] Their modest size too relates them: they are never printed in the rivalrous, painterly size of, say, a Boyd Webb.

Yet, if Aberhart's art *is* a kind of topography, it is a topography subject to time. Within its stillness, everything is subject to change. The change may be momentary, as in the flutter of the leaves to the right of the Maori cemetery gate, registered as a ghostly blur. Or it may be slow, as in the rotting away of the planks of the entrance bridge, leaving their harder grain outstanding. Even the distant funerary monument to which that leafy path leads will be subject to inexorable decay.

It is significant, too, that Aberhart includes the date in his titles. Time is the theme, quite as much as place. Given this titling convention, we may easily measure the time elapsed between photographs. This is especially significant when Aberhart returns to one of his earlier subjects since, when he shows us the same subject at different dates, we are encouraged to scrutinize for signs of change—a bush has grown in front of the Masonic lodge where before there was none, someone has taken the notice board down from that blind window on the façade. There will always be such changes, one after another, until the building is gone.

That Aberhart should so often depict funereal and war memorial monuments suggests a persistent strain of mourning.[39] We may sense something of the same pleasurable sorrow over ruination in his depictions of buildings: it might seem he saw little else worth photographing but ruin and decay. He proffers what Alan Mulgan nicely calls, in his poem "The Eye and the Land," "The history writ in sagging weatherboards."[40] Aberhart displays, even in all the calm of this pictured world, a kind of catastrophic imagination. His innumerable photographs of colonial churches in dilapidation seem to anticipate a time when New Zealand will be in its entirety a country in ruins, when these wooden buildings, made from the destruction of the native forest, will themselves be subject to ruin, and will be replaced by the returning trees.

His art everywhere implies that the works of the colonizer are fragile and under threat. The abandonment and decay of his buildings, and the solitude of his cemeteries in empty fields, seem to threaten all human dwelling, whether of the living or the dead, reverting to the pre-human. Of the colonial project ruination is all that remains: a necropolis in an empty field. Such is the end of the flight to the Promised Land. We might well compare this slow catastrophe to the celebrative, jubilant, even triumphal presentations of the early colonial topographers: the stumps of the native forest fresh in their fields, newly sown grass, sailboats and a steamer on the river, a raw clay road, a new bridge and school, the first church. And all this on land newly alienated—or after the Land Wars literally confiscated—from its Maori inhabitants.

History is seen by Aberhart much as by Walter Benjamin: as "irresistible decay."[41] Aberhart makes of it an allegory of ruin. As Benjamin has it, "the appreciation of the transience of things, and the concern to redeem them for eternity, is one of the strongest impulses in allegory."[42] Yet also, in a counter-weaving of this melancholy pleasure in ruination, Aberhart provides an answer to the stock Pakeha feeling that there is here no history: these dilapidated buildings, these cemetery statues, these war memorial monuments are what the English painter John Piper once called "the visible effects of history in terms of decay."[43]

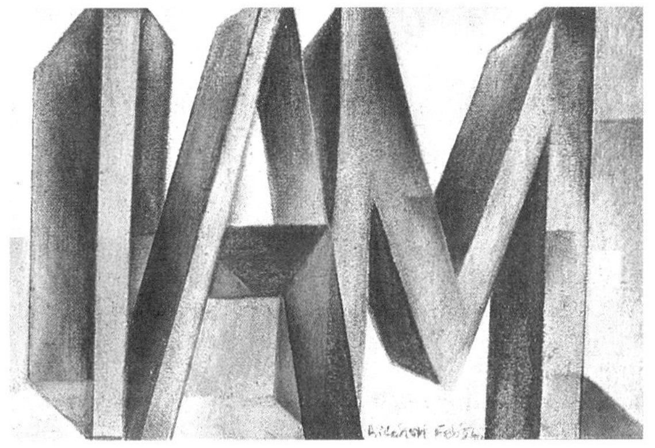

Colin McCahon
I Am, 1954
Oil on hessian
14 1/2 x 22 1/8 inches
Charles Brasch Bequest, 1973. Courtesy of the McCahon Research and Publication Trust

Michael Parekowhai's sculpture *The Indefinite Article* (1990) is closely based on McCahon's painting *I Am* (1954). In order to see what Parekowhai is up to here, we should establish who, or what, is *McCahon's* "I"?

McCahon's "I" is perhaps the "I" which has finally learned to stand upright in New Zealand, the "I" of which Curnow dreams, when he writes:

> Not I, some child, born in a marvelous year,
> Will learn the trick of standing upright here.[44]

It is, perhaps, that new New Zealand personage whom the Nationalists sought, now separable at last from Mother England, an example of that successful adaptation on these isles which may proudly proclaim the "I" at once of nation, of the New Zealand painter, and of New Zealand painting itself—and all this, most grandly, in the self-constituting Word of God announcing: *"I AM."*

Yet the way this "I AM" is woven from a self-contradictory, Cubist space, whose forms, given their ambiguous transparencies, are paradoxically at once behind and in front of each other, marks the very precariousness of any proper selfhood in a culture as yet insufficiently formed. The "I" named here behaves in time as its forms behave in the space of the picture: it is at once behind and before itself. One must say "I" in order that there be an "I" standing behind one, proven and made substantial by its lasting existence in time; and one must say "I" so as to enter the space of the future selfhood one's utterance simultaneously opens.

The task is to embody a new, properly national "I," as if, in poet Charles Brasch's words, in a "raw colonial society," "to create order for the first time, in a wilderness that is without form and very nearly void."[45] Into that void, which is the lack of a properly New Zealand culture, the original "I" of the artist's being must be placed, making the culture's first, self-constituting mark in the nothingness. This "I" of a new Nationalist culture creates itself, as in the self-creating Word of the Judeo-Christian God, announcing to Moses in Exodus 3:14: "I AM THAT I AM."

Despite its marks of uncertainty, what we see in McCahon's *I Am* is the moment of a particularly heightened consciousness: the self-inventing of a New Zealand "I"—that "I" which, so it is the artist's pride to say, might stand for all New Zealanders. As Declan Kebard has remarked of a similar Irish search for national self-identity: "In such a transaction, the 'I' is necessarily precarious or inchoate, disappearing or scarcely born; but it is the identity towards which the lyric moves that is its *raison d'être*."[46]

However, Parekowhai's *The Indefinite Article*, modeled though it flagrantly is on McCahon's *I Am*, is concerned with quite another politics of identity. It suggests that the New Zealand space into which McCahon plants his original "I" is not, after all, a "void," the empty space awaiting the Promised Land of a New Zealand culture. By means of a bilingual pun in its sculpted words, *The Indefinite Article* recalls that Maori culture was already present in this alleged void, and had been for centuries present, when Pakeha Nationalists took it upon themselves to invent a culture there.

In English, the sculpted words "I am he" might mean: "I am he, *I* am the one awaited—I, not McCahon." In Maori, on the other hand, they may mean "I am wrong," since one meaning of *he* is "wrong"—so completely undermining the high claim of the English sentence. If we hear the "he" in Maori, Parekowhai is *not* the one. Rather, he asserts "I am wrong in claiming to be so." Another meaning of the Maori *he*—and this is the meaning to which Parekowhai's title refers—is the indefinite article, as in "a" or "some." Accordingly, Parekowhai's sculpture might say: "I find my identity in a larger group—that of Maori." It might claim: "I am many." I am defined in relation to ancestors and kin.

Again, the letters "I am he" may be read as a near-miss anagram of their maker's first or "Christian" name, Michael: an anagram missing the C and L. What is missing is not random, however, nor the mark of an anagrammatical incompetence: it is the two letters of the name not present in the Maori alphabet. Of course, the artist's name is already a conjunction of disparate parts: Michael, European: Parekowhai, Maori. Parekowhai here deletes his Maori name or self, "Parekowhai," in offering the elements of only his first name, "Michael"; but he does so by means of the language of his Maori self, in its transcription into the English alphabet. This is a complex and weird self-structuring, in which Pakeha and Maori are shown to be inextricably intermeshed, definable only in relation to each other—each irretrievably changed by the other from the first moment of contact.

For Parekowhai, then, the self-constituting "I" is irreparably split. It exists only in its double reading. It is no longer possible, as the Pakeha McCahon tried to do, to assert an "I" for all New Zealanders. New Zealand now defines itself as *bi*-cultural—even in, or especially in, state ideology. And if

Parekowhai purely as an *artist* figure constructs a persona here, it too is split, arriving belatedly, finding itself only in reference to, in rivalrous struggle with, and in high homage to that other, prior, more famous McCahonian "I."

During the Nationalist time, the "grand view" came to be associated with the art of over-forties hobbyists.[47] It came to be tarred, too, with the touristic that roamed the country as if with a stranger's eye, seeking grandiose and spectacular spots; while the more subtle, vigilant, true artist's eye came to be praised for seeking, with a knowing love, the hidden truths of the non-touristic *spaces between.* As Auckland City Art Gallery Director Peter Tomory wrote, the "emphasis is on the hyphenations between the eye blinding attractions of the scenic tourist pamphlet."[48]

So, in *The Listener (Head)* and in *The Green Plain* (1948) McCahon could present the barest and dullest of plains, with the latter appearing, in its striking horizontality, as almost literally a hyphen between. Still more characteristically, he could offer no more than the silhouette of a dark hill against a white sky, that very "ordinariness" which a tourist's snap will ignore. And he could proclaim: "Nor is this the tourist's landscape we so often see painted. I am dealing with the essential monotony of this land, 'a landscape with too few lovers'..."[49] In *The Listener,* as in all of Nationalist art, the solitary sensibility is posed precisely *against* tourist chatter. It seeks a beauty less obvious, more difficult, more profound.

For a number of post-Nationalist artists, however, these imperatives have lost their force. For them, the fascinating thing is not "the hyphenations between," but rather the very thing the Nationalists disallowed—"the eye blinding attractions of the scenic." Forbidden to Nationalist high-art discourse—which indeed defined itself precisely against such low cultural forms—the mass-cultural rhetoric of tourism and the landscape of leisure are now examined—and enjoyed—by such artists as Gavin Hipkins.

If for McCahon and his peers the aim was to get behind or, rather, *between* the too-showy spectacles of the tourist in order to uncover a putative "real New Zealand," for post-Nationalist artists things are quite otherwise. There is no getting behind the cultural, so their art suggests, there is nothing behind. Nature comes to us already as Culture, as a picture of one kind or another, whether painted by art high or low: the task is to make critical and pleasurable play with this condition.

Hence Hipkins's investigation in *The Homely* (1998-2000) of the Promised Land of the postcard or "tourist pamphlet." His are not so much views of Nature than an investigation of the mass cultural codes of its viewing. For Hipkins, New Zealand is no longer as it had been for McCahon, "a landscape with too few

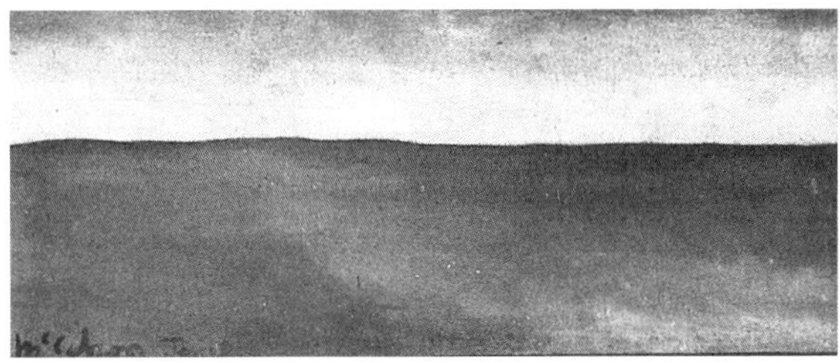

Colin McCahon
The Green Plain, 1948
Oil on canvas
13 7/8 x 35 inches
Courtesy of the McCahon Research and Publication Trust

lovers."[50] It is a landscape promiscuously loved.

If Hipkins shows a lighthouse, it is that famous one on New Zealand's northernmost tip at Te Reinga, the burden of innumerable postcards. If he treats a tree at night it will not be lit by moon and stars, it will be alive with "fairy lights," the product of human artifice rather than the divine illumination of a McCahon. A Hipkins tree trunk is found not in a forest but, more conveniently for the admiring eye, inside a building. And should he show a Maori gate, it will not be the gate to a Maori cemetery, Aberhart's melancholy site of history and death; rather, it will open to the pleasures of the narrow gauge rail of a park's miniature train. This is the topography of the leisure industry, or of touristic commerce—the landscapes of a Sublime, Ideal, and Picturesque fallen from the place they once enjoyed in high art. What remains after this fall is landscape not as site of the Spirit, but landscape as the site of Capital.

Of course, none of this denies the New Zealand landscape the remnants of a certain beauty. It is perhaps precisely such remnants that Hipkins seeks in the nostalgia of his soft-focus blur—a blur entirely un-topographic, in flight towards romance.

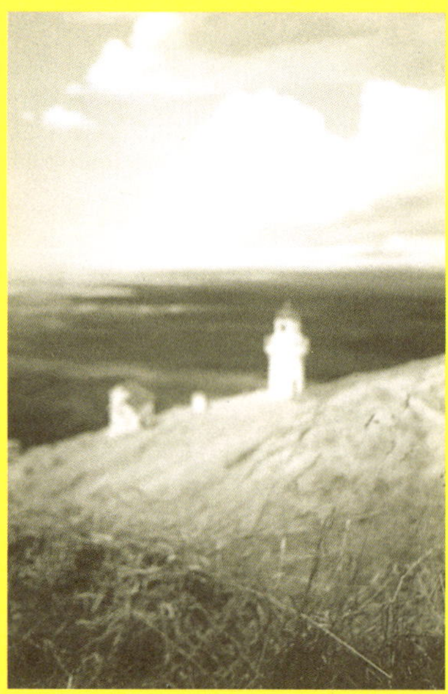

Gavin Hipkins
The Homely: Dunedin (Landscape), 1999
C-type print, edition of 12
15 5/8 x 23 3/8 inches
Courtesy of Hamish McKay Gallery, Wellington

The Nationalist dream of the "Promised Land" is now irreparably damaged or dead. If there is to be a New Zealand utopia, it will be one that has asked the question the Nationalists refused to: What *was* the "Great Silence" Nationalism heard in the land? Might it be, as Paul Carter harshly claims, no more than "a silencing of the other," a "villification and conquest of other sounds, the deafening accompaniment of colonialism"?[51] Today, one might say it was the silencing of Maori voice and Maori history so that the Nationalist movement might seem the first to speak in this place. At the very least, those who heard the "Great Silence" were deaf to all Maori voices. However, the very success of works like Parekowhai's and Fraser's makes such deafness impossible today: the presence of such works marks the end of the old Nationalist version of the flight to the Promised Land. Yet, the "better country" the Nationalists were seeking is perhaps still sought today, under different names and with different hopes.

1. New Zealand Nationalist high culture may be defined as that painting and writing, roughly between 1930 and 1970, which sought to define the essence of New Zealand and to create a specifically New Zealand School.
2. With that doubleness or tripleness of meaning typical of McCahon, the pillars of the airplane windows here may represent not only the "big tree" of the inscription, but also the pillar of cloud by day and fire by night of Exodus 13:21, in which God conceals and manifests Himself to lead the way through the wilderness. (I owe this suggestion to the late Bryce Nichol, from "The Smoke and the Fire," an unpublished essay held as a memorial to him in the School of Fine Arts Library, University of Auckland, 1996.)
3. The iconography comes from stock symbols of fifteenth-century Flemish and Italian paintings of the Annunciation, a fact that reinforces my reading of this painting as an Annunciation to McCahon, and a divine mandating of his vision.
4. *Was This The Promised Land?* (1962) is one of a group of related works—*The Promised Land; Another Promised Land; Was This The Promised Land (gold, white and black); The Promised Land (gold and black sky)*—exhibited at the Durham Street Gallery of the Canterbury Society of Arts, Christchurch, September 1962.
5. Colin McCahon, in a letter to Nola Barron, 19 December 1969, photocopy in my possession, kindly given to me by Barron.
6. European, or non-Maori, New Zealander.
7. Jacques Derrida, "This Strange Institution Called Literature: An Interview with Jacques Derrida," in *Acts of Literature*, ed. Derek Attridge (New York: Routledge, 1992), 299. (In the words quoted, Derrida was speaking of the writer's responsibility towards democracy.)
8. *Ibid.*
9. *Ibid.*
10. Allen Curnow, "The Axe," in *Four Plays* (Wellington: A. H. and A. W. Reed, 1972), 27.
11. Keith Sinclair, "Memories of T. H. Scott (1918–60)," *Landfall* 14, no. 2 (June 1960): 182.
12. M. H. Holcroft, *Discovered Isles: A Trilogy. The Deepening Stream; The Waiting Hills; Encircling Seas* (Christchurch: Caxton Press, 1950), 92.
13. Colin McCahon, *Necessary Protection*, exh. cat. (Auckland: Barry Lett Gallery, 1971), unpaginated. McCahon here refers to his Necessary Protection drawings which "began with one made for John Caselberg's book *Chart to My Country*."
14. Denys Trussell, "Landscape, Civilisation and New Zealanders," *Art New Zealand* 7 (1977): 17.
15. Allen Curnow, "Introduction," in *A Book of New Zealand Verse, 1923–45* (Christchurch: Caxton Press, 1945), 51.
16. *Ibid.*, 50–51.
17. Allen Curnow, "Introduction," in *The Penguin Book of New Zealand Verse* (Harmondsworth, England: Penguin, 1960), 20.
18. In the case, for instance, of the self-portrait spectator figure in the foreground of Augustus Earle's *Distant View of the Bay of Islands* (1827), it would be more exact to speak of the proto-colonial gaze, since New Zealand was not officially declared a colony until 1840. For these nineteenth-century spectator figures, see my *Frames on the Land: Early Landscape Painting in New Zealand* (Auckland: Collins, 1983), especially 12 and 42–44; and, for further detail, my "Spectator Figures in Some New Zealand Paintings and Prints," *Art New Zealand* 23 (1982): 40–45.
19. Allen Curnow, in Curnow and Ngaio Marsh, "A Dialogue by Way of Introduction," *First Yearbook of the Arts in New Zealand* (Wellington: H. H. Tombs, 1945), 2.
20. Matthew Arnold, cited as epigraph, in Curnow, *A Book of New Zealand Verse*, 15.
21. Holcroft, *Discovered Isles*, 86. My italics.
22. Curnow, *A Book of New Zealand Verse*, 15.
23. Denys Trussell, "Landscape, Civilisation and New Zealanders," 17.
24. These words were applied by Fraser to Goat Island (Mapoutahi) on ten drawings from a set accompanying her sculpture *The Benediction of Goat Island Our Saviour (With Three Sure Acts of Victory)*, in its exhibition of the same title at Sue Crockford Gallery, Auckland, 1998.
25. These words were applied by Fraser to Goat Island (Mapoutahi) on the wall text accompanying the exhibition "The Benediction of Goat Island Our Saviour."
26. "The Great Silence" is a sub-chapter heading and often-repeated phrase in Holcroft, *Discovered Isles*. See, for instance, chapter 5, sub-chapter 3, 146.
27. It should be acknowledged, however, that from 1962 onward McCahon's paintings began to include Maori motifs and Maori inscriptions. See Gordon H. Brown, Chapter 16, "Under the Prow of the Great Canoe," in *Colin McCahon: Artist* (Wellington: A.H. & A.W. Reed, 1984); and Francis Pound, Chapter 4, "McCahon and Maori," in *The Space Between: Pakeha Use of Maori Motifs in Modernist New Zealand Art* (Auckland: Workshop Press, 1994).
28. Of course, the question of the aesthetic quality, or its lack, of the original in Aberhart's *Mater Dolorosa* was hardly at issue when it fulfilled its initial function. This oleograph was once supra-aesthetically received—revered and exalted in the act of worship. Now its consumption is aesthetic alone. This shift—or fall, as some would say—is marked too by a radical shift in site. It has left the white wall of its church to alight on the white wall of the gallery, the museum, the modernist house, or, as here, the miniaturized white wall of the exhibition-catalogue page.
29. Alexa Johnson, "Christianity in New Zealand Art," in *Headlands: Thinking Through New Zealand Art*, exh. cat. (Sydney: Museum of Contemporary Art, 1992), 108. My italics.
30. Laurence Aberhart, in Johnson, "Christianity in New Zealand Art," 108.
31. Colin McCahon, "Beginnings," *Landfall* 20, no. 4 (December 1966): 363.
32. To a perhaps over-zealous iconographer, this ruination of "glory" by "gory" might seem a protest against the murderous history of the Christian faith and its nearly two thousand years of massacre.
33. Curnow, *The Penguin Book of New Zealand Verse*, 51.
34. *Ibid.*, 17.
35. Such surface inscriptions are confined to Aberhart's early works, between 1980 and 1984.
36. An instance of Aberhart's night exposures is *Taranaki from Oeo Road, Under Moonlight, 27–28 September 1999*.
37. Alfred Burton (1843–1914), for instance, in his gelatin-silver print *Te Tokanganui a Noho* from the series The Maori at Home, depicts the interior of a meeting house in a manner reminiscent of Aberhart's depictions of similar subjects.
38. As with the curved top, for instance, of the silver contact print, gold and selenium toned *Landscape near Mohaka, 5 June 1989*.
39. It is significant that Aberhart uses the French way of titling still life, *nature morte*. For instance: *Nature Morte (Silence), Wanganui, 10 February 1986; Nature Morte (Osteology), Wanganui Museum, 27 February 1986*; and *Nature Morte (Fish), Wanganui Museum, 11 February 1986*. Aberhart's Nature is a dead Nature.
40. Alan Mulgan, "The Eye and the Land," in *Golden Wedding and Other Poems* (Christchurch: Caxton Press, 1964), 46. Weatherboards are the New Zealand equivalent to American clapboards.
41. Walter Benjamin, *The Origins of German Tragic Drama* (London: New Left Books, 1977), 178.
42. Walter Benjamin, cited in Richard Wolin, *Walter Benjamin* (New York: Columbia University Press, 1982), 71.
43. John Piper, "Pleasing Decay," *Architectural Review* (September 1947), cited in Rose Macaulay, *The Pleasure of Ruins* (London: Thames and Hudson, 1984), 23.
44. Allen Curnow, "Attitudes for a New Zealand Poet," in *A Book of New Zealand Verse*, 166.
45. Charles Brasch, "Notes," *Landfall* 11, no. 1 (March 1957): 3.
46. Declan Kebard, *Inventing Ireland* (London: Jonathan Cape, 1995), 117. Kebard's book has been helpful throughout my analysis of the McCahonian "I".
47. Charles Brasch, "Notes," *Landfall* 4, no. 4 (December 1950): 281. Brasch was mocking the amateur art of the then-powerful Art Societies. Before the development of the gallery system, they were the main exhibiting and selling spaces for New Zealand art.
48. Peter Tomory, "Imaginary Islands and Floating Reefs: The Romantic Image in New Zealand Painting," *Ascent* 1, no. 2 (July 1968): 16.
49. McCahon, in Tony Green, "Colin McCahon's Paintings and Drawings at the Ikon Gallery," *Bulletin of New Zealand Art History* 2 (1974): 35.
50. This phrase is famously inscribed on Colin McCahon's *Northland Panels* (1958).
51. Paul Carter, "Repetitions at Night: Mimicry, Noise and Context," in Ross Gibson, ed., *Exchanges: Cross-Cultural Encounters in the Pacific* (Sydney: Museum of Sydney, 1996), 76–79.

Just What Is It that Makes the Term Global-Local So Widely Cited, Yet So Annoying?[1]

Lee Weng Choy

My title derives, of course, from the Richard Hamilton collage *Just what is it that makes today's homes so different, so appealing?* (1956)—you know, the one with the muscle-man holding a gigantic Tootsie Pop, the one that inaugurated the appearance of the word "Pop" in modern art. Initially, I had thought to call the essay "Citing and Re-siting Singapore in the Global-Local Spectacle." That title, while less catchy, would have better described my theme. But I decided against it because I didn't want to add to the circulation of the term "global-local" without at least qualifying it with some sarcasm. My problem with the term is that, for the most part, the global-local tensions it refers to are already subsumed by the logic of globalization and late capitalism. It signifies the further penetration of global capitalism into the "local," then presents this "local" as *authentic*. "Global-local" reminds me of that other buzzword, "New Asia." These terms suggest an increasing conflation of arts and cultural discourse with the idiom of national—even "transnational"—tourism boards. (What are today's spectacles—art biennials, world expos—if not *also* a form of transnational tourism?) The phenomena these terms refer to are arguably less the local vis-à-vis the global, or the contemporary renaissance of tradition, than, to coin another term, the "authenti-kitsch."[2]

But why Singapore? What could this small island city-state be representative of? How does it figure in the imagining of the "Pacific Rim," particularly in terms of topography and landscape? And what are the relationships between the "global-local," "spectacle," and "landscape"? I intend to address these questions by taking a look at certain images of Singapore. In the process, I hope to reveal the dynamics involved in *looking*, not just at this island that aspires to be a global city, but at the more global desire for the "local" and for "location." Moreover, I hope to look not just *at* Singapore, but *from* and *through* it.

To start an essay about Singapore and the global-local by citing Pop art may seem like forcing a tenuous connection. Singapore does not figure much in the history of Pop, nor does Pop figure all that much in Singapore art. What is at stake, however, is the condition of world art after Pop. Arthur Danto argues that Pop, together with Minimalism, marked a

mutation in the historical nature of art itself. For Danto, "Pop and Minimalism were in effect philosophical exercises, for each was groping toward something that had finally to be recognized by philosophy itself: whatever was to distinguish art from reality was not going to be something evident to the eye."[3] Andy Warhol's *Brillo Box* looks exactly like a commercially manufactured one. Danto privileges Pop and Minimalism not just because—like all modern art—they confront the art movements that precede them—but because they confront the *entire* self-revolutionizing history of modern art. Pop and Minimalism usher in the final break between "art" and "image," a break initiated decades earlier by Marcel Duchamp and his readymades. This break between "art" and "image" radically opens up the field of art; as Danto sees it, this opening is so radical, it marks the "End of Art," that is, the end of a particular history of art. Contemporary art, what Danto calls "post-historical art," is the art of radical pluralism: everything and anything, from every- and anywhere, can be, and does get cited and re-sited as art.

Contemporary art in Singapore is emblematic of this "post-historical" condition. On the one hand, this seems the most obvious point to make. Singapore, like any other contemporary metropolis, is a hyperreal city of signs—although thankfully the forces of late capitalism haven't quite finalized the break between "reality" and "image" On the other hand, the claim seems complicated, for how does the end of modern Western art history converge with contemporary art practice in a place like Singapore?

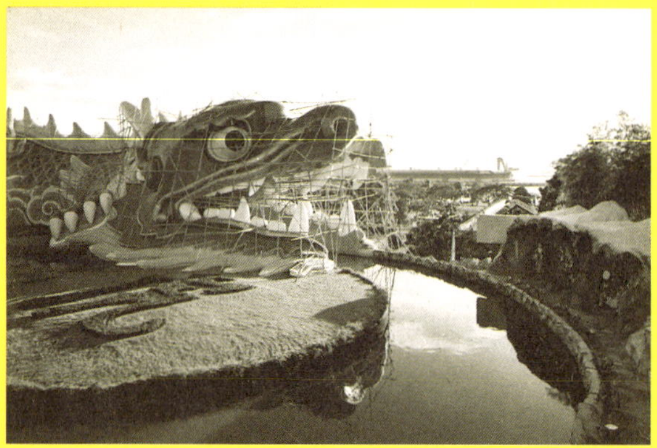

Lucas Jodogne
Untitled, from *Bodiless Dragon,* 1998

Throughout the 1990s, the Singapore government has increasingly emphasized the importance of the arts for the nation. In 1989, a landmark report by the Advisory Council on Culture and the Arts led to the creation of institutions like the National Arts Council, the National Heritage Board, the Singapore Art Museum, and the soon-to-be-completed, $300-million-plus arts center, The Esplanade. In March 2000, another report, the ostentatiously named "Renaissance City Report," presented an update of the government's vision to promote arts and culture. As Minister for Information and the Arts Lee Yock Suan announced, there are two aims: "First, it is to establish Singapore as a global city of the arts. We want to position Singapore as a key city in Asia and as one of the cultural centers in the world. The idea is to be one of the top cities in the world to live, work and play in... Second, it is to provide cultural ballast in our nation-building efforts."[4]

To those familiar with Singapore this script yields no surprise. Like most everything else, the arts are circumscribed by the instrumentalist logic of the trinity of state/government /ruling party (in Singapore these three political mechanisms have effectively merged into one). The development of the arts is subsumed by the always more primary agenda of fueling a vibrant economy and maintaining a politically "stable" society. As to be expected, the rise of East Asia's fortunes during the 1980s was accompanied by assertions from various quarters about

the ideology of "Asian Values." Disproportionate to its size in global affairs, Singapore claimed a place in the world's imagination by staking a vanguard role in articulating an *Asian* modernity. But developing an economy that, after a generation, can boast a per capita Gross National Product higher than that of Great Britain, its former colonizer, is not the same as becoming a cultural capital of Asia.

No doubt various individual artists and arts groups from Singapore will become better appreciated inside and outside the country. And in more than a few cases the acclaim will be well deserved. As for the Singapore "arts scene," the commonplace criticism is that one cannot *plan* the development of art and culture. Another criticism often made about the government's plans for the arts is that its dominant position and relatively closed-minded disposition is what will hold the arts back in the end, notwithstanding all the investment and hype. So if one made a comparison between Singapore and a city that has indeed "arrived" as a cultural capital—say London, Paris, or New York—one would expect the latter to have a more open society, the arts scene to have developed over time organically, and so on. Such a comparison, however, obscures other issues at stake.

I'm not sure if anyone talks about Brisbane as a "global city of the arts," but in the 1990s this relatively unheard-of Australian town put itself on the world art map as the host city of one of the most significant art events to represent the Asia-Pacific region. What Singapore says it wants to do, Brisbane seems to have done, at least in terms of contemporary visual art. Brisbane's Queensland Art Gallery (QAG) has been exhibiting the Asia-Pacific Triennial of Contemporary Art (APT) since 1993. Over 230 artists and 280 curators, advisers, and writers from twenty countries and regions have participated in the three triennials to date, and more than 350,000 persons have visited the exhibitions.[5]

Singapore has yet to make the material, social and intellectual investments in the visual arts that Brisbane has made. And the support from the Queensland government is far more hands-off than that of Singapore's. Given time, however, Singaporean society will become more open—even the government admits that. But rather than signal an impending transformation, this expectation belies a continuity. Since independence, Singapore has embraced globalization, and while that requires a certain openness (to foreign investment, markets, and business innovation), it has always also come with a high degree of control (of labor, politics, and society). When it comes to the arts, there is still the will to discipline, and ever more sophisticated forms of control are being devised. Nonetheless, rather than emphasize their differences in achievement, strategy, and agenda, my juxtaposition of Brisbane and Singapore is meant to suggest a common underlying logic: both cities are attempting to position themselves as gateways to "Asia"—and in Brisbane's case, the "Pacific" as well.

In her APT3 catalog essay, "Journey Without Maps: The Asia Pacific Triennial," QAG Deputy Director Caroline Turner contended that:

> Geography has not been an objective in itself, but a means of achieving a focus and allowing opportunities for artists from this region who had, and indeed still have, fewer opportunities for their work to be included in international exhibitions, although this is changing. Many of the artists represented in the three Triennials have an international reputation and, for some at least, the Triennial has played a part in bringing their work to world attention. The Triennial has never been a government-to-government project about official exchanges, and nor have artists been chosen to "represent" a country. Rather, invitations have been extended to them to participate as individuals, and this has meant that they can at times express their ideas in ways that are not possible in official exhibitions.[6]

Yet for all these assertions and efforts to emphasize "Crossing Borders"—a newly introduced curatorial category in addition to the previous national ones—APT3 still came across mainly as a collection of representations of ethnic and cultural geography. It's just that some of the stars of the show are now framed by cross-cultural rather than mono-cultural maps. APT3's curatorial interventions weren't radical enough—they didn't cut deep enough into the roots of the encompassing global-local spectacle. The APT—if not by expressed intent, then by structural default—still functions as a discursive and event center for *geo-graphing* the arts and culture of the Asia-Pacific in ways that *maintain* rather than undo boundaries.[7] The spectacle of the global-local is precisely about *consuming difference*. It's as if these hubs of global-local consumption—"hub" especially in the sense that there is a claim for a certain neutrality, universality or openness—take "nourishment from the margins," as Lucy Davis has put it.[8] The "Other" has to be maintained as different in order to be "Other," and yet this difference is homogenized through consumption; for rather than any *real* local, it is the re-framed and reconstituted global-local that is displayed for global and local consumption.

So how does one move beyond the consumerist geography of the global-local? I'm not sure. For APT3, I was the Singapore-based co-curator, and at the conference, my "representation" of the island city-state was deliberately problematic, although I didn't explicitly criticize the APT as a global-local spectacle. (At events like these, there's always at least one conference panelist who will present a critique of the whole thing. It's as if they are invited to do exactly that: the criticism of the spectacle is the last ingredient without which it could not be constituted.) For my own presentation, one could say that I speculated grandly on the future of world contemporary art. If I didn't speak about Singapore, I did speak somewhat like a Singaporean. Speculating about the future is what political and business leaders here like to do, even though their notion of the future is not always matched by a deep understanding of the past—Singapore is a society of "tomorrow." (Incidentally, Hamilton's *Just what is it* was first exhibited at a show called "This Is Tomorrow.") But the sense of time in Singapore is not like the time of Pop art. It is more like that of the *popularization* of Pop—an ahistorical contemporary.

Time in Singapore is unlike time anywhere else I've been. Whenever I visit, for example, a place where I used to live, like the San Francisco Bay Area, I experience multiple times—decades. I visit neighborhoods that seem largely unchanged since I first saw them. If I were to visit, say, London or Beijing, I'd expect to experience centuries; in Delhi, maybe millennia. But in Singapore, there seems to be only one time—the present—a hurried one, on the verge of tomorrow. Old buildings wear worried faces—from being under siege, waiting to be knocked down, or worse, "renovated." Life may be more hectic in Hong Kong, Tokyo, or New York, but I don't know of any other place where it feels like everyone marches in the same step. The pace, while not the fastest on the planet, is possibly the most persistent. This relentless "present" in Singapore is of course not entirely omnipresent; if it were, then this truly would be utopia.

As an ideal it characterizes a city of appropriation par excellence; past, future—all time is only one time, the present time. It is an ideal vividly manifest in Singapore's wish to become the most global-local place of them all. Sanjay Krishnan has written how "scaffolding seems the only unchanging feature in a city that sees itself in permanent transition… [it] is at once a symbol of the ugliness and the breathtaking energy of the desire for renewal or 'speed,' the desire to change rapidly and without remorse."[9]

In Lucas Jodogne's book of photographs, *Singapore: Views on the Urban Landscape*, [10] there is a picture of an open-mouthed, Chinese dragon statue covered by an almost delicate net of bamboo scaffolding. In the background a few loading cranes are in view, which resonate subtly with the bamboo stakes in the foreground. (Jodogne deliberately didn't caption his photos, so as not to map locations with their names, but give primacy to the pictorial composition.) Early traders found it difficult to sail into Keppel Harbor because of the rough tides, currents, and rocks, but also because of the *kelongs* and *pagar* (fish traps and wooden stakes) that radiated out from the capes at both entrances to the harbor. Indeed, it was these fang-like *kelongs* and *pagar* that gave rise to its old nickname, the "Dragon's Mouth."[11] The dragon statue in the photo is from the theme park Haw Par Villa, which means "Villa of the Tiger and Leopard." Created by Aw Boon Haw, who with his brother started the highly successful Tiger Balm ointment brand, the park has a collection of over one thousand painted cement statues and 150 giant tableaux centered around Chinese folklore, legends, history, and Confucian and Taoist ideology. Aw's intention for the park was to help teach and preserve Chinese values. In 1985, the government acquired and leased it to a publishing company, which then reconstructed it as a commercial theme-park enterprise. I think the aspiration was to turn it into something like a Disneyland of Chinese mythology. It has not been very profitable. Undaunted, the Singapore Tourism Board still pushes the park as a major tourist attraction; its official pocket-guide books beckon tourists to "enjoy the beautiful landscaping."

Jodogne's photos juxtapose the Singapore state's reflex to turn its cultural heritage into global-local authenti-kitsch with his own interest in classical, European landscape composition. While "landscape" is not "nature" so much as a convention of presenting it, the function of this convention has been to give the viewer *not* an *image* but a *sense* of rootedness. By "sense" I mean an embodiment of memory; landscapes are psychological constructions of a certain duration or permanence. In Singapore, "landscape" is like an oxymoron—not so much because the landscape changes rapidly, but because development has been so relentless that the island has become this global-local hub or interzone. Indeed, *spectacle*—which is about the triumph of the *image* over everything else—is a form of anti-landscape.

On one of my visits to San Francisco, I was reminded of an aspect of city life that is so obvious, but one that I had forgotten: that "nature" is not absent, but in fact abounds in the city. The city's most famous landmark, the Golden Gate Bridge, is spectacular precisely because of that combination of natural splendor and civil engineering. The bridge heightens, frames our awareness of the hills and mountains, the mouth of the bay opening into the Pacific; yet it is these same surroundings which frame and make the bridge so pretty. One is always looking at a view in San Francisco: whether at the Golden Gate and Marin County from some hill in the city, or the city itself while driving along a windy road in the Oakland hills. Sure, the San Francisco Bay Area is intensely developed and urban, but everywhere "nature" is there—indeed, it is the frame of almost every view.

We may think that concrete, steel, glass, and asphalt dominate the cityscapes of today, but sometimes what gives a particular corner of town its character are its trees or hills. What is a city without its parks? What apartment block is completely bereft of potted plants and pets? Much as we urban dwellers drive nature away, we also always try to reintroduce it into the metropolis. For all our efforts to control, to order, to be mechanical and technological, one could say that "nature"—in the many roles it plays, the many ways we imagine it (from the beautiful, pastoral, opposite-of-culture, or the unconscious)—is the repressed of the city, which inevitably returns.

In Singapore, one could exaggerate a little and say there is landscaping but no landscape. Of all the capital cities in Southeast Asia, Singapore is the greenest. The tree-lined drive from the airport into town certainly gives a good impression to the newly arrived. But somehow, I want more—this is the tropics. One of my fantasies is for the city's "Main Street," Orchard Road, to be covered by a canopy of tropical forest, with the buildings punching through. Nature is everywhere in Singapore, but the enduring experience of this city is of the single-minded will for mastery over it. This will is of course what has characterized urbanization. What is notable about Singapore is how thorough this will has been: hills have been flattened and land reclaimed to expand its surface area, and as I've suggested, even time—arguably nature at its most abstract—seems to have been "mastered."

The society of the spectacle isn't an invention of Singapore, of course, as much as it may sometimes feel that way for those of us who live here and read French theory. Miles Orvell, in "Understanding Disneyland: American Mass Culture and the European Gaze,"[12] argues how that quintessential American spectacle, Disneyland, is "a fateful symptom of postmodern culture." The occasion for Orvell's essay was the opening of EuroDisney in France. Obviously, many of Europe's intellectuals were not pleased. For Jean Baudrillard, "America functions, vis-à-vis Europe, as a kind of deliberate oxymoron… it is a sign of the primitive, yet also a sign of the future." Baudrillard still registers a distance between Europe and America. Umberto Eco, in contrast, "*connects* the two cultures, offering us a view of America that assimilates it to the popular European sensibility." That is, America is Europe remade as popular culture. Yet Orvell believes that EuroDisney is not simply "low" culture, but "a convergence of spheres, if not an erasure of the boundaries between the playful, historically allusive tendencies of postmodern art and the playful, thematically allusive nature of Disney." No longer just kitsch, Disney has evolved into authenti-kitsch.

Orvell's use of the term "postmodern," however, may no longer be adequate for theorizing globalization. The "post" tends to presume particular conditions of modernism from which it then takes off. Perhaps "schizo-chronic" might better describe how modernity continues to revolutionize itself of late. The "newest" arenas of modernity simultaneously advance the cultural forms of the past even as they lag behind the previous arenas in cultural development. The triumph of American painting in the 1950s was an overtaking of Europe without a catching-up. New York can never match the density of Paris's cultural history. But a certain erasure of boundaries does occur: "Europeanism" was modernity's first universalism, and while "Americanism" may have surpassed Europeanism, we don't use the phrase "American modernity" so much as "Western modernity." America has both assimilated Europe and been assimilated by the grand trajectory of Europe. And Asia? Or the rest of the world for that matter? The European gaze on America is now reproduced not just as a EuroAmerican but a *global* gaze on Asia. Asia is the new sign of the primitive and the future. Asia assimilates and has been assimilated. And Singapore? Singapore is the exemplary sign of Asian authenti-kitsch.

Can there be art in a world dominated by authenti-kitsch? I don't see why not. But for the contemporary artist who necessarily deals with representations always already inside the global-local spectacle, there is no "outside" from which to present a critique—though that doesn't mean one has to sit neatly within the boundaries. As part of Nokia Singapore Art 1999, the equivalent of the Singapore Biennial, Lim Tzay Chuen placed a gigantic, pink toy ladder up against the front of the Singapore Art Museum (SAM). Through a sheer contrast in scale, the oversized ladder reframed the entire museum, making it look like a big white dollhouse. *Time* magazine may have deemed, to the Tourism Board's delight, that Singapore is now "fun," but "play," in the fullest sense of the word, is arguably still something almost foreign to this society. There is an uneasy tension between the museum and Lim's installation. It is as if the staid colonial building can't stop taking itself seriously, even as it is being "belittled."

Lim's work, titled *"and the boy asked…,"* evokes Duchamp's *Fountain* (1917). Today, one finds all kinds of readymade and found objects in art spaces—stuffed goats and rubber tires, basketballs and aquariums—although that is not what links Lim to Duchamp; one doesn't find readymade gigantic ladders. One does, however, find readymade museums, and like Duchamp, Lim is concerned with the power of the institution to determine art. Found objects, as the name suggests, can be any object that an artist "finds" instead of "makes"; they are visually interesting, to the artist at least, if no one else. But Duchamp's readymades were chosen on a reaction of visual indifference. So if one reads Lim's work as a reframing of the museum as a readymade, the implication is that SAM, as the state's official art institution, cannot sustain visual interest. Instead of housing art, whatever is framed by it becomes rendered authenti-kitsch (though many of the over three hundred works shown at Nokia were arguably kitsch to begin with). Lim's work is especially provocative because it leans, both literally and metaphorically, against the boundary of the art institution.

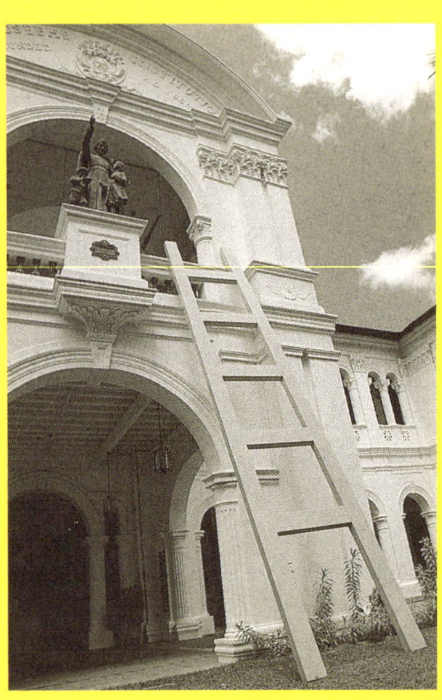

Lim Tzay Chuen
"and the boy asked…", 1999
Installation view, Nokia Singapore Art 1999, Singapore Art Museum, December 1999–January 2000
Steel and enamel paint

Also at Nokia was a brilliant parody of Singapore's obsession with the global-local: Lee Wen's video installation, *World Class* (1999). It comprised a stuffed white globe with wings, a stuffed star in a glass case, a bunch of survey forms posted onto a wall—asking people what they thought constituted "world class"—and a TV covered with a long cloth funnel, through which one could peer in. On screen was Lee Wen himself, preaching like a possessed propagandist. By virtue of the force of his insistence, he called forth Singapore as a "World-Class Society… with a world-class airport… a world-class government… world-class artists… and a world-class museum." Make no mistake, there are those in Singapore who take very seriously the question, "Just What Is It that Makes Certain Cities so World Class, so Global-Local?" In a 1997 National Day Dinner Speech, Prime Minister Goh Chok Tong highlighted the role of "foreign talent" in Singapore's future:

> To be a world-class business centre we must seek out world-class foreign talent to supplement our own. We must get them to work here, and better still, encourage some of them to sink roots here. The world-class foreign talent will help us to make Singapore a world class city and best home for Singaporeans.[13]

Statements like Goh's are a hard act to follow. The problem with parody is that sometimes the thing itself is inadvertently far more self-parodying than any intervention. Yet for all its inadvertent self-parody, Singapore sometimes seems like a nation without irony. It is as if irony is only latent and needs awakening, remembering or defamiliarization. Parody, like what Walter Benjamin once said of criticism, is a matter of the right distance. Mimic too closely and it's indistinguishable. Mimic too outrageously, and the joke is only one-dimensional. Lee Wen's video is almost hypnotic in its concentrated repetition, its language almost interchangeable with the state's. The white cloth funnel only intensifies the experience, making it less like watching a screen than being inside the dream world of ideology. Lee Wen's commentary/parody on the state's efforts to interpellate Singaporeans unmasks "world class" as ideological, but in its ironic way then shows how pervasive this ideology is—laughing at it doesn't distance us too far from it. It cuts very close.

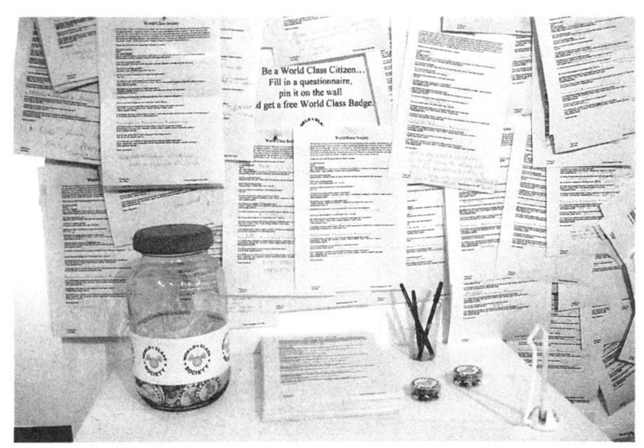

Lee Wen
World Class, installation view, 1999
Video and mixed media

On the subject of "foreign talent," given the state's low tolerance for criticism from anyone, let alone "foreigners," the American Ray Langenbach could be described as a not-so-desirable "foreign talent." An interesting juxtaposition is Lee Wen's performance of *Yellow Man* with Langenbach's performance of a "yellow woman," Lan Gen Bah. For APT3, Lee Wen presented the thirteenth edition of his *Journey of a Yellow Man* series. As *Yellow Man*, Lee Wen performs painted yellow all over, his head shaved bald, and usually stripped down to yellow painted briefs. His actions have ranged from walking around Brisbane carrying an ox's heart, to presenting a paper at a conference at The Substation arts center in Singapore. *Yellow Man* is an ambiguous and ironic figure. The all-over yellow may read like an exaggeration of ethnic identity, but more than that, Lee Wen poses and destabilizes all kinds of categories.

Unlike *Yellow Man*, who appears in the flesh, Lan Gen Bah exists only in the digital realm. She is purportedly a Chinese woman born in Singapore, a theorist and artist whose area of research is cognitive engineering and propaganda. Juxtaposing Lee Wen with Langenbach's double drag—"white man" as "yellow woman"—provokes the question: is *Yellow Man* a form of drag as well? And a double drag at that? On the surface we have a "yellow" man posing as a "yellower" man, but who is posing as the "yellow" man in the first place? Langenbach asks, does Lan Gen Bah function as a persona of "a particular author or of the (Singapore/American) body-politic and the state? Does she represent white desire for yellow attributes, or yellow desire for white attributes and privileges?"[14]

The question of "whiteness" in Singapore is indeed apropos. At APT3 I closed my conference presentation with a "thought performance": I asked the audience to imagine me doing something of a "white man" performance right there and then. I said that unlike Lee Wen, I did not need to cover myself in white poster paint and wear a white business suit. To *pose* as this "white man," all I had to do was appear as the curator from Singapore, to reveal Singapore as modernity's idealized *tabula rasa*.

Langenbach has commented that my argument,

> not only lays out 'appropriation' as Singapore, but your own need, Lan Gen Bah's need, and other people's need to appropriate Singapore. In fact, Singapore remains the place that everyone

> believes can be defined, described, nutshelled, reduced, objectified. From (former Sex Pistols manager) Malcolm McLaren to (international curator) Hou Hanru to (architect) Rem Koolhaas, and (science-fiction writer) William Gibson, and on and on, and especially the [ruling] People's Action Party. And each of us assume that we are the only ones who've got it right. Somehow, we all eat this meal, regurgitate it up and then consume it again or derive pleasure or horror in the fact that someone else is doing it too. So your argument, aware of its appropriational strategy, could, in a sense, end by appropriating itself.[15]

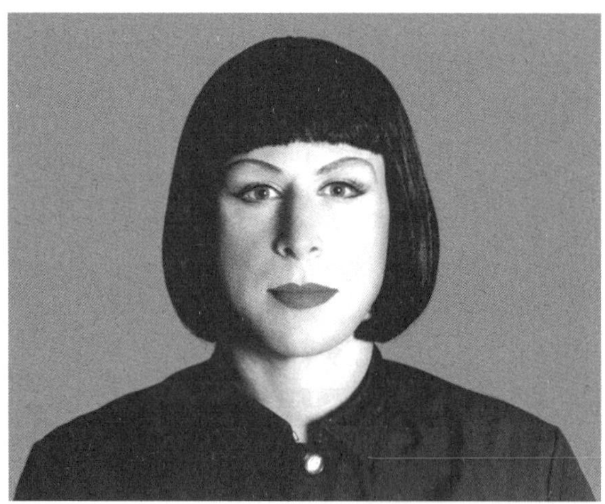

Ray Langenbach
Lan Gen Bah's portrait from *Re-engineering the Society of Mind*, 1999
Video and mixed-media installation

In the land of appropriation, is the only appropriate option to parody appropriation? Can one criticize Singapore without also somehow reproducing "Singapore"? Does everything come full circle: "late capitalism" = "appropriation" = "global-local" = "spectacle" = "authenti-kitsch"? Terms lose their specificity, equivocating one another when rendered equivalent. Yet that is the thing about spectacle: it is the ultimate view from above, it flattens out the panorama, conflates everything with everything else, yielding a spread of images that appear to vary but make no difference.

I am not, however, proposing the construction of a critical landscape for Singapore, so as to give some sense of rootedness in this global-local hub, some authenticity in this city of authenti-kitsch. Spectacle may be anti-landscape, but I don't think landscape is the antidote to spectacle. Perhaps I can respond to Langenbach with yet another trope—one he's used himself. (I'm being Singaporean-like here, mixing as many metaphors as I can, instead of using only one.) The parody of appropriation is a viral strategy: it aims to replicate levels of parody faster than the re-appropriations of parody into the spectacle. Although it's not just a game of speed, where artists have to be oh-so-modernist in being cutting edge, advanced guard. To replicate furiously and subversively is also to interrupt the host organism's functions. This strategy isn't new; the critical faculty has traditionally been about both thinking ahead and slowing down.

What I've tried to do in this essay is not to frame Singapore as representative—of the global-local, the authenti-kitsch—so much as to play with a certain reading of Singapore as an abstraction of these phenomena. At the same time, I've tried not to be reductive. On the contrary, my hope is to be suggestive, to open up looking—at Singapore, and at looking itself.

1. A shorter version of this essay was first published in *Artlink* 20, no. 2 (June 2000).
2. I have taken the term "authenti-kitsch" from a conversation with Lucy Davis.
3. Arthur C. Danto, *The Wake of Art: Criticism, Philosophy, and the Ends of Taste* (Amsterdam: G&B Arts International, 1998), 59. See also, Danto, *After the End of Art: Contemporary Art and the Pale of History* (Princeton: Princeton University Press, 1997).
4. The full text of Lee Yock Suan's speech can be found on the Singapore Government's web site: http://www.gov.sg/mita/renaissance.htm
5. Statistics are from the Queensland Art Gallery and taken from Caroline Turner, "Journey Without Maps: The Asia Pacific Triennial," in *Beyond the Future: The Third Asia-Pacific Triennial of Contemporary Art*, exh. cat. (Brisbane: Queensland Art Gallery 1999), 22.
6. Turner, "Journey Without Maps," 21.
7. In her forthcoming dissertation on culturalism, visual culture and political-aesthetic strategies in Singapore, "Making Difference—so easy to enjoy so hard to forget" (Roskilde University, Denmark, 2000), Lucy Davis notes that: "The trope of the pure organism, the boundaries of which are to be protected from the dangerous corruptions from outside, was theorized by Geoffrey Benjamin in 1970s as a trope that was analogously transferred to all aspects of Singapore life, from ethnic divisions to the length of male hair." [Benjamin, "The Cultural Logic of Singapore's Multiracialism," in Riaz Hassan, ed., *Singapore: Society in Transition* (Kuala Lumpur; New York: Oxford University Press, 1976)]. Such technologies of boundary maintenance of the local, the specific, the particular, and the policing of these "natural" boundaries against external, "unnatural" corruptions, are of course not unique to Singapore, and are themselves part of the particular logic of the eighteenth-century romanticist episteme. This split and struggle between the particular and the universal—in this case formulated as global and local—is of course the *constitutive split* of modernity itself. Technologies of boundary maintenance also occur in the late capitalist celebration of the "hybrid," "nomad," "creole," "mongrel," "inter-," "multi-," whereby the declaration of any one of these "bastard metaphors" is usually followed by a retroactive listing of all the various, clearly defined "identitarian components."
8. *Ibid*.
9. Sanjay Krishnan, "Singapore: Two Stories at the Cost of One City," *Commentary* [National University of Singapore Society] 10 (1992): 81.
10. Lucas Jodogne, *Singapore: Views on the Urban Landscape* (Antwerp: Pandora, 1998).
11. See Geraldene Lowe-Ismail, *Chinatown Memories* (Singapore: Singapore Heritage Society, 1998), 26.
12. Miles Orvell, *After the Machine: Visual Arts and the Erasing of Cultural Boundaries* (Jackson: University Press of Mississippi, 1995), 147–159.
13. The English text of Prime Minister Goh Chok Tong's National Day Dinner Speech (In Mandarin), 31 August 1997, can be found on the Singapore Government web site: http://www.gov.sg/mita/pressrelease/970901-1.htm.
14. From e-mail correspondence with Ray Langenbach.
15. *Ibid*.

Laurence Aberhart

Anderson's Bay Cemetery #2 [Southern Cross, Southern Sky, Southern Sea], Dunedin, December 1980, 1980
Gelatin-silver print
8 x 10 inches
Courtesy of the artist and Sue Crockford Gallery, Auckland, New Zealand

Lesley, Kamala, and Charlotte, South Springston, Canterbury, 1980, 1980
Gelatin-silver print
8 x 10 inches
Courtesy of the artist and Sue Crockford Gallery, Auckland, New Zealand

Old bridge structure from new bridge, Clutha River, Alexandra, December 1980, 1980
Gelatin-silver print
8 x 10 inches
Courtesy of the artist and Sue Crockford Gallery, Auckland, New Zealand

Auckland, 11 April 1982, 1982
Gelatin-silver print
8 x 10 inches
Courtesy of Don Higgins and Sue Crockford Gallery, Auckland, New Zealand

Carved Headboard #2, Pawarengo, Whangape Harbour, Northland, 10 May 1982, 1982/83
Gelatin-silver print
8 x 10 inches
Courtesy of the artist and Sue Crockford Gallery, Auckland, New Zealand

Interior #2, "Rongokarae," Waikirikiri, Bay of Plenty, 7 June 1982, 1982
Gelatin-silver print
8 x 10 inches
Courtesy of the artist and Sue Crockford Gallery, Auckland, New Zealand

Interior, church, Maraeroa, Hokianga Harbour, Northland, 2 May 1982, 1982
Gelatin-silver print
8 x 10 inches
Courtesy of the artist and Sue Crockford Gallery, Auckland, New Zealand

"Ripeka Tapu," Rangi Point, Hokianga Harbour, Northland, 3 May 1982, 1982
Gelatin-silver print
8 x 10 inches
Courtesy of the artist and Sue Crockford Gallery, Auckland, New Zealand

Te Hapuku, Te Hauke, Hawkes Bay, 17 June 1982, 1982
Gelatin-silver print
8 x 10 inches
Courtesy of the artist and Sue Crockford Gallery, Auckland, New Zealand

Hipango Monument, Korokota [Golgotha], Putiki, Wanganui, 31 January 1986, 1986
Gelatin-silver print
8 x 10 inches
Courtesy of the artist and Sue Crockford Gallery, Auckland, New Zealand

Midway Beach, Gisborne, 13 June 1986, 1986
Gelatin-silver print
8 x 10 inches
Courtesy of the artist and Sue Crockford Gallery, Auckland, New Zealand

Nature Morte [silence], Savage Club, Wanganui, 20 February 1986, 1986
Gelatin-silver print
10 x 8 inches
Courtesy of the artist and Sue Crockford Gallery, Auckland, New Zealand

Doug Aitken

blow debris, 2000
Video installation
Dimensions variable
Courtesy of the artist and 303 Gallery, New York

Center for Land Use Interpretation (CLUI)

The Desert Research Station, 2000
Mixed-media installation at The Museum of Contemporary Art, Los Angeles, and Hinkley, California
Dimensions variable
Courtesy of the artists

Miles Coolidge

Near Mattawa, 2000
14 C-prints
57 3/4 x 50 inches each
Courtesy of the artist, ACME., Los Angeles, and Casey Kaplan, New York

Caryl Davis

How Light Becomes Me (Lava), 1996–2000
Cibachrome print mounted on aluminum
17 x 26 inches each
Courtesy of the artist

How Light Becomes Me (Peak), 1996–2000
Cibachrome print mounted on aluminum
16 x 24 inches each
Courtesy of the artist

How Light Becomes Me (Pines), 1996–2000
Cibachrome print mounted on aluminum
26 x 40 inches each
Courtesy of the artist

How Light Becomes Me (Pink), 1996–2000
Cibachrome print mounted on aluminum
29 x 43 inches; 43 x 29 inches
Courtesy of the artist

How Light Becomes Me (Porch), 1996–2000
Cibachrome print mounted on aluminum
31 x 47 inches; 47 x 31 inches
Courtesy of the artist

Christina Fernandez

Manuela S-t-i-t-c-h-e-d, 1996
10 C-prints and wall mounted text
30 x 40 inches each
Courtesy of the artist

Simryn Gill

Forest, 1996–98
8 black-and-white photographs selected from a series of 16 images, edition of 15
Photographs taken by Nicholas Leong
48 x 38 inches each
Courtesy of the artist and Roslyn Oxley9 Gallery, Sydney, Australia

Rodney Graham

Edge of a Wood, 1999
Double video projection made from 16mm film; 7:54 minutes
Dimensions variable
Courtesy of the artist and Donald Young Gallery, Chicago

Anthony Hernandez

Public Fishing Areas: Herbert C. Legg Lake #1, 1979
Gelatin-silver print
16 x 20 inches
Courtesy of the artist and Grant Selwyn Fine Art, Los Angeles

Public Fishing Areas: Marina Del Mar, 1979
Gelatin-silver print
16 x 20 inches
Courtesy of the artist and Grant Selwyn Fine Art, Los Angeles

Public Fishing Areas: Public Park, San Bernardino, 1979
Gelatin-silver print
16 x 20 inches
Courtesy of the artist and Grant Selwyn Fine Art, Los Angeles

Public Fishing Areas: Catfish Corner, Near Lake Elsinore, 1981
Gelatin-silver print
16 x 20 inches
Courtesy of the artist and Grant Selwyn Fine Art, Los Angeles

Public Fishing Areas: Hansen Dam #1, 1981
Gelatin-silver print
16 x 20 inches
Courtesy of the artist and Grant Selwyn Fine Art, Los Angeles

Public Fishing Areas: Hansen Dam #2, 1981
Gelatin-silver print
16 x 20 inches
Courtesy of the artist and Grant Selwyn Fine Art, Los Angeles

Public Fishing Areas: Harbor Lake, 1981
Gelatin-silver print
16 x 20 inches
Courtesy of the artist and Grant Selwyn Fine Art, Los Angeles

Public Fishing Areas: Lake Casitas, 1981
Gelatin-silver print
16 x 20 inches
Courtesy of the artist and Grant Selwyn Fine Art, Los Angeles

Public Fishing Areas: Little Rock Reservoir #1, 1981
Gelatin-silver print
16 x 20 inches
Courtesy of the artist and Grant Selwyn Fine Art, Los Angeles

Public Fishing Areas: Little Rock Reservoir #2, 1981
Gelatin-silver print
16 x 20 inches
Courtesy of the artist and Grant Selwyn Fine Art, Los Angeles

Public Fishing Areas: Little Rock Reservoir #3, 1981
Gelatin-silver print
16 x 20 inches
Courtesy of the artist and Grant Selwyn Fine Art, Los Angeles

Public Fishing Areas: Puddingstone Reservoir #2, 1981
Gelatin-silver print
16 x 20 inches
Courtesy of the artist and Grant Selwyn Fine Art, Los Angeles

Public Fishing Areas: Puddingstone Reservoir #4, 1981
Gelatin-silver print
16 x 20 inches
Courtesy of the artist and Grant Selwyn Fine Art, Los Angeles

Public Fishing Areas: Hemet Lake, 1982
Gelatin-silver print
16 x 20 inches
Courtesy of the artist and Grant Selwyn Fine Art, Los Angeles

Public Fishing Areas: Lake Elsinore #1, 1982
Gelatin-silver print
16 x 20 inches
Courtesy of the artist and Grant Selwyn Fine Art, Los Angeles

Public Fishing Areas: Lake Elsinore #2, 1982
Gelatin-silver print
16 x 20 inches
Courtesy of the artist and Grant Selwyn Fine Art, Los Angeles

Public Fishing Areas: Lake Elsinore #3, 1982
Gelatin-silver print
16 x 20 inches
Courtesy of the artist and Grant Selwyn Fine Art, Los Angeles

Public Fishing Areas: Little Rock Reservoir #4, 1982
Gelatin-silver print
16 x 20 inches
Courtesy of the artist and Grant Selwyn Fine Art, Los Angeles

Public Fishing Areas: Peck Rd., Water Conservation Park #1, 1982
Gelatin-silver print
16 x 20 inches
Courtesy of the artist and Grant Selwyn Fine Art, Los Angeles

Public Fishing Areas: Peck Rd., Water Conservation Park #2, 1982
Gelatin-silver print
16 x 20 inches
Courtesy of the artist and Grant Selwyn Fine Art, Los Angeles

Public Fishing Areas: Puddingstone Reservoir #3, 1982
Gelatin-silver print
16 x 20 inches
Courtesy of the artist and Grant Selwyn Fine Art, Los Angeles

Public Fishing Areas: Salton Sea, 1982
Gelatin-silver print
16 x 20 inches
Courtesy of the artist and Grant Selwyn Fine Art, Los Angeles

Public Fishing Areas: Puddingstone Reservoir #1, 1983
Gelatin-silver print
16 x 20 inches
Courtesy of the artist and Grant Selwyn Fine Art, Los Angeles

Gavin Hipkins

The Homely: Auckland (Model), 1998; *Christchurch (Corridor),* 1998; *Christchurch (Icicles),* 1998; *Christchurch (Mask),* 1998; *Christchurch (Museum),* 1998; *Sydney (Dogs),* 1998; *Sydney (Heads),* 1998; *Wellington (Fern),* 1998; *Wellington (Museum),* 1998; *Auckland (Mount Eden),* 1999; *Auckland (One Tree Hill),* 1999; *Dunedin (Landscape),* 1999; *Huka (Falls),* 1999; *Melbourne (Cross),* 1999; *Melbourne (Wood),* 1999; *Napier (Tree),* 1999; *Near New Plymouth (Clouds),* 1999; *Porirua (Village),* 1999; *Rotorua (Fountain),* 1999; *Roturua (Gateway),* 1999; *Roturua (Mud),* 1999; *South Island (House),* 1999; *Sydney (Flower),* 1999; *Sydney (Harbour),* 1999; *Sydney (Lion),* 1999; *Sydney (Museum),* 1999; *Te Wairoa (Falls),* 1999; *Wellington (Path),* 1999; *Hokitika (Rocks),* 2000; *Westport (Curtain),* 2000
30 C-type prints selected from a series of 60
24 x 16 inches each
Courtesy of the artist and Hamish McKay Gallery, Wellington, New Zealand

Igloolik Isuma Productions

Nunaqpa (Going Inland), 1991
Videotape, 58:15 minutes
Courtesy of Igloolik Isuma Productions and V tape, Toronto

Episode 1: Qimuksik (Dog Team), Avaja (Avaja)—Nunavut (Our Land), 1995
Videotape, 52 minutes
Courtesy of Igloolik Isuma Productions and V tape, Toronto

Episode 4: Tugaliaq (Ice Blocks)—Nunavut (Our Land), 1995
Videotape, 28:50 minutes
Courtesy of Igloolik Isuma Productions and V tape, Toronto

Tim Johnson

Illusory City, 1983–85
Acrylic on canvas
71 x 59 inches
Courtesy of Parliament House Art Collection

Papunya, 1983–85
Synthetic polymer paint on linen canvas
35 x 24 inches
Sir James and Lady Cruthers, Perth, Australia

The Sun, 1994
Acrylic on canvas
60 x 96 inches
Private Collection, Sydney, Australia

Western Pure Land, 1999
Acrylic on canvas
72 1/2 x 60 inches
Private Collection, Sydney, Australia

Rachel Khedoori

Griffith Park, 1996
8 posters, 24 x 17 inches each; 16mm film, 16mm projector, looping mechanism, and reflective screen
Collection of Wilhelm and Gabi Schürmann, courtesy of David Zwirner, New York

Roy Kiyooka

Halifax Sea and Rock, 1971
35 gelatin-silver photographs
6 1/2 x 8 7/8 inches each
Vancouver Art Gallery Acquisition Fund VAG 98.27.1 a-jj

Long Beach to Peggy's Cove, 1971
Silver print
16 3/8 x 127 inches
Vancouver Art Gallery Acquisition Fund VAG 96.22 a-f

Small Harbour on Nomi Island, 1984
27 C-type photographs
Three sections, 9 x 99 1/2 each; text panel 9 x 10 inches
Vancouver Art Gallery Acquisition Fund VAG 98.27.5 a-x

David Lamelas

The Desert People, 1974
16mm film, 47:00 minutes
Courtesy of the artist and Galerie Kienzle & Gmeiner, Berlin

A Fiction, 1975
Eight color film stills from *The Desert People*
Courtesy of the artist and Galerie Kienzle & Gmeiner, Berlin

Simon Leung

Squatting Project/Wien, 1998
131 gelatin-silver prints and 50 projected images
Dimensions variable
Courtesy of the artist

Tracey Moffatt

Night Cries: A Rural Tragedy, 1989
Video projection, 19 minutes
Courtesy of the artist and Women Make Movies, Inc.

Invocations (2), 2000
Photo-silkscreen printed in ultra-violet inks on Textured Somerset Satin paper
57 3/4 x 48 inches
Courtesy of the artist and Matthew Marks Gallery, New York

Invocations (4), 2000
Photo-silkscreen printed in ultra-violet inks on Textured Somerset Satin paper
57 3/4 x 48 inches
Courtesy of the artist and Matthew Marks Gallery, New York

Invocations (10), 2000
Photo-silkscreen printed in ultra-violet inks on Textured Somerset Satin paper
42 x 39 inches
Courtesy of the artist and Matthew Marks Gallery, New York

Invocations (11), 2000
Photo-silkscreen printed in ultra-violet inks on Textured Somerset Satin paper
57 3/4 x 48 inches
Courtesy of the artist and Matthew Marks Gallery, New York

Lee Mullican

Agawam, 1950
Oil on canvas
50 x 40 inches
Collection of Mr. and Mrs. Hoberman, Los Angeles

Section From the Burlap Plain, 1951
Oil on canvas
40 x 50 inches
Beverly and Mel Rosenthal, Malibu

Asia Minor, 1953
Oil on canvas
50 x 40 inches
Estate of Lee Mullican, courtesy of Grant Selwyn Fine Art, Los Angeles

Drum Bazaar, 1953
Oil on canvas
49 1/2 x 39 1/2 inches
Estate of Lee Mullican, courtesy of Grant Selwyn Fine Art, Los Angeles

Passage Factor, 1953
Oil on canvas
50 x 40 inches
Estate of Lee Mullican, courtesy of Grant Selwyn Fine Art, Los Angeles

Paul Outerbridge

Docks, Mexico, c. 1955
Digital cibachrome print
11 x 14 inches
Courtesy of Graham Howe and the estate of Paul Outerbridge

Mexico, c. 1955
Digital cibachrome print
11 x 14 inches
Courtesy of Graham Howe and the estate of Paul Outerbridge

Mexico, c. 1955
Digital cibachrome print
11 x 14 inches
Courtesy of Graham Howe and the estate of Paul Outerbridge

Mexico, c. 1955
Digital cibachrome print
11 x 14 inches
Courtesy of Graham Howe and the estate of Paul Outerbridge

Mexico, c. 1955
Digital cibachrome print
11 x 14 inches
Courtesy of Graham Howe and the estate of Paul Outerbridge

Mexico, c. 1955
Digital cibachrome print
11 x 14 inches
Courtesy of Graham Howe and the estate of Paul Outerbridge

Mexico, c. 1955
Digital cibachrome print
11 x 14 inches
Courtesy of Graham Howe and the estate of Paul Outerbridge

Mexico, c. 1955
Digital cibachrome print
11 x 14 inches
Courtesy of Graham Howe and the estate of Paul Outerbridge

Michael Parekowhai

The Indefinite Article, 1990
Acrylic on wood
90 x 240 x 7 inches
Jim Barr and Mary Barr loan collection, Dunedin Public Art Gallery

Allan Sekula

from *TITANIC's wake*, 1998–2000

Regular dockworkers' dispatch board, Seattle
Cibachrome photograph
48 x 60 inches

Casual dockworkers' dispatch, Seattle (diptych)
Cibachrome photograph
26 x 68 inches

31 December 1999, off the Albanian coast (diptych)
Cibachrome photograph
38 x 87 inches

Portrait of Kaela Economou, beaten by the Seattle police, 2 December 1999
Cibachrome photograph
29 x 40 inches

Assemblage made by coal dock workers, Vancouver
Cibachrome photograph
29 x 40 inches

Shipwreck and worker, Istanbul
Cibachrome photograph
48 x 60 inches

All works in edition of 5
Courtesy of the artist and Christopher Grimes Gallery, Santa Monica

Dear Bill Gates, 1999
Cibachrome photograph and typewritten letter
Photo 28 x 103 inches; letter 12 x 9 inches; edition 3 of 5
Courtesy of the artist and Christopher Grimes Gallery, Santa Monica

Waiting for Tear Gas, 2000
Slide projection; 81 color transparencies projected continuously at 13-second intervals, wall-mounted text, edition of 5
Projection size 72 x 108 inches
Courtesy of the artist and Christopher Grimes Gallery, Santa Monica

Yuk King Tan

The Picturesque, 1997/2000
Mixed-media performance/installation with fireworks
Dimensions variable
Courtesy of the artist and Sue Crockford Gallery, Auckland, New Zealand

Glen Wilson

Desert Fishing, 2000
Video installation
Dimensions variable
Courtesy of the artist

Only selected exhibitions since 1990 are listed with the exception of Roy Kiyooka, Zacharias Kunuk, Lee Mullican, and Paul Outerbridge.

Laurence Aberhart

1949 Born, Nelson, New Zealand
Lives and works in Russell, Bay of Islands, Northland, New Zealand

Selected One-Person Exhibitions

2000 *Northland, Part One–The Eighties*, Sue Crockford Gallery, Auckland
1999 *Where Shadows Dream of Light*, Dunedin Public Art Gallery, Dunedin, New Zealand
Anonymous Architecture & Other Fables, Sue Crockford Gallery, Auckland
Dark Stuff, Darren Knight Gallery, Sydney
1998 *Photographs of USA, Europe & New Zealand*, The American Club, Hong Kong
Sampling, Darren Knight Gallery, Sydney
All Gates Open, Fisher Gallery, Pakuranga, Auckland
1997 *Enamels and Cameos*, Sue Crockford Gallery, Auckland
Interiors, Whangarei Art Museum, Whangarei, New Zealand
1996 Darren Knight DKW Gallery, Melbourne
1995 Peter McLeavey Gallery, Wellington, New Zealand
Mission Heliographique, Aberhart North Gallery, Auckand
1994 *Platinum Print Photographs*, Aberhart North Gallery, Auckland
Darren Knight DKW Gallery, Melbourne
1993 Peter McLeavey Gallery, Wellington, New Zealand
Danceland, Bathhouse, Rotorua, New Zealand
The Contact Print 1993, Aberhart North Gallery, Auckland
1992 *Mass Update*, Aberhart North Gallery, Auckland
1991 *Taranaki Project*, Govett-Brewster Art Gallery, New Plymouth, New Zealand
1990 *Nature Morte*, National Art Gallery, Wellington, New Zealand
Vestiges From The Last Colonial Culture: Photographs of New Zealand, Pacific Design Center, Los Angeles
Peter McLeavey Gallery, Wellington, New Zealand
Park-Royal Hotel, Wellington, New Zealand
Sarjeant Art Gallery, Wanganui, New Zealand
1990 Remix, Aberhart North Gallery, Auckland

Selected Group Exhibitions

2000 *Drive*, Govett-Brewster Art Gallery, New Plymouth, New Zealand
The Promised Land, The Bishop Suter Art Gallery, Nelson, New Zealand
25th Anniversary Ex, Brooke Gifford Gallery, Christchurch, New Zealand
1999 *Three Photographers*, John Batten Gallery, Hong Kong
People, Places, Pastimes: Challenging Perspectives of Ispswich, Global Arts Link, Ipswich, Australia
WORD, Museum of Contemporary Art, Sydney
Mapping Our Countries, National Museum of Australia, Sydney
1998 *Dream Collectors*, Museum of New Zealand Te Papa Tongarewa, Wellington, New Zealand, and Auckland City Art Gallery, Auckland
Outside the Circle, Whangarei Art Museum, Whangarei, New Zealand
1970s, Sue Crockford Gallery, Auckland
Folklore: The New Zealanders, Artspace, Auckland, and Sarjeant Art Gallery, Wanganui, New Zealand
1997 *Family Values*, Peter McLeavey Gallery, Wellington, New Zealand
Recent Acquisitions in Context, Auckland City Art Gallery, Auckland
1996 Govett-Brewster Art Gallery, New Plymouth, New Zealand
Seven New Zealand Artists, Dogget Street Studio, Brisbane, Australia, and Mornington Peninsula Regional Gallery, Melbourne
1995 *Australia Felix Festival*, Benalla, Australia
Symbolist Photography, Fisher Gallery, Auckland
Waikato Te Awa: The People and The River, Waikato Museum of Art and History, Hamilton, New Zealand
Sight Seeing, Australia Post National Philatelic Centre, Melbourne
Currencies, PhotoForum, Auckland, and Auckland War Memorial Museum, Auckland
1994 *Letters from Ronald's Room*, Gallery Seventy Nine, Hawera, New Zealand
Station to Station: The Way of the Cross, Auckland Art Gallery, Auckland
Masons of the Grand Lodge, Page 90 Artspace, Wellington, New Zealand
1992 *Peebles, Peers and Contemporaries*, Centre for Contemporary Art, Christchurch, New Zealand
Headlands: Thinking through New Zealand Art, Museum of Contemporary Art, Sydney, and National Art Gallery, Wellington, New Zealand
Contemporary Update, Sarjeant Art Gallery, Wanganui, New Zealand
Whatu Aho Rua, Sarjeant Art Gallery, Wanganui, New Zealand
1991 *A Private View*, Gisborne Museum and Arts Centre, Gisborne, New Zealand
175 East, Sarjeant Art Gallery, Wanganui, New Zealand
Laurence Aberhart and Bill Hammond, Brooke Gifford Gallery, Christchurch, New Zealand
Old Fashioned, Aberhart North Gallery, Auckland
1990 *Situation and Style*, Jonathan-Jensen Gallery, Christchurch, New Zealand
Acquisitions Review 1988-90, Auckland Art Gallery, Auckland
Now See Hear, Wellington City Gallery, Wellington, New Zealand
200 Years of N.Z. Landscape, Auckland Art Gallery, Auckland
Art in the Sub-Antarctic, Southland Museum and Art Gallery, Southland, New Zealand

Doug Aitken

1968 Born, Redondo Beach, California
Lives and works in Los Angeles

Selected One-Person Exhibitions

2000 Galerie Hauser & Wirth & Presenhuber, Zurich
Vienna Secession, Vienna
Taka Ishii Gallery, Tokyo
1999 *Concentrations 33: Doug Aitken, Diamond Sea*, Dallas Museum of Art, Dallas, Texas
Victoria Miro Gallery, London
Lawing Gallery, Houston, Texas
Pitti Discovery Series, Pitti Immagine Discovery, Florence, Italy
1998 303 Gallery, New York
Jirí Svestka Gallery, Prague
Taka Ishii Gallery, Tokyo
Gallery Side 2, Tokyo
1997 303 Gallery, New York
1996 Taka Ishii Gallery, Tokyo
1994 303 Gallery, New York
1993 AC Project Room, New York

Selected Group Exhibitions

2000 *Whitney Biennial*, Whitney Museum of American Art, New York
1998 *New Selections from the Permanent Collection*, Walker Art Center, Minneapolis
Portrait—Human Figure, Galerie Peter Kilchmann, Zurich
La Voie Lactée, Alleged, New York
L.A. Times, Palazzo Re Rebaudengo, Guarene, Italy
New Visions: Video 1998, Long Beach Museum of Art, Long Beach, California
Unfinished History, Walker Art Center, Minneapolis
I Love New York—Crossover of Contemporary Art, Museum Ludwig, Cologne, Germany
Speed, The Photographers' Gallery, London
Poor Man's Pudding; Rich Man's Crumbs, AC Project Room, New York
1997 *Whitney Biennial*, Whitney Museum of American Art, New York
One Minute Scenario, Le Printemps de Cahors, Saint-Cloud, France
Doug Aitken and Peter Gehrke, Galleri Index, Stockholm
Camera Oscura, San Casciano dei Bagni, Italy
Doug Aitken, Alex Bag, Naotaka Hiro, Taka Ishii Gallery, Tokyo
Video Divertimento, San Casciano dei Bagni, Italy
(re)Mediation: The Digital in Contemporary American Printmaking, Cankarjev Dom Gallery, Ljubljana, Slovenia
1996 *Campo 6: The Spiral Village*, Galleria Civica d'Arte, Moderna e Contemporanea, Turin; and Bonnefanten Museum, Maastricht, The Netherlands

29′–0″/East, Kunstraum Wien, Vienna
a/drift: Scenes from a Penetrable Culture, Bard Center for Curatorial Studies, Annandale-on-Hudson, New York
Art in the Anchorage, Brooklyn Bridge Anchorage, Brooklyn, New York
Doug Aitken, Mariko Mori, Ricardo Zulueta, Elga Wimmer Gallery, New York

1995 *La Belle et la Bête*, Musée d'Art Moderne de la Ville de Paris, Paris
The Image and The Object, Museo Laboratorio di Arte Contemporanea, Rome

1994 *Beyond Belief*, Lisson Gallery, London
Audience 0.01, Flash Art, Milan
still, Espace Montjoie, Paris
New York, New York, Ma'nes Space, Prague
Out West and Back East, Santa Monica Museum of Art, Santa Monica, California
Not Here Neither There, LACE, Los Angeles

1993 *Okay Behavior*, 303 Gallery, New York
Underlay, 15 Renwick Street, New York
Doug Aitken and Robin Lowe, AC Project Room, New York

1992 *Multiplicity*, Christopher Middendorf Gallery, Washington, D.C.
The Art Mall: A Social Space, The New Museum of Contemporary Art, New York
Invitational 92, Stux Gallery, New York

1991 *Artworks/Artworkers*, AC Project Room, New York

Center for Land Use Interpretation (CLUI)

1994 Founded, Oakland, California
Based in Los Angeles

Selected Exhibitions and Projects

2000 *The Interpretive Arena of the American Landscape*, Witte de With, Rotterdam, The Netherlands

1999 *The Nellis Range: Landscape of Conjecture*, CLUI, Los Angeles and Las Vegas, Nevada
100 Places in Washington, Center on Contemporary Art, Seattle, Washington
Territory in Photo Color: The Postcards of Merle Porter, CLUI, Los Angeles
More Than Meets the Eye, Triennal der Photographie, Hamburg, Germany
Commonwealth of Technology, MIT List Visual Arts Center, Cambridge, Massachusetts
Recent Work of the Wendover Residents, CLUI, Wendover, Utah
Monuments of Displacement: Mining Landforms of Nevada, As Seen Through the Aerial Photographs of F.E. DuBois, CLUI, Los Angeles
Not Photography, Rosamund Felsen Gallery, Santa Monica, California
As Far as the Eye Can See, Atlanta Gallery of Art, Atlanta

1998 *Subterranean Renovations*, CLUI, Los Angeles
VORs of Texas, CLUI, Los Angeles
Model of Decay: The Chesapeake Bay Hydraulic Model, CLUI, Los Angeles
Nuclear Proving Grounds of the World, CLUI, Los Angeles

1997 *Around Wendover: An Examination of the Anthropic Landscape of the Great Salt Lake Desert Region*, CLUI, Wendover, Utah
Hinterland: A Voyage into Exurban Southern California, LACE, Los Angeles

1996 *Concentric Restrictions*, CLUI, Specter Range, Nevada
Around Wendover: An Examination of the Anthropic Landscape through Maps and Photographs, CLUI, Wendover, Utah
Group show, Visual Art Department, University of California, San Diego, California

1995 *5th Avenue Peninsula Tour*, Oakland, California
Model Earth II, CLUI, Oakland, California
Re:Zone, DiverseWorks Art Space, Houston
Denaturalized Sites II, CLUI, Oakland, California

1994 *Various Ephemeral Land Uses*, CLUI, Oakland, California
Denaturalized Sites I, CLUI, Oakland, California
Model Earth I, CLUI, Oakland, California

Miles Coolidge

1963 Born, Montreal, Quebec
Lives and works in Los Angeles

Selected One-Person Exhibitions

2000 Orange County Museum of Art, Newport Beach, California
Galerie Jennifer Flay, Paris

1998 *Central Valley*, ACME., Los Angeles
James Van Damme Gallery, Brussels, Belgium
Moundbuilder's Golf Course, ACME., Los Angeles

1996 *Garage Pictures*, Casey Kaplan, New York
Safetyville, ACME., Los Angeles

1994 *Elevator Pictures*, Los Angeles Center for Photographic Studies, Los Angeles

1992 *In Its Place*, California Institute of the Arts, Valencia, California
Palindromes, Carpenter Center for the Visual Arts, Cambridge, Massachusetts

Selected Group Exhibitions

2000 *Unapocalyptic: The Future That Never Was*, Fisher Gallery, University of Southern California, Los Angeles

1999 *C.O.L.A. Individual Artist Grants 1999*, Los Angeles Municipal Art Gallery, Los Angeles
Photography: An Expanded View—Recent Acquisitions, Guggenheim Museum Soho, New York, and Guggenheim Museum Bilbao, Bilbao, Spain
Tomorrow Forever—Photography as Ruin, Kunsthalle Krems, Kremstein, Austria
Sliding Scale, Southeastern Center for Contemporary Art, Winston-Salem, South Carolina

1998 *L.A. or Lilliput?*, Long Beach Museum of Art, Long Beach, California
Thinking Aloud, Kettles Yard, Cambridge, England
Jeff Burton, Miles Coolidge, Annika von Hausswolf, Jonathan Monk, Karen Yasinsky, Casey Kaplan, New York
Urban Landscapes: Miles Coolidge, Marin Kasimir, Katja Liebman, Steven Pippin, Victoria Miro, London
LA on Paper 2: Fantastic Matter of Fact, Galerie Krinzinger, Vienna
The Campaign Against Living Miserably, Royal College of Art, London
Sightings, ICA, London

1997 *Stills*, Walker Art Center, Minneapolis
Vaknin Schwartz, Atlanta
Rena Bransten Gallery, San Francisco
Elsewhere, Carnegie Museum of Art, Pittsburgh, Pennsylvania
Transport, Post, Los Angeles
Angel Hair, Dogenhaus Galerie, Leipzig, Germany
The Big Picture: Recent Acquisitions in Photography, Albright-Knox Art Gallery, Buffalo, New York
World Speak Dumb, Karyn Lovegrove Gallery, Melbourne
Defamiliar, Regen Projects, Los Angeles

1996 *The Lie of the Land*, University Art Museum, Santa Barbara, California
Location, Location, Institute of Contemporary Art, San Jose, California
Skin Deep, Thomas Solomon's Garage, Los Angeles
Left of Center: New Art from L.A., 10 in 1 Gallery, Chicago

1995 *Hollywood Boulevard Is Sinking*, Three Day Weekend, Los Angeles
Redevelopment, Victoria Room, San Francisco
Late Photography, Foodhouse, Santa Monica, California

1994 *Rundgang*, Kunstakademie Düsseldorf, Düsseldorf, Germany

1993 *LACPS Members' Exhibition*, Santa Monica Museum of Art, Santa Monica, California

Caryl Davis

1958 Born, Schenectady, New York
Lives and works in Los Angeles

Selected One-Person Exhibitions

1996 Susanne Hilberry Gallery, Birmingham, Michigan

1995 Dan Bernier Gallery, Santa Monica

1990 Richard/Bennett Gallery, Los Angeles
MFA Thesis exhibition, UCLA Wight Gallery

Selected Group Exhibitions

2000 *Fissure*, Staff Projects—Staff USA, New York

1998 *Pollution*, Gian Ferrari Arte Contemporanea, Milan

1997 *Invited*, Joseph Helman Gallery, New York
Discomfort, Santa Barbara Contemporary Arts Forum, Santa Barbara, California
California Currents, Armand Hammer Museum of Art, Los Angeles
Ideologies of Seeing Faculty Works, Southern California Institute of Architecture, Los Angeles

1996 *The Lie of the Land*, University Art Museum, Santa Barbara, California
Selections Fall '96, The Drawing Center, New York
Embedded Metaphor, Independent Curators Incorporated, New York
Documenta, Huntington Beach Art Center, Huntington Beach, California

1995 *The Big Night*, The Bradbury Building, Los Angeles

1994 *LACE 8th Videoannuale*, Wexner Center for the Arts, Columbus, Ohio and LACE, Los Angeles

1993 *FAR BAZZAR*, The Brewery, Los Angeles

1992 *Seven Los Angeles Artists: LAX at LACE*, LACE, Los Angeles
Tattoo, Foodhouse, Santa Monica, California

Bedroom Eyes, California State University, Fullerton, California
The Store Show, Richard/Bennett Gallery, Los Angeles
1991 *Comfort*, Christopher Grimes Gallery, Santa Monica, California
1990 *Drawing the Line*, Richard/Bennett Gallery, Los Angeles

Christina Fernandez
1965 Born, Los Angeles
Lives and works in Los Angeles

Selected One-Person Exhibitions
1999 *Ruin*, Los Angeles Center for Photographic Studies, Los Angeles
1998 *The Body Is an Analog & Bend: Two Works on Sight*, California State University, Northridge, California
1993 *Sin Cool/Without Cool*, Daniel Saxon Gallery, Los Angeles
1992 *Hidden Crimson*, Daniel Saxon Gallery, Los Angeles

Selected Group Exhibitions
2000 *Tethered to the Logic of Homo Sapiens*, Riverside Art Museum, Riverside, California
1999 *Intermission Projections*, Side Street Projects, Laemmle Grand Theatres, Los Angeles
Aztlan Today: Chicano Post-nation, Canal Isabel Segunda, Madrid
Not on Any Map, The School of the Art Institute of Chicago, Chicago
1998 *I to Eye III*, Cirrus Gallery, Los Angeles
Women Who Shoot, Newspace, Los Angeles
1997 *Public Image, Private Focus*, California State University, Los Angeles
Significant Departures, Cerritos College, Norwalk, California
1996 *The Virgin, Frida, and Me*, Saddleback College, Mission Viejo, California
Working Histories: Labor in Southern California, Los Angeles Center for Photographic Studies, Los Angeles
Here Now... Y Que?, Centro Cultural de la Raza, San Diego, California
Intersecting Identities, University of Southern California, Los Angeles
Chicanolandia, University of California at Santa Cruz, Santa Cruz, California
1995 *WestWorld: Emerging Los Angeles Artists*, Cal Poly Pomona, Pomona, California
Iconography as Metaphor, Los Angeles Pierce College Art Gallery, Woodland Hills, California
Chicanolandia, Los Alamos Historical Society, Los Alamos, New Mexico, and Peoria Arts Commission, Peoria, Arizona
From the West, The Mexican Museum, San Francisco
1994 *Mi Gente*, Breeden Gallery, Orange, California
Encuentro, University of Guadalajara, Guadalajara, Mexico
1993 *Chicano Aesthetic—4 Artists: A Dialogue*, Georgia State University School of Art and Design Galleries, Atlanta
Chicano/Chicana: Visceral Images, The Works Gallery, Costa Mesa, California
1992 *Chicano Y Latino: Parallels and Divergence*, Kimberly Gallery of Art, Washington, D.C., and El Paso Museum of Art, El Paso, Texas
Ojo Abierto/Open Eye, Santa Barbara Contemporary Arts Forum, Santa Barbara, California
Breaking Barriers, Santa Monica Museum of Art, Santa Monica, California
New Photographers, Los Angeles Center for Photographic Studies, Los Angeles
1991 *Chicano & Latino: Parallels and Divergence*, Daniel Saxon Gallery, Los Angeles
L.A. Illuminado: Eight Los Angeles Photographers, Otis Gallery, Los Angeles
ExVotos y Ofrendas—Día de los Muertos: A Woman's Point of View, Galería de la Raza, San Francisco

Simryn Gill
1959 Born, Singapore
Lives and works in Sydney

Selected One-Person Exhibitions
2000 *Simryn Gill*, Ikon Gallery, Birmingham, England
Roadkill, Project Gallery, CCA Kitakyushu, Japan
Natural Resemblance: Some Recent Photo Work, Experimental Art Foundation, Adelaide, Australia
1999 *Simryn Gill*, Bluecoat Gallery, Liverpool, England
Simryn Gill, Slow Release, Bishopsgate Goods Yard, London
Vegetation, ArtPace, San Antonio, Texas
Rampant, Institute of Modern Art, Brisbane, Australia
1998 *Self-seeds*, Kiasma Museum of Contemporary Art, Helsinki
Forest, Roslyn Oxley9 Gallery, Sydney
1997 *Body Politic*, Scapular Gallery Nomad, Manila, Philippines
1996 *Blank Verse*, Fort Canning Park, Singapore
Wonderlust, Artspace, Sydney
1995 *Out of My Hair?*, Institute of Modern Art, Brisbane, Australia
1994 *Heart of the Matter*, The Substation, Singapore
Local Ginger, Sussex Estate, Singapore
1992 *Pooja/Loot*, Experimental Art Foundation, Adelaide, Australia
Deep Thoughts, Post West, Adelaide, Australia

Selected Group Exhibitions
1999 *Gang of Four*, Roslyn Oxley9 Gallery, Sydney
Au-Delà, Galerie Martin Klosterfelde, Berlin
Babel, Ikon Gallery, Birmingham, England
Asia-Pacific Triennial, Queensland Art Gallery, Brisbane, Australia
Australian Perspecta, Museum of Contemporary Art, Sydney
Letter To Picasso, Post Master Gallery, Melbourne
1998 *Close Quarters: Contemporary Art from Australia & New Zealand*, Monash University Gallery, Melbourne, and Australian Centre for Contemporary Art, Melbourne
Transit, The Art Gallery of New South Wales, Sydney
Schools, Valentine Willie Fine Art, Kuala Lumpur, Malaysia
1997 *Wardrobe*, Mad Love, Adelaide, Australia
Thin Skin, The Performance Space, Sydney
Web Sites, Australian Perspecta, The Art Gallery of New South Wales, Sydney
On Life, Beauty, Translations and Other Difficulties: 5th Istanbul Biennial, Istanbul
Cities On The Move, Weiner Secession, Vienna
1996 *Above & Beyond*, Australian Centre for Contemporary Art, Melbourne
1995 *Litteraria*, South Australian Museum, Adelaide, Australia
TransCulture, Naoshima Contemporary Art Museum, Naoshima, Japan
Skin Trilogy, National Art Gallery, Kuala Lumpur, Malaysia
1994 *Biodata, Adelaide Biennial*, Contemporary Art Centre of South Australia, Adelaide, Australia
Localities of Desire, Museum of Contemporary Art, Sydney
Jemmy, Ebenezar Studios, Adelaide, Australia
Let Me Speak, Matic, Kuala Lumpur, Malaysia
Vision & Idea: Relooking Modern Malaysian Art, National Art Gallery, Kuala Lumpur, Malaysia
1993 *What About Converging Extremes?*, Galeriwan, Kuala Lumpur, Malaysia
Here Not There, Institute of Modern Art, Brisbane, Australia
Images of a First Language, Prospect Gallery, Adelaide, Australia
1992 *Artist's Regional Exchange*, Perth Institute of Contemporary Arts, Perth, Australia
1991 *Possessed*, Bullring Gallery, Adelaide, Australia
Pastiche, Club Foote, Adelaide, Australia

Rodney Graham
1949 Born, Vancouver
Lives and works in Vancouver

Selected One-Person Exhibitions
1999 Museum of Contemporary Art, Miami
Donald Young Gallery, Chicago
1998 Johnen & Schöttle, Cologne, Germany
Wexner Center for the Arts, Columbus, Ohio
1997 303 Gallery, New York
Lisson Gallery, London
Angles Gallery, Santa Monica, California
Canadian Pavilion, XLVII Venice Biennale, Venice
1996 The Renaissance Society at the University of Chicago, Chicago
FRAC Basse-Normandie, Caen, France
Nicole Klagsbrun, New York
Morris and Helen Belkin Art Gallery, Vancouver
1995 303 Gallery, New York
Galerie Rüdiger Schöttle, Munich
Johnen & Schöttle, Cologne, Germany
Musée Départemental de Rochechouart, Rochechourart, France
1994 Art Gallery of York University, Toronto
Fundacio Espai Poblenou, Barcelona
Rodney Graham: Works from the Permanent Collection, Art Metropole, Toronto
Rodney Graham, Bernhard Starkmann, Boston
1993 Angles Gallery, Santa Monica, California
School of Velocity, Lisson Gallery, London

Concordance to the Standard Edition, Galerie Micheline Szwajcer, Antwerp, Belgium

1992 *Adjacent Film Frames*, Galerie One Five, Antwerp, Belgium
Galerie Nelson, Lyon, France

1991 *Stanley Park Cedars*, La Maison de la Culture et de la Communication de Saint-Etienne, Saint-Etienne, France
Ponderosa Pines, Galerie Rüdiger Schöttle, Munich

1990 *Parsifal*, Johnen & Schöttle, Cologne, Germany
Books, Lisson Gallery, London
Oxfordshire Trees, Christine Burgin Gallery, New York

Selected Group Exhibitions

2000 *Making Time*, Museum of Contemporary Art, Lake Worth, Florida

1999 *Time Traced*, Dia Center for the Arts, New York
Searchlight: Consciousness at the Millennium, California College of Arts and Crafts, San Francisco

1998 *La space de l'intime*, Printemps de Cahors, Cahors, France
The Serial Attitude, Wexner Center for the Arts, Columbus, Ohio, and Addison Gallery of American Art, Andover, Massachusetts
Dust Breeding, Fraenkel Gallery, San Francisco
Sharawadgi, Felsenvilla, Baden, Germany
Projected Allegories, Contemporary Arts Museum, Houston

1997 *Citta/Natura*, Palazzo delle Esposizioni, Rome
Wood Work, Fisher Landau Center, Long Island City, New York
Patrick Painter Editions, S.L. Simpson Gallery, Toronto
Niemandsland, Krefelder Kunstmuseum, Krefeld, Germany

1996 Johnen & Schöttle, Cologne, Germany
Lesen!, Kunsthalle St. Gallen, St. Gallen, Switzerland
Victor Burgin, Dan Graham, Rodney Graham, John Hilliard, Lisson Gallery, London
The Architecture of Dreams, Museo Regional de Guadalajara, Guadalajara, Mexico
Topographies, Vancouver Art Gallery, Vancouver
Rodney Graham, Geoffrey James, Richard Long, Angles Gallery, Santa Monica, California

1995 Centre Genevois de Gravure Contemporaine, Geneva, Switzerland
About the Place: Recent Art in the Americas, The Art Institute of Chicago, Chicago
Les fragments du désire, Futur Musée des Instruments, Brussels
Spirits at the Crossing, Setagaya Art Museum, Tokyo
Artistes/Architects, Le Nouveau Musée, Villeurbanne, France
Seeing Things, Galerie Antoni Estrany, Barcelona

1994 *Dan Graham, Rodney Graham, Jenny Holzer, Fotografien und Multiples*, Galerie Rüdiger Schöttle, Munich
In the Field, Margo Leavin Gallery, Los Angeles
Serial, Angles Gallery, Santa Monica, California
Beeld, Museum voor Hedendaagse Kunst, Gent, The Netherlands
Nicole Klagsbrun Gallery, New York
Des objects sans fondation, Residence Secondaire, Carrée Saint-Nicholas, Paris

1993 *Hans-Peter Feldmann, Rodney Graham, Allen Ruppersberg*, 303 Gallery, New York
Canada, Une Nouvelle Génération, Musée Municipal, La Roche sur Yon, France
Binaera; 14 Interaktionen—Kunst und Technologie, Kunsthalle Wien, Vienna
Second Tyne International, Newcastle-upon-Tyne, England
Voyage to Cythera, Vendremin Calergi Palace, Venice Biennale, Venice
Corners filled with what is swept into corners, Galerie Micheline Szwajcer, Antwerp, Belgium

1992 *Documenta IX*, Kassel, Germany
Rodney Graham et Ken Lum, Galerie Nelson, Paris
Cameres indiscrete: Rodney Graham, Ken Lum, Jeff Wall, Ian Wallace, Centre Santa Monica, Barcelona
Art by Numbers, Angles Gallery, Santa Monica, California
Los ultimos dias, Galeria del Arenal, Seville, Spain
Stars Don't Stand Still in the Sky—Hommage à Stêphane Mallarmé, Kunstmuseum, Winterthur, Switzerland
C'est pas la fin du monde, Rennes, France
Une seconde pensée du paysage, Centre d'Art Contemporain, Locriné, France
Inscapes, De Appel Foundation, Amsterdam
Acquisitions: 1989–1993, Stedelijk Van Abbemuseum, Eindhoven, The Netherlands

1991 *Le diaphane: Une reflexion, une collection, une exposition, un lieu*, Musée Municipal des Beaux-Arts and ERSEP-Ecole d'Art, Tourcoing, France
Rodney Graham, Stephen Prina, Christopher Williams, S.L. Simpson Gallery, Toronto
Learn to Read Art, Dia Center for the Arts, Basel Art Fair, Basel, Switzerland
La revanche de l'image, Galerie Pierre Huber, Geneva, Switzerland
Vanitas, Galerie Crousel-Robelin, Paris
Nieuwe vieugel, Stedelijk Van Abbemuseum, Eindhoven, The Netherlands
Crossroads, Art Gallery of York University, Toronto
Lost Illusions, Vancouver Art Gallery, Vancouver

1990 *Rodney Graham, Ian Wallace*, Rüdiger Schöttle Gallery, Munich
Weitersehen, Museum Haus Esters and Museum Haus Lange, Krefeld, Germany
Hanne Darboven, Rodney Graham, Antonio Muntadas, Lawrence Weiner, Galeria Marga Paz, Madrid
Oeuvres sur papier, Galerie Philip Nelson, Lyon, France
Real Allegories, Lisson Gallery, London
Figures et lectures, Galerie Samia Saoumia, Paris
Hacia el Paisaje, Centro Alantico de Arte Moderno, Canary Islands

Anthony Hernandez

1947 Born, Los Angeles
Lives and works in Los Angeles

Selected One-Person Exhibitions

2000 *Pictures for Rome*, Grant Selwyn, Beverly Hills, California, and Grant Selwyn, New York

1999 *City Point-Rome*, Galerie Polaris, Paris

1998 *The 70's*, Dan Bernier Gallery, Los Angeles

1997 Galerie Polaris, Paris
Craig Krull Gallery, Santa Monica, California
Centre National de la Photographie, Paris

1996 Musée de l'Elysée, Lausanne, Switzerland

1995 Craig Krull Gallery, Santa Monica, California
The Sprengel Museum Hannover, Hannover, Germany

1993 Turner/Krull Gallery, Los Angeles

1991 Turner/Krull Gallery, Los Angeles

1990 The Opsis Foundation, New York

Selected Group Exhibitions

2000 *Beyond Boundaries: Contemporary Photography in California*, Ansel Adams Center for Photography, San Francisco
Made in California 1900-2000, Los Angeles County Museum of Art, Los Angeles
Identification of a Landscape: Venezia-Marghera, Photography and the Transformation of the Contemporary City, Documents and Beyond, Museo Nacional Centro de Arte Reina Sofía, Madrid

1999 *C.O.L.A. Awards Show*, Los Angeles Municipal Art Gallery, Los Angeles
Two-person show with Jack Risley, Franco Riccardo, Naples, Italy

1998 *Radical Past*, Armory Center for the Arts, Pasadena, California

1997 *TRASH: When Waste Materials Become Art*, Museo d'Arte Moderna e Contemporanea, Rovereto, Italy
Scene of the Crime, Armand Hammer Museum of Art, Los Angeles

1996 *Long Beach: A Photographic Survey*, University Art Museum, California State University, Long Beach, California
Crossing the Frontier: Photographs of the Developing West, 1849 to the Present, San Francisco Museum of Modern Art, San Francisco
Herkunft?, Fotomuseum Winterthur, Winterthur, Switzerland

1995 *Street Engagements: Social Landscape Photography of the Sixties*, The Parrish Art Museum, Southhampton, New York

1994 *Love in the Ruins: Art and Inspiration of LA*, Long Beach Museum of Art, Long Beach, California

1993 *Wasteland: Landscape from Now On*, Fotografie Biennale III, Rotterdam, The Netherlands

1992 *Between Home and Heaven: Contemporary American Landscape Photography*, National Museum of American Art, Washington, D.C.

1991 *The City Life of Flora and Fauna*, The Seagram Gallery, New York
From the West, Gail Severn Gallery, Sun Valley, Idaho
Las Vegas, Mark Masuoka Galley, Las Vegas, Nevada

Gavin Hipkins

1968 Born, Auckland, New Zealand
Lives and works in Vancouver and Wellington, New Zealand

Selected One-Person Exhibitions

2000 *The Shaft*, Hamish McKay Gallery, Wellington, New Zealand
The Habitat, Artspace, Auckland, and Adam Art Gallery, Victoria University of Wellington, Wellington, New Zealand
1999 *The Pack*, Artspace, Sydney
The Circuit, Dunedin Public Art Gallery, Dunedin, New Zealand
The Well, Hamish McKay Gallery, Wellington, New Zealand
The Drop, Ivan Anthony Gallery, Auckland
Machine Art: Recent Work by Gavin Hipkins, Govett-Brewster Art Gallery, New Plymouth, New Zealand
1998 *The Coil*, Hamish McKay Gallery, Wellington, New Zealand
The Trench, Physics Room, Christchurch, New Zealand
1997 *The Tunnel*, Artspace, Auckland
The Blue Light, Hamish McKay Gallery, Wellington, New Zealand
Panorama, Teststrip, Auckland
1996 *The Field*, Dunedin Public Art Gallery, Dunedin, New Zealand
Third Party, James Smith Council Carpark, Wellington, New Zealand
1995 *The Vision*, Manawatu Gallery, Palmerston North, New Zealand
The Field, Teststrip, Auckland
Pictorial, Hamish McKay Gallery, Wellington, New Zealand

Selected Group Exhibitions

2000 *Guarene Arte 2000*, Palazzo Re Rebaudengo, Turin, Italy
Crystal Chain Gang, Auckland Art Gallery, Auckland
Grid Visions, Poole Arts Centre, Dorset, England
1999 *Fear and Beauty: New Zealand Art at the End of the Millennium*, The Suter Gallery, Nelson, New Zealand
Hothouse Deluxe, Wellington City Gallery and Michael Hirschfeld Gallery, Wellington, New Zealand
The Collected Works: Going Public at the Govett-Brewster Art Gallery 1970–2000, Govett-Brewster Art Gallery, New Plymouth, New Zealand
1998 *Every Day: 11th Biennale of Sydney*, Museum of Contemporary Art, Sydney
Leap of Faith: Contemporary New Zealand Art, Govett-Brewster Art Gallery, New Plymouth, New Zealand
F: Divergent Abstraction and the Photographic Project, University of Tasmania Plimsoll Gallery, Hobart, Australia
Media(tion): New Zealand Photographies, Blair Wakefield Exhibitions, Wellington, New Zealand
1997 *Killroy*, High Street Project, Christchurch, New Zealand
Signs of the Times: Sampling New Directions in New Zealand Art, Wellington City Gallery, Wellington, New Zealand
Visa Gold Art Award, Wellington City Gallery, Wellington, New Zealand, and Auckland Art Gallery, Auckland
Currents, Govett-Brewster Art Gallery, New Plymouth, New Zealand
1996 *Black Grams*, 23A Gallery, Auckland
Nostalgic, Monash University Gallery, Melbourne
A Selection of New Zealand Photography, Hamish McKay Gallery, Wellington, New Zealand
1995 *Currency—Contemporary Photographic Art*, Auckland Institute and Museum, Auckland
Symbolist Photography, Fisher Gallery, Auckland
1994 *Lest We Forget: Photography, Memory and National Character*, Wellington City Gallery, Wellington, New Zealand
Station to Station: The Way of the Cross, 14 Contemporary Artists, Auckland City Art Gallery, Auckland
Open the Shutter: Auckland Photographers Now, Auckland Institute and Museum, Auckland
Ten Years On, Contemporary Auckland Artists, Fisher Gallery, Auckland
Circle of Confusion: 7 Photographers, Hamish McKay Gallery, Wellington, New Zealand
Striptease, Teststrip, Auckland
1993 *Composition as Explanation*, George Fraser Gallery, Auckland, and High Street Project, Christchurch, New Zealand
Comfort Zone, Govett-Brewster Art Gallery, New Plymouth, New Zealand
In Three Acts, Artspace, Auckland
Suffer, Teststrip, Auckland, and Hamish McKay Gallery, Wellington, New Zealand
1992 *Scenes—From Real and Imaginary Lives: Recent Photography*, Wellington City Art Gallery, Wellington, New Zealand
False Horizons, Artspace, Auckland
Caterpillar Landscape, Auckland Society of Arts, Auckland, New Zealand

Igloolik Isuma Productions

Zacharias Kunuk, Norman Cohn, Paulossie Qulitalik
All members live and work in Igloolik, Nunavut, Canada

Selected Videography

1999 *NIPI (Voice)*, 51:00
1995 *Episode 1: Qimuksik (Dog Team)—Nunavut (Our Land)*, 28:50
Episode 2: Avaja (Avaja)—Nunavut (Our Land), 28:50
Episode 3: Qamaq (Stone House)—Nunavut (Our Land), 28:50
Episode 4: Tugaliaq (Ice Blocks)—Nunavut (Our Land), 28:50
Episode 5: Angiraq (Home)—Nunavut (Our Land), 28:50
Episode 6: Auriaq (Stalking)—Nunavut (Our Land), 28:50
Episode 7: Qulungisi (Seal Pups)—Nunavut (Our Land), 28:50
Episode 8: Avamuktalik (Fish Swimming Back and Forth)—Nunavut (Our Land), 28:50
Episode 9: Aiviaq (Walrus)—Nunavut (Our Land), 28:50
Episode 10: Qaisut—Nunavut (Our Land), 28:50
Episode 11: Tukutuliaq (Caribou Hunt)—Nunavut (Our Land), 28:50
Episode 12: Unaaq (Harpoon)—Nunavut (Our Land), 28:50
Episode 13: Quviasuvik (Happy Day)—Nunavut (Our Land), 28:50
1993 *Saputi (Fish Traps)*, 30:30
1991 *Nunaqpa (Going Inland)*, 58:15
1989 *Qaggiq (Gathering Place)*, 58:00

Tim Johnson

1947 Born, Sydney
Lives and works in Sydney

Selected One-Person Exhibitions

2000 Tolarno Galleries, Melbourne
1998 *The Sources Are Real*, Mori Gallery, Sydney
Alien Land, Tolarno Galleries, Melbourne
Tim Johnson and Karma Phuntsok, Bellas Gallery, Brisbane, Australia
1997 *On the Internet*, Mori Gallery, Sydney
CD installation, Tolarno Galleries, Melbourne
1996 Chapman Gallery, Canberra, Australia
1995 *4 Directions*, Mori Gallery, Sydney
Tolarno Galleries, Melbourne
Non La, Bellas Gallery, Brisbane, Australia
1994 *Tim Johnson*, Glasgow Museum, Glasgow
Asia, Mori Gallery, Sydney
Chapman Gallery, Canberra, Australia
1993 *Shareware*, Tolarno Galleries, Melbourne
Across Cultures, Ian Potter Gallery, University of Melbourne, Melbourne
1992 *Visualisation*, Mori Gallery, Sydney, and Bellas Gallery, Brisbane, Australia
1991 *Armageddon*, Mori Gallery, Sydney
Chapman Gallery, Canberra, Australia

Selected Group Exhibitions

1999 Tolarno Galleries at the Perth Festival, Perth, Australia
Bright and Shining, 4A Gallery, Sydney
Global Arts Link, Ipswich, Australia
The Rose Crossing, Queensland Art Gallery, Brisbane, Australia
What John Berger Saw, Australian National University, Canberra, Australia
The Chartwell Collection, Auckland Art Gallery, Auckland
Asia-Pacific Triennal, Brisbane, Australia
1998 *Mingling of Cultures*, Australian National Gallery, Canberra, Australia
Crossing Boundaries, with Zen Yipu and My Le Thi, Australian National University, Canberra, Australia
Wilderness Society Exhibition, Mori Gallery, Sydney
Verve, S.H. Erwin Gallery, Sydney
Be Seeing You…, Mori Gallery, Sydney
Dylan, Tim Johnson and Greg Weight, Michael Nagy Fine Art, Sydney
Ways of Being, Ivan Dougherty Gallery, Sydney
1997 *Spirit + Place*, Museum of Contemporary Art, Sydney
Objects + Ideas, Museum of Contemporary Art, Sydney
Plastic Fantastic, Museum of Contemporary Art, Sydney
Inside, University of Kassel, Kassel, Germany
Similar, with My Le Thi, 4A Gallery, Sydney
Dead Sun, The Art Gallery of New South Wales, Sydney
MacCaughey Prize Exhibition, National Gallery of Victoria, Melbourne
1996 *Hidden Treasures II*, S.H. Erwin Gallery, Sydney
Colonial, Post-Colonial, Museum of Modern Art at Heide, Melbourne

Australia: Familiar and Strange, Seoul Arts Center, Seoul, South Korea

1995 *Antipodean Currents*, Guggenheim Museum Soho, New York
Asia & Oceania Influence, Ivan Dougherty Gallery, Sydney

1994 *Light and Movement*, Museum of Contemporary Art, Sydney
25 Years of Performance Art in Australia, Ivan Dougherty Gallery, Sydney

1993 *Identities: Art from Australia*, Taipei Fine Arts Museum, Taiwan
Wits End, Museum of Contemporary Art, Sydney
Art Frankfurt, Messe Frankfurt, Frankfurt
Art Cologne, Köln Messe, Cologne, Germany
Luminaries, Monash University Gallery, Melbourne
Inaugural Exhibition, Museum of Modern Art at Heide, Melbourne

1992 *Ninth Biennale of Sydney: The Boundary Rider*, The Art Gallery of New South Wales, Sydney
Documenta IX, Kassel, Germany
Domino I: Collaborations Between Artists, Ian Potter Gallery, Melbourne

1991 *Off the Wall/In the Air: A Seventies Selection*, Monash University Gallery, Melbourne
Artists Make Books, Linden Gallery, Melbourne
Rivers, Australian Centre for Contemporary Art, Melbourne

1990 *Paraculture*, Artists Space, New York
Art Frankfurt, Kunstmesse Frankfurt, Frankfurt
Out of Asia, Heide Gallery, Melbourne
L'été australien à Montpellier, Musée Fabre, Montpellier, France
Balance, Queensland Art Gallery, Brisbane, Australia
Art Dock, Noumea, New Caledonia

Rachel Khedoori

1964 Born, Sydney
Lives and works in Los Angeles

Selected One-Person Exhibitions

2000 Galerie Gisela Capitain, Cologne, Germany

1999 *Rachel Khedoori*, David Zwirner, New York

1997 *Rachel Khedoori*, Galerie Hauser & Wirth, Zurich

1995 Association of the Museum van Hedendaagse Kunst, Gent, Belgium
Rum, Malmö, Sweden

Selected Group Exhibitions

2000 *Sammlung (1), The Oldest Possible Memory*, Sammlung Hauser & Wirth, St. Gallen, Switzerland

1999 *Forget About the Ball and Get On with the Game*, Kunsthaus Nürnberg, Nürnberg, Germany
Los Angeles, Philomene Magers Projekte and Galerie Sabine Kunst, Munich

1997 *Kunstausstellung Holderbank*, Holderbank, Switzerland

1996 *Wanås 1996*, The Wanås Foundation, Knislinge, Sweden
Inklusion Exklusion: Kunst im Zeitalter von ostkolonialismus und globaler Migration, Sterischer Herbst 96, Graz, Austria

1994 *Rachel Khedoori and Toba Khedoori*, David Zwirner, New York

Roy Kiyooka

1926 Born, Moose Jaw, Saskatchewan
1994 Died, Vancouver

Selected One-Person Exhibitions

1999 *Works by Roy Kiyooka*, Concourse Gallery, organized by Charles H. Scott Gallery, Vancouver
Selected Work, Catriona Jeffries Gallery, Vancouver

1998 *Photographic Works 1970–1994*, Catriona Jeffries Gallery, Vancouver

1992 *Hoarfrost*, University of British Columbia Fine Arts Gallery, Vancouver

1990 *Roy Kiyooka, Intersections: Interventions*, Artspeak Gallery and Or Gallery, Vancouver

1985 *In/Around/My Japan: A Canadian/Japanese Artist's Color Prints Taken Between 1969–1984 by Roy Kiyooka*, Richmond Art Gallery, Richmond, British Columbia

1981 University of Toronto Art Gallery, Scarborough, Ontario

1975 *Roy Kiyooka: 25 Years*, Vancouver Art Gallery, Vancouver

1970 *World Expo 70*, Osaka, Japan
StoneDGloves: alms for soft palms, University of British Columbia, Vancouver

Selected Group Exhibitions

1999 *War Zones, Bearing Witness*, Presentation House Gallery, North Vancouver
Out of this Century, Vancouver Art Gallery, Vancouver

1992 *The Crisis of Abstraction in Canada: The 1950s*, National Gallery of Canada, Ottawa, Ontario, Canada
Visions of the Prairie Landscape, Art Gallery of Windsor, Windsor, Ontario, Canada

1990 *Yellow Peril Reconsidered*, Oboro, Montreal, Quebec, Canada

1989 *The Flat Side of the Landscape*, Mendel Art Gallery, Saskatoon, Saskatchewan, Canada

1986 *Founders of the Alberta College of Art*, Alberta College of Art Gallery, Calgary, Alberta, Canada

1978 *13 Cameras*, Vancouver Art Gallery, Vancouver

1974 *477-74-7 B.F.A. Faculty Show*, University of British Columbia Fine Arts Gallery, Vancouver

1973 *Japanese Artists of the Americas*, National Museum of Modern Art Kyoto, Kyoto, Japan
Emma Lake Workshops 1955–1973, Norman Mackenzie Art Gallery, Regina, Saskatchewan, Canada
Mystic Circle Exhibition, Burnaby Art Gallery, Burnaby, British Columbia, Canada

1972 *Halifax/Vancouver Exchange*, Vancouver Art Gallery, Vancouver

1971 *Faculty Show*, Nova Scotia College of Art, Halifax, Nova Scotia

1970 *B.C. Almanac(h) C.B.*, National Film Board Still Photography Division, Ottawa, Ontario, Canada

David Lamelas

1946 Born, Buenos Aires
Lives and works in Los Angeles, Brussels, and Berlin

Selected One-Person Exhibitions

2000 *Projects on Canvas and Paper, 1984–1990*, Galerie Kienzle & Gmeiner, Berlin
The Invention of Dr. Morel, Neue Nationalgalerie, Berlin

1999 *Berlin, Time as Activity*, Galerie Gisela Capitain, Cologne, Germany
L'invention, Centre d'Art Contemporain, Brussels

1998 *time cuts*, Künstlerhaus Stuttgart, Stuttgart, Germany
Galerie Kienzle & Gmeiner, Berlin
DAAD Galerie, Berlin
Filme, Institut für Gegenwartskunst, Vienna
Cinefrac 1998, FRAC Film Script, Bordeaux

1997 *A New Refutation of Time: Werke 1963–76*, Wanderausstellung Kunstverein München, Munich
House—People, Encore Bruxelles, Brussels

1995 *Lecture "Reading Films,"* APP.BXL LOBBY, Brussels

1993 Galleria Fac Simile, Milan
8 Disegni, Studio Michela Scotti, Milan

1991 *Lavandula, Labiatae, Lamiales*, Palais des Beaux-Arts, Brussels

Selected Group Exhibitions

2000 *Live In Your Head*, The Whitechapel Art Gallery, London
The Sleep of Reason, Norwich Gallery, Norwich, England
Making Time: Considering Time as a Material in Contemporary Film and Video, Palm Beach Institute of Contemporary Art, Palm Beach, Florida

1999 *Serein und Konzepte in der Photo-und Videokunst*, Museum Ludwig Köln, Cologne, Germany
Art/Film, Art 30 Basel, Kunsthalle Basel, Basel, Switzerland
Children of Berlin, Kunst-Werke Berlin, Berlin, and P.S. 1 Contemporary Art Center, New York

1998 *Raum/Schnitt/Denken 3—David Lamelas/Marguerite Duras*, Deutsches Architektur Zentrum, Berlin

1997 *The Impossible Document: Photography and British Conceptual Art in Britain 1966-1976*, Camerawork, London
InSite97, Installation Gallery, San Diego, California
OPEN MUSEUM, Provinciaal Centrum voor Beeldende Kunsten, Hasselt, Belgium

1996 *Quaisiasi cosa vi venga in mente*, Galleria Fac Simile, Milan
Zoersel '96, Domein Kasteel van Halle, Zoersel, Belgium
Perfect, Galerie Mot & Van den Boogaard, Brussels

1995 *Reconsidering the Object of Art, 1965–1975*, The Museum of Contemporary Art, Los Angeles
Fundacion Baur Patucus, Buenos Aires

1994 *Cuarte Pared*, Museum Jacobo Borges, Caracas, Venezuela
Leandro Katz, David Lamelas, Liliana Porter, ICI, Buenos Aires
Dialogues, Provinciaal Museum Hasselt, Hasselt, Belgium

M.A.C. (Galeries contemporaines des Musées des Marseille), Marseille, France
1993 Palais des Beaux-Arts, Brussels
1992 *America: Bride of the Sun*, Royal Museum of Fine Arts, Antwerp
Lichtspiele, Kunsthalle Wien, Vienna
1991 Carla Stellweg Gallery, New York
1990 *David Lamelas/Luis Camnitzer*, Carla Stellweg Gallery, New York
Au commencement, Centre d'Art de Guerigny, Guerigny, France

Simon Leung

1964 Born, Hong Kong
Lives and works in Los Angeles and New York

Selected One-Person Exhibitions

1998 *Surf Vietnam*, Huntington Beach Art Center, Huntington Beach, California
1997 *Proposal for Surf Vietnam*, Refusalon, San Francisco
1996 *Call to Glory...or Afternoon Tea with Marcel Duchamp*, Pat Hearn Gallery, New York
1991 *Memories of the Sea*, N.A.M.E., Chicago

Selected Group Exhibitions

1999 *O Melancholy Bitter Wall of Eagles*, Rosamund Felsen Gallery, Santa Monica, California
DR. KRENSLOVE: or how I learned to stop worrying and love the MU$EUM, American Fine Art Co., New York
RE-MIX, Popular Mechanics, Los Angeles
The Manchurian Candidate, 30 Paris House, London
1998 *The Making Of*, Generali Foundation, Vienna
Trash, Los Angeles Municipal Art Gallery, Barnsdall Park, Los Angeles
Surfboards Unique and Unusual, International Surfing Museum, Huntington Beach, California
E Pluribus Nihil, American Fine Art Co. and Colin De Land Fine Art, New York
1997 *Figure*, Betty Rymer Gallery, School of The Art Institute of Chicago, Chicago
Blind Date, California Institute of the Arts, Valencia, California
Hollywood Premiere, Just For the Night, Popular Mechanics, Los Angeles
Webradio for Do It Yourself, thing.net, New York
The Gramercy International, Los Angeles, Chateau Marmont, West Hollywood, California
1996 *Thinking Print*, The Museum of Modern Art, New York
The Male Gaze from y to z, Galerie Jennifer Flay, Paris
Disappeared, Randolph Street Gallery, Chicago
1995 *Dennis Balk/Simon Leung/Nils Norman*, Pat Hearn Gallery, New York
In the Flesh, Aldrich Museum of Contemporary Art, Ridgefield, Connecticut
Desiring Authors, Enveloping Myths, Bernard Toale Gallery, Boston
50, Storefront for Art & Architecture, New York
Page 12, 450 Broadway Gallery, New York
1994 *GEWALT/Geschäfte*, Neue Gesellschaft für Bildende Kunst, Berlin
Bioinformatica, Sandra Gering Gallery, New York
ACT UP Art Box, Josh Baer Gallery and Fawbush Gallery, New York
Taste/Venue, Pat Hearn Gallery, New York
1993 *Whitney Biennial*, Whitney Museum of American Art, New York
Ciphers of Identity, University of Maryland, Baltimore, Maryland
Futura Book Collection, Air de Paris, Nice, France
CHANGING I-dense cities, Shedhalle, Zurich
Studio Programs, P.S. 1 Contemporary Art Center, New York
The Shooting Gallery, Los Angeles Center for Photographic Studies, Los Angeles
The Return of the Cadavre Exquis, The Drawing Center, New York
1992 *The Auto-Erotic Object*, Hunter College, New York
Still, Andrea Rosen Gallery, New York
The Big Nothing, The New Museum of Contemporary Art, New York
Benefit Exhibition, The New Museum of Contemporary Art, New York
Simon Leung/Andrea Zittel, Andrea Rosen Gallery, New York
1991 *Gretchen Faust/Simon Leung/Jonathan Genkin*, Nicole Klagsbrun Gallery, New York
(Dis)member, Traditional Values and Simon Watson, New York
All Grown Up, City University of New York, New York
Art Joven en Nueva York, Sala Mendoza, Caracas, Venezuela
1990 *Viral Infection: The Body and Its Discontents*, HALLWALLS, Buffalo, New York
INSTALLATIONS, The Drawing Center, New York
Stendhal Syndrome: The Cure, Andrea Rosen Gallery, New York
Manipulation and Photography, THE Gallery, New York

Tracey Moffatt

1960 Born, Brisbane, Australia
Lives and works in New York

Selected One-Person Exhibitions

2000 Matthew Marks Gallery, New York
1999 *Laudanum*, Ulmer Museum, Ulm, Germany
Tracey Moffatt, Institute of Contemporary Art, Brisbane, Australia
Kunstverein Freiburg, Freiburg, Germany
L.A. Galerie, Frankfurt
Fundació Caixa de Pensions, Barcelona
Rena Bransten, San Francisco
Torch Gallery, Amsterdam
Lawing Gallery, Houston, Texas
Free Falling, Institute of Contemporary Art, Boston
Paul Morris Gallery, New York
Roslyn Oxley9 Gallery, Sydney
Fundació "la Caixa," Sala San Juan, Barcelona
Centre National de la Photographie, Paris
Galerie Salomon Laage, Paris
1998 Arnolfini, Bristol, England
Roslyn Oxley9 Gallery, Sydney
Victoria Miro Gallery, London
L.A. Galerie, Frankfurt
Württembergischer Kunstverein, Stuttgart, Germany
Magazin 4, Volarlberger Kunstverein, Bergenz, Austria
Le Case d'Arte, Milan
Monash University Gallery, Melbourne
Curtin University Gallery, Perth, Australia
Galleri Larsen, Stockholm
1997 *Free Falling*, Dia Center for the Arts, New York
L.A. Galerie, Frankfurt
Fond Regional d'Art Contemporain Bourgogne, Dijon, France
Casino Luxembourg, Luxembourg
Musée d'Art Contemporain, Lyon, France
1995 *Guapa (Goodlooking)*, Karyn Lovegrove Gallery, Melbourne
Short Takes, ArtPace, San Antonio, Texas
1994 *Scarred for Life*, Karyn Lovegrove Gallery, Melbourne
1992 *Pet Thang*, Mori Gallery, Sydney
Tracey Moffatt, Centre for Contemporary Arts, Glasgow

Selected Group Exhibitions

1999 *Wohin Kein Auge Reicht*, Deichtorhallen, Hamburg
1998 *Das Versprechen der Photographie, Die Sammlung der DG Bank*, Hara Museum of Contemporary Art, Tokyo
Rosa für Jungs, Hellblau für Mädchen, Neue Gesellschaft für Bildende Kunst, Berlin
Présumés innocentes, Capc Musée d'art Contemporain, Bordeaux, France
Roteritos' x 7, XXVI Bienal de São Paolo, São Paolo
Portraits, Paul Morris Gallery, New York
Fleeting Portraits, Neue Gesellschaft für Bildende Kunst, Berlin
Horizont, Brecthaus am Weissensee, Berlin
The Human Being, Kunstverein, Schloss Plö, Germany
Life Is a Bitch, De Appel Foundation, Amsterdam
Family Viewing, The Museum of Contemporary Art, Los Angeles
Nature of Man, Lunds Konsthall, Lund, Sweden
1997 *Site Santa Fe*, Santa Fe, New Mexico
Campo 6, The Spiral Village, Bonnefanten Museum, Maastricht, The Netherlands
Subject to Representation, Gallery 101, Ottawa, Canada
Venice Biennale, Venice
1996 *Fundacao Biennal de São Paulo*, São Paulo
Campo 6, The Spiral Village, Museum of Modern Art, Turin, Italy
Jurassic Technologies, Tenth Biennale of Sydney, Sydney
Prospect 96, Schirn Kunsthalle Frankfurt, Frankfurt
Short Stories, Altes Rathaus, Göttingen, Germany
1995 *Familiar Places*, Institute of Contemporary Art, Boston
'95 Kwangju Biennale, Kwangju, Korea
New Works 95, ArtPace, San Antonio, Texas
Perspecta 95, Art Gallery of New South Wales, Sydney

1994 *Antipodean Currents*, The John F. Kennedy Center for the Performing Arts, Washington, D.C.
Power Works, Govett-Brewster Art Gallery, New Plymouth, New Zealand
1993 *The Boundary Rider*, Ninth Biennale of Sydney, Sydney
1992 *Artist's Projects*, Adelaide Festival of the Arts, Adelaide, Australia
1991 *From the Empire's End*, Circulo de Bellas Artes, Madrid
1990 *Satellite Cultures*, The New Museum of Contemporary Art, New York

Lee Mullican

1919 Born, Chickasha, Oklahoma
1998 Died, Los Angeles

Selected One-Person Exhibitions

2000 *Lee Mullican: Work from the 1950s*, James Kelly Contemporary, Santa Fe, New Mexico
Turning Worlds to Fable: Paintings and Drawings from the 1940s and 1950s, Grant Selwyn, New York
1999 *Lee Mullican: Paintings from the 1940's and 1950's*, Grant Selwyn, Los Angeles
Lee Mullican: Selected Drawings 1945-1980, The Armand Hammer Museum of Art, Los Angeles
1985 Herbert Palmer Gallery, Los Angeles
1977 Stables Gallery, Taos Art Association, Taos, New Mexico
1976 *Paintings and Drawings in the Museum's Collection*, Santa Barbara Art Museum, Santa Barbara, California
1973 *Retrospective: Selected Works*, Santa Barbara Art Museum, Santa Barbara, California
1972 Patrick Shannon, Santa Fe, New Mexico
1971 Jodi Scully Gallery, Los Angeles

Selected Group Exhibitions

2000 *The Influence of Native American Art on 1930s and 1940s Modernists*, David Findlay Jr. Fine Art, New York
Themes Out of School: Art & Education in Los Angeles, Creative Artists Agency, Los Angeles
1999 *The American Century, Art & Culture 1900–2000*, Whitney Museum of American Art, New York
1997 *Sculpture Exhibition*, Phoenix Gallery, Taos, New Mexico
1995 *Pacific Dreams, Currents of Surrealism and Fantasy in California Art, 1934–1957*, Oakland Museum of California, Oakland, California
1989 *Mullican + Mullican*, Lee Mullican and Matt Mullican, Jonson Gallery, University Art Museum, University of Albuquerque, New Mexico
1978 *Creation*, with Gordon Onslow Ford, Galerie Gerard Schreiner, Basel, Switzerland
1977 *Private Images—Photographs by Painters*, Los Angeles County Museum of Art, Los Angeles
Dynaton Re-Viewed, Three Painters, Lee Mullican, Gordon Onslow Ford, Wolfgang Paalen, Paule Anglim Gallery, San Francisco
Photographs by Southern California Painters and Sculptors, College of Creative Studies, University of California, Santa Barbara, California
1976 *California Painting and Sculpture, The Modern Era*, San Francisco Museum of Art, San Francisco
1975 *The Artist Collects*, Newport Harbor Museum, Newport Beach, California
1974 Rose Rabow, San Francisco
1970 Rose Rabow, San Francisco

Paul Outerbridge

1896 Born, New York
1958 Died, Laguna Beach, California

Selected One-Person Exhibitions

1959 The Smithsonian Institution, Washington, D.C.
1923 Art Center, New York

Selected Group Exhibitions

1979 G. Ray Hawkins Gallery, Los Angeles
1978 Rotterdamse Kunstichting, Rotterdam, The Netherlands
Tyler Museum of Art, Tyler, Texas
Center for the Visual Arts, Illinois State University, Normal, Illinois
1977 G. Ray Hawkins Gallery, Los Angeles
The Corcoran Gallery of Art, Washington, D.C.
1951 Los Angeles County Fair, Los Angeles
1944 *Third National Print and Drawing Exhibition*, Laguna Beach, California
1940 *Photographic Society of America Invitational Salon*, New York World's Fair, New York
1932 *Exhibition of Advertising Art*, Art Center, New York
Brooklyn Museum of Art, Brooklyn, New York
1931 Albright Art Gallery, Buffalo, New York
Third Annual Exhibition of Contemporary Photography, The Ayer Galleries, Philadelphia
Eleventh Annual Exhibition of Advertising Art, Art Center, New York
1930 American Designers Gallery, New York
1929 *Film und Foto*, Werkbundausstellung, Stuttgart, Germany
1928 First Independent Salon of Photography, Salon d'Escallier, Paris
1924 First International Salon of the Pictorial Photographers of America, New York
Society of Independent Artists, New York
1923 John Wanamaker Gallery, New York
Society of Independent Artists, New York

Michael Parekowhai

1968 Born, Petone, New Zealand
Nga-Ariki, Ngati Whakarongo
Lives and works in Auckland, New Zealand

Selected One-Person Exhibitions

1999 *Patriot: Ten Guitars*, Artspace, Auckland
Kitset Cultures, djamu Gallery, Sydney
1998 *Recent Paintings*, Jonathan Smart Gallery, Christchurch, New Zealand
1997 *Recent Paintings*, Gow-Langsford Gallery, Auckland
1994 *Kiss the Baby Goodbye*, Govett-Brewster Art Gallery, New Plymouth, New Zealand
A Capella, Gregory Flint Gallery, Auckland

Selected Group Exhibitions

2000 *Simpson Grierson Season—Works from the Collection*, Auckland Art Gallery, Auckland
Wonderlands, Govett-Brewster Art Gallery, New Plymouth, New Zealand
1999 *Beyond the Future: The Third Asia-Pacific Triennial*, Queensland Art Gallery, Brisbane, Australia
Home and Away, Auckland Art Gallery, Auckland
Taonga Mauri, Artstation, Auckland
Who Do I Think I Am, Artspace, Auckland
Wonderlands: Views on Life at the End of the Century, at the End of the World, Govett-Brewster Art Gallery, New Plymouth, New Zealand
1998 *Dream Collectors*, Museum of New Zealand Te Papa Tongarewa, Wellington, New Zealand
1996 *The World Over/De Wereld Bollen: Art in the Age of Globalisation*, Wellington City Gallery, Wellington, New Zealand
Here I Give Thanks, Dunedin Public Art Gallery, Dunedin, New Zealand
1995 *Cultural Safety*, Waikato Museum of Art and History, Hamilton, New Zealand
The Nervous System, Govett-Brewster Art Gallery, New Plymouth, New Zealand
Korungi, Auckland Art Gallery, Auckland
1994 *Art Now*, National Gallery, Wellington, New Zealand
Changing Signs, Artspace, Auckland
1993 *After McCahon*, Cubism, Wellington, New Zealand
Shared Pleasures, Waikato Museum of Art and History, Hamilton, New Zealand
International Festival of the Arts, Wellington, New Zealand
Stop Making Sense, Wellington City Gallery, Wellington, New Zealand
1992 *Homemade Home*, Wellington City Gallery, Wellington, New Zealand
Vogue/Vague, C.S.A., Christchurch, New Zealand
Hit Parade: Contemporary Art from the Paris Family Collection, Wellington City Gallery, Wellington, New Zealand
W.A.R. Whatu Aho Rua, Tandanya Gallery, Adelaide, Australia
Headlands: thinking through New Zealand Art, National Art Gallery, Wellington, New Zealand
1991 *Light Sensitive*, Artspace, Auckland
Cross-pollination, Artspace, Auckland
1990 *Kohia ko Taikaka Anake*, National Art Gallery, Wellington, New Zealand
Choice! Artspace, Auckland
Light'arted, Artspace, Auckland

Allan Sekula

1951 Born, Erie, Pennsylvania
Lives and works in Los Angeles

Selected One-Person Exhibitions

2000 Christopher Grimes Gallery, Santa Monica, California
Tours Art Vivant C.C.C., Tours, France
Dear Bill Gates, Museum Boymans-van-Beuningen, Rotterdam, The Netherlands
1999 *Freeway to China (Version 2 for Liverpool)*, Open Eye Gallery, Liverpool, England
Fish Story, Henry Art Gallery, Seattle
1998 *Dead Letter Office*, Palais des Beaux-Arts, Brussels
Deep Six/Passer au bleu, Musée des Beaux-Arts et de la Dentelle, Calais, France
Dead Letter Office, Galerie Michel Rein, Tours, France

1996 *Dismal Science: Photo Works 1972–1996*, University Galleries, Illinois State University, Normal, Illinois
Middle Passage, Museum Boymans-van-Beuningen, Rotterdam, The Netherlands
Fish Story, Santa Monica Museum of Art, Santa Monica, California
1995 *Fish Story*, Witte de With Center for Contemporary Art, Rotterdam, The Netherlands
1993 *Fish Story (Work in Progress)*, University Art Museum, Berkeley, California
1991 *Geography Lesson: Canadian Notes* and *Aerospace Folktales*, Vancouver Art Gallery, Vancouver

Selected Group Exhibitions

2000 *Made in California*, Los Angeles County Museum of Art, Los Angeles
Desert and Transit, Kunsthalle zu Kiel, Kiel, Germany
Die Regierung/The Government, Kestner Gesellschaft, Hannover, Germany
Rotterdam Foto Biennial, Rotterdam, The Netherlands
Seascape, Christopher Grimes Gallery, Santa Monica, California
1999 *Trace: Liverpool Biennial*, Liverpool, England
1998 *Voyage: de l'exotisme aux non lieux*, Musée de la Valence, Valence, France
La mer n'est pas la terre, La Criée, Rennes, France
Port and Corridor: Work Sites in Los Angeles: Robbert Flick and Allan Sekula, The Getty Research Institute, Los Angeles
Scratches on the Surface of Things, Museum Boymans-van-Beuningen, Rotterdam, The Netherlands
1997 *InSite 97*, San Diego/Tijuana, Centro Cultural Tijuana, Tijuana, Mexico
1996 *Face à l'histoire*, Centre Pompidou, Paris
1994 *Propositions I*, One Five, Brussels
1993 *Trade Routes*, The New Museum of Contemporary Art, New York
Whitney Biennial, Whitney Museum of American Art, New York
1992 *Wasteland: Landscape from Now On*, Fotografie Biennale Rotterdam, Rotterdam, The Netherlands
Proof: Los Angeles Art and the Photograph 1960–1980, Laguna Art Museum, Laguna Beach, California
1991 *A Dialogue About Recent American and European Photography*, The Museum of Contemporary Art, Los Angeles
The Power of Words: An Aspect of Recent Documentary Photography, P.P.O.W., New York
Critical Realism, Perspektief, Rotterdam, The Netherlands

Yuk King Tan

1971 Born, Townsville, Australia
Lives and works in Auckland, New Zealand

Selected Solo Exhibitions

1999 *instant!*, Ludwig Forum für Internationale Kunst, Aachen, Germany
badsituationism, Mehrwerrt Vitrine, Aachen, Germany
1997 *The Picturesque*, The Govett Brewster Art Gallery, New Plymouth, New Zealand
sleepeasy, Dunedin Public Art Gallery, Dunedin, New Zealand
1996 *bodyblow*, Johnathon Smart Gallery, Christchurch, New Zealand
Escape Velocity, Sue Crockford Art Gallery, Auckland
1995 *Combination no.3—hot off the shelf*, Manawatu Public Art Gallery, Palmerston North, New Zealand
1994 *Artistical and Orna Mental*, Artspace, Auckland

Selected Group Exhibitions

1999 *More Than Ever*, Fiat Lux Gallery, Auckland
Who Do I Think I Am, Artspace, Auckland
James Wallace/Visa Gold Awards Exhibition, Wellington City Gallery, Wellington, New Zealand
Robert McDougall Gallery, Christchurch, New Zealand
Take 5, Museum of New Zealand Te Papa Tongarewa, New Zealand
New Work, Hamish McKay Gallery, Wellington, New Zealand
Toi Toi Toi, Museum Fridericianum, Kassel, Germany
badsituationism 10min 26sec, Ludwig Forum für Internationale Kunst, Aachen, Germany
1998 *Grapple*, Pinnacles Gallery, Townsville, Australia
Pasifica, Canberra Contemporary Artspace, Canberra, Australia, and Gallery 4A, Sydney
Take-away Symbols, Govett-Brewster Art Gallery, New Plymouth, New Zealand
1997 *The Oriental Room*, Auckland War Memorial Museum, Auckland
4 Artists, Sue Crockford Gallery, Auckland
1996 *Fusion*, Auckland Art Gallery, Auckland
Asia-Pacific Triennial, Queensland Art Gallery, Brisbane, Australia
TransFusion, Hong Kong Arts Centre, Hong Kong
Heirloom, Monash University Gallery, Melbourne
No.3 De Etalagg, Den Haag, The Netherlands
The Concrete Deal, James Smith Carpark, Wellington, New Zealand
New Zealand/New China, International Festival of the Arts, Wellington, New Zealand
1995 *The New Temple—I Give So That You Give, I Give So That You May Go and Stay Away*, Window Project, Auckland Art Gallery, Auckland
Fleshly Worn—Bodies in Question, ASA, Auckland
The Nervous System, Govett-Brewster Art Gallery, New Plymouth, New Zealand, and Wellington City Gallery, Wellington, New Zealand
Northern Exposure, McDougall Art Annex, Christchurch, New Zealand
Sculpitecture, Hamish McKay Gallery, Wellington, New Zealand
WOW! Yuk and Ani's Show, Teststrip Gallery, Auckland
1994 *Localities of Desire—Art in an International World*, Museum of Contemporary Art, Sydney
Knight Landesman Exhibition, Teststrip Gallery, Auckland
Taking Stock of the 90's, Sarjeant Art Gallery, Wanganui, New Zealand
4 Artists, Hamish McKay Gallery, Wellington, New Zealand
1993 *Suffer II*, Hamish McKay Gallery, Wellington, New Zealand
a. genda, Artspace, Auckland
1992 *Chemical and Catalyst*, Chemistry Building, Auckland

Glen Wilson

1969 Born, Columbus, Ohio
Lives and works in Los Angeles

Selected One-Person Exhibitions

1999 *Origins Malagache?*, North Park Studio, San Diego, California
1997 *drum: a photo-based installation*, Los Angeles Center for Photographic Studies, Los Angeles
1996 *free (a site-specific performance)*, University of California, San Diego, California
Beyond the Pale (a three act protest), University of California, San Diego, California
1995 *Giant Inflatable Thing*, Visual Arts Center, University of California, San Diego, California
drum: a photo-based installation, Visual Arts Center, University of California, San Diego, California
1994 *Speakin' of Change: A Spoken Work Event*, Intersection Gallery, San Diego, California
1993 *I-NOMA*, Spring Site, Chicago

Selected Group Exhibitions

2000 *iNSITE2000, Interstice 2001: The Nomad Project*, Installation Gallery, San Diego, California
1998 *Xtrascape*, Los Angeles Municipal Art Gallery, Los Angeles
Summer Collections, The Los Angeles Center for Photographic Studies, Los Angeles
1997 *iNSITE97, You Are Here/Estas Aqui*, Installation Gallery, San Diego, California
Community Engagement Projects, Southwestern College, San Diego, California
1996 *Graduate Fellows Show*, The American Photography Institute, Tisch School for the Arts, New York University, New York
Minimal, Beautiful, Obscene, Visual Arts Center, University of California, San Diego, California
1995 *Young and Gifted*, Flavor Gallery, Harlem, New York
1994 *Works-In-Progress*, Visual Arts Center, University of California, San Diego, California
1993 *Vital Expressions*, The San Diego African-American Museum of the Lyceum, San Diego, California

ACKNOWLEDGEMENTS

It has been a great pleasure to work on this exhibition and a privilege to work with the great artists who generously participated in it. I am delighted to create a context within which to situate their varied practices, and I thank each of them for contributing their work.

Each exhibition at MOCA is also a collaboration of the museum's tremendous staff. I thank our Director Jeremy Strick, who was supportive of this project since his arrival at MOCA and with whom it has been a pleasure to work. Assistant Director Kathleen S. Bartels provided crucial administrative support and Chief Curator Paul Schimmel enthusiastically encouraged the exhibition from its early stages and as it grew in scope and ambition. His genuine love of the curatorial process and his animated discourse about works of art is always appreciated. I am particularly grateful to Rebecca Morse, whose enormous assistance and good nature makes each project a pleasure. Senior Editor Stephanie Emerson works tirelessly producing beautiful and intelligent books for the museum, and Assistant Editor Jane Hyun and Editorial Assistant Elizabeth Hamilton somehow cobble together an impossible amount of publication details with grace and good humor. Curatorial Interns Tone O. Nielsen, Lorilei Stewart, and Kelly Carmichael provided invaluable research assistance at crucial stages during exhibition preparation. Also I would like to acknowledge Colette Dartnall, Russell Ferguson, Ann Goldstein, Alma Ruiz, and Stacia Payne, members of the curatorial staff, whose collegial support is always felt and appreciated. Our registrarial staff ensures that every work of art arrives safely, and in particular I thank Chief Registrar Robert Hollister and Assistant Registrar Rosanna Hemerick for their diligence. MOCA's installation staff is unparalleled, and Acting Exhibitions Production Manager Jang Park, Media Arts Technical Manager David Bradshaw and Media Arts Technical Assistant Tina Bastajian, and Exhibitions Production Coordinator Zazu Faure worked tirelessly to make a beautiful and smooth installation. In the education department I thank Director of Education Kim Kanatani and Adult Programs Coordinator Caroline Blackburn for their support of the project. Other staff critical to the success of the exhibition include former Acting Director of Development Ed Patuto, former Grants Officer Jillian Spaak, Grants Coordinator Mike Urban, Media Relations Coordinator Katherine Lee, and Director of Travel and Support Programs Leslie Marcus.

I thank our catalogue essayists Lee Weng Choy and Francis Pound for their insightful texts on the landscapes and landscape traditions in Singapore and New Zealand, respectively. Michael Worthington designed this publication with great sensitivity and, as always, a willingness to make the production of each book an ongoing dialogue.

For their introductions, invaluable commentary, friendship, and support of this project, I thank the following: Judy Annear; Roy Arden; Asia-Pacific Triennial exhibition and conference; Jim and Mary Barr; Chuck Betlach and The Betlach Family Foundation; Sheryl Conkleton; Diane Cornwell; Wystan Curnow; Jan de Bont; Juliana Engberg; Paul Foss; Jacqueline Fraser; M.A. Greenstein; Dana Friis-Hansen; Jeff Gibson; Ihor Holubizky; Giovanni Intra; Peter Krapp and Catherine Liu; Karyn Lovegrove; Geoff Lowe and Jacqui Riva; Gary and Tracy Mezzatesta; Helen Molesworth and Frazer Ward; Tina Petra; Cay Sophie Rabinowitz; David Schafer; Merry Scully; and Trevor Smith.

For their assistance with loans and myriad other details without which this project would never have been possible: I thank Daina Augaitis, Alf Bogusky, Bruce Grenville, Vancouver Art Gallery; Ron Brownson, Auckland Art Gallery; Greg Burke, Hanna Scott, Govett-Brewster Art Gallery; Hanna Schouwink, David Zwirner, David Zwirner Gallery; Erin Collins, Rodney Graham studio; Sally Couacaud; Sue Crockford, Isha Welsh, Sue Crockford Gallery; Chris Dikeakos;

Louise Dauth, Parliament House Art Collection; Brian Doyle, Lisa Spellman, 303 Gallery; Peggy Gale; Gow Langsford, Auckland; Randy Green, Muse X Editions; Bob Gunderman and Randy Sommer, ACME.; Deborah Hennessy, Roslyn Oxley, Roslyn Oxley9 Gallery; Mr. & Mrs. David Hoberman; Graham Howe, Curatorial Assistance; Sir James and Lady Cruthers; Catriona Jeffries, Catriona Jeffries Gallery; Jochen Kienzle, Galerie Kienzle and Gmeiner; Chris Kennedy, Kim Tomczak, V tape; Robert Leonard, Artspace, Auckland; Robert Linsley; Ewen McDonald; Matthew Marks, Jeffrey Peabody, Adrian Rosenfeld, Matthew Marks Gallery; Hamish McKay, Wellington, New Zealand; Museums Aotearoa, New Zealand; Wilhelm and Gabi Schürmann; Luke Parker, Stephen Mori, Stephen Mori Gallery; Maureen Pskowski, Donald Young, Donald Young Gallery; Beverly and Mel Rosenthal; Marc Selwyn, Stephen Hilger, Grant Selwyn Fine Art; John Timmins, Justin Paton, Dunedin Public Art Gallery; Hetti Perkins; Women Make Movies, Inc.; and Kelly Wood.

I thank the Fellows of Contemporary Art for their generous support of the exhibition, as well as Creative New Zealand, The MOCA Projects Council, the New Media Project, KLON-FM 88.1, Erik and Heidi Murkoff, and Audrey M. Irmas, whose great commitment to MOCA and to contemporary art I deeply respect.

Connie Butler

Associate Curator

Exhibition History
Fellows of Contemporary Art

The concept of the Fellows of Contemporary Art, as developed by its founding members in 1975, is unique. Monies received from dues are used to underwrite exhibitions, catalogs and videos at non-profit contemporary museums and galleries. The Fellows do not give grants or maintain a permanent facility or collection. In addition to the exhibition schedule, the Fellows have an active membership education program.

1976
"Ed Moses Drawings, 1958–1976"

1977
"Unstretched Surfaces/Surfaces Libres"

1978–80
"Wallace Berman Retrospective"

1979–80
"Vija Celmins, A Survey Exhibition"

1980
"Variations: Five Los Angeles Painters"

1981–82
"Craig Kauffman: A Comprehensive Survey, 1957–1980"

1981–82
"Paul Wonner: Abstract Realist"

1982–83
"Changing Trends, Content and Style: Twelve Southern California Painters"

1983
"Variations II: Seven Los Angeles Painters"

1984
"Martha Alf Retrospective"

1985
"Sunshine and Shadow: Recent Painting in Southern California"

1985–86
"James Turrell"

1986
"William Brice"

1987
"Variations III: Emerging Artists in Southern California"

1987–88
"Perpetual Motion"

1988
"Jud Fine"

1989–90
"The Pasadena Armory Show, 1989"

1990
"Lita Albuquerque: Reflections"

1991
"Facing the Finish: Some Recent California Art"

1991–93
"Roland Reiss: A Seventeen Year Survey"

1992–94
"Proof: Los Angeles Art and the Photograph, 1960–1980"

1993–94
"Kim Abeles: Encyclopedia Persona, A Fifteen-Year Survey"

1994–95
"Plane/Structures"

1995–96
"Llyn Foulkes: Between a Rock and a Hard Place"

1997
"Scene of the Crime"

1998
"Access All Areas"

1999
"Bruce and Norman Yonemoto: Memory, Matter, and Modern Romance"

1999
"Eleanor Antin"

Future Exhibitions:

2001–02
"George Stone: Probabilities—A Twenty-Year Survey"

2002
"On Wanting to Grow Horns: The Little Theatre of Tom Knechtel"

For additional information about these exhibitions and our videos, visit www.focala.org

Board of Directors
Fellows of Contemporary Art

Front cover
detail, *31 DECEMBER 1999, OFF THE ALBANIAN COAST* (diptych)
from *TITANIC's wake*, 1998-2000
Allan Sekula

Back cover
MEXICO, c. 1955
Paul Outerbridge

Inside details pages 1–12
THE HOMELY: TE WAIROA (FALLS), 1999
Gavin Hipkins

ILLUMINATED RAVINE, 1979/1991
Rodney Graham

DRUM BAZAAR, 1953
Lee Mullican

HOW LIGHT BECOMES ME (PINK), 1996-2000
Caryl Davis

from *GRIFFITH PARK*, 1996
Rachel Khedoori

NATURE MORTE [SILENCE], SAVAGE CLUB, WANGANUI, 20 FEBRUARY 1986, 1986
Laurence Aberhart

SQUATTING PROJECT/WIÉN, 1998
Simon Leung

HINKLEY VIEW from *The Desert Research Station*, 2000
Center for Land Use Interpretation

from *NEAR MATTAWA, #8*, 2000
Miles Coolidge

MANUELA S-T-I-T-C-H-E-D: SAN PEDRO FASH., EASTERN LOS ANGELES, CA, 1996
Christina Fernandez

INVOCATIONS (4), 2000
Tracey Moffatt

from *BLOW DEBRIS*, 2000
Doug Aitken

All photographs appear courtesy of the artists and/or lenders of the works. The following list, keyed to page numbers, applies to photographs for which a separate acknowledgement is due:

Brian Forrest, pp. 9, 32–35 all, 46–49 all; courtesy of Catriona Jeffries Gallery, pp. 54 top, 56 top, 57 all; Teresa Healy, pp. 54 bottom, 55; Simon Leung, pp. 58–59 all, 60 bottom, 61; Werner Kaligofsky, p. 60 top; Ron Gordon, p. 68 bottom; Sue Black, p. 92 bottom; Bryan James, pp. 104–105; Bill Nichol, p. 118; by permission of the National Library of Australia, p. 125; Ruth Soh, p. 140; and Lee Wen, p. 141.

Roster of Members
Fellows of Contemporary Art

Dean Victor Ambrose
Dewey E. Anderson
Barbara & Charles Arledge
Shirley Martin Bacher
Mr. & Mrs. W.G. Barker
Irene & Jerry Barr
Ann & Olin Barrett
Binnie Beaumont
Kay Sprinkle Beaumont
& Geoffrey C. Beaumont
Lanie & Lazare Bernhard
Ellie Blankfort & Peter Clothier
Marsha & Vernon Bohr
Mary Lou & George Boone
Suzanne & David Booth
Etan Boritzer
Linda Brownridge
& Edward Mulvaney
Gay & Ernest Bryant
Bente & Gerald E. Buck
Betye Burton
Susan & John Caldwell
Susan B. Campoy
Maureen & Robert Carlson
Mary & Gus Chabre
Charlotte Chamberlain
& Paul Wieselmann
Leigh Charlton and Sam Joseph
Sara Muller Chernoff
and Dennis Muller
Kitty Chester
Hyon Chough and Bernie Sacharski
Paul Cohart
Barbara Cohn
Susan and Michael Connell
Diane & Michael Cornwell
Zoe & Donald W. Cosgrove
Beryl Cowley
Peggy & Timm Crull
Christina R. Davis
Marina Forstmann Day
Betty & Brack Duker
Sandra A. and Victor Ell
Lulu Epstein
William D. Feldman & Joan Blum
Kathryn Files
Joanne & Beau France
Mardi & Merrill Francis
Joan & Ken Frankel
Mrs. & Mr. James Robert Frazer
Judy & Kent Frewing
Linda Genereux & Timur Galen
Homeira & Arnold Goldstein
Nancy Goodson
Linda & Arthur Goolsbee
Dr. & Mrs. David Gottlieb
Mariana & Ron Grant
Randall Green
Bill Griffin
Stephanie & Ken Grody
Pat & Eugene Hancock
Mary Elizabeth & Alfred Hausrath
Dr. Randal Haworth
Carol & Warner Henry
Niki Horwitch & Stephen Berg
Joan & John Hotchkis
Roberta Huntley
Mr. & Mrs. William H. Hurt
Michelle and Bud Isenberg
Linda & Jerry Janger
Gloria & Sonny Kamm
Stephen A. Kanter
Tobe & Greg Karns
Mickey Katz & Stan May
Suzanne and Ric Kayne
Teri & John Kennady
Tracy & Christopher Keys
Barbara & Victor Klein
Phyllis & John Kleinberg
Susan & Allan Klumpp
Virginia Krueger
Hannah & Russel Kully
Anne Lasell
Larry Layne
Dawn Hoffman Lee & Harlan Lee
Lydia & Charles Levy
Bernard & Peggy Lewak
Bobbi Linkletter & Guy Blase
Linda Lucus Lund
Penny & Jay Lusche
Molly & Leon Lyon
Gloria and Richard Mahdesian
Dena & Louis Marienthal
Barbara & Terry Maxwell
Dee Die & Ted McCarthy
Amanda & Jim McIntyre
Elizabeth Michelson
Tressa R. Miller & Wm.B. Schwartz
Carolyn & Charles Miller
Donna & Clinton Mills
Rochelle & Jeff Mills
Harry Montgomery
Hilarie & Mark Moore
Laura Donnelley-Morton
and John Morton
Caroline Labiner Moser
Garna & Steven Muller
Ann and Bob Myers
Grace & Richard Narver
Lois & Richard Neiter
Dr. and Mrs. Robert H. Newhouse
Sandra Kline Nichols & Peter
Eileen & Peter Norton
Richard Orselli, M.D.
Cathie & David Partridge
Suzanne & Theodore Paulson
Joan Payden
Putter & Blair Pence
Marisa & Jacques Perret
Ellie & Frank Person
Tom Peters
Tina Petra & Ken Wong
Peggy Phelps & Nelson Leonard
Linda & Reese Polesky
Gina & Irv Posalski
Dallas Price
Kathy Reges & Richard Carlson
Joan B. Rehnborg
Joan & Tom Riach
Debby & Bill Richards
Carol & John Richards
Helen & David Rifkind
Christy & Gary Roeber
Gayle & Ed Roski
Barbara & Martin Schechter
Cinda & Stephen Schrader
Gloria Sedaghat
Anton David Segerstrom
Patricia Shea
Corrinne and Tony Shukartsi
Marjorie and David Sievers
Miriam L. Smith & Douglas Greene
Theodore E. & Mary S. Smith
Annette & Russell Dymock Smith
Penny & Ted Sonnenschein
Ronnie & Joe Stabler
Laurie Smits Staude
Patricia & Charles Steinmann
Margarita & David Steinmetz
Gretel & George Stephens
Ginny & Richard Stever
Arthur Strick
Ann E. Summers
Laney & Thomas Techentin
Elinor & Rubin Turner
Sheryle Ulyate
Jolly Urner
Donna Vaccarino
Carolyn & Bob Volk
Magda & Frederick Waingrow
Carole Walker
Kathleen Watt
Linda and Tod White
Mili Julia Wild
Jene M. Witte
Laura-Lee & Robert Woods
Mrs. Paul K. Yost